Advance Praise

Well before Austin became the venue for Formula One, the city's leadership considered it important to focus on our globalization efforts and develop an internationally inclusive mindset. We at the Chamber of Commerce know the importance of building trust, inspiring respect and creating long-lasting business relationships with the many international communities that choose to invest here. That is why we are excited that one of our own, international etiquette expert and intercultural consultant Sharon Schweitzer, has stepped up to author such a detailed, resource-rich book. Access to Asia will be invaluable to anyone who understands that today's business, whether corporate or civic, depends on developing sound, long-term relationships. We know from having watched our diverse community grow exponentially how important this is to business success today.

— **Michael W. Rollins, CCE, President & CEO, Austin Chamber of Commerce. Austin, Texas USA**

China in 24 pages? Didn't think it could be done? Sharon Schweitzer presents what the visiting business person needs to know with her clear, comprehensive, no-nonsense advice. In just this one chapter, she has incorporated Chinese expectations, communication patterns and work organisation in a simple, succinct way (including some useful phrases in Mandarin.) I found her commentary on key differences between the Chinese and Western way of doing things highly illuminating and her references to experts in the field very appropriate and useful. The 8 point self-awareness exercise at the end of each chapter is a good way to check how close or how far apart you are to your Chinese partners or those in the other nine Asian countries offered in this book. Such a wealth of information!

— **Barry Tomalin, Author of World Business Cultures: A Handbook (3rd Ed. 2014). Redhill, United Kingdom**

"After more than three decades helping business travelers better understand their colleagues in other cultures, I know how vital it is to understand country-specific customs and avoid costly international faux pas. It is refreshing to see that in addition to the invaluable insights and practical advice offered in Access to Asia, Ms. Schweitzer helps readers to assess their own readiness for working with Asian cultures, acknowledging the most important requirement for cross-cultural success: know yourself first, in order to know others!"

—**Dean Foster**, President, DFA Intercultural Global Solutions, and author of the John Wiley Global Etiquette Guide series, USA

"Unlike typical regional business guides, *Access to Asia* focuses on the deeper side of cultural understanding. It goes beyond rules and facts and helps the reader make sense of the often subtle, yet profound, cultural differences found in Asia—something that's critical for building successful relationships. Sharon Schweitzer understands that cultural understanding is not just a set of techniques to use, facts to learn, or rules to follow. By learning the cultural perspective of others, we explore the hidden parts of our cultural self. *Access to Asia* provides a great starting point for this profoundly satisfying journey."

—**Joseph Shaules,** director, Japan Intercultural Institute, Author of *The Intercultural Mind: Connecting Culture, Cognition and Global Living*, Tokyo, Japan

"*Access to Asia* is like the Lonely Planet for business travelers—an essential handbook. In the West if you have the business logic set in place that is enough for business to get done. But in Asia, typically, you much establish a route to the heart of the person you are dealing with. Only then will business happen. Sharon Schweitzer understands this and offers readers a very clear and invaluable guidebook."

—**Srikanth Bhagavat**, Managing Director and Principal Advisor, Hexagon Wealth, Bangalore, India

"As we emphasize through our Gateway program, today's higher education institutions must graduate globally competent students with an awareness of and adaptability to diverse cultures. *Access to Asia's* focus on relationship building makes it essential reading for global citizens–current and future–so they understand how success in Asia depends on cultural awareness."

—**Dr. William I. Brustein,** Vice Provost, Global Strategies and International Affairs, The Ohio State University, Columbus, Ohio, USA

"Success in today's business world is increasingly dependent upon foundations of deep social and cultural understanding, particularly in Asia's business environment. Having a highly organized, detailed and focused multicultural guide is invaluable. *Access to Asia* is that invaluable book of significant educational value for budding entrepreneurs, universities and colleges offering undergraduate, graduate and MBA courses focusing on international business. *Access to Asia* is a must-have resource for international travelers looking to boost their business interests in Asia."

—**Dr. Steve Leslie,** Former Executive Vice-President and Provost, The University of Texas, Austin, Texas, USA

"As the world grows smaller and smaller the understanding of different cultures, especially those so different from our own, has never been more vital. Access to Asia is the must-read book for any traveller to the East, however much they think they already know. There has been nothing like it for some time and the literary world has been crying out for such a book. It is teeming with invaluable gold dust that has made Sharon Schweitzer's stellar work one of the 21st century's best promotions of cross-cultural awareness."

—**William Hanson,** British etiquette consultant, broadcaster and author of The Bluffer's Guide to Etiquette (Bluffer's Media, 2014) Manchester, England

"As the President of The Protocol School of Washington, I am thrilled one of our great graduates, Sharon Schweitzer is now making significant contributions to our field with the publication of her book Access to Asia.
I strongly endorse the focus in Sharon's timely book toward building trust and inspiring respect in the international business arena, in addition to stressing the importance of developing strong business relationships with counterparts in Asia. After all, we are not "going" global—we are global! The same deep knowledge and enthusiasm for developing truly unique, captivating advice that Sharon shares with her clients can be found in this book. As a current or future business leader with an eye to cultural competence, you will find the insightful advice in this practical resource invaluable."

—**Pamela Eyring**, Owner and President, The Protocol School of Washington, USA

"The importance of understanding different cultures around the world has never been greater. Learning to discern the subtle differences within Asian cultures enables us to understand and appreciate better the opportunities such diversity affords. Sharon's life experience, research and resultant depth of understanding and clarity of Asian cultures, within a framework of eight crucial questions, makes this book a must have for anyone interested in expanding their understanding of global affairs."

—**Jay Remer,** Canada's Etiquette Guy, Author of *The Six Pillars of Civility,* St. Andrews, New Brunswick, Canada

"*Access to Asia* by Sharon Schweitzer fills a much needed information gap for international business travelers.

Frequently, CEOs and other high level executives, during programs or coaching sessions, ask me for an information source for specific hard facts about a country. Usually travel time is very short and they are focused on strategic results. But during the non-task interactions, ignorance about the basic facts of the country could be embarrassing as well as erode trust. I think this book provides pertinent information quickly prior to a business trip or hosting international counterparts. Also, this book creates the awareness that besides the hard facts of business such as legal regulatory and financial aspects of doing business in a country, we must be aware of the cultural factors or "Smart factors" such as: differences in decision making, communication, or establishing a relationship of confidence and trust. Access to Asia by Sharon Schweitzer will help to remove the blind spots that are impediments to success in doing business in Asia."

—**Sheida Hodge,** Author, *Global Smarts: the art of communicating and deal making anywhere in the world*, Seattle, Washington USA

"Access to Asia is. . . bursting with authentic information."

—**Richard D. Lewis**, author of *When Teams Collide: Managing the International Team Successfully* and *When Cultures Collide*

ACCESS *to* ASIA

ACCESS *to* ASIA

YOUR MULTICULTURAL GUIDE TO
BUILDING TRUST, INSPIRING RESPECT,
AND CREATING LONG-LASTING
BUSINESS RELATIONSHIPS

SHARON SCHWEITZER, J.D.
LIZ ALEXANDER, Ph.D.

WILEY

Published by John Wiley & Sons, Inc., Hoboken, New Jersey
Published simultaneously in Canada

For general information about our other products and services, please contact our Customer Care
Department within the United States at (800) 762-2974, outside the United States at (317) 572-3993
or fax (317) 572-4002.

Wiley publishes in a variety of print and electronic formats and by print-on-demand. Some material
included with standard print versions of this book may not be included in e-books or in
print-on-demand. If this book refers to media such as a CD or DVD that is not included in the
version you purchased, you may download this material at http://booksupport.wiley.com. For more
information about Wiley products, visit www.wiley.com.

Library of Congress Cataloging-in-Publication Data:

Schweitzer, Sharon
    Access to Asia : your multicultural guide to building trust, inspiring respect, and creating
long-lasting business relationships / Sharon Schweitzer, Liz Alexander.
        pages cm
    Includes bibliographical references and index.
    ISBN 978-1-118-91901-9 (cloth); 978-1-118-91902-6 (epdf); 978-1-118-91904-0 (epub)
1. Business etiquette–Asia. 2. Corporate culture–Asia. 3. Management–Asia. 4. Management–
Cross-cultural studies. 5. Intercultural communication. I. Alexander, Liz. II. Title.
    HF5389.3.A78S39 2015
    395.5'2095–dc23

                                                                                    2014039933

Printed in the United States of America
10 9 8 7 6 5 4 3 2

Contents

Foreword

As the Founder of itim International, which has been associated with the work of Professor Geert Hofstede for the past 30 years, we have long emphasized that when it comes to national cultural differences, culture only exists by comparison. We human beings have much in common, but we are also all unique. Culture, in this regard, describes the differences that exist between groups—be they nations, regions, or organizations.

When visiting the 10 Asian countries showcased in this book, as a potential business partner, or business colleague, or because you've been seconded abroad for a longer period of time, Sharon Schweitzer's *Access to Asia* will be of considerable benefit. Adopt the advice offered within these pages and it will empower you as a global professional by helping you understand the breadth and depth of successful intercultural relationships.

We are all busy people, often feeling that we have little time to focus on strategy when tactical matters are pressing. Sharon Schweitzer demonstrates that she understands this. Not only is *Access to Asia* packed full of information you may not have come across elsewhere, those nuggets are presented in a readily accessible way. Ms. Schweitzer comprehensively covers the building blocks needed in order to get a true sense of each of these 10 important Asian markets through the Country Basics sections. She has gone even further, however, by amassing considerable on-the-ground insights related to eight important questions.

In many books covering the differences between values patterns of different cultures, many of the most important dos and don'ts are overlooked. This is not the case with *Access to Asia,* which is why I highly recommend this book to everybody who truly desires to build trust, inspire respect, and create long-lasting business relationships in this important region of the world.

Bob Waisfisz
Managing Partner of The Hofstede
Helsinki, Finland

About the Authors

Sharon Schweitzer, J.D., is an international business consultant focusing on intercultural communication and global etiquette for future and current international leaders within Global 2000 companies. Her practice, during earlier years as an employment attorney, involved cultural dynamics and communication within groups and between individuals. Sharon is a popular radio and TV guest, conference speaker, and columnist. She consults throughout the U.S., as well as in Asia, Europe, and the U.K. Sharon's website is www.sharonschweitzer .com

Liz Alexander, PhD, is the multiple award-winning author of 14 books, and co-founder of boutique consulting firm Leading Thought. She directs her gifts and passion to helping aspiring thought leaders harness strategically valuable, actionable insights to grow their businesses and boost revenue. Liz also acts as book strategist and consulting co-author to business leaders, entrepreneurs, and consultants worldwide. Please connect with her at info@leadingthought.us.com.

Acknowledgments

The time I have spent writing and researching this book has been a personally fulfilling experience as well as a professionally beneficial one. Not least because of the rich, deep, wonderful relationships worldwide that I have been lucky enough to develop and will cherish for the rest of my life. Over 100 interviewees are mentioned individually in the Contributors section at the back of this book. While there is not sufficient space to mention all of you again here, please collectively accept my heartfelt thanks for so generously sharing your insights with us. This includes those of you who, because of professional or cultural constraints, did not wish to be named. Quite honestly, this book could not have been written without you!

The same is true of the following people, each of whom have made significant contributions, if not directly to the content of this book, then certainly to my sanity.

First, I would like to thank my consulting co-author Dr. Liz Alexander who has been a coach, mentor, friend, guiding light, and true pleasure throughout this journey. During our lifetimes we meet special spirits who touch our lives deeply, and Dr. Liz is one of those life-transforming gurus for me. I am forever indebted.

I also remain extremely grateful to the support given by Cathy Hoover and Courtney Harris and the team at Regus.

Thank you, Jerald Wrightsil, for your generosity of spirit in introducing us to so many wonderful people within your extensive Asian networks. Liz and I can never thank you enough for always being there when we needed you.

Other people and organizations that I would like to single out for their contributions to this project are: Korena Garcia, director of Custom Intelligence Services, Stratfor; A. J. Gallerano and Bryan Campbell of DuBois, Bryant & Campbell, L.L.P.; Jamie Nanquil and the team at Social Media Delivered; Deborah Wallis of One-on-One Transcription; and Kathy Wood and her team at

KatzTranscription—as well as Priya Kumar, who designed the beautiful maps that grace each of our country chapters.

Where would I be without my assistant Vaughn Bradley, researcher Kristen Eggers, and author's assistant Leah Haney all of whom have been pivotal in getting this book completed and in on time? You are all greatly appreciated, as is Kristen's mom, Julie Smith, whose phenomenal administrative services I cannot praise highly enough.

Deserving special mention, too, is everyone who has helped me at The University of Texas at Austin, with special mentions to Kevin Hegarty and Dr. Steve Leslie; The Ohio State University, with special thanks to Dr. William Brustein; and the leadership of the City of Austin.

Thank you to the team at John Wiley & Sons. This first-time author is honored to be published by such a well-respected name in the publishing industry; your support and guidance have left me feeling confident that my work could not have found a better home: Elizabeth Gildea, Brian Neill, Christine Moore, and Chaitanya Mella.

Finally, I am indebted to my friend Mary Scott Nabers; my supportive and loving family: my phenomenal parents, Ted and Lynn Schweitzer—it all started with you; my brothers and sisters; my amazing niece, Erica Schweitzer-Wirth; John Robinson III; and Deborah Schons.

Above all, I would like to express my huge gratitude to my brilliant, loving husband, John Robinson, and to Charm, the world's most beautiful golden retriever.

Introduction

In the world of high-speed motor brands dominate—Formula One and NASCAR. Both require skill, strategy, and intense focus. In all other respects, they couldn't be more different.

Formula One is the racing equivalent of a Louis Vuitton store: high class, with European roots and international appeal. Formula One races, known as Grand Prix, showcase technologically sophisticated, single-seat, purpose-built cars driven by men like Prost, Villeneuve, and Schumacher with engines designed by world-class talent at Alfa Romeo, Ferrari, Maserati, Lotus, and Mercedes-Benz. The only two U.S. Americans who have won in Formula One's 62-year history are Phil Hill in 1961 and Mario Andretti in 1978.

NASCAR (the National Association for Stock Car Auto Racing), on the other hand, is an all-American phenomenon whose heroes have first names such as Denny, JJ, and Kyle. Stock cars are almost indistinguishable from those you'd find in a Chevrolet, Ford, or Dodge showroom. In contrast to Formula One, almost all NASCAR Sprint Cup Series winners have been U.S. Americans. Whereas attendees at Formula One races can enjoy four-star hotels, expensive restaurants, suites and grandstand seats, NASCAR fans tend to prefer an RV, eat BBQ, and drink beer.

When Formula One announced that it would race again in the U.S. at the purpose-built track named Circuit of the Americas in Austin, Texas, many were surprised. Other U.S. venues were under consideration to host the race. However, misperceptions of Texas as a state with cactus, men in cowboy hats, and armadillo were shown to be wrong. Austin's reputation as the Live Music Capital of the World is just one indication of the city's culture of inclusiveness, sophistication, and willingness to embrace new experiences. Formula One held its inaugural race in Austin in 2012 and given its ten-year contract with Texas, racing is expected through 2022 and beyond.

The awareness, flexibility, understanding, and a willingness to adapt are similarly essential when conducting business across different world cultures. If you have ever traveled to China, India, Japan, or any of the other Asian countries explored in this book, you will appreciate how important it is to travel with an open mind and not to expect that domestic business practices are understood elsewhere.

Where there are cultural differences, there is the potential for misunderstanding. That is why the overarching question at the heart of this book is: What do I need to know, think, and do to build trust, inspire respect, and create long-lasting business relationships in Asia?

A Journey of Passion

As the daughter of a military officer, Sharon has spent her life exposed to different cultures—she's a real "third culture kid."[1] Her passion for helping others professionally benefit from enhanced cross-cultural relationships began in 1989, the year she graduated from law school. After spending a month that summer experiencing China, Hong Kong, and Thailand with a fellow summer associate, she wrote in her journal: "I need to be doing something where I'm traveling and working with people in different cultures."

Nevertheless, back in the U.S., Sharon did what most recently-graduated lawyers do: She joined a law firm. Two years later, she began working for the Texas Attorney General's office, which reignited her fascination with the way different mindsets and priorities impact how people communicate and resolve conflict.

By early 2008, Sharon had visited all seven continents and over 30 countries, and had gained a professional understanding of how to bridge the gap between people from different cultures. Taking a two-year sabbatical from the law, she visited the Czech Republic and immersed herself in family and culture. Then she embarked on a series of courses at the Protocol School of Washington to emerge as a newly minted corporate-etiquette and international-protocol consultant, and a protocol officer.

From Etiquette to Intercultural Exchange

For the first six years after launching Protocol and Etiquette Worldwide, Sharon was influenced by experts in the field of international etiquette and intercultural awareness. What she found was that her clients wanted more than third-hand advice. They were hungry for realistic, practical, and implementable guidance that would enable them to be more successful in our globalized economy. They wanted to hear Sharon's experiences and stories!

---

[1] David C. Pollock and Ruth E. Van Reken, *Third Culture Kids: Growing Up Among Worlds* (Boston: Nicholas Brealey Publishing, 2009).

In 2012, the city of Austin asked Sharon to present on cross-cultural awareness in readiness for the inaugural Formula One races. Her interest in the research of social psychologist Geert Hofstede and his son (Gerte Jan), as well as that of cross-communication consultants Fons Trompenaars and Charles Hampden-Turner deepened. Sharon's lifelong cross-cultural experience, training, and research have been funneled into this book.

From our great personal love of Asia, and in light of the increased interest worldwide in doing business across that continent, we chose to focus this book on Asia. By crafting material that engages, educates, and entertains, we intend to take you on a personally fulfilling journey.

A Questioning Framework

As the eighteenth-century French philosopher Voltaire said, "Judge a man by his questions rather than his answers." After interviewing over 100 international professionals for this book, we noticed a pattern emerging: eight core questions whose answers were essential in attracting and building the relationships upon which today's successful businesses depend. Having researched many of the models offered by cultural gurus such as Edward Hall, Florence Kluckhohn, Fred Strodtbeck, Geert Hofstede, Fons Trompenaars and Charles Hampden-Turner, George Simons, Janet Bennett, and Milton Bennett, we found these eight questions reflect topics vitally important for culturally aware businesspeople.

Why *These* Asian Countries?

To counter the desire to cover every country as if they were equally important to U.S. business interests, Sharon engaged the global intelligence firm Stratfor, asking them to produce a report on U.S. American business travel to Asia in order to identify the current and future top-ranking countries for U.S. investment and travel.[2] Six countries—China, Hong Kong,[3] Japan, India, South Korea, and Taiwan—accounted for over 70 percent of all U.S. business travel to Asia and represented the top U.S. regional trade partners, as well as key

---

[2]"American Business Travel to Asia: A Look at Top-Ranking Countries for U.S. Investment and Related Travel," Stratfor Global Intelligence, August 24, 2012.

[3]Although sovereignty of Hong Kong was passed from the United Kingdom to China in 1997, the rules of transfer stated that the region would remain self-governing until July, 2047. Hong Kong maintains its own legal system, taxation, currency, and business guidelines. Although technically a Special Autonomous Region (SAR) of the People's Republic of China, Hong Kong will be treated as a separate country throughout this book.

destinations for U.S. investment. According to Stratfor, business travel to these countries, with the possible exception of Taiwan, is not expected to decline significantly over the next two decades.

However, we also wanted to include countries that were likely to emerge as increasingly important destinations for U.S. business travelers over the next 20 years. Among these top-ranking countries are Singapore, the Philippines, and Malaysia. Finally, it was Sharon's personal fascination with the mysterious Myanmar, formerly known as Burma, which led to our inclusion of that country here.

How This Book Is Structured

This book opens with an overview on culture, which explains why cultural awareness is important to establishing successful relationships, followed by an introduction to our eight-question framework. For all readers who seek an understanding of the United States, in addition to the 10 Asian countries, we have included a chapter on U.S. culture. U.S readers will gain a better self-awareness and understanding of their own culture. Overview of Concepts and Terms, offers an alphabetical collection of key concepts. Please contact Sharon at sharon@sharonschweitzer.com with your suggestions and insights for improving this list.

Each of the 10 country chapters that follow help expand your knowledge through the eight-question framework. Topics in these chapters include

- A brief historical overview
- The names of heroes and sports figures
- An explanation of etiquette and protocol
- Insider tips on socializing
- Fiscal calendars and a list of important holidays

There is also a quiz in each chapter together with a Self-Awareness Profile.

Self-Awareness Profiles

This simple exercise prompts you to self-identify where you currently stand on topics related to the eight-question framework. This visual comparison will help you discover your current mindset and behavior to help develop more robust business relationships in each country. You will find these graphics after the eight-questions section and the cultural summary within each country chapter. We suggest photocopying the graphics or using a pencil within the book so that you can see, over time, how you have adjusted your mindset.

Here is an example, concerning formality within Japanese business:

Example

How **formal** do the **Japanese** tend to be in business? (Note: numbers set in bold indicate the prevailing cultural preference.)

Very informal   **Highly formal**

    1   2   3   4   5   **6**

If you fall within the range of 5 or 6 on this continuum, you will likely easily adapt to Japanese formalities within business. If you are someone more comfortable with showing emotion in business dealings, expressing strongly held opinions, and acting assertively with others, you may need to consider seeking intercultural training.

Business *Is* Relationships

Regardless of home country, human beings share a common desire to *relate*. In their work identifying the universal attributes called *strengths*, the Gallup Organization found that out of the 34 personal themes described by the Strengths-Finder assessment tool, the top five were common internationally: Achiever, Learner, Relator, Responsibility, and Strategic. The placement of these themes in the top five differed slightly according to whether it is U.S. or international data, but whether we're from Baltimore or Bangalore, San Francisco or Shanghai, achieving, learning, and relating appear to be primary concerns for us all.

Regardless of the industry, then, we are *all* in the relationship business. Understanding this is even more salient when operating abroad. As Professor Christine Uber Grosse points out: "Personal relationships matter in Asian business, in contrast to their lesser role in U.S. business. As a result, U.S. managers do not always understand the need to establish trust and build business relationships with Asian partners and clients."[4]

From Theory to Practice

Prior to the launch of the inaugural Formula One U.S. Grand Prix at Austin's new Circuit of the Americas, Sharon was asked to write a series of articles and

---

[4]Christine Uber Grosse, "US-Asian Communication Strategies to Develop Trust in Business Relationships," *Global Business Languages* 10, no. 5 (2005), http://docs.lib.purdue.edu /gbl/vol10/iss1/5. (accessed January 10, 2015)

to conduct workshops on international protocol and etiquette, to help prepare Austin's business community for welcoming international visitors. While
speaking privately with various attendees, Sharon shared the following story to
illustrate how intercultural respect and courtesy play a huge role in establishing
long-lasting business relationships:

Some years ago, on a tour of American cities, a Chinese delegation visited
Austin. On the final night of their stay, after attending well-organized business and government events around the city, the delegates were treated to a
banquet featuring Texas BBQ at a real estate broker's private residence. Each
delegate received individually-wrapped gifts of memorabilia unique to Texas.
The organizers even supplied slippers so everyone could remove their shoes
before entering the private residence, if desired. Everything went smoothly
and the delegation traveled to the next stop on their national tour. Their next
experience was quite different, however. On one occasion the Chinese delegation waited thirty minutes before someone realized they were in the wrong
downtown high-rise—they'd ended up next door. The delegates were not as
impressed as they had been in Austin. When the Chinese returned home, they
invited the Austin real estate host to make presentations and talks in China.
These opportunities have subsequently boosted her business internationally.

While Robert Burns wrote in Scottish dialect, fellow Scot Liz has angli-
cized this quote from one of his poems to make it more understandable: "Oh,
would some Power the gift to give us/to see ourselves as others see us!"[5]

With that in mind, the chapters that follow help you learn about the values
held by your Asian clients and partners, but they also encourage you to view
U.S. cultural values in a new way. With a willingness to adapt, this material
can help you develop strong, long-lasting business relationships for powerful,
mutual benefit.

---

[5]"To a Louse," RobertBurns.org, www.robertburns.org/works/97.shtml (accessed November 21,
2014).

1

A Question of Culture

When we marry, most of us discover that our spouse's family has a different set of expectations, values, and beliefs, ranging from broad topics, such as boundaries to specific subjects such as shared holidays. Invariably, these are different from the way *we* were raised. If we can reconcile our own values with those of our new extended family, we avoid the potential culture clash; if not, and things escalate, the end result can be unpleasant. The same holds true in business.

J.B. (not his real name) is a factory owner in Chennai, in southern India, whose mid-sized business produces revenues of around $250 million a year and has two joint venture agreements. One relationship, with a German company, has happily lasted 18 years. The other, with a U.S.[1] company, he wants to draw to a close, because of their less than desirable approach to doing business.

For example, on one occasion, J.B. wanted to spend $5,000 to manufacture a tool for a particular project and was questioned at length by his U.S. partners as to why he didn't just buy the tool from vendors overseas. J.B. responded that these vendors did not allow him to purchase a single item, only items in bulk, which he felt was wasteful and would incur unnecessary shipping costs. Overall, it was going to be considerably less expensive to make the part. After further laborious discussions, his U.S. partners reluctantly agreed.

---

[1] The United States of America has been abbreviated to "U.S." in this book.

1

In contrast, J.B.'s experience with the Germans is such that, "If I make a request, they will ask me if that is the best solution in my opinion. If I say yes, they trust my expertise." Why would J.B.'s experience with the Germans be so different than the experience with his U.S. partners? In short: cultural differences. But before examining this example further, let's explore what we mean by the word *culture*.

We use the word *culture* in many different contexts, including countries, organizations, and groups, and we talk about *cultural misunderstandings, cultural clashes, cultural fit,* and even *culture shock.* However, books and articles focused on cultural topics often neglect to define the term. Perhaps that is not surprising, considering the complexities involved in explaining culture.

Culture was originally an agricultural term, used in the Middle Ages, stemming from the Latin word *cultura,* meaning the care, cultivation, or honoring of the land; we still talk about *cultivating* plants. But since the early nineteenth century, culture also became associated with the beliefs, values, and customs of different civilizations. Culture is complex and hard to pin down with a single definition because it encompasses many subcomponents.

Culture

"Culture is the accumulation of life experiences spanning generations."
Sheida Hodge, *Global Smarts*[2]

One place to start is to compare culture with similar but not synonymous concepts, such as identity, nationhood, values, and norms. Renowned intercultural researcher and the author of numerous books on this topic, including *Culture's Consequences,*[3] Geert Hofstede advises that culture is distinct from identity: Your identity has more to do with where and with whom you belong, as in *national identity,* or your identity within a particular group. Culture, on the other hand, is concerned with "the collective programming of the mind that distinguishes the members of one group or category of people from another."[4] In that regard, Hofstede considers culture to consist of "the unwritten rules of the social game."[5] These are the rules we learn from observing what goes on in our specific environment, together with the learning

---

[2]Sheida Hodge, *Global Smarts: The Art of Communicating and Deal Making Anywhere in the World* (New York: John Wiley & Sons, 2000).
[3]Geert Hofstede, *Culture's Consequences: Comparing Values, Behaviors, Institutions, and Organizations Across Nations,* 2nd edition (Thousand Oaks, CA: Sage Publications, 2001).
[4]"Culture," Geert Hofstede, www.geerthofstede.nl/culture (accessed November 21, 2014).
[5]Ibid.

we get from others, rather than something we are born knowing, such as the human propensity for smiling, or the fear of death, which are innate across all races.

Some of the earliest influences of Hofstede and others stemmed from research conducted by cultural anthropologists. For example, Florence Kluckhohn and Fred Strodtbeck's (1961) *value orientations* theory postulated six different types of beliefs, influences, and relationships. Kluckhohn and Strodtbeck differentiated them according to the following dimensions:

- Relationship with nature—especially the need for control
- Social structure—whether focused mostly on individuals or groups
- Appropriate goals—being or doing
- Time—past (traditions), present (current circumstances), or future (desires/goals)
- Basis of human nature—good or evil
- Conception of space—public or private

These anthropologically sound dimensions speak to all forms of community, including our business lives.

Culture is not synonymous with nationhood for the simple reason that just under 200 countries exist in the world today,[6] whereas, according to Richard Lewis, there are some 700 national and regional cultures.[7] Additionally, culture is not synonymous with concepts such as norms and values; it *encompasses* them.

Pattern Interrupt

"(M)any Japanese executives are reserved, polite, quiet, and rarely display emotion. Somewhere there is probably a loud, boisterous, gesticulating Japanese manager who is as emotional and imperious as any prima donna. Just because we haven't met him (or her) doesn't mean that no such person exists."

Terri Morrison and Wayne A. Conaway[8]

---

[6]"How Many Countries?," Infoplease, www.infoplease.com/ipa/A0932875.html (accessed November 21, 2014).

[7]Richard D. Lewis, *When Cultures Collide: Leading Across Cultures* (Boston: Nicholas Brealey International, 2006).

[8]Terri Morrison and Wayne A. Conaway, *Kiss, Bow, or Shake Hands,* 2nd edition (Avon, MA: Adams Media, 2006).

Many commentators, including Fons Trompenaars[9], Geert Hofstede,[10] George Simons,[11] and Sheida Hodge[12] have represented culture as a multi-layered model. Depictions of these representations are either in the form of concentric circles or an iceberg, and highlight the difference between the cultural components of which we are aware and those that are subconscious. Think of a peach with three layers: the outer skin, the flesh, and the innermost pit or stone, as in Figure 1.1:

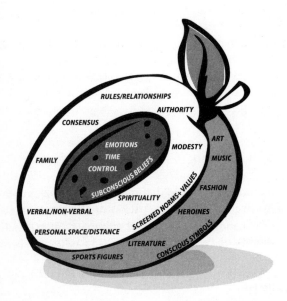

© PROTOCOL & ETIQUETTE WORLDWIDE LLC | SHARON M. SCHWEITZER, JD

Figure 1.1

This approach aligns with Edward T. Hall's three levels of culture, outlined in *The Dance of Life: The Other Dimension of Time*.[13] As you can see in the peach graphic, the outer skin represents the conscious or visible *manifestations* of culture, including literature, food, music, fashion, and art. These are often

[9]Fons Trompenaars and Charles Hampden-Turner, *Riding the Waves of Culture: Understanding Diversity in Global Business*, 3rd ed. (New York: McGraw-Hill, 2012).

[10]Geert Hofstede, Gert Jan Hofstede, and Michael Minkov, *Cultures and Organizations: Software of the Mind-Intercultural Cooperation and Its Importance for Survival*, 3rd edition (New York: McGraw Hill, 2010).

[11]George Simons, *Cultural Detective*, http://diversophy.com/ (accessed November 21, 2014).

[12]Hodge, *Global Smarts*.

[13]Edward T. Hall, *The Dance of Life: The Other Dimension of Time* (New York: Anchor Books, 1984, 1989).

visible, such as the *kimono* in Japan, the *sari* in India or the *hijab* in Malaysia. The middle layer or *flesh* comprises norms and values that are often unknown to people outside that culture. Examples include authority, consensus, family, modesty, personal space, and spirituality.

The innermost pit or stone represents the hidden or subconscious assumptions held by a culture about how the world *works*, such as fatalism, environmental control, and notions of time. Consider the analogy of a goldfish in water. That medium is pivotal to the way the goldfish lives and breathes until the water evaporates or the bowl breaks. This is similar to the culture shock that many experience when moving to a different culture.

Let's now consider the less-than-desirable relationship J.B. has with his U.S. partners and contrast that with his more satisfactory dealings with the German company. How can this be, when you would expect there to be greater similarities between Germany and the U.S. than between Germany and India?

Many factors are involved in business dealings with culturally different partners. One model was developed by Geert Hofstede, who, having analyzed cultural differences since the late 1960s, identified six "dimensions of national cultures,"[14] three of which are especially pertinent to the J.B. example.

The first of these is what Hofstede identified as *uncertainty avoidance,* meaning the degree to which a culture is tolerant of ambiguity and feels comfortable with unknown situations. Ironically, the United States and India are closer to each other in terms of their comfort with uncertainty than either of them is with the Germans. However, as Hofstede explains, the Germans compensate for their desire to avoid uncertainty by relying on others' expertise. This aligns well with the Indian preference for *power,* another of Hofstede's dimensions. In India, power is unequally distributed throughout the culture, with the *boss* (J.B.) being the final decision maker. When the Germans asked J.B. if his suggestion was the best option, and he confirmed that it was, they accepted his opinion. The Germans were presumably able to reduce their level of uncertainty by giving credence to the power differential that J.B. is afforded in Indian society as the head of the company.

The third relevant dimension to mention here is that of *short-term* or *long-term orientation*. Germany and the U.S. are both examples of the Western tendency for seeking results in the short-term. In comparison, many Asian cultures, such as India, prefer to take a long-term view. As one Indian executive explained:

"By taking the long view, Indians are apt to make allowances for the fact that not everything is always going to go to plan. That includes the fact that early on in a relationship there are bound to be hiccups. This is only to be expected, given the complexity of human interactions. Yet it's remarkable

---

[14]Ibid.

to us how Americans hold to the belief in one Truth, whereas we Indians know there to be many Truths, each one applicable according to the context in which it is applied."

Again, why is there more alignment between the Indian and German executives, and more friction between J.B. and his U.S. partners? Perhaps because of J.B.'s industry experience and expertise, the Germans received assurance that their short-term needs would be met. Trust is highly relevant here. Former President Ronald Reagan's comment, "Trust but verify," is anathema to Indians, who would not consider the need for verification to be indicative of trust.

Why This? Why Now?

Cultural considerations vary geographically in many countries. In the U.S., for example, conducting business in the Midwest is different from doing so in Texas or California. As the former CEO of Coca-Cola, Doug Ivester, said, "As economic borders come down, cultural barriers go up, presenting new challenges and opportunities in business."[15] According to Athanasios Vamvakidis, an economist in the International Monetary Fund's Asia and Pacific Department, "Alongside the globalization process, countries have been increasing their regional economic links through regional trade agreements."[16]

As economic borders have come down, what about the cultural barriers? The authors of *Getting China and India Right,* Anil K. Gupta and Haiyan Wang, stated that any organization looking to make progress in these markets needs to embrace the kind of long-term orientation typical of India and China and rarely found in Western countries:

According to Gupta and Wang: "Most companies will find that their existing knowledge about how to succeed in other markets teaches them little about how to succeed in China and India. If they want to aim for market leadership rather than merely skimming the cream at the top, they will need to engage in considerable learning from scratch."

With that in mind, you are about to discover a little more about the ways U.S. culture compares with Asian cultures. What you find out will create a baseline for understanding the different perspectives among these cultures and help create deeper, more lasting, and more trusted relationships. After all, in order to know how to relate to other cultures, you first need to know where *you* are standing.

---

[15] Robert Rosen, *Global Literacies* (New York: Simon & Schuster, 2000), 21.
[16] "Regional Trade Agreements or Broad Liberalization: Which Path Leads to Faster Growth?" *IMF Staff Papers* 46, no. 1 (March 1999).

So, here's a question for you:

Who Are "Americans"?

The term *American* is very broad and includes the inhabitants of Central, Latin, North, and South America. It doesn't just refer to people who live in the U.S., as the following table illustrates.

Table 1.1

North America	A continent with 23 countries (Antigua and Barbuda; Bahamas; Barbados; Belize; Canada; Costa Rica; Cuba; Dominica; Dominican Republic; El Salvador; Grenada; Guatemala; Haiti; Honduras; Jamaica; Mexico; Nicaragua; Panama; St. Kitts & Nevis; St. Lucia; St. Vincent and the Grenadines; Trinidad and Tobago; United States) and dozens of possessions and territories.[17]
South America	A continent with 12 countries (Argentina; Bolivia; Brazil; Chile; Columbia; Ecuador; Guyana; Peru; Paraguay; Suriname; Uruguay; Venezuela) and three territories (Falkland Islands; French Guiana; Galapagos Islands).[18]
Central America	A region comprising seven countries (Belize; Costa Rica; El Salvador; Guatemala; Honduras; Nicaragua; Panama).[19]
Latin America	A region comprising: Mexico, Central America, South America, and "the islands of the Caribbean whose inhabitants speak a Romance language."[20]

There are numerous *Americans* in the world who have cultural customs and ways of interacting that are quite different from those found in the U.S. This is why, for this book, we have elected to use a more specific term and refer throughout to *U.S. Americans*.

Bear this in mind as you turn to the next chapter, in which we explore a little more about how U.S. Americans *think*.

---

[17]"North America," Worldatlas, www.worldatlas.com/webimage/countrys/na.htm (accessed November 21, 2014).

[18]"South America," Worldatlas, www.worldatlas.com/webimage/countrys/sa.htm (accessed January 9, 2015).

[19]"Central America," Worldatlas, www.worldatlas.com/webimage/countrys/camerica.htm (accessed January 9, 2015).

[20]Roger A. Kittleson, "History of Latin America," Encyclopedia Britannica, April 10, 2014, www.britannica.com/EBchecked/topic/331694/history-of-Latin-America (accessed January 9, 2015).

2 | Exploring Country Cultures

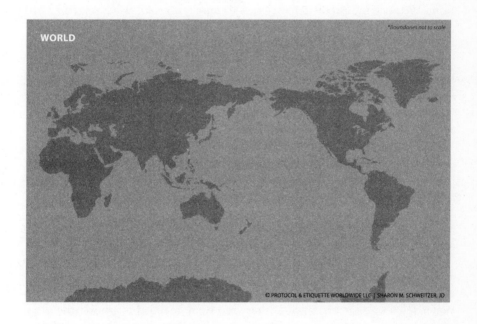

WORLD

*Boundaries not to scale

© PROTOCOL & ETIQUETTE WORLDWIDE LLC | SHARON M. SCHWEITZER, JD

"The most interesting thing about cultures may not be in the observable things they do—the rituals, eating preferences, codes of behavior, and the like—but in the way they mold our most fundamental conscious and unconscious thinking and perception."
—Ethan Watters, "We Aren't the World"[1]

---

[1] Ethan Watters, "We Aren't the World," *Pacific Standard*, February 25, 2013, www.psmag .com/magazines/pacific-standard-cover-story/joe-henrich-weird-ultimatum-game-shaking-up -psychology-economics-53135 (accessed November 20, 2014).

The Machiguenga, who live in a part of Peru close to the borders of Bolivia and Brazil, enjoy lives many of us would envy. Each family member has the freedom to choose what they work on and when to work. They balance their lives, men as planters and hunters and women as harvesters and cooks, with time for relaxation and fun. Given their relative isolation and self-sufficiency, the tribe has little need for cash.

Most Western scientists who visit this *living Eden* do so to conduct pharmacological research. UCLA anthropology graduate student Joe Henrich's interest in visiting the Machiguenga, however, was very different.[2] Henrich wanted to explore whether human beings were psychologically hard-wired to respond universally. In particular, he was interested in knowing whether concepts like fairness and cooperation were basic to *all* cultures, from Western industrialized societies to more isolated *exotic* ones like the Machiguenga.

Henrich devised an ultimatum game that is similar to what game-theory buffs and economists call *the prisoner's dilemma*. The game involved two players, unknown to each other, one of whom would receive the equivalent of several days' wages. The recipient would then decide how much cash to share with the other player, who had the option of accepting or refusing that sum. The dilemma was that if the second player refused the money, the first player forfeited his or her share.

Henrich had great difficulty getting the Machiguenga volunteers to understand the rules, saying: "They just didn't understand why anyone would sacrifice money to punish someone who had the good luck of getting to play the other role."

This is not how U.S. Americans typically think when it comes to these kinds of games.

For example, when an online article about Henrich's study appeared in *Pacific Standard*[3] in February 2013, hundreds of comments from U.S. readers largely confirmed what researchers already knew about our culture: We prefer splits to be made 50-50; otherwise, we're inclined to punish the other player, even if it means losing money ourselves. We also tend to view someone's behavior as being indicative of a personality trait or disposition as opposed to a situational response. Psychologists call this the *fundamental attribution error*, or FAE.

---

[2] "The People of Manu," PBS Online, www.pbs.org/edens/manu/people.htm (accessed November 20, 2014).

[3] Ethan Watters, "We Aren't the World," *Pacific Standard*, February 25, 2013, www.psmag.com/magazines/pacific-standard-cover-story/joe-henrich-weird-ultimatum-game-shaking-up-psychology-economics-53135 (accessed November 20, 2014).

Some of the comments on Henrich's research included (italics are ours to highlight examples of FAE)

- "(T)his *hypothetical tightwad* offered you nothing. If he's that *greedy and indifferent to the lives of others,* how do you think he'll use the money once he gets it?"
- "The other person has *proven themselves unusually greedy and selfish.* They've also done nothing to deserve having this fortune showered upon them."
- "I can only speculate on why this other person wouldn't offer a fair share of this fortune that fell into their lap through no merit of their own, and I find *self-absorption a more likely explanation* than them needing every last dollar in that fortune for completely altruistic reasons."

Note how these commentators jumped to conclusions and made assumptions about *greed, selfishness, and self-absorption* based on the sketchiest of information.

Thinking Is Not Universal

The Machiguenga study helps highlight the erroneous assumption that there are *universal* ways of thinking, feeling, and behaving. This bias is played out in organizations day after day, especially as it relates to leadership and management research and advice.

Consider this quote from a *New York Times* interview with the director of the U.S.-based NeuroLeadership Institute:

"Certainty is a constant drive for the brain . . . the feeling of uncertainty feels like pain . . . that turns out to be cognitively exhausting. . . . The less we can predict the future, the more threatened we feel . . . so we are driven to create certainty."[4]

Did you assume the *we* in that quote meant *we humans*? Actually, it more accurately refers only to certain cultures.

---

[4]Adam Bryant, "A Boss's Challenge: Have Everyone Join the 'In' Group," The New York Times, March 23, 2013, www.nytimes.com/2013/03/24/business/neuroleadership-institutes -chief-on-shared-goals.html?_r=2& (accessed November 20, 2014).

Geert Hofstede's studies over a 40-year span resulted in various dimensions of national cultures. These cultural dimensions must be compared within the context of other country scores and not analyzed as a standalone dimension. As mentioned previously, one of Hofstede's dimensions looks at the issue of uncertainty avoidance by measuring the extent to which people across 76 countries and regions "feel uncomfortable with uncertainty and ambiguity."[5] According to Hofstede's model, the higher the score, the more people within that culture will be uncomfortable with the new, unknown, and surprising. Such cultures deal with that discomfort with strict laws and rules; they also tend to espouse one unassailable *truth*. For more on this topic, see Chapter 3, pages 45–46. Scores on the uncertainty avoidance dimension range from cultures like Greece and Portugal, which scored 112 and 104 respectively, to Singapore and Jamaica, which scored 8 and 13 respectively.

The U.S. score on the uncertainty avoidance dimension is 46, which Hofstede describes as the medium to low range, similar to Indonesia (48), the Philippines (44), and India (40). The U.S. score is quite different from that of Japan (92), South Korea (85), Taiwan (69), China (30), and Hong Kong (29). As these data illustrate, there are considerable variations of tolerance of uncertainty and ambiguity throughout Asia. To assert that all human beings are "driven to create certainty" is misleading at best.

Relationships Are Dynamic

Access to Asia offers you an education in what we're calling the Global Three Rs:

- Engaging in sufficient *research* (due diligence) about a culture
- Showing *respect* for differences
- Enhancing *relationships* through interaction

Think about the word *relationship* for a moment. A relationship is a dynamic, involving two or more individuals or things. We cannot determine where we stand in *relation* to another culture until we have a better handle on ourselves. It is for that reason that this chapter does something few other books do: It holds up a mirror to U.S. culture.

---

[5]"Dimensions," The Hofstede Center, http://geert-hofstede.com/dimensions.html (accessed November 20, 2014).

"A fish discovers its need for water only when it is no longer in it. Our culture is like water to a fish . . . What one culture may regard as essential—a certain level of material wealth, for example—may not be so vital to other cultures."

— *Trompenaars and Hampden-Turner, Riding the Waves of Culture*[6]

We are often oblivious to what *we* think, what *we* value, and what *we* are motivated by because we take them for granted. We are like the goldfish mentioned in the previous chapter. We don't realize that we're swimming in water until the glass bowl is overturned—a feeling that is analogous to doing business in a new culture.

Remaining unaware of how we see the world puts us all at a huge disadvantage—like the new recruit who is ignorant of organizational culture, also known as "the way things are done around here." That's an alienating position to be in until you learn to adapt. But how can you possibly learn what you need to do to develop and maintain meaningful relationships with global clients, customers, and partners?

This is where the eight questions can help – questions that surfaced after interviewing more than 100 people for this book. These questions speak to many of the dimensions identified by the work of Geert Hofstede, Fons Trompenaars, Michele J. Gelfand, Richard Nisbett, Robert J. House, Peter Dorfman, Mansour Javidan, Paul J. Hanges, Mary F. Sully de Luque,[7] and George Simons.[8] Think of them as the beginning of holding up a mirror to *yourself*, with the goal of succeeding in business in Asia.

1. How Do We Prefer to Act—Individually or as a Group?

You may already be familiar with the terms *individualism* and *collectivism* or *communitarianism*[9] that refer to the tendency for cultures to be oriented toward the self or the group. In individualistic societies like the U.S., U.K., and Canada, for example, decisions are made, contracts are negotiated, and deals are cut for which people consider themselves individually responsible. Business people from collectivist cultures, like those covered among the 10 countries featured

---

[6]Fons Trompenaars and Charles Hampden-Turner, *Riding the Waves of Culture: Understanding Diversity in Global Business* (New York: McGraw-Hill, 2012), 27.
[7]Robert J. House, et al., *Strategic Leadership Across Cultures: GLOBE Study of CEO Leadership Behavior and Effectiveness in 24 Countries* (Thousand Oaks, CA: Sage Publications, Inc., 2013).
[8]See: http://diversophy.com.
[9]Ibid., 65–85.

in this book, prefer group representation and group negotiations. In most cases, making a decision without group input is to be avoided.

People in each of these two cultural dimensions have developed different social skills that, although essential to success in one's own culture, are not necessarily understood elsewhere. As Richard Brislin, professor of management and industrial relations at the University of Hawaii at Manoa, advises

> To transcend the distance between self and others, people in individualistic societies have to develop a certain set of social skills. These include public speaking, meeting others quickly and putting them at ease . . . making a good impression . . . These skills are not necessary for collectivists. When it comes time for a person to meet unknown others in a larger society, members of the collective act as go-betweens and make introductions, describe the person's accomplishments and abilities, and so forth. In short, individualists have to rely on themselves. . . . Collectivists have a supportive group that assists in this same goal.[10]

If you are wondering what individualism and collectivism have to do with expanding into international business markets and boosting sales in Asia, know that when you sit at the negotiating table with your Asian partners, your conversation should not be about you and your company but about collaboration and working in harmony with them.

Table 2.1 on page 15 shows the Individualism Index from Geert Hofstede's research on cultural differences, including the rankings of the U.S., Great Britain, Canada, and eight of the Asian countries included in this book (Myanmar and The Philippines were not part of the original Hofstede study). In this index, the higher the number, the greater the degree of individualism. Countries positioned lower on this index are more focused on making sure that you will be consensus-seeking and team-focused before they commit to doing business with you long-term.[11]

2. How Are Power and Authority Viewed?

Many cultures around the globe are ascriptive. In *ascriptive* cultures, characteristics including class, age, sex, higher education, and religion are considered more important than in achievement-oriented cultures. In some ascriptive cultures, power is held *over* people. In others, including many of the Asian countries included in this book, power is considered to be *participative.*

---

[10]Richard Brislin, *Cross-Cultural Encounters: Face-to-Face Interaction* (New York: Pergamon Press, 1981), pp 21-22.
[11]Geert Hofstede, Gert Jan Hofstede, and Michael Minkov, *Cultures and Organizations: Software of the Mind,* 3rd edition. (New York: McGraw-Hill, 2010), 95–97.

Table 2.1   The Individualism Index

World Rank	Country	Index
1	United States	91
3	Great Britain	89
4–6	Canada	80
33	India	48
35–37	Japan	46
54	Malaysia	26
55–56	Hong Kong	25
58–63	China	20
58–63	Singapore	20
58–63	Thailand	20
58–63	Vietnam	20
65	South Korea	18
66	Taiwan	17

Myanmar Individualism Index

World Rank	Country	Index
N/A*	Myanmar	51**

*Myanmar does not have a world ranking because it was not included in Hofstede's cultural dimensions work,[12] or the GLOBE Studies.[13]

**This score is from an exploratory study of Myanmar culture by Dr. Charles Rarick,[14] which uses Hofstede's value dimensions. Refer to Chapter 10 for more information.

As Michael DeCaro, former Chief Audit Executive and VP of Finance, Asia Pacific, and Japan, for Dell, explains

"Western leaders that arrive on the scene and simply announce decisions without getting everyone involved have a much greater likelihood of finding it difficult to achieve their objectives in Asia. For example, in Japan, a position of authority simply allows a leader to take the lead in gaining and developing consensus as to what the ultimate decision will be."

---

[12]"Dimensions," The Hofstede Center, http://geert-hofstede.com/dimensions.html (accessed November 20, 2014).

[13]Robert J. House, Paul J. Hanges, Mansour Javidan, Peter W. Dorfman, and Vipin Gupta, *Culture, Leadership, and Organizations: The GLOBE Study of 62 Societies*, (Thousand Oaks, CA: Sage Publications, Inc., 2004); Robert J. House, Peter W. Dorfman, Mansour Javidan, Paul J. Hanges, and Mary Sully de Luque, *Strategic Leadership Across Cultures: GLOBE Study of CEO Leadership Behavior and Effectiveness in 24 Countries*, (Thousand Oaks, CA: Sage Publications, Inc., 2013).

[14]C. Rarick and I. Nickerson, "An Exploratory Study of Myanmar Culture Using Hofstede's Value Dimension" (February 20, 2006), doi:10.2139/ssrn.1114625.

The differences in *perceived* inequalities between people in Asian countries are captured by Geert Hofstede's Power Distance (PDI) dimension, reflecting the degree to which a culture is comfortable with power inequalities. The higher the PDI number, the greater the power distance, meaning members of a culture "expect and accept that power is distributed unequally." For example, the U.S. score of 40 on the PDI in Table 2.2 is relatively low on the PDI,

Table 2.2   The Power Distance Index

World Ranking	Country	Index
1–2	Malaysia	104
5	Philippines	94
12–14	China	80
15–16	Indonesia	78
17–18	India	77
19	Singapore	74
22–25	Vietnam	70
27–29	Hong Kong	68
34–36	Thailand	64
41–42	S. Korea	60
43–44	Taiwan	58
49–50	Japan	54
59–61	United States	40
62	Canada	39
65–67	Great Britain	35

Myanmar Power Distance Index

World Rank	Country	Index
N/A*	Myanmar	26**

*Myanmar does not have a world ranking because it was not included in Hofstede's cultural dimensions work,[15] or the GLOBE Studies.[16]
**This score is from an exploratory study of Myanmar culture by Dr. Charles Rarick,[17] which uses Hofstede's value dimensions. Refer to Chapter 10 for more information.

---

[15]"Dimensions," The Hofstede Center, http://geert-hofstede.com/dimensions.html (accessed November 20, 2014).
[16]Robert J. House, Paul J. Hanges, Mansour Javidan, Peter W. Dorfman, and Vipin Gupta, *Culture, Leadership, and Organizations: The GLOBE Study of 62 Societies*, (Thousand Oaks, CA: Sage Publications, Inc., 2004); Robert J. House, Peter W. Dorfman, Mansour Javidan, Paul J. Hanges, and Mary Sully de Luque, *Strategic Leadership Across Cultures: GLOBE Study of CEO Leadership Behavior and Effectiveness in 24 Countries*, (Thousand Oaks, CA: Sage Publications, Inc., 2013).
[17]C. Rarick and I. Nickerson, "An Exploratory Study of Myanmar Culture Using Hofstede's Value Dimension" (February 20, 2006), doi:10.2139/ssrn.1114625.

reflecting the belief that 'all men are created equal.' Nevertheless, reality teaches us that there will be inequalities in society.

3. How Do We Compare Rules and Relationships?

Fons Trompenaars and Charles Hampden-Turner speak of this distinction in terms of *universalist* and *particularist* cultures (see Table 2.3). As they point out in *Riding the Waves of Culture:*

"One serious pitfall for universalist cultures in doing business with more particularist ones is that the importance of the relationship is often ignored. The contract will be seen as definitive by the universalist, but only a rough guideline or approximation by the particularist."

The authors have identified different countries' cultural preferences with respect to rules and relationships. In one example, they discovered which cultures would follow the rule of law and which would consider the circumstances to protect a friend from the police. Table 2.3 indicates where some Western cultures fall on this universalist-particularist continuum, together with the six Asian cultures included in Trompenaars and Hampden-Turner's study.[18] The higher the number, the more universalist the culture.

Table 2.3   Universalism–Particularism Chart

Country opting for universalist ("rules-based") system	Percentage of Respondents
South Korea	37
China	47
India	54
Indonesia	57
Japan	68
Singapore	69
U.K.	91
U.S. and Canada	93

4. How Do We View Time?

One key subtlety about time concerns the concepts of *monochronic* and *polychronic*. In the West, we expect an executive stopped by another colleague en

---

[18] Adapted from Fons Trompenaars and Charles Hampden-Turner's *Riding the Waves of Culture: Understanding Diversity in Global Business* (New York: McGraw-Hill, 2012), 46.

route to a meeting, to say that he or she can't stop to chat. In polychronic cultures, such as those in Asia, it's common for several things to happen at once and punctuality is not as essential. People in the U.S. tend to be less comfortable with constant interruptions; such simultaneous comings and goings are common in polychronic societies like India and Malaysia.

Like cocktail party guests, some of whom arrive promptly whereas others only show up after the event is in full swing, there are considerable variations within as well as between cultures when it comes to perceptions of time.

With respect to the concepts of monochronic time, meaning linear or sequential, doing one thing at a time, and polychronic or *synchronic* time, meaning doing several things at a time or *multitasking*, a study published in the *Journal of Consumer Research* found that the U.S. falls within the middle of the continuum (3.18, where 1.0 is monochronic and 5.0 is polychronic).[19] In Asian countries, the equivalent figure was 4.0. Given the central theme of this book—relationships—this movement is a good thing.

As Trompenaars and Hampden-Turner point out, polychronic cultures are less focused on punctuality. Although recent research indicates that the U.S. is moving toward a more polychronic orientation,[20] the culture has typically been monochronic. Although you may not ever need to use either of these terms directly, what we are stressing here is encapsulated by this quote of Hall's:

> "It is impossible to know how many millions of dollars have been lost in international business because monochronic and polychronic people do not understand each other or even realize that two such different time systems exist."[21]

Table 2.4 on page 19 shows different concepts for monochronic and polychronic time.

5. How Do We Typically Communicate?

One important topic to consider with respect to communication is what anthropologists have termed *low-context* and *high-context*. Here's an analogy to illustrate the difference between the two:

As a lawyer, Sharon frequently read witness testimony transcripts. These documents capture the witnesses' spoken word, *not* body language such as hand gestures, eye movements, shrugs, finger-pointing, eye-rolling or other nonverbal communication. Only observing the witness provides awareness of the

---

[19]Kaufman, C.F., Lane, P.M., and Lindquist, J. "Exploring More Than 24 Hours a Day: A Preliminary Investigation of Polychronic Time Use," *Journal of Consumer Research*, 18 (1991): 392–401.
[20]Ibid.
[21]Edward T. Hall, *The Dance of Life: The Other Dimension of Time* (New York: Anchor Books, 1984).

Table 2.4   Monochronic and Polychronic Time

Monochronic	Polychronic
Traditional Examples: Canada, Germany, U.S., Northern and Western Europe	**Traditional Examples:** Arab countries, Asia, Middle East, Latin America, Southern and Eastern Mediterranean, Turkey
Focus is on doing one thing at a time	Focus is on doing many things at once
Attention given mostly to ■ The project ■ Priorities ■ The task ■ Procedures	Attention given mostly to ■ Relationships ■ Clients, patrons, customers ■ Friends and colleagues ■ Family members
Appointments, milestones, and deadlines are scheduled because they are important.	Appointments are flexible; meetings may be postponed or missed.
Everyone expected to adhere to clock time and be punctual, prompt. Schedules are followed.	Time is seen as fluid, punctuality not so important. Schedules may be modified.
Time is a limited commodity and quantifiable.	Time is limitless, unquantifiable.
Behaviors include ■ Time management ■ Setting deadlines and schedules and discouraging interruptions ■ Creating agendas	**Behaviors include** ■ Avoiding being too busy to socialize ■ Changing deadlines and schedules ■ Comfortable with interruptions ■ Dispensing with agendas

enormous effects of such subtleties on the jury, the judge, and the observers. The same is true of interoffice-communication.

The U.S., for example, is considered a relatively low-context culture in which direct communication is rewarded and the emphasis is placed on words. In contrast, Asian cultures are high-context, meaning communication is indirect and words can only be understood in context. Body language and facial expressions all have a major part to play. Few cultures, or the people living in them, fall at one end of the spectrum or the other. Most people have a combination of high- and low-context characteristics in communication. Table 2.5 on page 20 shows the key differences.

**Table 2.5   Communication Characteristics of
High–Context and Low–Context Cultures**

High–Context	Low–Context
Traditional Examples: Eastern Asia, Japan, China, South Korea	**Traditional Examples:** Canada, Germany, Scandinavia, Switzerland, U.K., U.S.
Communication as an art form	Communication as a way to brainstorm
Implicit:	Explicit:
• Indirect, nonverbal messages	• Direct, verbal message
• Finessed, vague, indefinite, imprecise	• Specific, precise, to the point, definite
• Nonverbal cues highly significant (tone of voice, facial expressions, gestures, eye movements all impact conversation)	• Nonverbal cues not as significant (the actual words spoken are crucial)
Situation and people more important than actual words spoken	Greatest importance placed on words; "What did he *say*?"
Disagreement is personalized	Disagreement is depersonalized
Sensitivity to conflict expressed nonverbally	Withdrawal from conflict or work on project; focus on logical task, not personal conflict
Behaviors include	**Behaviors include**
• Silence in meetings	• Speaking to fill void in conversation
• Inhaling through pursed lips to show displeasure	• Spoken displeasure
• Using eyes to indicate close of conversation/meeting	• A direct statement that the meeting is over
• Inhaling with a hissing sound to indicate difficulty	• A direct statement that something isn't possible

6. How Formal or Informal Are We?

Professor Michele Gelfand and her colleagues at the University of Maryland's Department of Psychology have made a distinction between tight and loose cultures. *Tight* cultures are those with strong social norms and a low tolerance for any behavior that does not conform to those norms. An example would be the

Japanese, with their higher degree of structure, and formality. *Loose* cultures are the polar opposite, with weak social norms and high tolerance. These cultures are more likely to be comfortable with informalities.

Table 2.6 gives a sense of the informality or "looseness" between countries in the West and the eight Asian countries included in Gelfand's study.[22] The higher the number, the tighter the culture. Richard Lewis has categorized country cultures into three broad categories: linear-active, multi-active, and reactive.[23]

Table 2.6   Continuum of Tight and Loose Scores

Country	Tightness Score
Pakistan	12.3
Malaysia	11.8
India	11.0
Singapore	10.4
South Korea	10.0
Japan	8.6
China	7.9
U.K.	6.9
Hong Kong	6.3
United States	5.1
Australia	4.4
[Mean of 33 countries studied]	6.5

7. How Aligned Are Our Social and Business Lives?

In the same way that people in the East and West have different concepts of time (see our discussion of question 4 on page 17), the ways we choose to spend that time in the workplace are diverse.

Researchers from the University of Delaware[24] asked workers how many of their working hours were spent on work-related tasks as opposed to social activities, such as informal chatting, celebrating coworkers' birthdays

---

[22]Reproduced from Michele J. Gelfand, Michele J., et al., "Differences Between Tight and Loose Cultures: A 33-Nation Study," *Science* 332 (May, 2011) 1100, 1103.

[23]Richard D. Lewis, *When Teams Collide: Managing the International Team Successfully* (Boston: Nicholas Brealey Publishing, 2012), 10.

[24]L. Manrai and A. Manrai, "Effects of Cultural-Context, Gender, and Acculturation on Perceptions of Work versus Social/Leisure Time Usage," *Journal of Business Research*, no. 32, 1995: 115–128.

and anniversaries, and enjoying tea or coffee together. U.S. respondents working for companies in major cities typically said they spent 80 percent of their time on business tasks and the remaining 20 percent on socializing. In Asian countries, including India, Indonesia, and Malaysia, the answer was 50/50.

This study also found that many international business travelers believed that socializing on the job was an inefficient way to spend time in today's competitive world. As Richard Brislin and Eugene Kim of the University of Hawaii at Manoa, Hawaii, point out, "The problem with such reactions is that they are ethnocentric: People are making conclusions based on the norms and values of their own cultures."[25]

The importance of the 50:50 balance that some consider "aimless socializing and chatting" becomes clear when you realize how much more important relationship-building is in collectivist cultures than in individualist ones. In China, for example, the culture depends largely on *guanxi* networks through which favors and influence are passed from one person to another.

Westerners often don't appreciate how important it is in Asian cultures to spend more time developing and maintaining relationships. This difference was highlighted in a cross-cultural communication course attended by an Indian interviewee who was surprised and interested to learn one of the "key elements of U.S. business culture"[26] was the separation of our work and private lives. In contrast, one U.S. executive who is currently establishing connections in Myanmar pointed out that he will likely spend the next two years in meetings, having talks, hosting delegations, and attending dinners and luncheons before any business is secured.

As Andy Molinsky so eloquently states in his book *Global Dexterity*,[27] "adapting to new cultures without losing yourself in the process" requires establishing personal boundaries and knowing just how far you are prepared to modify them as situations arise. Some activities may not be for you. Knowing this beforehand will save grief and *face* for you and your Asian business partners. It is possible to refrain from participating without judging other cultures. Often the wise and more successful approach is to keep an open mind to new experiences, as the pioneering work of Stanford psychology professor Dr. Carol Dweck highlights.

---

[25]Richard W. Brislin and Eugene S. Kim, "Cultural Diversity in People's Understanding and Uses of Time," *Applied Psychology: An International Review* 52, no. 3 (2003): 363–382.

[26]Karine Schomer, "Working with Americans, Change Management Consulting and Training, LLC," www.cmct.net (accessed November 20, 2014).

[27]Andy Molinsky, *Global Dexterity: How to Adapt Your Behavior Across Cultures without Losing Yourself in the Process* (Boston: Harvard Business School Publishing, 2013).

Mindset and Success

According to Dweck's research, people who hold rigid beliefs as to what they can or can't (should/shouldn't) achieve have *fixed* mindsets. They tend to be less successful in the areas of business, education, and sports than people with *growth* mindsets. *Growth* people consider challenging experiences to be essential to developing new abilities. "Virtually all great people have had these qualities," writes Dweck on her website.[28]

Table 2.7 contains example statements to help you identify how open or fixed your mindset may be to growth. Responses to these statements range from Strongly Agree, Agree, and Mostly Agree to Mostly Disagree, Disagree, and Strongly Disagree. To complete the entire quiz, visit url http://mindset online.com and click the Test Your Mindset link.[29]

Table 2.7   Statements for Determining a Fixed or Growth Mindset

- You can learn new things, but you cannot really change your basic intelligence.
- Your talent in an area is something about you that you cannot change very much.
- You can change even your basic level of talent considerably.

8. How Is the Concept of Women in Business Handled?

Life is not as black-and-white as we would like it to be. The extent to which a female professional may experience challenges in Asia because of her gender depends on many things.

The challenges that impact women in their home country often shed light on the business environment for international businesswomen. There is no hard-and-fast rule on the topic of how women are treated in the world of work, as you will discover when we ask this question again in each of the 10 country-specific chapters. In the meantime, look at Table 2.8 on page 24, the Booz & Company Third Billion Index, to see rankings for the Canada, U.K., and U.S., and eight of the Asian countries covered in this book. The Third Billion Index is compiled from a myriad of indicators that affect women's

---

[28]"Mindset for Achievement," Mindset, http://mindsetonline.com/howmindsetaffects/mindset forachievement/index.html (accessed November 20, 2014).

[29]"Test Your Mindset," Mindset, http://mindsetonline.com/testyourmindset/step1.php (accessed November 20, 2014).

Table 2.8   Third Billion Index Scores and Rankings

Rank	Country	Score
7	Canada	67.2
13	United Kingdom	64.9
30	United States	58.0
32	Hong Kong/China	57.4
37	Singapore	55.6
43	Japan	54.1
48	Thailand	53.3
50	Republic of Korea	52.4
54	Philippines	51.7
58	China	50.9
—	*Mean*	50.0
75	Vietnam	47.9
80	Cambodia	47.0
82	Malaysia	46.0
90	Indonesia	43.7
94	Laos	42.4
115	India	37.3

economic standing, including entrepreneurial support and equal pay. It features 128 countries whose scores range from 70.6 (Australia and Norway, ranked number one and number two, respectively) to 26.1 (Yemen, with the lowest score).[30]

Global flexibility research conducted by social psychologist Richard E. Nisbett, anthropologist Joe Henrich, and many others show that different cultures not only think differently, but they actually see the world differently. Yet this thinking, whether Eastern or Western, can be modified fairly easily. To demonstrate that, consider Hong Kong. Given its exposure to the influences of both East (China) and West (Great Britain), Hong Kong proves to be "an interesting laboratory for purposes of cross-cultural study."[31]

By priming student participants with pictures associated with U.S. culture (images of Mickey Mouse) or Chinese culture (images of dragons),

---

[30]"Third Billion Index Rankings," Booz & Company, 2012, http://www.strategyand.pwc.com/media/file/Strategyand_2012-Third-Billion-Index-Rankings.pdf (accessed November 20, 2014).

[31]Richard Nisbett, *The Geography of Thought: How Asians and Westerners Think Differently . . . and Why* (New York: The Free Press, 2003), 118–119.

Ying-yi Hong[32] and her University of Hong Kong colleagues discovered something interesting during their studies. Those students who were primed with the U.S. images quickly adapted to the individualistic thinking indicative of the West, whereas those primed with Eastern images continued to embrace the context-dependent way of thinking that typifies Asia.

Cognitive and cultural neuroscience is shedding light on the hidden workings of the mind and the hidden role of deep culture on cognition and behavior.[33]

This book is designed to serve as a similar kind of primer, one that will help you be flexible in your thinking, motivations, feelings, and behaviors when doing business in Asia, while maintaining the values and morals you hold dear.

Now let's explore what U.S. Americans specifically need to be aware of when attempting to develop relationships with business people in Asia. The next chapter, as well as the 10 country-specific chapters in this book, provide responses to these eight questions, along with valuable country basics and international etiquette.

---

[32]Y. Hong, C. Chiu, and T. Kung, "Bringing Culture out in Front: Effects of Cultural Meaning System Activation on Social Cognition," *Progress in Asian Social Psychology* 1, eds. K. Leung, Y. Kashima, U. Kim, and S. Yamaguchi (Singapore: John Wiley & Sons, 1997), 135–146.

[33]Joseph Shaules, *The Intercultural Mind: Connecting Culture, Cognition and Global Living* (Boston: Intercultural Press 2015).

3 | United States of America

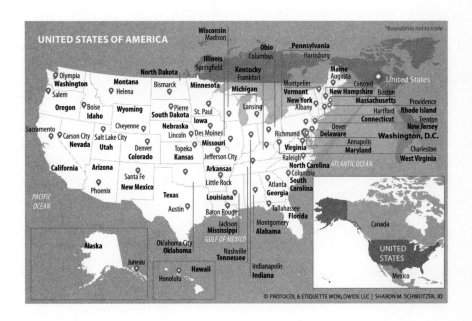

UNITED STATES OF AMERICA

Boundaries not to scale

Wisconsin — Madison
Ohio — Columbus
Pennsylvania — Harrisburg
Illinois — Springfield
Kentucky — Frankfort
Maine — Augusta
North Dakota — Bismarck
Washington — Olympia
Salem
Montana — Helena
Minnesota
Michigan
Montpelier
Vermont
New Hampshire — Concord
Boston
United States
Oregon — Boise
Idaho
Wyoming — Cheyenne
South Dakota — Pierre
St. Paul
Iowa
Lansing
New York — Albany
Massachusetts
Hartford
Connecticut
Rhode Island — Providence
Trenton
New Jersey
Sacramento
Carson City
Nevada
Salt Lake City
Utah
Denver
Colorado
Nebraska — Lincoln
Des Moines
Missouri
Topeka
Kansas
Jefferson City
Richmond
Virginia
Dover
Delaware
Annapolis
Maryland
Washington, D.C.
Charleston
West Virginia
California
Arizona — Phoenix
Santa Fe
New Mexico
Texas — Austin
Arkansas — Little Rock
Louisiana — Baton Rouge
Raleigh
North Carolina
Columbia
South Carolina
Atlanta
Georgia
ATLANTIC OCEAN
PACIFIC OCEAN
Tallahassee
Florida
Jackson
Mississippi
Montgomery
Alabama
Canada
Alaska — Juneau
Oklahoma City
Oklahoma
GULF OF MEXICO
Nashville
Tennessee
Indianapolis
Indiana
Hawaii — Honolulu
UNITED STATES
Mexico

© PROTOCOL & ETIQUETTE WORLDWIDE LLC | SHARON M. SCHWEITZER, JD

"The thing that I learned as a diplomat is that human relations ultimately make a huge difference. No matter what message you are about to deliver somewhere, whether it is holding out a hand of friendship, or making clear that you disapprove of something, is the fact that the person sitting across the table is a human being, so the goal is to always establish common ground."

—Madeleine Korbel Albright, Former United States Secretary of State

Introduction

One of the things that is well known about the United States,[1] even in other cultures, is how little U.S. Americans[2] seem to know about the world. For example, during one of Sharon's business trips to China, she visited the Haidian District office of a long-standing female colleague. As they were finishing their discussion, her Chinese colleague asked, "Americans are still learning about world geography, yes?" In her polite, face-saving, indirect way, what she was *really* asking was why Westerners are sometimes ignorant of other cultures. This led to a fascinating discussion about the differences between Eastern and Western thought.

This need to understand the differences in Western thought and action is fundamental to establishing long-term relationships in Asia. As we explained in the Introduction, this book offers in-the-trenches information focused around eight questions. The culturally focused themes that these address are covered in each of the 10 Asian country chapters. It is important to review these themes as they relate to U.S. culture too, to gain awareness of aspects of culture U.S. Americans often don't think about until we are doing business in countries whose attitudes and behaviors are quite different from ours, and when we must be more culturally fluent.

There is a dual purpose to this chapter: To address the eight question framework as it relates to the U.S. American way of doing business, but also as a primer to doing business in the U.S. for Asian readers or indeed anyone visiting from another culture.

Quiz

How much do you know about the U.S.? Answer the following questions as True or False to test your knowledge (the Answer Key that follows the quiz includes page references where you can find more information.):

_____1. The U.S. is one of only three countries still using the Imperial system of measurement instead of the international metric system.

_____2. In the U.S., English is the official national language.

_____3. There are three U.S. territories: American Samoa, Guam, and the U.S. Virgin Islands.

---

[1]As mentioned in Chapter 1 on page 1, the United States of America has been abbreviated to "U.S." in this book.

[2]As mentioned in Chapter 1 on page 7, there are numerous "Americans" in the world who have cultural customs that are quite different to those in the United States. This is why we have elected to use a more specific term and refer to "U.S. Americans."

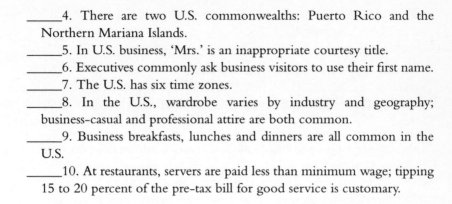

_____4. There are two U.S. commonwealths: Puerto Rico and the Northern Mariana Islands.

_____5. In U.S. business, 'Mrs.' is an inappropriate courtesy title.

_____6. Executives commonly ask business visitors to use their first name.

_____7. The U.S. has six time zones.

_____8. In the U.S., wardrobe varies by industry and geography; business-casual and professional attire are both common.

_____9. Business breakfasts, lunches and dinners are all common in the U.S.

_____10. At restaurants, servers are paid less than minimum wage; tipping 15 to 20 percent of the pre-tax bill for good service is customary.

Answer Key: 1. T (p. 33); 2. F (p. 33); 3. T (p. 29–30); 4. T (p. 30); 5. T (p. 38); 6. T (p. 38); 7. F (p. 34); 8. T (p. 36); 9. T (p. 39); 10. T (p. 40).

Country Basics

This section provides key knowledge in an easy-to-read format to help you quickly grasp some of the basics necessary to navigate this culture.

Historical Timeline

A critical way to show respect for another person's culture is to have knowledge of their country's history and current affairs. Table 3.1 on page 30 outlines a few key U.S. events along with concurrent world events.

Full Country Name and Location

The United States of America is the world's third largest nation. It borders the Atlantic Ocean and the Pacific Ocean, between Canada and Mexico. Alaska and Hawaii are the only non-contiguous states. Hawaii is an island archipelago of 8 major islands, 137 in all.[3] Alaska is located in the northwest corner of the North American continent, bordered by Canada, the Arctic Ocean and the Pacific Ocean. There are three U.S. territories: American Samoa, Guam,

---

[3]"Hawaii Facts & Figures," State of Hawaii Department of Business, Economic Development & Tourism, September 2011, http://files.hawaii.gov/dbedt/economic/library/facts/2011-facts-cropped.pdf (accessed November 20, 2014).

and the U.S. Virgin Islands; and two commonwealths: Puerto Rico and the
Northern Mariana Islands.[4]

Table 3.1   Key Historical Events

Period/ Dates	Description/Events	World Events
1776	Declaration of Independence signed.	*The Wealth of Nations* is published.
1783	U.S. independence recognized by Britain.	Beethoven's first works are printed.
1788	The Constitution is ratified.	Mozart releases the three "great" symphonies: E-flat, G minor, and "Jupiter."
1861	Civil war breaks out after several southern states secede from the union.	The Kingdom of Italy is founded.
1865	End of Civil War, slavery is abolished.	Joseph Lister pioneers antiseptic surgery.
1964	Civil Rights Act is enacted.	Olympics held in Tokyo, Japan.
1969	United States puts first man on the moon.	U.S. and Japan agree on return of the Ryukyu Islands to Japan.
2001	Sept. 11 terrorist attacks on the World Trade Center in New York City and the Pentagon in Washington, D.C.	People's Republic of China is admitted to the World Trade Organization.
2008	Barack Obama elected as first African-American president.	Olympics held in Beijing, China.
2016	Presidential and legislative elections scheduled.	Elections scheduled for Japan, Malaysia, the Philippines, and Taiwan.
2018	Legislative elections scheduled.	Elections scheduled for China and Malaysia. PyeongChang, South Korea to host the XXIII Olympic Winter Games.

[4]"Territories of the United States," Encyclopedia.com, 2005, www.encyclopedia.com /topic/Territories_of_the_United_States.aspx (accessed November 20, 2014); "Commonwealths & Territories of the United States of America," U.S. Government Printing Office, February 13, 2012, http://bensguide.gpo.gov/3-5/state/territories.html (accessed November 20, 2014).

Government / Political Structure

The U.S. is a constitution-based federal republic with strong democratic traditions. A president, elected by a college of representatives from each state, serves as both the head of state and head of government. The president serves a four-year term, with eligibility for a second term. Most recent elections were held November, 2012. The bicameral legislature, or Congress, consists of the Senate and House of Representatives.

Population and Economic Centers

The 2014 *CIA World Factbook* estimates the U.S. population at 319 million people, with 82.4 percent living in urban areas.[5] The country is divided into 50 states and one district (District of Columbia).

According to the *CIA World Factbook*, ethnicities among this population are: White (79.96 percent), Black (12.85 percent), Asian (4.43 percent), American Indian and Alaska native (0.97 percent), native Hawaiian and other Pacific islanders (0.18 percent), and two or more races (1.61 percent). *Note*: a separate listing for Hispanic is not included here because the U.S. Census Bureau considers the term *Hispanic* to refer to persons living in the U.S. of Spanish/Hispanic/Latino origin, including those of Mexican, Cuban, Puerto Rican, Dominican Republic, Spanish, and Central or South American origin, who may be of any race or ethnic group (White, Black, Asian, and so on); about 15.1 percent of the total U.S. population is Hispanic.[6]

The major business centers and populations (as of 2010) are shown in Table 3.2 on page 32.[7]

Economy

The U.S. is ranked 7th out of 189 economies in terms of ease of doing business, according to the World Bank Group's *Doing Business 2015* report.[8] Its 2013

---

[5]CIA, *The World Factbook*, "United States," www.cia.gov/library/publications/the-world-factbook/geos/us.html (accessed November 20, 2014).
[6]Ibid.
[7]"United States Census 2010," U.S. Census Bureau, www.census.gov/2010census (accessed November 20, 2014).
[8]World Bank Group, *Doing Business 2015*, published October 29, 2014, http://www.doingbusiness.org/~/media/GIAWB/Doing%20Business/Documents/Annual-Reports/English/DB15-Full-Report.pdf, p.4, (accessed November 20, 2014).

Table 3.2   Major Business Centers

Business Centers	Population (millions)
Chicago, IL	2.7
Houston, TX	2.1
Los Angeles, CA	3.8
New York City, NY	8.2
Philadelphia, PA	1.5
San Francisco, CA	0.8
Washington, DC	0.6

GDP was ranked number one by the World Bank,[9] and the composition of its GDP by sector was services (79.4 percent), industry (19.5 percent), and agriculture (1.1 percent).[10]

Corruption Perceptions Index

The U.S. ranked 19th least corrupt out of 177 countries and territories with a score of 73 out of 100.[11] This annual index, compiled by Transparency International, measures perceived levels of public sector corruption.

The Criminal Division of the Department of Justice and the Federal Bureau of Investigation are the anticorruption agencies that conduct investigations in the United States.

Human Development Index

The U.S. ranked fifth out of 187 countries and territories.[12] The HDI, compiled by the United Nations Development Programme, is a composite index of life expectancy, education and income statistics.

---

[9]The World Bank, Data, GDP Ranking, "Gross Domestic Product Ranking Table," last updated September 24, 2014, http://data.worldbank.org/data-catalog/GDP-ranking-table (accessed November 20, 2014).

[10]CIA, *The World Factbook*, "United States," www.cia.gov/library/publications/the-world-factbook/geos/us.html (accessed November 20, 2014).

[11]Transparency International, "Corruption Perceptions Index 2013," www.transparency.org/cpi2013/results (accessed November 20, 2014).

[12]United Nations Development Programme, *Human Development Report 2014*, http://hdr.undp.org/sites/default/files/hdr14-report-en-1.pdf, p. 160–63, (accessed November 20, 2014).

Global Gender Gap Index

The U.S. ranked 20th out of 142 countries in terms of gender equality with a score of 0.7463.[13] This annual index, compiled by the World Economic Forum, assesses gender gaps based on economic, political, educational, and health-based criteria.

System of Measurement

When shipping or transporting materials to and from the U.S., be aware that it is one of only three countries using the Imperial system of measurement instead of the international metric system. (The other two countries are Myanmar/Burma and Liberia.)

Climate

The U.S. has a varied climate: Tropical in Hawaii and Florida; arctic in Alaska; semi-arid in the Great Plains west of the Mississippi River; arid in the Great Basin of the southwest; and low winter temperatures in the northeast and northwest.

Languages

English is widely spoken in the U.S. (82.1 percent), along with Spanish (10.7 percent), other Indo-European (3.8 percent), Asian and Pacific Island (2.7 percent), and others (0.7 percent). The U.S. has no official national language, although English is official in 28 of the 50 states.[14]

Belief Systems, Philosophies, and Religions

The country breakdown is as follows: Christian Protestant (51.3 percent), Roman Catholic (23.9 percent), Mormon (1.7 percent), other Christian (1.6

---

[13]World Economic Forum, *The Global Gender Gap Report 2014*, www3.weforum.org /docs/GGGR14/GGGR_CompleteReport_2014.pdf, p.8-9, (accessed November 20, 2014).
[14]"United States Census 2010," U.S. Census Bureau, www.census.gov/2010census (accessed November 20, 2014).

percent), Jewish (1.7 percent), Buddhist (0.7 percent), Islam (0.6 percent), other or unspecified (2.5 percent), unaffiliated (12.1 percent), none (4 percent).[15]

For an overview of belief systems, philosophies, and religions, please refer to Chapter 4, pages 64–65.

Time Zones/Daylight Savings

The U.S. has five time zones:

- Hawaii Standard Time (HST) UTC/GMT −10
- Pacific Standard Time (PST) UTC/GMT −8
- Mountain Standard Time (MST) UTC/GMT −7
- Central Standard Time (CST) UTC/GMT −6
- Eastern Standard Time (EST) UTC/GMT −5

Note that the standard formula to calculate local time is to add or subtract a certain number of hours from the UTC (Coordinated Universal Time)/GMT (Greenwich Mean Time).

Daylight Savings Time in the U.S. begins at 2:00 a.m. local time on the second Sunday in March. It ends at 2:00 a.m. on the first Sunday in November when clocks turn back one hour. Arizona, Puerto Rico, Hawaii, the U.S. Virgin Islands, and American Samoa do not observe Daylight Savings Time.[16]

For more information, see www.timeanddate.com/worldclock.

Telephone Country Code and Internet Suffix

The U.S. telephone country code is 01 and the Internet suffix is .us.

Currency

The U.S. currency is the U.S. dollar (USD). One dollar is divided into 100 cents.

Business Culture, Etiquette, and Customs

This section covers business culture, etiquette and customs.

---

[15] Ibid.

[16] "Daylight Saving Time in the United States," Timetemperature.com, www.time temperature.com/tzus/daylight_saving_time.shtml. (accessed November 20, 2014).

Fiscal Year

The U.S. fiscal year may vary by company or government type and industry. Dates are commonly written as month/day/year: for example, April 1, 2020 is 04/01/2020.

Working Week

The structure of the typical U.S. working week is outlined in Table 3.3.

Table 3.3   The U.S. Working Schedule

Industry	Business Hours	Days of the Week
Businesses	08:00–17:00	Monday–Friday
Banks	09:00–17:00	Monday–Friday
	09:00–14:00	Saturday
Retail shops	10:00–21:00	Monday–Saturday
	12:00–18:00	Sunday

Holidays and Festivals

Common U.S. holidays and festivals appear in Table 3.4.

Table 3.4   U.S. Holidays and Festivals

Date	Name
January 1	New Year's Day
Third Monday of January	Martin Luther King Day
Third Monday of February	Presidents Day
March/April	Easter
May 5	Cinco de Mayo
Last Monday in May	Memorial Day
July 4	Independence Day
First Monday in September	Labor Day
November 11	Veteran's Day
Fourth Thursday in November	Thanksgiving Day
December 25	Christmas Day

Business Dress/Appearance

Wardrobe varies by industry and geography; business-casual and professional attire are both common. Professional dress for men is a suit (matching slacks and coat) with a white or light-colored shirt, a quality silk tie, polished shoes that match the belt, and socks.

Professional attire for women includes a suit (matching skirt and jacket) or a conservative dress, minimal jewelry and closed-toed shoes with a two- to three-inch heel. In certain industries, bare legs are acceptable for a professional woman in summer months.

Men's business-casual attire includes collared shirts, pressed trousers, or jeans. For women, short sleeved (not sleeveless) dresses, pants (not leggings), sweaters, and open toed shoes (not sandals) are appropriate.

In professional circles, both men and women wear high-quality watches and carry leather portfolios or briefcases. Tailor suits to fit; suggested suit colors are navy, black, dark gray, or brown. Men are clean-shaven or have neatly trimmed facial hair. Women wear neutral makeup. Both men and women cover tattoos, remove piercings, and keep their fingernails trimmed and clean; they avoid black and patterned nail polish.

News Sources

Common news sources in the U.S. include the following:

- *Wall Street Journal*: http://online.wsj.com/home-page
- *Financial Times*: www.ft.com/home/us
- *The Economist*: www.economist.com
- *New York Times*: www.nytimes.com
- *Los Angeles Times*: www.latimes.com
- *Chicago Tribune*: www.chicagotribune.com
- *Dallas Morning News*: www.dallasnews.com
- *USA Today*: www.usatoday.com

Business Cards

Exchanging business cards occurs in professional or international trade circles. Carrying 50 or more cards in a neutral colored, quality card case is common.

With cards printed in another language, present the English side to your U.S. counterpart when meeting.

Technology

According to Akamai Technology's *State of the Internet Report,* the U.S. has the 10th-fastest average Internet connection speed in the world.[17] Latest figures rank the U.S. second in the world for the number of Internet users[18] and first globally for the number of Internet hosts.[19]

Gifts

Appropriate corporate gifts tailored to the recipient include coffee table books, office or desk accessories (pen sets, paperweights, etc.). Cash or personal clothing is inappropriate. When considering boxed candy or liquor, research health, religious, or personal habits.

Corporate gifts are given for holidays, retirements, birthdays, births, marriage, or promotion. Buy moderately priced gifts. Send a thank-you note within 48 hours. Never give gifts or cash to a government official.

Introductions, Greetings, Personal Space, and Eye Contact

Introduce yourself using both first and last name. Greet with "Hello," "Good morning," or "Good afternoon." Avoid "Hey there," and "How ya doin?"

Personal space is 'an arm's length.' A handshake is the appropriate touch in the U.S. workplace. However, after a relationship is established, people in the southern, western, and southwestern U.S., who commonly are more demonstrative with greetings, may offer a light hug or an air-kiss.

---

[17] Akamai Technologies, "State of the Internet Q4 2013," published April 2014, http://www.akamai.com/dl/akamai/akamai-soti-q413.pdf?WT.mc_id=soti_Q413 (accessed November 20, 2014).

[18] CIA, *The World Factbook*, "Country Comparison: Internet Users," information dated 2009, www.cia.gov/library/publications/the-world-factbook/rankorder/2153rank.html (accessed November 20, 2014).

[19] CIA, *The World Factbook*, "Country Comparison: Internet Hosts," information dated 2009, www.cia.gov/library/publications/the-world-factbook/rankorder/2184rank.html (accessed November 20, 2014).

Useful Phrases

Phrases useful for travelers to the U.S. include the following:

- Good morning/afternoon
- Nice/pleasure to meet you
- Please and thank you
- Hello/Goodbye
- I look forward to seeing you soon

Names

Executives commonly ask business visitors for permission to use their first names. Avoid shortening a name, such as Michael to Mike, unless invited to do so. It's best to use a courtesy title, such as Mr., or Ms. However, Mrs. is not used in U.S. business.

Meetings and Negotiations

In U.S. American business terms, time is money, so punctuality is highly valued. Scheduled meetings begin promptly, often despite the absence of latecomers. Traditionally, leaders send draft agendas for meetings in advance, and run them from the head of the conference table. The goal for these meetings commonly is to set a plan of action.

Negotiations are structured and results-oriented, and they can be direct, forceful, and explicit. Confrontations should be avoided.

Presentation Styles, Conversational Topics, and Humor

Appropriate conversation topics include sports, weather, restaurants, films, music, pets, vacations, and hobbies. Inappropriate topics include sex, religion, politics, gossip, and health concerns. Humor is often used to defuse tense situations.[20]

Successful presentations deliver facts, statistics, and data in engaging, humorous, and entertaining ways, often using interactive tools such as SlideShare, PowerPoint, photos, and handouts.

---

[20]Mary M. Bosrock, *Put Your Best Foot Forward USA: A Fearless Guide to Understanding the United States of America,* (St. Paul, MN: International Education Systems, 1999).

Gestures

Common gestures in the U.S. include the following:

- Touching your index finger to your thumb with your three remaining fingers flexed out is a sign of approval (the okay sign).
- Making a fist with your thumb pointing up is also a sign of approval.
- Raising your index and middle fingers in a *V* shape, palm outward, can be a sign for victory or Peace.
- Waving *hello* or *goodbye* by raising your arm and moving it, palm outward, from side to side.
- Curling your index finger in and out, palm facing upward, means "Come here."

Notable Foods and Dishes

The U.S. is a *melting pot* influenced by numerous cultures. Accordingly, Chinese, Czech, Indian, Korean, Japanese, Thai, Brazilian, Mexican, and Vietnamese food is available nationwide. Health-conscious consumers often request gluten-free menus. Organic-food stores, restaurants, and juice bars are popular.

Specialty Dishes

Favorite dishes in U.S. cuisine include the following:

- **Steak:** Different cuts of beef, seared or grilled
- **Roasted chicken:** Chicken with spices
- **Fish:** Blackened, grilled, or broiled with spices
- **Cobb salad:** Lettuce, tomato, ham, turkey, blue cheese, eggs, dressing
- **Mashed potatoes:** Potatoes, mashed, mixed with butter and cream
- **Hamburgers:** Grilled beef placed in a round bun
- **Hot dogs:** Frankfurters in a long bread bun
- **Macaroni and cheese:** Cooked pasta, melted cheese, and cream
- **Ice cream:** Sweetened milk or cream-based frozen dessert

Dining Etiquette

When invited to business-related breakfast, lunch, or dinner at a residence or restaurant, RSVP within 48 hours. In the U.S. style, you hold the fork in the left hand and the knife in the right. Secure the food item with your fork, and cut it with the knife, then place the knife down at the top of the plate and switch the fork to your right hand to eat. Pass dishes counter-clockwise. Watch the host for cues; do not begin eating until all diners have been served. Dinner typically ends after dessert and coffee. The host or person extending the invitation pays the bill discretely.

Drinking and Toasting

Hosts often make brief toasts for the guest of honor at an event. Raise your glass and join in, or, if honored yourself, respond with a thank-you toast. Toasts include "To your health," "Cheers," and "To a long life." "Clinking" glasses is not required. Follow the host's lead in ordering alcohol or wine. Moderation is key.

Tipping and Bill-Paying

Tipping is customary and expected. At restaurants, servers are paid less than minimum wage because tips are expected to make up the difference; tip 15 to 20 percent of the pre-tax bill for good service. In parties of six or more, an 18- to 20-percent tip is often added to the bill automatically. Save one-, two-, and five-dollar notes for tipping. To reserve a specific table; tip the *maître d'* prior to guest arrival. Tip guidelines:

- **Hotel bellmen:** $1–$2 per bag
- **Airport skycaps:** $1–$2 per bag
- **Taxi drivers:** 15%–20%
- **Valets:** $2–$5
- **Cloakroom attendants:** $2–$5
- **Maids:** $2–5 day

Smoking

Government bodies have voted to restrict smoking in public places, including restaurants and bars, and to limit smoking within certain distances of a building or doorway. Because smoking laws are governed by county and city municipalities, each city is different. Ask before lighting up.

Taboos

Cultural taboos in the U.S. include

- Using ethnic slurs
- Drunkenness
- Displaying a clenched hand, with the middle finger extended
- Bending the right arm at elbow, slapping the left hand over the bicep, and then raising the right arm
- Slapping someone on the back
- Pointing or shaking a finger at someone, in particular, in someone's face
- Failing to tip for service provided
- Failing to make eye contact in a conversation
- Asking about age, income, pregnancy, weight
- Arriving late or too early
- Talking with your mouth full of food
- Failing to cover your mouth when sneezing or coughing
- Smoking without asking permission
- Interrupting a conversation

Heroes and Sports

Knowing about another country's heroes and sports offers opportunities to incorporate culture-specific references into your conversations and presentations.

Heroes

According to an article by Thaddeus Wawro in *Entrepreneur* magazine,[21] U.S. American heroes are typically "visionaries and dreamers, innovators and inventors, mavericks and rebels, trailblazers and pioneers . . . (who) knew how to use their talent, drive, ingenuity, and desire to make dreams come true . . . and influence the course of history."[22] Some examples of U.S. heroes include the following:

George Washington (1732–1799): "Founding Father" and first U.S. president (1789–97). Commander-in-chief of the Continental Army

---

[21] Thaddeus Wawro, "Hero Worship," *Entrepreneur*, March 1, 2000 http://www.entrepreneur.com/article/19266 (accessed November 20, 2014).
[22] Allyson Stewart-Allen and Lanie Denslow, *Working with Americans: How to Build Profitable Business Relationships,* (London: Pearson Education, 2002).

during the Revolutionary War, and led U.S. Americans to independence. As head of the Constitutional Convention and first president of the U.S., he played a critical role in setting the foundation for the country.

Martin Luther King, Jr. (1929–1968): Civil rights activist. Leader in the African-American civil rights movement. His nonviolent activism inspired the Civil Rights Act of 1964, which outlawed discrimination based on race, color, religion, sex, or national origin. Recipient of the Nobel Peace Prize in 1964.

Oprah Winfrey (1954-present): Self-made billionaire and award-winning talk show host. Self-made billionaire, actress, producer, author, and influential role model and activist, whose philanthropy has raised millions of dollars for charitable funds. In 2013, she received the nation's highest civilian award, the Presidential Medal of Freedom. Former host of multi-award-winning *The Oprah Winfrey Show* (1986–2011), and CEO of the *Oprah Winfrey Network* since 2011.

Steve Jobs (1955–2011): Entrepreneur and inventor. Cofounder and former CEO of Apple, Inc.; played a part in revolutionizing modern technology with products such as the Macintosh computer and iPhone. Often described as an innovator, a pioneer, and a visionary for his contributions to the field of consumer electronics.

Sports

Some examples of popular U.S. sports include the following:

Sports

Baseball: "America's pastime" has grown into a major professional sport, with games broadcast on television and radio. The U.S. has two prominent baseball organizations: Major League Baseball, which is the professional league, and the minor leagues, whose teams are based in smaller cities.

Football: Originally only a college sport, U.S. American football now enjoys national popularity via the National Football League (NFL), which is divided into two conferences, the National Football Conference (NFC) and the American Football Conference (AFC). At season's end, the winning teams from each conference play for the title in the Super Bowl.

Basketball: Invented in 1891 in the U.S, basketball is now a popular college and international sport. The national professional league is the National Basketball Association (NBA).

Sports Figures

George Herman "Babe" Ruth, Jr. (1895–1948): Professional baseball player, one of the inaugural inductees into the National Baseball Hall of Fame in 1936. He broke many of baseball's most important slugging records, including career home runs (714) and two others still standing today.

Michael Jordan (1963–present): Former professional basketball player, acclaimed as the greatest basketball player of all time.[23] With five Most Valuable Player awards, six NBA champion titles, six NBA finals MVP awards, and two Olympic gold medals, among numerous others, his record is unparalleled.

Serena Williams (1981–present): Professional tennis player, ranked No. 1 in women's singles tennis. With 63 singles titles, 22 doubles titles, 4 Olympic gold medals, and 18 Grand Slam titles, she holds the record for most titles among active players.

Eight-Question Framework

Chapter 2 introduced you to some of the differences in the way that Westerners and Asians see the world and operate within it in the larger cultural context. The following approach to the eight-question framework for the U.S. mirrors what you will find in each of the following 10 Asian country chapters. As such, each of the eight questions addresses one or more business topics to help you attract and build the relationships with your Asian counterparts, upon which today's successful businesses depend.

1. How Do U.S. Americans Prefer to Act: Individually or as a Group?

"And so, my fellow Americans: ask not what your country can do for you—ask what you can do for your country."
   —*John F. Kennedy*, Inaugural address, January 20th, 1961

"What's on Americans' Minds? Increasingly, 'Me,'"[24] was the heading of an article reporting how, since 1960, incidences of the use of 'I' had substantially

---

[23] NBA Encyclopedia Playoff Edition, www.nba.com/history/players/jordan_bio.html (accessed November 20, 2014).
[24] Sharon Jayson, "What's on Americans' Minds? Increasingly, 'Me,'" USA Today, July 10, 2012, http://usatoday30.usatoday.com/news/health/story/2012-07-10/individualist-language-in -books/56134152/1 (accessed November 20, 2014).

increased in more than 750,000 U.S. books. In the article, author and psychologist Jean Twenge said this trend suggested that U.S. Americans were far more than just independent-minded; it indicated that a specific type of individualistic thinking—"I come first," and "I'm the best"—had increased over the years.

Beliefs likes these inhibit our ability to bridge the cultural divide between ourselves and people from other countries. Broadening our own awareness is the first step in the journey. Few understand this better than those tasked with preparing current and future generations for life in the global arena. University provosts and academics are expanding international and cultural awareness programs because, as Dr. Steven W. Leslie, former provost and executive vice president at The University of Texas at Austin, said, "We are now in a situation where we can't just insulate ourselves and say, 'We are the United States. We're the place the world comes for leadership, innovation, and education.'"

Dr. William I. Brustein, the vice provost for global strategies and international affairs at The Ohio State University agrees: "There's that perception around the world of the United States, and of Western culture, as coming in only thinking of its own self-interest, not thinking of things that may be mutually beneficial."

This kind of posturing will *not* achieve the business outcomes desired in Asia. What will achieve them is collaborating in a way that is respectful and with an eye to building long-lasting relationships.

2. How Are Power and Authority Viewed in the U.S.?

"It is often difficult for those from highly centralized nations to understand, but the fact is that final power really *does* lie in the hands of the people in the United States. This is true whether one speaks of political, economic, or social power."

—*Jef C. Davis and Alison R. Lanier,* Living in the U.S.A.

In their book *Riding The Waves of Culture: Understanding Diversity in Global Business,* world-renowned international management experts Fons Trompenaars and Charles Hampden-Turner relate the story of a Western general manager (GM) who failed to understand that the concept of status has a different meaning in the East than it does in the West. The new GM's arrival in Thailand prompted the company's finance manager to ask him which Mercedes model the GM would like to order. The GM said he preferred to drive a car that was relatively small and easy to handle in Bangkok traffic; he suggested they order him a Suzuki or Mini Cooper.

The new car seemed to be taking a while to arrive. When the GM questioned the finance manager, he had the distinct impression that it would be quicker if he just went with the Mercedes rather than a less expensive car.

After another month of no news, the GM raised the question of his car at a management meeting. Other members of the management team "somewhat shyly . . . explained that they could hardly come to work on bicycles." The message became crystal clear: After the GM was seen driving an inexpensive compact car, his subordinates would be reduced to riding two-wheelers.

There is an interdependence of status in Asian countries that is foreign to the way we think and act in the U.S. This kind of deference to authority is contrary to what many of us were taught at an early age: Challenge people in supposed positions of *power.*

The achievement-oriented culture of the U.S., where accomplishments are college degrees, awards, and beyond, reinforces the belief that anyone with the desire and drive can become anything they wish.

Pulitzer Prize winner Nelle Harper Lee discovered something similar. In 1960, Ms. Lee published her novel, *To Kill a Mockingbird,* a book so successful that former first lady Laura Bush described it decades later as having "changed how people think." However, this did not stop the media from continually asking when Ms. Lee would write another book. One mark of an achievement-oriented culture is the expectation that the *next* achievement will quickly follow the previous ones.

3. How Do We Compare Rules and Relationships in the U.S.?

"I once asked a Chinese philosopher why he thought the East and the West had developed such different habits of thought. 'Because you had Aristotle and we had Confucius,' he replied."
   —Richard E. Nisbett, The Geography of Thought[25]

Imagine you had participated in intense negotiations with a Chinese supplier and just finalized the price of a commodity over a three-year contract. Then the bottom dropped out of the market, and the Chinese asked you to renegotiate the price. They argued that conditions had changed and that the existing contract was nothing more than a *guideline.* Your response may well be to refuse—because a binding agreement is a binding agreement, right? That the price would drop so dramatically is not your problem.

Again, this goes back to our U.S. way of thinking, which is consistent with the ancient Greek philosopher Aristotle's considerable influence on Western thought. He explained the world in terms of logical rules that allow us to better control our environment. As Sharon Jackson Wendell, an attorney at Vorys,

---

[25]Richard E. Nisbett, *The Geography of Thought: How Asians and Westerners Think Differently . . . and Why,* (New York: The Free Press, 2003), 29.

pointed out, "Americans have the sense that we control our environment and therefore need to address all possible eventualities before they arise, along with resolutions in the event something goes awry." To maintain control, we regard written *rules* to be sacrosanct and for most U.S. businesspeople, the contract *is* the relationship. But the Chinese, influenced by the Confucian desire to seek consensus, would be surprised by your refusal to renegotiate the commodity contract. In China, an executed contract may be modified later because it is only a set of specifications. They see the world holistically and comprised of interdependent relationships, whereas Westerners view the world as populated by independent individuals responding to logical rules. Yes, U.S. Americans are crazy for rules and love to make laws in the U.S.[26]

4. How Do We View Time in the U.S.?

"As Americans are trained to see things, the future will not be better than the past or the present unless people use their time for constructive, future-oriented activities. Thus, Americans admire a "well organized" person . . ."
— *Gary Althen,* American Ways: A Cultural Guide to the United States

When Sharon owned her first small business, she worked with a CFO named Tim, the type of man who packed his day with obligations and who had little time to spare. Like many U.S. Americans, Tim viewed time as a commodity: "Time is money." Inevitably, Tim would call at the eleventh hour with a project on a short runway. His time was precious and Sharon would joke, "Should I remain standing, or do you have enough time for me to sit down today?" When appropriate, she'd even drive Tim to the airport to facilitate a longer conversation because she respected Tim's concept of time.

Consider the following:

- FedEx's original branding campaign included the line *When it absolutely, positively has to be there overnight.*[27]
- An AT&T television ad claimed "Faster is better."
- A Booz & Company strategy/business magazine article, titled 'What You Should Accomplish in Your First 10 Days,' argued that leaders can no

[26]Diane Asitimbay, *What's Up, America? A Foreigner's Guide to Understanding Americans,* (San Diego: Culturelink Press, 2009).

[27]Dick Maggiore, "FedEx's Strategic Positioning Concept Absolutely, Positively Disrupted," Innis Maggiore Group, Inc., October 22, 2012, www.innismaggiore.com/positionistview/read.aspx?id=104 (accessed November 20, 2014).

longer afford the luxury of being *in situ* for 100 days before achieving results.[28]

- The concept of time management as a business imperative is attributed to naturalized U.S. citizen Peter F. Drucker.[29]

No doubt about it, Western perspectives of time have been hugely influential for branding, management processes, and leadership thinking. In some parts of the world, time relates to natural cycles and "flows" like a river. In the U.S. and some other Western cultures, however, time has been commoditized and mechanized.

Adjusting Your Sense of Time

In the same way you adjust your watch to a different time zone when traveling internationally, you must adjust your attitude about time in Asia. As social psychologist Robert V. Levine of California State University, Fresno, points out, time is "a wonderful window on culture. You get answers to what cultures value and believe in."[30]

On the same topic, Professor Antonio R. Damasio of the University of Southern California writes: "We wake up to time, courtesy of an alarm clock, and go through the day run by time—the meeting, the visitors, the conference call, the luncheon are all set to begin at a particular hour."[31] This may be true in the West, but it is not necessarily the way business life is viewed elsewhere.

Generally speaking, compared with our Asian colleagues, Westerners place a premium on such things as punctuality; accomplishing projects quickly; being more short term–oriented; using apps, organizers, and planners to keep track of professional and personal lives; and adhering to maxims like "Time is of the essence."

Much of this has been attributed to Aristotle's influence, who is credited with promoting the Western view that humans can and should master their external environment, hence the obsession with *managing* time. This is why participants from different cultural backgrounds attending meetings in the U.S. may need to be reminded that U.S. time is "fixed" as opposed to *fluid*. In the

---

[28]Eric J. McNulty, "What You Should Accomplish in Your First 10 Days," *strategy+business*, June 11, 2013, www.strategy-business.com/blog/What-You-Should-Accomplish-in-Your-First -10-Days (accessed November 20, 2014).

[29]"The Wisdom of Peter Drucker from A to Z," Inc., November 19, 2009, www.inc .com/articles/2009/11/drucker.html (accessed November 22, 2014).

[30]Carol Ezzell, "Clocking Cultures," *Scientific American*, February 2006, www.nature.com /scientificamerican/journal/v16/n1s/full/scientificamerican0206-42sp.html (accessed November 20, 2014).

[31]Antonio R. Damasio, "Remembering When," *Scientific American*, February 2006, http:// www.nature.com/scientificamerican/journal/v16/n1s/full/scientificamerican0206-34sp.html (accessed November 20, 2014).

global arena, meeting times may be posted as *9:00 a.m. U.S. time*, indicating a prompt start time, or *9:00 a.m. Malaysian time*, indicating a flexible start time.

Westerners shortcutting the trust-building process is not uncommon. But from the Asian perspective, a Westerner visiting an Asian partner only once a year is not enough: It means the relationship is superficial because you are not prepared to invest sufficient time. Remember, *our* way is not the only way of viewing the world.

5. How Do We Typically Communicate in the U.S.?

"When an American says, 'Pass that file!" it's just her way of saying, 'Could I trouble you to just pass me that file, please?' They're not being discourteous: Dutch, Scandinavians and Spanish people tend to have the same speech patterns."
— *Barry Tomalin & Mike Nicks*, World Business Cultures: A Handbook

Ice is ice and snow is snow—except to the Inuit and the Yupik peoples living in the Arctic Circle. The Inuit and Yupik have many different words for ice and snow—ice that never melts, ice with holes like Swiss cheese, wet snow, soft powdered snow, and so on—because for them, these distinctions could mean life or death. Anthropologists have discovered that the Eskimos have more than 50 words for snow and 70 words for ice. The Sami tribe, living in northern Scandinavia and Russia, has more than 1,000 words for reindeer!

On the other end of the spectrum, consider the absence of the word *no* in many Asian cultures. For example, Sharon is frequently asked by clients and executives why people in Asia have difficulty being straightforward. What they really mean is: why do they have such trouble saying no? The short answer is that this is about *face*. Look at it from the reverse viewpoint. When we Westerners communicate in upfront and direct ways, we are, to the Asian worldview, causing the rejected party to lose face.

In corporate America, speaking your mind is generally encouraged, because in our culture we prefer people to get to the point. U.S. Americans use direct communication and launch into speech with business or selling in mind.[32] This goes back to the concept that *time is money*. Offering a customer a straightforward rejection, such as, "No. I apologize, but that's not possible," is not unusual. However, assuming that this kind of direct communication is universal is a big mistake—especially when doing business in Asia. As Richard Nisbett points out in *The Geography of Thought:*

---

[32]Richard D. Lewis, *When Teams Collide: Managing the International Team Successfully* (Boston: Nicholas Brealey Publishing, 2012), 185.

"Westerners—and especially Americans—are apt to find Asians hard to read because Asians are likely to assume that their point has been made indirectly and with finesse. Meanwhile, the Westerner is very much in the dark. Asians, in turn, are apt to find Westerners—perhaps especially Americans—direct to the point of condescension or even rudeness."[33]

Also, bear in mind that using sports analogies in phrases such as "He doesn't pull any punches" or "Shoot straight!" is likely to confuse Asians.

6. How Formal or Informal Are We in the U.S.?

"(American) culture is generally informal, with first names almost always used except by children addressing adults."
  —*Milena Bočánková a kolektiv, Intercultural Communication*

A story in David A. Ricks's book *Blunders in International Business*[34] concerns a U.S. manager who was sent to Malaysia to close a major deal. Unfortunately, he had neglected to do his homework on Malaysian forms of introduction and name pronunciations. After hearing what he believed was the name *Roger* when being introduced to a potential business client, the U.S. manager, in his friendly, informal way, proceeded to call the man *Rog*.

The U.S. manager here made two missteps. First, he slipped into the informal practice of using a first name, which is not common in Asian countries. Second, he misheard the client's name, which was actually *rajah*, a title of nobility. With this overly familiar and culturally insensitive approach, the U.S. manager's *faux pas* irrevocably damaged that relationship. To the Malaysians, his level of informality was disrespectful.

Before a trip to China, Sharon researched professional titles to show respect. Even when Chinese people have known each other professionally for years, they may continue to use titles such as *Boss Lady* or *Madame* in the presence of others. In China, as in other Asian cultures, this honors professional status. Follow the lead of those more experienced. Avoid thinking informality is acceptable worldwide.

In certain U.S. industries, informal greetings such as "Hi" and "Hey" have become increasingly common. However, in professional and international trade circles, formal greetings such as "Good morning" and "Good afternoon," are still the standards. U.S. informality like this often comes across to our Asian counterparts as rude. Also many U.S. executives do not greet international business counterparts at the airport or provide small welcome gifts (see Chapter 4 page 57 for gift-giving in Asia). One U.S. businessman even said he considered

---

[33] Nisbett, *The Geography of Thought,* 61.
[34] David A. Ricks, *Blunders in International Business,* 4th edition (Malden, MA: Blackwell, 2006).

these activities to be unnecessary and unimportant. However, this is not a universally accepted view. U.S. Americans often extended what sounded like verbal invitations to lunch, dinner, or a drink, but failed to follow up.

Sharon's U.S. clients often ask her whether it's appropriate to end a business conversation with "Let's get together for lunch or coffee." Her advice is to avoid phrases like this unless it is sincere and you intend to follow up. A better conversation closer is to say, "Thank you for your time. I've enjoyed visiting with you," or "I look forward to seeing you at the next meeting."

Nevertheless, inviting your Asian colleagues for lunch or dinner can be a good idea. Specifically, inviting business colleagues to dinner in your home is an exceptional method for building trust. It provides overseas colleagues with insight into local customs, and satisfies their innate curiosity in ways that no restaurant visit can possibly match because, in Asia, being invited to someone's home is the ultimate honor.

7. How Aligned Are Our Social and Business Lives in the U.S.?

"Most companies have a "no drinking" of alcoholic beverages policy during regular business hours."
—*Mary Murray Bosrock,* Put Your Best Foot Forward: U.S.A. A Fearless Guide to Understanding the United States of America (1999)

Considerable regional and corporate cultural variations exist even within the U.S., ranging from the relaxed atmosphere of Silicon Valley to the intense, incessant focus of New York's Wall Street. Generally speaking, however U.S. employers do not expect their employees to fraternize during work hours, let alone spend time with coworkers outside the office. Depending on the corporate culture, upper management is actively discouraged from befriending subordinates to avoid claims of inappropriate behavior.

From that perspective, it is hard for many Westerners to see an advantage to socializing with colleagues during the working day.

8. How Is the Concept of Women in Business Handled in the U.S.?

"Historically, American women have been independent from the time the first colonists came to the United States."
—*Diane Asitimbay,* What's Up America?

Global consulting firm Booz & Company issued a report titled *Empowering the Third Billion: Women and the World of Work in 2012.*[35] The 'Third

---

[35]"The Third Billion," strategy&, www.booz.com/global/home/what-we-think/third_billion (accessed November 20, 2014).

Billion' refers to women being as significant to the global economy over the next decade as the populations of India and China. The purpose of the report was to highlight the need for "smarter policies that can remove social, cultural, and professional constraints on women and foster greater economic opportunities."

Sheryl Sandberg's bestseller, *Lean In: Women, Work, and the Will to Lead*, speaks to the way women may have held themselves back in U.S. business. U.S. girls are often taught that passivity makes them more appealing and *feminine*. As *The Third Billion* report shows, women have made great strides by positioning themselves in greater numbers in lower and middle-management positions, but they have done less well in achieving senior positions. For example, as the Booz report points out, "In 2011, women held 16.1 percent of board seats at Fortune 500 companies and 14.1 percent of executive officer positions." In entrepreneurial life, "Just 1.8 percent of women-owned firms have more than \$1 million in revenues, compared with 6.3 percent of men-owned firms."

How do U.S. American businesswomen approach and adapt to culturally diverse international environments? As Andy Molinsky stresses in *Global Dexterity*, there comes a point at which you have to decide how much *cultural adaptation* you are prepared to do without violating your deepest values.

CEO Melanie Barnes asks herself whether the right thing for her to do as a female leader is to delegate authority to a male executive so that the business can get done. This is a consideration she makes constantly as her business establishes and maintains strong relationships in Japan:

"Let's say I already have someone in Japan who is interested in a deal that I'm working on and they have approached our company. Would it be a deal killer if there is a woman CEO on this side? Would it make them more likely to dismiss this opportunity even if it's something they would normally want to do? Would the right thing for the company be for me to get out of the way and put a man in my place so that the deal could be made? Should I even be the lead negotiator? Or is that automatically giving an advantage to a team that has a male negotiator?"

Even in the U.S., adds Ms. Barnes, "There is a really fine line to walk for women when it comes to being confident and not coming across as cocky or strident. I think women in the U.S. aren't given very much tolerance when it comes to having a variety of styles. You can be dismissed as passive, silly, angry, or a lot of things just because the culture doesn't allow us the wide range of behaviors without getting stereotyped. I think being aware of that is a good thing."

Cultural Summary

Here are some key points to remember:

- Individualism impacts business relationships, decision making, and negotiating.
- Be aware of the vast differences in U.S. corporate culture based on industry as well as geography.
- Time is money in the U.S., and plays a part in relationship-building and maintaining networks professionally as well as personally.

Self-Awareness Profile

Be sure to use this Self-Awareness Profile to help you become more aware of what you may need to focus on to relate more comfortably with business connections in the United States.

This simple exercise prompts you to self-assess where you currently stand on topics related to the eight-question framework and *compare* this with the country culture. This visual will help you discover the extent to which you may need to adapt your current mindset and behavior to develop more robust business relationships. For details on how to complete this graphic, see the instructions given in the Introduction on pages xviii–xix.

Consider copying the 8-question Profile or using a pencil so that you can see, over time, how you have adjusted your cultural mindset. You might also wish to create unique graphics related to each of the businesses you work with, as these cultural positions vary depending upon geographic location, industry, generational factors, and corporate profile.

Q1: What is your preferred way of doing business?

As an individual making autonomous decisions					As a team member who seeks group consensus
1	2	3	4	5	6

Q2: How comfortable are you in hierarchies in which power is distributed unequally?

Very uncomfortable					Very comfortable
1	2	3	4	5	6

Q3: How closely do you follow rules and obey the law?

Almost always					It depends
1	2	**3**	4	5	6

Q4: What is your general attitude toward time?

**I prefer
agendas, schedules,
planning**

**I prefer flexibility,
fluidity without
scheduling**

1	**2**	3	4	5	6

Q5: What is your preferred way to communicate?

Very diplomatically					Very candidly
1	2	3	4	**5**	6

Q6: What is your interpersonal style or level of formality in business interactions?

Very formal					Very informal
1	2	3	4	**5**	6

Q7: What is your view on socializing within business?

A waste of time					Essential
1	2	3	**4**	5	6

Q8: Should a woman defer to a man as the lead, if winning business in a certain culture depended on it?

Never					Yes, absolutely
1	2	**3**	4	5	6

The Journey Continues . . .

Now that you have been introduced to the eight-question framework as it relates to U.S. culture, you should feel more confident as you explore each of the ten Asian countries that follow. This involves more than passive reading, however. Please take the opportunity to test your knowledge at the beginning of each country-specific chapter with the quiz and finish each chapter with your personal self-awareness profile.

4

Overview of Concepts and Terms

This chapter contains an alphabetical list of concepts and terms that will help you better understand how to build trust, inspire respect, and create long-lasting business relationships in Asia. Please note, however, that these are offered only as guidelines, and that not every concept will apply universally across all Asian cultures. Supplement what you find here by reviewing each of the following country chapters and develop the Asian contacts that can provide you with an even deeper cultural understanding.

Business Cards

Out of respect for your Asian counterparts, print your business cards in English on one side and in their language on the other. Always present and receive business cards with the right hand, or both hands (not the left), with the text facing toward the recipient. When receiving a card, review it carefully for a moment (to show respect for the person named) before placing it in a business card case, portfolio, or on the table in front of you.

Colloquialisms

The playwright George Bernard Shaw once described the relationship between England and the United States as "two countries divided by a common language." If this linguistic chasm can be said to exist between the interpretations of English in two Western countries, imagine the divide between English and the languages of Asia. Avoid using slang words or colloquialisms, both from your own culture (because the listener will not know what you mean) and from the Asian culture (because you may not fully understand subtle nuances in meaning).

Communication

Breakdowns in communication often result from misunderstanding. During conversations with your Asian counterparts, listen with the desire to understand, rather than with impatience as you wait to talk next. Avoid trying to reinforce your existing beliefs. This is particularly important given the weight Asian cultures put on mutually beneficial relationships.

Eye Contact

Direct or prolonged eye contact may be considered aggressive, threatening, or impolite. Lowering your eyes is often a sign of respect for superiors or elders.

Foreign Corrupt Practices Act (FCPA)

Do not offer gifts to government officials in any country. The U.S. Foreign Corrupt Practices Act of 1977[1] imposes severe penalties on companies and persons who promise, offer, or give anything of value to foreign government officials for the purpose of seeking business.

Formal and Informal

Many Asian cultures observe hierarchies that govern behavior and expectations in business and in life. These standards of formality are deep-rooted, having been established long ago, and come in part from the belief that power should be centralized. Formality is traditionally the way in which people within the hierarchy have reached more central and influential positions.

---

[1]"Foreign Corrupt Practices Act," U.S. Department of Justice, www.justice.gov/criminal /fraud/fcpa/ (accessed November 21, 2014).

Gender

Historically, given the importance of family in Asian cultures, a woman's role has been to manage the home and take care of her family.[2] Women tended to work outside of the home within family businesses, or as assistants. You may find that these traditional beliefs are still held by people born before 1960, but younger people are much more receptive to equality and the role of women in the workplace. Given these diverse and changing attitudes, be sure to check the section on women in business (Question 8) within each country chapter.

Gestures

Gestures considered acceptable in your own culture may be misconstrued or viewed as obscene in Asia. Using the wrong gesture has been known to incite fights, riots—or even death.[3] For example, beckoning someone by curling an index finger is considered rude in Asia, because it is more often associated with beckoning an animal. A more-acceptable gesture involves placing the hand out, palm down, and curling the fingers a few times in a scratching motion. Be sure to review the relevant sections on gestures and taboos in each country chapter and consider additional reading.[4]

Gifts

Gifts have always been an important aspect of business in Asia, where they are a way of showing respect for your host. Asians give gifts to people they *want* to have a good relationship with, whereas in the West people tend to give gifts to those with whom they *already* have a close relationship. Here are some tips about giving and receiving gifts in Asia:

- Gifts should be opened at a later time, in private, to save face if the gift is less than perfect.

---

[2] Roger E. Axtell et al., *Do's and Taboos Around the World for Women in Business* (New York: John Wiley & Sons, 1997).

[3] Kerim Friedman, "How (Not) to Signal 'Stop,'" Savage Minds, September 28, 2008, http://savageminds.org/2008/09/28/how-not-to-signal-stop/ (accessed November 21, 2014).

[4] Roger E. Axtell, *Gestures: The Do's and Taboos of Body Language Around the World* (New York: John Wiley & Sons, 1998); Romana Lefevre, *Rude Hand Gestures of the World* (San Francisco: Chronicle Books, 2011); and Nancy Armstrong and Melissa Wagner, *Field Guide to Gestures* (Philadelphia: Quirk Books, 2003).

- It is a common custom to use both hands to give and receive gifts (unless the recipient is Muslim and then the right hand only is used).
- Clocks are bad luck (except in Korea).
- Cutlery, scissors, knives, and any sharp objects represent the severing of ties in a relationship.
- The recipient may decline three times before politely accepting a gift, so be sure to gently persevere with your offer three times.
- If you prefer not to give one gift to each person present, you may offer a single group gift to the highest-ranking person.
- Give gifts from *our company to your company.*

Greetings

The proper protocol for greetings depends on the country. Be sure to do your research and ask your host how best to greet people in their country.

Be observant; in Asia, men commonly wait for a woman to offer her hand before attempting to shake hands. Do not take offense if a woman does not offer.

Unless you know how to bow correctly, do not attempt something outside your comfort zone. A courteous nod may be a good substitute for bowing.

Guanxi

The concept of *guanxi* (gwan–SHEE), which originated in China, refers to networks of trust that have reciprocal obligations. It remains a crucial concept to be aware of when developing relationships in the Asian business world.

Head, Hands, and Feet

Head: In Asia, the top half of a person's body is generally held in higher esteem than the bottom half. The head is considered the most sacred part of the body. It is taboo to pat or touch someone's head in any way, especially the top of the head. Similarly, avoid passing objects or reaching over the head of anyone, especially a monk. (Females should never touch any part of a monk's robes or body.)

Hands: Depending on the country and culture, use both hands simultaneously, or the right hand only, to receive and accept gifts, and to dine and pass or receive food and beverages. However, be aware that in some cultures, the left hand is used for personal hygiene and is viewed as unclean. (Left-handed children may be trained to use their right hands when dining and passing food). Due to these cultural differences, when dining, with or without silverware or chopsticks, use both hands, or your right hand only.

Feet: The bottom half of the body is considered inferior because feet touch the street and are therefore unclean from their proximity to dirt and vermin. Never show the soles of your feet or shoes, and don't place them on an office desk or table. Remove shoes when entering a temple or shrine. Avoid gesturing or pointing at a person or spiritual object with your shoes or feet, because this is considered highly disrespectful.

High Context or Low Context

For a fuller explanation of the concepts, please refer to Chapter 2, page 18.

Humor and Jokes

Humor is culture-specific, meaning that most jokes tend to be funny only among people who share experiences in that culture. For instance, an Eskimo may not understand a joke about the desert. Jokes referencing Western culture, stereotypes, and slang may be misunderstood by or lost on audiences in Asia. Many interpreters do not bother to interpret jokes, instead telling audiences to "please laugh, the speaker just told a culture-specific joke that we don't understand."

International Standard for Date and Time Notation

When communicating internationally, be aware of the following International Standard (ISO 8601:2004) for the numeric format of dates and times:[5]

International standard *date* notation: *YYYY-MM-DD*
International standard *time* notation: *hh:mm:ss*

---

[5]Markus Kuhn, "A Summary of the International Standard Date and Time Notation," December 19, 2004, www.cl.cam.ac.uk/~mgk25/iso-time.html.

Interpreters

Pace is crucial when giving a presentation or negotiating in Asia. Your interpreter will smoothly interpret approximately two short sentences at a time, so keep your ideas and concepts succinct. Stop after two short sentences to allow your translator time to relay the idea to your audience. Relay concepts in two-sentence spurts and your audience will appreciate your concise communication. Avoid elaborate or highly personal presentations; a simple presentation in which numbers and facts are accompanied by black-and-white graphics will be appreciated.

Introductions

Each country has specific rules for formal introductions. Review the relevant country chapter.

Laws and Regulations

Throughout Asia, honor is a virtue, and integrity is considered important. Dishonorable deeds in business may be severely punished. In some countries, although the view of Westerners is generally positive, nationals may be wary and suspicious of your motivations. To prove you are trustworthy, adhere to local laws and regulations.

Names

In U.S. names, the surname, or family name, generally appears after an individual's given name. In Asia, however, this order varies, and no set rule exists. Some Asians have adopted Westernized names. Because naming conventions vary, review the relevant chapter for the country you are visiting. Never address someone by their first name before you've been invited to do so. Also, research a country's courtesy titles and culture-specific honorifics and use them when appropriate.

Organization for Economic Co-Operation and Development (OECD)

Countries belonging to the OECD[6] developed an anti-bribery measure similar to the FCPA in 1977. Japan and Korea are current members *See FCPA* on page 56.

---

[6] Organization for Economic Co-Operation and Development. www.oecd.org/ (accessed November 21, 2014).

Other-Dependent and Other-Independent

In Asia, individuals are *other-dependent*—they consider themselves to be a part of a bigger collective in which each person contributes to their family, business, and country. Individuals in the U.S. and many other Western nations, on the other hand, are *other-independent,* meaning that they consider themselves responsible for being independent and self-sufficient.

Personal Appearance and Wardrobe

In the West, individuality is encouraged, and people often express it through hair design, clothing, and jewelry. In Asia, on the other hand, priorities are more group-related: self-sacrifice; focusing on the *we,* not the *I*; and joining the *in-group.* Looking different and standing out with bright colors or ostentatious jewelry is inconsistent with group conformity. When visiting Asia, observe the country dress code expectations to demonstrate appreciation for each culture's values.

Women visiting Muslim or Hindu cultures should dress especially modestly. Read the country chapters and research prior to travel; do not wait until arrival.

Relationships

Without the firm foundation of respect and trust, business transactions are like houses built on sand. In Asia, establishing solid relationships is the building block of business, and this includes the giving of gifts, understanding the concept of *face,* and a considerable amount of socializing. Asian cultures are relationship-oriented, rather than strictly bound by rules. Although Westerners typically think of relationships as transactional, especially in terms of nurturing ongoing collaborations after a deal has been struck, the opposite is true in much of Asia.

Silence

Peace and serenity are highly valued in Asia, where as much emphasis is placed on the spaces between the words as on the words themselves. Never interrupt your Asian counterpart's silence with talk, because he or she may be cogitating or communicating non-verbally. Be patient; allow your host to break the silence first.

Smiling

Bear in mind that a smile can mean or mask many things besides joy in Asia: embarrassment, irritation, commiseration, anxiety, happiness, or even unhappiness.

Specially Designated Nationals (SDN) List

Learn how to navigate and use the SDN list of the Office of Foreign Assets Control of the U.S. Department of Treasury.[7] This list, also known as the 'Blocked Persons' list, contains the names of people or entities with whom U.S. companies and individuals are prohibited from doing business.

Spitting

In Asia, spitting has historically been viewed as a means of ridding the body of excess bodily fluid and is an acceptable act of hygiene. Spitting is most common in India, China, and South Korea.[8]

Superstition

In some Asian cultures, meetings may be postponed or cancelled and contracts delayed because the time, day, or month is not fortuitous. In some cases, your Asian counterpart may consult an astrologer to check whether a particular day or month is good for negotiating transactions. Also, certain numbers may be associated with good or bad luck.

Time

The concept of time varies from culture to culture, but punctuality on your part is expected. Allow extra time for delays, traffic, or detours. Double-check

---

[7]"Sanctions List Search," U.S. Office of Foreign Assets Control, http://sdnsearch.ofac.treas.gov (accessed November 21, 2014).
[8]Paula Cocozza, "Spitting in Public: Disgusting and Antisocial—or a Great British Tradition?," *The Guardian*, September 25, 2013, www.theguardian.com/law/shortcuts/2013/sep/25 /spitting-in-public-disgusting-antisocial-tradition.

addresses and locations prior to departure in the event Wi-Fi or Internet unavailability prevents access while en route. If a delay occurs, contact your counterpart so they know that you are en route.

One practice to consider is to meet with prospective business associates in your hotel lobby or cafe. This provides a comfortable, air-conditioned environment while avoiding city traffic and allows you to continue working if your counterpart is delayed.

For details about monochronic time and polychronic time, refer to Chapter 2, page 17.

Tipping

Tipping expectations vary among Asian cultures. Review the material on tipping in the specific country chapters.

Touching

Public displays of affection are taboo. Hugging, kissing, or touching a member of the opposite sex in public is inappropriate, and may even be illegal in certain countries.

Voice

In Asia, senior members of the business and social cultural hierarchy do not raise their voices or shout. Speaking with a soft voice is a signifier of higher rank, so practice using a restrained and moderate tone as a more effective way of communicating. Avoid shouting or raising your voice to members of staff. In Asia, raised, loud, or angry voices lead to a loss of face.

Belief Systems

Table 4.1 offers a brief overview of the main belief systems, philosophies, and religions in Asia, together with the specific countries to which they apply.[9]

---

[9]Robert Pollock, *World Religions: Beliefs and Traditions from Around the Globe* (New York: Fall River Press, 2008).

Table 4.1   Belief Systems, Philosophies, and Religions[10]

Belief System/ Philosophy/ Religion	Definition	Countries
Buddhism	Belief system that originated in northern India from the teachings of Buddha, or the *Enlightened One* (Siddhartha Gautama; sixth-century BCE). Buddha's Four Noble Truths focus on ending suffering and achieving enlightenment. Devotional practices include meditation, chanting, and adhering to the Noble Eightfold Path.	China, Hong Kong, India, Japan, South Korea, Malaysia, Myanmar, Singapore, South Korea, Taiwan, Thailand
Christianity	Religion based on the Bible and the New Testament teachings of Jesus Christ. Focuses on the existence of God and his son, Jesus, who died for the forgiveness of humanity's sins. Devotional practices include prayer, fasting, and congregational worship.	China, Hong Kong, India, Japan, Malaysia, Myanmar, Philippines, Singapore, South Korea, Taiwan
Confucianism	Belief system based on the philosophical and ethical teachings of Confucius or Kong Qui (551–479 BCE). Described variously as a 'worldview, social ethic, political ideology, scholarly tradition, and way of life.'[11]	China, Hong Kong, South Korea
Hinduism	Cultural approach or way of life (*dharma*) that embraces many ancient traditions. Has no founder or single spiritual text. Despite embracing many deities, it is not considered polytheistic.[12] The Vedas are the sacred texts. Ceremonial practices for worship vary.	India, Hong Kong, Malaysia, Myanmar, Singapore
Islam	The most sacred text is the Qur'an, the word of God as revealed to Muhammad. Islamic theology and practice also embraces the Hadith, or recorded sayings of Muhammad.	China, Hong Kong, India, Malaysia, Myanmar, Philippines, Singapore, Thailand

[10] Ibid.

[11] Tu Weiming, "Confucianism," Encyclopedia Britannica, October 31, 2014, www.britannica.com/EBchecked/topic/132104/Confucianism.

[12] Subhamoy Das, "Common Myths About Hinduism," About.com, http://hinduism.about.com/od/basics/a/hinduism.htm (accessed November 21, 2014).

Table 4.1 *(Continued)*

Belief System/ Philosophy/ Religion	Definition	Countries
Jainism	Indian religion, also known as *Jaina dharma,* which began between the seventh and fifth centuries BCE. Teaches that spiritual purity and enlightenment is achieved through disciplined nonviolence (the Sanskrit word *ji,* from which the term *Jaina* derives, means *to conquer*).	India
Judaism	A religion developed among ancient Hebrews focusing on a single, all-powerful God and the coming of the Messiah. Jewish scriptures are found in the Torah (*to teach*), which includes the Five Books of Moses and the Ten Commandments. Founded over 3,500 years ago by Moses, Judaism is one of the 'three Abrahamic religions'[13] (along with Christianity and Islam).	China, Hong Kong, Singapore
Shinto	Sometimes referred to as *Shintoism,* (or *way of the spirits*), this Japanese devotional practice enables humans to communicate with invisible spirits called *kami,* as a means of achieving needs like good health and business success.	Japan
Sikhism	Founded in India by Guru Nanak in the fifteenth century. *Sikh* is a Punjabi word meaning *disciple.* Male adherents of Sikhism wear turbans (females wear headscarves) to protect the hair (*kes),* which is never cut. The religion's historical center is the Golden Temple at Amritsar.	India, Malaysia, Singapore, Thailand, Hong Kong
Taoism (Daoism)	Philosophical and ethical belief based on the *Tao Te Ching,* written by Lao Tzu, thought to be a contemporary of Confucius. From Taoism we get the concepts of yin and yang, or opposite and complementary forces. The word *Tao* means *the way.* Focus is on the Three Treasures: compassion, moderation, and humility.	China, Hong Kong, Singapore, Taiwan

---

[13]"Judaism at a Glance," BBC, June 12, 2009, www.bbc.co.uk/religion/religions/judaism /ataglance/glance.shtml.

5 | China

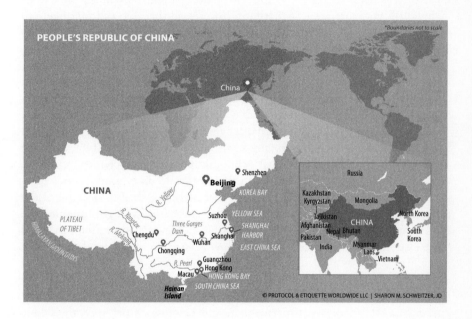

All people are the same; only their habits differ.

—Confucius

Introduction

More than 40 million people worldwide are currently learning to speak Mandarin, reflecting the monumental growth of China, that usurped the long-standing status of the U.S. as the world's leading economic power.[1] In late 2014, the International Monetary Fund (IMF) reported that when adjusting for purchasing power, China's economy had overtaken that of the United States. However, the IMF also estimated that it will be some time before China surpasses the U.S. in terms of the raw market value of China's currency,[2] "China still sits more than $6.5 trillion lower than the U.S. and isn't likely to overtake for quite some time."[3] This momentum is likely to increase given that 200 million people are predicted to enter the Chinese middle class by 2026, joining the 300 million who have done so in the past 30 years. Additionally, in the Forbes 2014 list of the *World's 100 Most Powerful Women,* nine are from China, nearly 10 percent of the list. In 2012, *Forbes* reported that the most female billionaires come from China.

China has money and lots of it: The country is sitting on more than $15 trillion in bank deposits growing $2 trillion annually.[4] The Chinese middle class and wealthy wield individual economic power. As McKinsey reported, China is predicted to surpass Japan as the world's leading luxury goods market, and account for over 20 percent of that market globally.[5] Because of the tremendous increase in the amount of international travel by its people, due to their increased wealth, China's National Tourism Administration published more elaborate *Guidelines on Civilized Travel Abroad*[6] in their latest booklet.

China is one of the oldest civilizations worldwide, with a written history dating over 4,000 years. Engineering feats include the Three Gorges Dam, the Great Wall of China, and the Terracotta Warriors. China is the birthplace of gunpowder, the compass, papermaking, and printing. More recently, China successfully hosted the 2008 Olympic Games in Beijing, where more than 11,000 elite athletes competed in over 300 events.

Confucianism originated in the Shandong province and influences Chinese family, social, and business life. Confucius proposed five "great relationships":

---

[1] October 2014 or December 2014.

[2] *World Economic Outlook: Legacies, Clouds, Uncertainties,* International Monetary Fund, October 2014, www.imf.org/external/pubs/ft/weo/2014/02/pdf/text.pdf (accessed January 10, 2015).

[3] http://www.businessinsider.com/china-overtakes-us-as-worlds-largest-economy-2014-10#ixzz 3OjotqhMH (accessed January 20, 2015)

[4] Jeffrey Towson and Jonathan Woetzel, *The 1 Hour China Book: Two Peking University Professors Explain All of China Business in Six Short Stories* (Cayman Islands: Towson Group LLC, 2013).

[5] McKinsey & Company, "Understanding China's Growing Love for Luxury," March 2011, http://mckinseyonmarketingandsales.com/understanding-chinas-growing-love-for-luxury.

[6] China National Tourism Administration, "Outbound Travel of Chinese Citizens to Improve the Quality of Civilization," July 15, 2013, www.cnta.gov.cn/html/2013-7/2013-7-15-9 -58-46078.html.

Ruler/subject; father/son; elder brother/younger brother; husband/ wife; friend/friend. Every individual action affects someone else, which leads to the Chinese aversion to responding without taking other perspectives into account. Chinese values include group harmony, courtesy, patience, sincerity, consensus, and cooperation.

Quiz

How much do you know about China? Answer the following questions as True or False to test your knowledge. (The Answer Key at the bottom includes page numbers that refer to the topic):

_____1. Social media sites such as Facebook and Twitter are popular with Chinese citizens.

_____2. In China, brands signify your rank and status in the hierarchy.

_____3. China is one of only five remaining Communist regimes.

_____4. Chinese family and society-oriented values take higher priority than those of the individual.

_____5. According to the IMF, adjust for purchasing power, China's economy overtook the U.S. in 2014 (it will be some time before China surpasses the U.S. in raw terms)

_____6. The concept of *Guanxi* originated in China and refers to networks of trust and relationships with reciprocal obligations.

_____7. In China, decisions are made during negotiations because on-site participants have the authority to do so.

_____8. Handshakes in China are not as firm as in the West; expect a softer and briefer handshake.

_____9. The People's Republic of China includes more than 6,500 islands.

_____10. In China, an executed contract may be modified later because it's only a set of specifications.

Answer Key: 1. F (p. 77–78); 2. T (p. 76); 3. T (p. 70); 4. T (p. 68–69, 85); 5. T (p. 71, 68); 6. T (p. 87–88); 7. F (p. 79–80, 80); 8. T (p. 78–79); 9. T (p. 70); 10. T (p. 86, 45).

Country Basics

This section provides key knowledge in an easy-to-read format to help you quickly grasp some of the basics necessary to navigate this culture.

Historical Timeline

A critical way to show respect for another person's culture is to have knowledge of her country's history and current affairs. Table 5.1 on page 71 outlines a few key events related to China, together with concurrent world events.[7]

Full Country Name and Location

The People's Republic of China occupies one fifteenth of the world's land mass and includes more than 6,500 islands. It borders the East China Sea, Korea Bay, Yellow Sea, and South China Sea. It shares land borders with Afghanistan, Bhutan, Burma, India, Kazakhstan, Kyrgyzstan, Laos, Mongolia, Nepal, Pakistan, Russia, and Tajikistan.

Government/Political Structure

The government structure includes a president and vice president, a premier, executive vice premier and several vice premiers, and a state council. A single legislative body, the National People's Congress, is made up of almost 3,000 elected members. The president and vice president are elected by the National People's Congress for five-year terms, with eligibility for a second term. China is one of only five remaining Communist regimes, along with Cuba, Laos, North Korea, and Vietnam.[8]

Population and Economic Centers

China has the world's largest population of approximately 1.36 billion, according to July 2014 estimates, cited in the *CIA World Factbook*. The main ethnic group is Han Chinese (91.5 percent). Minority groups include Zhuang, Manchu, Hui, Miao, Uighur, Tujia, Yi, Mongol, Tibetan, Buyi,

---

[7]China Timeline Sources: The State Council of the People's Republic of China, http://english .gov.cn/ (accessed November 12, 2014); BBC News Asia, "China Profile: Timeline," last updated October 2, 2014, www.bbc.com/news/world-asia-pacific-13017882 (accessed November 12, 2014); Bernard Grun, *The Timetables of History* (New York: Touchstone Press, 2005); BBC History, www.bbc.co.uk/history/0/ (accessed November 12, 2014). Encyclopedia Britannica, www.britannica.com/ (accessed November 12, 2014); and May-lee Chai and Winberg Chai, *China A to Z: Everything You Need to Know to Understand Chinese Customs and Culture* (New York: Plume, Penguin Group, 2007).

[8]CIA, *The World Factbook*, "Government Type," www.cia.gov/library/publications/the-world -factbook/fields/2128.html (accessed November 12, 2014).

Table 5.1   Key Historical Events

Period/ Dates	Description/Events	World Events
1644–1911	Qing Dynasty period.	British Industrial Revolution (1760–1840).
1839–1842	Opium War; China cedes Hong Kong to Britain.	Tea from India first arrives in Britain.
1911–1912	Chinese Revolution; the Republic of China is formed.	Royal Flying Corps (later RAF) established in Britain (1912).
1949	Mao Zedong leads the Communists to victory in civil war and founds the People's Republic of China.	India adopts new constitution after independence from British rule.
1958	Mao launches the "Great Leap Forward," a five-year economic plan to collectivize farming and introduce labor-intensive industry.	First radio broadcast is sent from space.
1972	The U.S. and China desire to resume trade after a 20-year hiatus.	India and Bangladesh sign a friendship treaty.
2001	China joins the World Trade Organization.	The first draft of the complete Human Genome is published.
2011	China becomes the world's second-largest economy.	The world population reaches seven billion.
2018	National elections scheduled.	Malaysia's elections scheduled; PyeongChang, South Korea, to host the XXIII Olympic Winter Games.

Dong, Yao, and other nationalities. About half of the population lives in urban areas.[9]

Administrative Divisions or Regions

China is divided into six traditional regions: East, North, Northeast, Northwest, South Central, and Southwest. While the *CIA World Factbook* lists Taiwan as a separate country,[10] China identifies it among its 23 provinces: Anhui, Fujian, Gansu, Guangdong, Guizhou, Hainan, Hebei, Heilongjiang, Henan, Hubei, Hunan, Jiangsu, Jiangxi, Jilin, Liaoning, Qinghai, Shaanxi, Shandong, Shanxi, Sichuan, Taiwan, Yunnan, and Zhejiang.[11]

China's five autonomous regions are: Guangxi Zhuang, Nei Mongol (Inner Mongolia), Ningxia Hui, Xinjiang Uygur, and Xizang (Tibet).[12]

China's four municipalities which fall directly under the authority of central government: Beijing,* Chongqing, Shanghai,* and Tianjin* (*provincial status).[13]

China lists Macao and Hong Kong as two special administrative regions.[14]

The major business centers and populations (2010) are outlined in Table 5.2.[15]

Table 5.2   Major Business Centers

Business Centers	Population (millions)
Beijing (capital)	16.4
Chengdu	6.3
Chongqing	6.3
Guangzhou	9.7
Shanghai	20.2
Shenzhen	10.4
Suzhou	4.0
Wuhan	6.8

[9]CIA, *The World Factbook*, "China," www.cia.gov/library/publications/the–world–factbook/geos /ch.html (accessed November 12, 2014).

[10]Ibid.

[11]The State Council of the People's Republic of China, "Administrative Division," last updated August 29, 2014, http://english.gov.cn/archive/china_abc/2014/08/27/content _281474983873401.htm (accessed November 12, 2014).

[12]Ibid.

[13]Ibid.

[14]Ibid.

[15]National Bureau of Statistics of China, *2010 Population Census*, www.stats.gov.cn/english /Statisticaldata/CensusData (accessed November 12, 2014).

Economy

China is ranked 90th out of 189 economies in terms of ease of doing business, according to the World Bank Group's *Doing Business 2015* report.[16] Its 2013 GDP was ranked 2nd by the World Bank[17] and the composition of its GDP by sector was services (46.1 percent), industry (43.9 percent), and agriculture (10 percent).[18]

Corruption Perceptions Index

China ranked 80th least corrupt out of 177 countries and territories with a score of 40 out of 100.[19] This annual Index, compiled by Transparency International, measures perceived levels of public sector corruption.

The Central Commission for Discipline Inspection of the Communist Party of China is the anti-corruption agency that conducts investigations.

Human Development Index

China ranked 91st out of 187 countries and territories.[20] The HDI, compiled by the United Nations Development Programme, is a composite index of life expectancy, education, and income statistics.

Global Gender Gap Index

China ranked 87th out of 142 countries in terms of gender equality with a score of 0.6830.[21] This annual index, compiled by the World Economic Forum, assesses gender gaps based on economic, political, educational, and health-based criteria.

---

[16]World Bank Group, *Doing Business 2015* (October 29, 2014): 4, www .doingbusiness.org/~/media/GIAWB/Doing%20Business/Documents/Annual-Reports/English /DB15-Full-Report.pdf.

[17]The World Bank, Data, GDP Ranking, "Gross Domestic Product Ranking Table," last updated September 24, 2014, http://data.worldbank.org/data-catalog/GDP-ranking-table (accessed November 12, 2014).

[18]CIA, *The World Factbook*, "China," www.cia.gov/library/publications/the-world-factbook/geos /ch.html (accessed November 12, 2014).

[19]Transparency International, "Corruption Perceptions Index 2013," www.transparency .org/cpi2013/results (accessed November 11, 2014).

[20]United Nations Development Programme, *Human Development Report 2014*, 160–163, http://hdr.undp.org/sites/default/files/hdr14-report-en-1.pdf (accessed November 11, 2014).

[21]World Economic Forum, *The Global Gender Gap Report 2014*, 8–9, www3.weforum.org /docs/GGGR14/GGGR_CompleteReport_2014.pdf (accessed November 11, 2014).

Climate

Extremely diverse; subtropical in the south to subarctic in the north. Monsoons during March/April and September/October.

Languages

The official national language is *Putonghua*, or Mandarin Chinese (Beijing dialect), and it is the *lingua franca*. Other languages include Cantonese (Yue), Shanghainese (Wu), Fukienese, Hakka, Hokkien, and Chin Chow.

Spoken Chinese may not be understandable because of numerous dialects; for example, the Shanghainese spoken in Shanghai may not be understandable by a Cantonese speaker in Hong Kong.

The *Pinyin* system was adopted in 1979 to standardize the spelling of Chinese words into Western languages. For example, China's capital Peking was pronounced *Beijing,* so the spelling was changed.

Written Chinese consists of characters known as pictographs and ideographs that are recognized nationwide.

Belief Systems, Philosophies, and Religions

The country breakdown is as follows: Unaffiliated (52.2 percent), folk religion (21.9 percent), Buddhist (18.2 percent), Christian (5.1 percent), Islam (1.8 percent), Hindu (less than 0.1 percent), Jewish (less than 0.1 percent), and other (includes Daoist/Taoist) (0.7 percent).[22]

Note: After 1949, China became an officially atheist country with the government discouraging religious practices.

For an overview of belief systems, philosophies, and religions, please refer to Chapter 4, pages 64–65.

Time Zones/Daylight Savings

Although geographically it spans five time zones, China has one time zone, China Standard Time (CST), which is eight hours ahead of GMT (Greenwich Mean Time)/UTC (Coordinated Universal Time). It does not operate under Daylight Savings Time.

It is 13 hours ahead of U.S. Eastern Standard Time (12 hours ahead in Daylight Savings Time). See www.timeanddate.com/worldclock.

To calculate time in China, add eight hours to UTC/GMT.

---

[22]CIA, *The World Factbook,* "China," www.cia.gov/library/publications/the-world-factbook/geos/ch.html (accessed November 12, 2014).

Telephone Country Code and Internet Suffix

The Chinaese telephone country code is 86, and the Internet suffix is .cn.

Currency

The Chinese currency is the *Renminbi* (RMB) and the unit of currency of the RMB is the *yuan* (CNY). One Yuan is divided into 10 Jiao, or 100 *fen*.

Business Culture, Etiquette, and Customs

This section covers business culture, etiquette, and customs.

Fiscal Year

The fiscal year is January 1 through December 31. Dates are written day, month, and year. For example, April 10, 2020 is written 10/04/20.

Working Week[23]

The structure of the Chinese working week is outlined in Table 5.3.

Table 5.3   The Chinese Working Schedule

Industry	Business Hours	Days of the Week
Business	9:00–18:00	Monday–Friday
Government	8:00–17:00	Monday–Friday (40-hour work week)
Banks	10:00–18:00	Monday–Friday
Shops	9:00–19:00	Daily (open until 22:00 in major cities)
Lunch (public sector)	12:00–13:00	
Lunch (private sector)	11:30–13:30	

---

[23]HSBC Bank & PricewaterhouseCoopers, *Doing Business in China,* 2012.

Holidays and Festivals

Some Chinese holidays are determined by the lunar calendar and change from year to year. Floating holidays are designated with an asterisk. On certain holidays, an office may remain open with limited staff. Check with your embassy or trade office before planning business travel.

Chinese business slows considerably during the Spring Festival. Avoid business visits during this two- to three-week holiday period. Key Chinese holidays are outlined in Table 5.4.

Table 5.4   Chinese Holidays and Festivals

Date	Name
January 1–2	New Year's Day
Late January/February	Spring Festival and Chinese New Year*
April	Ching Ming Festival (Tomb Sweeping Day)*
March 8	International Women's Day
May 1	Labor Day
May 4	Youth Day
June 1	Children's Day
June	Duanwu Festival or Dragon Boat Festival*
July 1	Anniversary of Founding of the Communist Party of China
August 1	People's Liberation Army Day
September	Mid-Autumn Festival*
October 1-3	National Day*

Business Dress/Appearance

The Mao jacket has gone and conservative professional attire is now seen in the commercial world. Appearance and first impressions are important in Chinese business circles. Wealth is admired. Men and women wearing tailored, well-made suits are considered successful. Men usually wear suits and ties in conservative and neutral colors. Most women wear modest suits, pantsuits, dresses or skirts with low two- to three-inch heels. For men and women, lightweight suits are appropriate during the summer and in southern regions. Designer clothing, high-quality shoes, and minimal accessories are recommended. Name brands signify your rank and status in the hierarchy.

News Sources

Here are some of China's most popular news sources:

- *South China Morning Post*: www.scmp.com
- *China Daily*: www.chinadaily.com.cn
- *Financial Times Asia Edition*: www.ftasia.net
- *Shanghai Daily*: www.shanghaidaily.com

Business Cards

Business cards are known as *ming pian*, or name cards, in China. If your company is prominent (for example, has the biggest market-share, is the oldest or the highest-ranking), include this distinction on the *ming pian*. Meetings start with a card exchange and it is especially important to pronounce Chinese names correctly. Cards should have information printed in English on one side and Mandarin on the other. Color is significant: Gold is the highest honor, black is most common. Avoid printing names in red ink. When handing your card, start with the most senior person and use both hands with print facing the receiver. When receiving, accept the card graciously with both hands, study the card and place it on the table or in a cardholder.

Technology

According to Akamai Technology's *State of the Internet Report*, China has the 66th fastest average Internet connection speed in the world.[24] Latest figures rank China 1st of 217 worldwide for the number of Internet users, just above the U.S.[25] and 5th of 232 globally for the number of Internet hosts.[26] The Internet is censored and monitored by the Chinese government. Domestic website content is controlled, and it is said that the *Great Firewall of China* blocks many

---

[24]Akamai Technologies, "State of the Internet Q4 2013," April 2014, www.akamai.com/dl/akamai/akamai-soti-q413.pdf?WT.mc_id=soti_Q413 (accessed November 12, 2014).

[25]CIA, *The World Factbook*, "Country Comparison: Internet Users," information dated 2009, www.cia.gov / library / publications / the - world - factbook / rankorder / 2153rank.html (accessed November 12, 2014).

[26]CIA, *The World Factbook*, "Country Comparison: Internet Hosts," information dated 2009, www.cia.gov / library / publications / the - world - factbook / rankorder / 2184rank.html (accessed November 12, 2014).

foreign websites,[27] including Facebook, Twitter, Instagram, and other social media sites. Weibo is a hybrid of Facebook and Twitter for Chinese citizens. Wechat is popular in China. Alibaba is the world's largest e-commerce website.

Gifts

Gifts are exchanged at initial and later meetings; coordinate these in advance with an internal source. Purchase more gifts than anticipated for those you may meet unexpectedly. Use both hands to present and receive. More senior members receive different gifts that are not expensive. Beautifully wrap gifts in red or gold; avoid black or white paper.

Business gift ideas include items made domestically and small office items including pens, trays, bowls, and corporate and desk memorabilia. Businesswomen enjoy cosmetics and silk scarves. Avoid Scotch, clocks, straw sandals, a stork or crane, or handkerchiefs. White and black items represent mourning; scissors, knives, and cutlery represent the severing of relationships.

Introductions, Greetings, Personal Space, and Eye Contact

In China, greetings include a slight bow of 30 degrees from the shoulders, for three seconds. Observe whether your host offers to shake hands. International businesswomen may need to extend a hand to indicate they are willing to shake hands. Handshakes are not as firm as in the West; expect a softer, briefer handshake. Applause may occur as a greeting; applaud in response.

Introductions are formal and usually involve an intermediary. Rank and status determine greeting. Not everyone present may necessarily be greeted or introduced. Chinese stand two arms' lengths apart and avoid physical contact. Lower your eyes when bowing.

Useful Phrases

Table 5.5 on page 79 contains a collection of useful phrases for travel in China, including their translations and pronunciation.

---

[27] Ted Plafker, *Doing Business in China: How to Profit in the World's Fastest Growing Market* (New York: Hachette Book Group, 2007).

Table 5.5   Useful Phrases for Chinese Travel

English	Chinese (Mandarin)	Pronunciation
Hello	*Ni hao*	NEE-how
Good morning	*Zao shang hao*	zhow-shang HOW
Good afternoon	*Xia wu hao*	she-ah-woo HOW
Good evening	*Wanshang hao*	wahn-shang HOW
Goodbye	*Zaijian*	dzeye zhee-EHN
Please	*Qing*	Cheen
Thank you	*Xie xie*	See-EH see-EH
You're welcome	*Bu yong xie*	boo yohn see-EH
Yes	*Shi*	Shih
Excuse me	*Qing rang / Qing rang yi xia*	shing ree-AH/EE-SHAH

Names

Pronouncing names correctly is important in Chinese culture. Wang, Zhang, and Li are the most common family names. Chinese names are printed in order of the generational or family name first, plus the given or first name second. A family name may precede the given name with a hyphen.

For example, Deng Xiaoping is Mr. Deng; Xiaoping is his first name. In China, the names are blended together (Dengxiaoping). In Hong Kong and Taiwan, a hyphen separates the first and second names (Deng-Xiaoping).

Job titles are symbols of honor and respect. When addressing someone in person or in writing, give face by using a professional title and family name: Doctor Hsu, Accountant Li, or Engineer Wong. Courtesy titles include *Xiansheng* (shee-ehn-SHUNG, similar to Mr.) and *Xiaojie* (shee-OW-jyeh, similar to Miss).

Meetings and Negotiations

First meetings are formal. Seniority, rank, and status are important with each team's highest-ranked member entering first and departing last. Follow the lead of the Chinese host to bow, shake hands, make introductions, and exchange cards with their team. Prior to doing business, be prepared to conduct small talk on appropriate topics including Chinese culture and cuisine, the 2008 Olympics in Beijing, Chinese sports figures, and global interest in learning Mandarin. Avoid human rights, politics, religion, sex, and the Communist Party.

Because English is not the *lingua franca*, hire a trusted translator. Determine the meeting attendees and e-mail translated materials with a proposed agenda in advance. Send technical experts and senior team leaders to match their negotiating team. The final decision maker may not be present at these meetings.

Presentation Styles, Conversational Topics, and Humor

Formality, modesty, and simplicity are recommended in your business dealings with the Chinese. Professional speaking consultant Angela DeFinis recommends toning down hand movements, focusing on facts, and using a pragmatic approach.[28] Ruben A. Hernandez suggests using real examples and being explicit because abstract ideas can be misinterpreted.[29] When presenting, Hernandez advises starting with a clear outline and explanation of background. Because rank and status are valued, your company's history, reputation, and your role need to be clarified. Explain any graphics used with visual aids. DeFinis points out that colors have special meaning, so use traditional black type on a white background for visuals to avoid offending. At the end, have a question-and-answer period: the Chinese consider interrupting a presentation with questions to be rude. Avoid sarcasm as humor.

Gestures

- Instead of pointing, use the whole open hand at waist level.
- To beckon someone, extend your hand, palm down and curl your four fingers together several times.
- Friends of the same gender will walk together holding hands.
- Spitting is still considered an act of hygiene.

Notable Foods and Dishes

Chinese cuisine is diverse. A few of the differences in regional cuisines include:[30]

---

[28]DeFinis Communications publication, "How to Create and Deliver Business Presentations for an Asian Audience," www.definiscommunications.com/pdf/How-to-Create-and-Deliver-Business-Presentations-for-an-Asian-Audience.pdf (accessed November 12, 2014).

[29]Ruben Hernandez, *Presenting Across Cultures: How to Adapt Your Business and Sales Presentations in Key Markets Around the World* (Tertium Business Books, 2013).

[30]Dean Foster, *The Global Etiquette Guide to Asia* (New York: John Wiley & Sons, 2000); China Highlights, "China Regional Cuisines," www.chinahighlights.com/travelguide/chinese-food/regional-cuisines.htm (accessed November 14, 2014).

- **Northern (Beijing):** Rich and elegant Mandarin dishes, including Peking duck. Typical ingredients include wheat flour, beef, lamb, duck, scallions, leeks, and garlic.
- **Shanghai (central):** Fine cuisine known for fresh taste and sweet sauces. It features a variety of local fish, seafood and vegetables.
- **Cantonese (Guangzhou):** Light, sweet cuisine with food often braised, stewed, or sautéed. Subtle sauces are used, including hoisin, oyster, plum, and sweet-and-sour.
- **Szechuan/Hunan (south-central):** Bold cuisine using a variety of poultry, pork, beef, vegetables, and tofu. It has notably spicy flavors from use of red chilies.

Specialty Dishes

Favorite dishes in Chinese cuisine include:[31]

- **Peking duck:** A national dish; seasoned, roasted duck with crispy skin served with scallions, sweet bean paste, and thin pancakes
- **Sweet-and-sour pork:** Deep-fried pork and vegetables, stir-fried in a sauce of sugar, ketchup, white vinegar, and soy sauce
- **Gong bao chicken:** Stir-fried chicken, peanuts, chili peppers, and vegetables

Dining Etiquette

Eat first, talk later!
—*Confucius, reflecting the Chinese belief that food is "the first pleasure"*

Cuisine is the epicenter of business relationships in China. Be prepared for lunch, tea, and a banquet. When reciprocating, coordinate with your host or hotel concierge to order one dish for every guest expected, plus one extra dish with additional noodles and rice.

Twelve-course banquets are declining in popularity and have been reduced to five courses in some cities, including Shanghai. Protocol requires the guest of honor to arrive on time and observe the host for direction. Allow the host to seat you and wait for an invitation to begin. The host sits with his or her

---

[31]Devine and N. Braganti, *The Traveler's Guide to Asian Customs & Manners*, Revised Edition (New York: St. Martin's Griffin, 1998); China Highlights, "Eight Most Popular Chinese Dishes," www.chinahighlights.com/travelguide/chinese-food/eight-chinese-dishes.htm (accessed November 14, 2014).

back to the exit door, at the dinner table, facing the honored guest seated on the opposite side, facing the door. The remaining guests are seated by rank and status on both sides of the host and guest. The host offers a welcome speech, and the honored guest stands and reciprocates with a thank-you speech and toast. Traditionally, hosts pick up chopsticks in a silent signal to begin dining or say, *Rang* (rahng derr chee), which means "Let's eat."

Learn local specialties and practice with chopsticks, which reverse for use as serving tongs. Taste every dish. Offer dining companions food before serving yourself; pour and refill others' drinks before your own. Serving dishes remain in the table center; not lifted or passed; the last morsel remains uneaten. When finished, place chopsticks on the chopstick rest or table.

Drinking and Toasting

Formal Chinese banquets include Chinese Baijiu, the world's most-consumed liquor, accounting for more than one-third of all spirits consumed in the world, according to International Wine & Spirit Research. The most common liquor is *mao tai,* which is made from fermented rice.

The toast *Ganbei* (Ghan-bay) means 'bottoms up' and *kai pay* (ki pay) means 'empty your glass' with the expectation that you *do a shot* or empty the glass all at once. To discontinue the bottoms up approach, say *sui bian*, which roughly translates to "Please proceed in your way, and I will do it my way."

When reciprocating the host's opening toast, lift the glass with both hands to shoulder-height and toast to the health of all and business prosperity.

In business meetings that Sharon attended everyone drank tea. Many times, the hot water was ready and the tea was immediately poured as soon as the meeting began.

Tipping and Bill-Paying

Tipping is not customary in China. In international cities, high-end restaurants and hotels may include a 10 to 15 percent service charge. When dining, do not ask for the bill, (or *Fapiao*), receipt until you are ready to leave: It is considered rude to receive the bill and stay at the table. For cab drivers, round up or tip 10 percent. Tip small change to bellhops, barbers, personal drivers, and maids.

Smoking

Smoking is common in restaurants and at formal events.

Taboos

The following are taboo in Chinese culture:

- Using the word "comrade" or the phrase "mainland China"
- Standing with your hands in your pockets
- Having a hairy nose or picking your nose in public
- Picking your teeth with your fingers
- Ignoring or rearranging seating positions
- Speaking loudly or acting rambunctiously
- Interrupting conversations or periods of silence
- Giving gifts in multiples of four, the numbers 44 or 444, and uneven numbers
- Boasting, bragging, or arrogance
- Pointing with your index finger
- Placing your feet on anything or using a shoe to move an item
- Placing a purse, briefcase or portfolio on the floor

Heroes and Sports

Knowing about another country's heroes and sports offers opportunities to incorporate culture-specific references into your conversations and presentations.

Heroes

Heroes from China's history include:

Guan Yu (162–219): Military general and idolized deity. Key general in the civil war leading to the collapse of the Han Dynasty. Served under Liu Bei, first emperor of the state of Shu Han in the Three Kingdoms period. Best known as a strong warrior loyal to his rulers. The subject of Luo Guan Zhong's *The Romance of the Three Kingdoms.* Worshipped as a god by many in southern China, Taiwan, and Hong Kong.

Yue Fei (1103–1142): Military general and national folk hero. General under the Song Dynasty. Yue Fei prevented enemy advances and continued to lead successful offensives into northern China to secure territories that had been captured. Widely known for his integral part in this resistance against foreign invaders and the survival of the Song Dynasty.

Sports

Sports

Kung Fu (or Wushu): A Chinese martial art form, originally intended as a means of self-defense.

Dragon boat racing (Sai Longzhou): Dating back 2,500 years, this custom continues during the annual Dragon Boat Festival held in late May to early June.[32]

Other popular modern sports include football (U.S. soccer), table tennis (U.S. ping-pong), badminton, swimming, and basketball.

Sports Figures

Den Yaping (1973–present): Table tennis player who, in China, was voted Female Athlete of the Century.[33] Nationally-prized sports figure in China. Began playing table tennis at five and overcame small stature (1.5 m or 4′11″) to win. Won six world championships, four Olympic championships, and 18 world titles. Retired at age 24 with more titles than any other table tennis player worldwide.

Li Na (1982–present): Chinese professional tennis player. Female trailblazer who launched a tennis craze across China. First Chinese player, male or female, to win a Grand Slam Title (the French Open). Ranked number two in the world by the Women's Tennis Association.

Yao Ming (1980–present): Retired Chinese professional basketball player. Played for the Chinese Basketball Association (CBA) and the U.S. NBA. Tallest NBA player at retirement at 7′6″ (2.9 m). Subject of the documentary *Year of the Yao*.

Eight-Question Framework

This section reviews the framework to which you were introduced earlier in this book. Each of these questions addresses one or more business topics to help you attract and build the relationships upon which today's successful businesses depend.

---

[32]Travel China Guide, "Dragon Boat Festival," www.travelchinaguide.com/essential/holidays/dragon-boat.htm (accessed November 12, 2014).

[33]BBC Nottingham Citylife, "University High Flyers," September 24, 2014, www.bbc.co.uk/nottingham/spotlight/2002/05/highflyer_nottingham.shtml (accessed November 12, 2014).

1. How Do the Chinese Prefer to Act: Individually or as a Group?

Here in China it is all about how you fit in; in the U.S. it is more about how to be yourself.
　　—*Phoebe You, Director and Chief Representative,*
　　　OSU China Gateway (Shanghai) Co., Ltd.

After hosting a Chinese delegation in Austin, Texas, real estate broker Helen Jobes received a reciprocal invitation to speak at a senior housing conference on Hainan Island, China. Conference delegates received gifts, including a golf shirt embroidered with the host's logo. The next morning, Ms. Jobes wore a simple blouse and skirt in neutral colors and was surprised to see everyone else wearing the golf shirt, including the chairwoman and former president of the China Real Estate Chamber of Commerce. At lunch, Ms. Jobes changed into the logo golf shirt because "I thought, 'I'm out of step here.'"

This story illustrates the importance of group identity in Chinese culture and the ways in which decisions are made as a group rather than individually. When a Chinese person loses face within their community, it potentially represents a lifetime of shame for them. Conforming, albeit subconsciously, as Ms. Jobes discovered, is more than showing politeness to your host. It signals that you understand and embrace a key value in Chinese culture.

Making decisions that take into account group loyalties is reflected by Geert Hofstede's findings on the Individualism index (See Chapter 2, page 15). As he reported, China's *highly collectivist* score reflects that people act in the interests of the group and not necessarily of themselves. In collectivist societies, people belong to *in groups* that take care of them in exchange for loyalty.[34]

2. How Are Power and Authority Viewed in China?

When a Chinese business leader makes a decision, they must be sure it does not offend anyone.
　　—*Phoebe You, Director and Chief Representative,*
　　　OSU China Gateway (Shanghai) Co., Ltd.

The prevailing belief that the Beijing government controls everything in China is only partly true. "To be sure, if Beijing truly wants something to

---

[34]The Hofstede Center, "What About China," http://geert-hofstede.com/china.html (accessed November 15, 2014).

happen, it will," writes INSEAD professor Michael A. Witt. "At the same time, Beijing recognizes that decentralization of power plays an important role in taking economic reforms forward."[35] In this respect, political power and authority tends to be *bottom-up,* whereas decision making within organizations is *top-down.*

According to one Chinese investor and executive who serves on the board of several Fortune 500 companies, where power and authority reside depends on whether it is a state-owned enterprise (SOE), joint venture, wholly-owned company, or private company.

Since 1978, China has gradually reduced the number of SOEs, down from over 75 percent of China's industrial output thirty years ago to 46 percent today.[36] Local governments invest and have control in SOEs through the funding of ventures that contribute to Beijing's desire to balance out development gaps in far-flung and rural areas.

Because privatization is in its infancy, local, provincial, and national officials retain power and authority over seemingly private business transactions. The power to make decisions is held by those with numerous loyalties. As the previously mentioned Chinese investor advises, "High-level corporate positions in Chinese business organizations are usually influenced by an invisible leadership group of government officials. Their power and authority reach well beyond their corporate board seat."

Turning to internal decision making, another Chinese professional described it as "very hierarchical with report to boss, to report to boss, to report to boss, to avoid taking blame."

Gabe Higham, who worked in China on behalf of Dell, observed, "Company decisions are typically reached in a top-down manner, with only the very top of the pyramid involved in decision making." The mid-level manager or supervisor has little authority; their role is to communicate instructions from the top and make sure these are executed.

Mr. Higham found Chinese bosses reluctant to delegate authority to subordinates, leaving many Chinese managers and supervisors unwilling to take action without instruction. This is especially true in new or uncertain situations where "the potential for criticism and job loss outweigh the potential for a fantastic result."

[35]INSEAD Knowledge, "The Ten Principles for Doing Business in China," February 22, 2012, http://knowledge.insead.edu/world/china/the-ten-principles-for-doing-business-in-china-757.

[36]Economy Watch, "China Economy," June 4, 2013, www.economywatch.com/world_economy/china.

The external and internal stakeholders holding the power and authority that impact business organizations require business leaders to gain consensus and avoid offense before making decisions.

3. How Do the Chinese Compare Rules and Relationships?

Rules and laws here are just suggestions. We write laws with lots of flexibility.
— *Chinese professional*

One Asian who travels frequently to China says that U.S. businesspeople often get angry, thinking the Chinese system is unfair. "But here in China everybody understands the system, so my advice to Westerners is to stop thinking the way you do in your own country and adopt the thinking of how to do business in China. Because when a Chinese businessperson comes up against a problem, they don't look for a lawyer, they look for someone to have a relationship with."

He added that: "Foreigners cannot do business here without a Chinese partner. People from the U.S. don't believe us when we tell them that business *is* politics in China. Our government has power and if you don't have the right relationships, the regulations are difficult and they can close you down. So I make it easy to do business in China by establishing relationships with government officials, and have Chinese partners based in Beijing, Shanghai, and Qingdao. They know what forms we need to fill out and will work with us to meet all the various regulations and other hurdles we face. For those who don't have these relationships in place, getting a decision might take many months when it might take us only 15 days."

'Thinking like a Westerner' caused challenges for one U.S. business professional who opened an office in Beijing and tried to do things herself

Most Westerners here have experienced the proverbial "knock on the door" when a government official or regulator visits. We got a call to say that the authorities wanted to talk about our medical license, which we have in addition to our business license.

We recently moved our premises to a new address but hadn't informed the authorities. We were told this was a major oversight and we needed a secure storage facility and a larger office to meet the licensing requirements. These officials even brought along a tape measure to check the regulated size according to the number of employees we had.

What she learned was something that the Asian businessman quoted above already knew: Grease the wheels of commerce by finding a local manager; know the right relationships to nurture; recognize that *guanxi* is a reciprocal obligation. China's business world is based on *guanxi*, or networks of trust, and creating these networks is crucial.

4. How Do the Chinese Regard Time?

The past, which continues to animate Chinese life in so many striking, unexpected, or subtle ways, seems to inhabit the people rather than the bricks and stones.
    —*Pierre Rykmans, Belgian scholar on China*[37]

China has been called the world's oldest living civilization. One aspect of time that Western businesses often fail to acknowledge—the past—is extremely important to Chinese culture. This story from Dr. Patricia Sieber, former director of the East Asian Studies Center at The Ohio State University (OSU) illustrates how one enduring U.S.-China relationship was built through patience and a reverence for history.

Some years ago, a member of OSU's faculty received an inquiry about an esteemed Chinese lady who wanted to visit and conduct research on her renowned Chinese playwright and filmmaker father, Hong Shen (1894–1955). He produced one of China's first sound films and is known for exemplifying film techniques learned in Hollywood. Several members of OSU's faculty and graduate students from the East Asian Studies Center and Institute for Chinese Studies collaborated to ensure this lady's visit was memorable and productive.

Adds Dr. Sieber: "We went into the archives with her and discovered that while teaching an English class here, Hong Shen had written his first play in English and had staged it in front of 1,300 people in the University Hall in 1919. Over time, he grew this Chinese community of playwrights and scriptwriters at Harvard and in New York. According to his daughter, Hong Qian, this was the happiest time of his life as he moved between all these different organizations, developing a greater global awareness. He took all of this experience and was pivotal in developing the fledgling film industry and dramatic community back home in China."

As a result of OSU's warmth and sensitivity to her request, Hong Qian subsequently donated part of her father's collection to their rare book library—the first special collections donation from China. Other collaboration benefits include helping OSU recruit students from China by pointing out

---

[37] China Heritage Quartely, "The Chinese Attitude Towards the Past," last updated March 14, 2014, www.chinaheritagequarterly.org / articles.php?issue = 014&searchterm = 014_chineseAttitude.inc (accessed November 12, 2014).

that OSU's ties to the Chinese student community date back to the first and second decades of the twentieth century, when Hong Shen found a home abroad and achieved great things with the knowledge he acquired.

"Patience, open-mindedness, willingness to experiment, and perhaps some humility are all necessary to achieving the fullest potential in a bilateral relationship," says Dr. Sieber. "It's always very hard to know exactly what's going to happen. High-risk, high-reward situations take more resources and more time."

5. How Direct Is Communication in China?

> To speak Chinese is not to know China.
> —*Dr. Geoff Raby, Australia's Ambassador to China (2011)*

Lily Li, CEO of China's top professional networking site Tianji, recommends taking the time to learn to communicate the "Chinese way," as patience is required: "Foreign CEOs are always confused and frustrated when they send out an e-mail [to someone in China] and expect a simple yes/no answer. Instead they get a very long reply that does not answer their initial question. Chinese people do not like to take responsibility. They are scared to lose their jobs and don't like to be forced into saying something they don't want to."[38]

One U.S. businesswoman based in Beijing agreed: "The thing I have observed is that I will ask a question for which I just expect a 'yes' or 'no' answer, but they'll just sit and talk among themselves in Chinese. When I ask what they're talking about I'm told they are discussing how to answer me." On one occasion, she wanted to thank her Chinese accountants for staying past midnight finishing an important project. She asked her Chinese accountants' U.S. liaison to arrange a debriefing to "talk about what went right and what didn't" during their first 30 days. He said this was a U.S. concept that the Chinese don't like. The debriefing with the accountants didn't go ahead because of the need to save face.

Indeed, direct communication and candor are viewed as rude by the Chinese. Historically, the Chinese have stayed in the same geographical area and have not relocated for business purposes, so losing face at age 30 within your community could last another 50 years! While mobility has increased, the Chinese continue to learn early on to be indirect and avoid losing face or offending. When negotiating, words and phrases like "maybe," "possibly," "it is inconvenient," "I am not sure," and "perhaps," often mean "no." This is not to say that the Chinese cannot be direct and blunt. Some prefer delivering negative news through an intermediary.

---

[38]BBC Capital, "An Expert's Insight: Thriving as a Foreign CEO in China," February 26, 2014, www.bbc.com/capital/story/20140205-thrive-as-a-foreign-ceo-in-china.

6. How Formal or Informal Do Businesspeople in China Tend to Be?

> I am constantly bemused at the sight of Western business people who come
> to China thinking that so long as they know to exchange name cards with
> two hands, everything is under control.
> — *Ted Plafker,* Doing Business in China[39]

Wishing to make a good impression and establish rapport with her Chinese audience, Helen Jobes sought advice from a professional speaker before making a presentation about senior housing in Sanya, Hainan Province. Unfortunately, the suggestion of informality by using humor, while sound for a U.S. audience, was not suitable for China.

Furthermore, given the importance of relationships within Confucianism, Ms. Jobes thought she was on safe ground by drawing on her experience as a grandmother. Within her slide deck, she included pictures of her grandchildren to support the message that as we age we need a place for family. She even included a slide of her rollerblading to communicate staying active, regardless of age.

The audience response was different than what Ms. Jobes expected: "You know how you try to be funny and it doesn't go anywhere? what I found during this day-long conference was that the Chinese presented in a very formal, factual way. I learned to keep hand movements to a minimum because they are distracting and may be disrespectful."

Remember that the Chinese are data-driven and expect to receive facts presented seriously and serenely, not accompanied by personal anecdotes that we might think are more engaging. Also, although experiences vary, depending on whether you are working with more formal state-owned businesses or newer, informal private companies, remember the Chinese prefer to show restraint and avoid emotion. Laughter during a business meeting may be an expression of embarrassment in response to a breach of etiquette or protocol.

Chinese Forms of Address

According to Phoebe You, "In Chinese culture, rarely do we address people with their first names. It is common to address people with their family name and work title. For instance, for a person who is a general manager at a company and whose family name is Song, it is fine to address this person as 'Song Zong,' which means 'General Manager Song,' or 'Song Jingli,' which means Manager Song.'"

---

[39]Ted Plafker, *Doing Business in China: How to Profit in the World's Fastest Growing Market* (New York: Hachette Book Group, 2007).

7. *How Aligned Are Chinese Social and Business Lives?*

With guanxi, nothing matters; without guanxi, everything matters
— *Chinese Proverb*

Dining and drinking after office hours is a big part of conducting business, including sampling the unique regional specialties, as John Melanson, a veteran of the semiconductor and electronics industry, discovered:

"You have to be a good sport. You have to try their specialties. The easiest thing is just do what they do. When they bring you a bowl of something unidentifiable, just dump it in the hot pot and go with it. I discovered that the Chinese find it fun to test you; some of it is just plain fun for them, and some of it is to find out what your limit is. They're watching you all the time, observing. But it's not mean-spirited at all. It's their way of pushing you to the point where you lose your inhibitions so they can figure out who you really are."

Derek Sandhaus, author of *Baijiu: The Essential Guide to Chinese Spirits*, points out some differences involved in drinking in China: "You drink at meals, and you always drink with someone else. You don't drink when you want to; you drink when other people want you to. That's uncomfortable for a lot of Westerners."

Nevertheless, dining is central to establishing business relationships and you may find your visit includes several lunches and at least one evening banquet. Because dining in the company of others is the grandest gesture of hospitality in China, reciprocity on your part is vital.

8. *How Is the Concept of Women in Business Handled in China?*

When a Chinese team hears that a CEO is coming from overseas they assume it's a man. But, culturally they don't have an issue if it's a woman.
— *Lily Li, Tianji CEO*[40]

Grant Thornton's International Business Report 2014 ranked China sixth in the world, tying with Thailand, for the number of women in senior management roles. As a top performing country this ranking reflects Chinese women's upward mobility in senior positions, boosting their numbers to 38 percent in 2014, up from 25 percent in 2012.[41] China's one-child policy has impacted the

[40]BBC Capital, "An Expert's Insight: Thriving as a Foreign CEO in China," February 26, 2014, www.bbc.com/capital/story/20140205-thrive-as-a-foreign-ceo-in-china.
[41]Grant Thornton, "United States Ranks in Bottom 10 Performing Countries for Women in Senior Management Roles," March 7, 2014, http://news.grantthornton.com/press-release/united-states-ranks-bottom-10-performing-countries-women-senior-management-roles.

female labor force, including direct effects on the number of women as business professionals in China.[42]

Contributing to this tremendous result is the fact that when the People's Republic of China was established in 1949, one of the goals was to promote equality between the sexes.[43] As one Shanghai business owner pointed out: "In China, we believe in the yin and yang, so from a cultural perspective life is a balance. The male in China has dominated things for so long. Women are the future business leaders, and I want to encourage that."

When asked how she held her position for 11 years, Madame Nie Meisheng, President and Chairperson of the China Real Estate Chamber of Commerce, echoed a view that businesswomen globally can relate to: "You've got to be good". In China, she says, "Women do not have much sexual discrimination. Of course, the female percentage is lower than the male, but from the government perspective and from some official institutes, a certain percentage of seats for women is reserved to keep a balance. Within the real-estate industry, in the higher positions, for example CFO or Board of Director, there are a lot of females. There is a huge population with a higher education level."

Ms. Phoebe You, Director of China Gateway, Office of International Affairs for The Ohio State University, also shared positive experiences and optimism. She paraphrased Chairman Mao Zedong by saying: "Chinese women get to share the other half of the sky with men in business, especially in the Shanghai area."

One Chinese investor's advice to international businesswomen is: "Just be yourself, be nice and respectful, and you will do very well." And a Beijing-based U.S. businesswoman found even fewer challenges as a female boss, saying: "In the U.S., I would be the only female in a meeting. Here our main distributor is a woman who owns that business."

Sharon, who has been engaging with her Chinese network for over 20 years, has found the best way to smooth a path in China as an international businesswoman is to establish your credentials and gain credibility well in advance of your arrival by:

- Having an awareness of women's history and current status in Chinese business culture
- Researching and cultivating local business connections and contacts in your Chinese host city

---

[42]Wang, Hui, *Fertility and Female Labor Force Participation: Evidence from the One-Child Policy in China*, dated November 14, 2014, http://econ.msu.edu/seminars/docs/WangPaper.pdf (accessed January 16, 2015).

[43]China Internet Information Center, "China Publishes Gender Equality White Paper," August 24, 2005, www.china.org.cn/english/2005/Aug/139404.htm.

- Having a mutual contact forward your CV and business qualifications prior to introductions
- Finding local contacts to act as intermediaries and accompany you to meetings and negotiations
- Understanding Chinese hierarchy and, as the female business leader or top negotiator, requesting male team members enter *after* you to communicate your senior rank and avoid expressing disagreement
- Learning a few Mandarin greetings—the effort will be appreciated and help to break the ice
- Nothing is black or white; business operates in a gray area.

Cultural Summary

Here are some key points to remember:

- The Chinese way of doing business includes the core value of harmony so when negotiating with local government, include the mayor and key officials.
- China is a collectivist culture. Be sure senior executives receive deference from younger members of your team. While in China, team members should avoid expressing disagreement when a decision is reached.
- When determining where power and authority rests, hire a Chinese firm to research when the company started, previous ownership, and investor and banking relationships.

Self-Awareness Profile

This simple exercise prompts you to self-assess where you currently stand on topics related to the eight-question framework and *compare* this with the country culture. This visual will help you discover the extent to which you may need to adapt your current mindset and behavior to develop more robust business relationships. For details on how to complete this graphic, see the instructions given in the Introduction on pages xviii–xix.

Consider copying the eight-question Profile or using a pencil so that you can see, over time, how you have adjusted your cultural mindset. You might also wish to create unique graphics related to each of the businesses you work with, as these cultural positions vary depending upon geographic location, industry, generational factors, and corporate profile.

Q1: What is your preferred way of doing business?

As an individual making autonomous decisions					**As a team member who seeks group consensus**
1	2	3	4	5	**6**

Q2: How comfortable are you in hierarchies in which power is distributed unequally?

Very uncomfortable					**Very comfortable**
1	2	3	4	5	**6**

Q3: How closely do you follow rules and obey the law?

Almost always					**It depends**
1	2	3	4	**5**	6

Q4: What is your general attitude toward time?

I prefer agendas, schedules, planning					**I prefer flexibility, fluidity without scheduling**
1	2	3	4	**5**	6

Q5: What is your preferred way to communicate?

Very diplomatically					**Very candidly**
1	**2**	3	4	5	6

Q6: What is your interpersonal style or level of formality in business interactions?

Very formal					**Very informal**
1	**2**	3	4	5	6

Q7: What is your view on socializing within business?

A waste of time   **Essential**

1   2   3   4   5   **6**

Q8: Should a woman defer to a man as the lead, if winning business in a certain culture depended on it?

Never   **Yes, absolutely**

1   2   3   4   **5**   6

6

Hong Kong

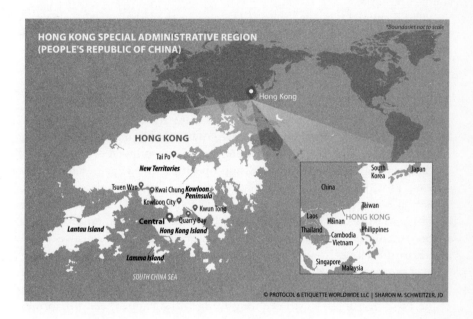

You can leave Hong Kong, but it will never leave you.

Nury Vittachi, *Hong Kong: The City of Dreams*

Introduction

The sun rises in the east, sets in the west, and meets in Hong Kong, also known as the pearl of the Orient. The island is a harmonious fusion of Eastern and Western cultures, the stepping-stone port of entry into China. Hong Kong's beautiful skyline, new airport, natural harbor, world-renowned shopping centers, and film industry all made it an international hub. There is little doubt that this East-West mindset is reflected in the way Hong Kongers conduct business.

This bicultural mindset has helped to create a flourishing service-oriented economy, representing one of the highest per-capita incomes in the world.[1] Hong Kong is ranked first in the world, the top-rated economic freedom according to the Index of Economic Freedom, a spot it has held for 20 consecutive years.[2] The economy is bolstered by the fact that it is a free port without customs tariffs or value-added taxes imposed. This market opens its arms wide to foreign investments without undue regulations and is a direct channel for investment in China. All these things have contributed to making Hong Kong a place with the 'highest level of economic freedom worldwide.'[3]

Hong Kong is a world financial hub operating under 'one country, two systems,' providing autonomy in economic and social systems. Here's the short version of how this occurred: After the first Opium War, China ceded Hong Kong Island to Britain in what may have been the world's largest drug transaction. Britain then added parts of the Kowloon Peninsula and many smaller islands to the Hong Kong territory. During the 1970s, exceptionally strong economic growth caused Hong Kong, along with Singapore, South Korea, and Taiwan to became one of four *Asian Tigers*. In 1997, Britain's 99-year lease of the New Territories north of Hong Kong Island expired, and the former British colony became a Special Administrative Region of China under the Basic Law until 2047. Hong Kong has been referred to as the 'Wall Street of Asia,' given the many multinationals that have established financial powerhouses there. As Sharon has discovered during her business travel to Hong Kong, it is not difficult to be successful in Hong Kong. The Milken Institute's 2013 Global Opportunity Index: *Attracting Foreign Investment Report* rated Hong Kong number one.[4]

---

[1] The World Bank, Data, "Hong Kong SAR, China," http://data.worldbank.org/country /hong-kong-sar-china (accessed November 13, 2014).
[2] The Heritage Foundation, *2014 Index of Economic Freedom*, "Hong Kong," www.heritage .org/index/country/hongkong (accessed November 13, 2014).
[3] Ibid.
[4] Milken Institute press release, March 19, 2013, www.globalopportunityindex.org/opportunity .taf?page=press.

Quiz

How much do you know about Hong Kong? Answer the following questions as True or False to test your knowledge. (The Answer Key at the bottom includes page numbers that refer to the topic.)

_____1. Cantonese is currently the predominant language in Hong Kong.

_____2. Hong Kong's economy is service-oriented.

_____3. Although Hong Kong is a Special Administrative Region of China, its constitution guarantees complete autonomy.

_____4. Hong Kong includes the New Territories, the Kowloon Peninsula, Hong Kong Island, Lantau Island, Lamma Island, and more than 200 smaller islands.

_____5. The honorific *Madame* is a diplomatic legacy.

_____6. For business proposals, use the good-luck numbers three (life), eight (prosperity), or nine (eternity).

_____7. Hong Kongers prefer to receive simple modest business gifts instead of high-quality luxury items.

_____8. More than 65% of Hong Kongers agree that more successful women in the workplace is a positive social phenomenon.

_____9. Fashion and style are important in Hong Kong, with emphasis on tailor made suits and designer labels.

_____10. Gifts are presented from "our company" to "your company" at meetings or banquets.

Answer Key: 1. T (p. 103); 2. T (p. 98); 3. F (p. 101); 4. T (p. 101); 5. T (p. 108); 6. T (p. 109); 7. F (p. 107); 8. T (p. 118); 9. T (p. 105); 10. T (p. 107).

Country Basics

This section provides key knowledge in an easy-to-read format to help you quickly grasp some of the basics necessary to navigate this culture.

Historical Timeline

A critical way to show respect for another person's culture is to have knowledge of their country's history and current affairs. Table 6.1 on page 100 outlines

Table 6.1   Key Historical Events

Period/ Dates	Description/Events	World Events
Circa 1700	Britain begins using Hong Kong's harbor for trade with China.	The Great Northern War begins.
1842	China cedes Hong Kong Island to Britain after the First Opium War.	Treaty between Britain and the U.S. defines Canadian frontier.
1860	Southern Kowloon is ceded to Britain after the Second Opium War.	Abraham Lincoln elected 16th president of the U.S.
1898	China leases Northern Kowloon, the New Territories, and 235 islands to Britain for 99 years.	Pierre and Marie Curie discover radium and polonium.
1984	Conditions are set for Hong Kong's return to China in 1997.	Apple introduces the original Macintosh microcomputer.
1990	Hong Kong's constitution, the Basic Law, is drafted.	Germany celebrates its formal reunification.
1995	Elections are held for new Legislative Council.	The World Trade Organization is established.
1997	Hong Kong becomes a Special Administrative Region of China.	Asian financial crisis occurs.
2007	Chinese government proposes to allow direct elections in Hong Kong by 2017.	Pratibha Patil is sworn in as India's first female president.
2011	Ordinance sets first statutory minimum wage.	The world population reaches 7 billion inhabitants according to the United Nations.
2012	Pro-democracy parties win the majority of votes and retain power of veto.	NASA's Curiosity rover successfully lands on Mars.
2014	Hong Kong is ranked number one city destination by Euromonitor International.	The XXII Olympic Winter Games take place in Sochi, Russia.
2016	Legislative elections scheduled.	Laos scheduled to be ASEAN Chair.
2017	Chief executive elections scheduled.	Indian, South Korean, and Singaporean presidential elections scheduled.
2047	Special Administrative Region status under Basic Law expires.	

a few key events related to Hong Kong, together with concurrent world events.[5]

Full Country Name and Location

The Hong Kong Special Administrative Region of the People's Republic of China is a little less than half the size of Luxembourg and a quarter of the size of the State of Rhode Island in the U.S. Bordering the South China Sea, it shares its only land border with China's southern coast. Hong Kong includes the New Territories (part of the mainland), the Kowloon Peninsula, Hong Kong Island, Lantau Island, Lamma Island, and more than 200 smaller islands.

Government/Political Structure

As a special administrative region of China since 1997, Hong Kong has a limited democracy that guarantees autonomy except in defense and foreign affairs. Its constitution, the Basic Law, was drafted in 1990 by the Chinese government and put into effect in 1997 when China regained administrative control over Hong Kong. The head of state is the president of China, and a Hong Kong resident is elected as the head of government, or chief executive. There is a single Legislative Council of 70 members. National elections were held March 25th, 2012; the next elections are scheduled for March of 2017.

Population and Economic Centers

The Hong Kong government reported the population to be 7.07 million in a 2011 census.[6] The *CIA World Factbook* (July 2014) estimates the population of Hong Kong to be approximately 7.11 million. Hong Kong is an urban nation with 100 percent of the population living in urban areas.[7]

The main ethnic group is Chinese (94 percent), followed by Filipino (2 percent), and Indonesian (2 percent).[8]

The major business centers are shown in Table 6.2 on page 102.

---

[5] *CultureGrams World Edition 2014: Hong Kong* (Ann Arbor: ProQuest, 2014); Bernard Grun, *The Timetables of History*, (New York: Touchstone Press, 2005); and BBC News Asia, "Hong Kong Profile: Timeline," last updated October 14, 2014, www.bbc.com/news/world-asia-pacific-16526765 (accessed November 13, 2014).

[6] Hong Kong Census and Statistics Department, *2011 Population Census: Summary Results*, February 2012, www.census2011.gov.hk/pdf/summary-results.pdf (accessed November 13, 2014).

[7] CIA, *The World Factbook*, "Hong Kong," www.cia.gov/library/publications/the-world-factbook/geos/hk.html (accessed November 13, 2014).

[8] Ibid.

Table 6.2   Major Business Centers

Business Centers	Population (millions)
Central	*
Kowloon City	*
Kwai Chung	*
Kwun Tong	*
Quarry Bay	*
Tai Po	*
Tsuen Wan	*

*Hong Kong's 2011 Population Census does not provide a breakdown for cities and towns, only main districts. See the Hong Kong Census and Statistics Department website for more information.[9]

Economy

Hong Kong is ranked 3rd out of 189 economies in terms of ease of doing business, according to the World Bank Group's *Doing Business 2015* report.[10] Its 2013 GDP was ranked 39th by the World Bank.[11] The composition of GDP by sector is services (93 percent), industry (6.9 percent), and agriculture (0 percent).[12]

Corruption Perceptions Index

Hong Kong ranked 15th least corrupt out of 177 countries and territories with a score of 75 out of 100.[13] This annual index, compiled by Transparency International, measures perceived levels of public sector corruption.

The Independent Commission Against Corruption is the anticorruption agency that conducts investigations in Hong Kong.

---

[9] Hong Kong Census and Statistics Department, "2011 Population Census," last revised April 18, 2013, www.census2011.gov.hk/en/index.html (accessed November 13, 2014).

[10] World Bank Group, *Doing Business 2015* (October 29, 2014): 4, www.doingbusiness.org/~ /media/GIAWB/Doing%20Business/Documents/Annual-Reports/English/DB15-Full-Report .pdf (accessed November 11, 2014).

[11] The World Bank, Data, GDP Ranking, "Gross Domestic Product Ranking Table," last updated September 24, 2014, http://data.worldbank.org/data-catalog/GDP-ranking-table (accessed November 13, 2014).

[12] CIA, *The World Factbook*, "Hong Kong," www.cia.gov/library/publications/the-world-factbook /geos/hk.html (accessed November 13, 2014).

[13] Transparency International, "Corruption Perceptions Index 2013," www.transparency .org/cpi2013/results (accessed November 11, 2014).

Human Development Index

Hong Kong ranked 15th out of 187 countries and territories.[14] The HDI, compiled by the United Nations Development Programme, is a composite index of life expectancy, education and income statistics.

Global Gender Gap Index

Hong Kong was not included in the Global Gender Gap Index.

Climate

Hong Kong's climate is tropical with seasonal monsoons (May–November) and four seasons: Spring (March–May) has rising temperatures with cool evenings; summer (June–August) is hot, humid, sunny, and rainy; fall (September–November) is the most pleasant with warm temperatures and sunshine; winter (December–February) is cool, dry, and cloudy.

Languages

The official languages are Cantonese (89.5 percent) and English (3.5 percent). Mandarin (1.4 percent) and other Chinese dialects (4 percent) are also spoken.[15] Hong Kong uses classical Chinese characters in writing, unlike the simplified characters used in China. English is the *lingua franca* for business. Mandarin is becoming more prevalent.

Belief Systems, Philosophies, and Religions

The country breakdown is as follows: mix of Buddhism, Taoism, Confucianism, Animism, and other local religions (90 percent) and Christianity (10 percent).[16]

---

[14]United Nations Development Programme, *Human Development Report 2014*, http://hdr.undp .org/sites/default/files/hdr14-report-en-1.pdf, p. 160–63 (accessed November 11, 2014).
[15]CIA, *The World Factbook*, "Hong Kong," www.cia.gov/library/publications/the-world-factbook /geos/hk.html (accessed November 13, 2014).
[16]Ibid.; *CultureGrams World Edition 2014: Hong Kong* (Ann Arbor: ProQuest, 2014).

The Hong Kong government also reports small numbers of Islams, Hindus, Jews, and Sikhs.[17]

For an overview of belief systems, philosophies, and religions, please refer to Chapter 4, pages 64–65.

Time Zones/Daylight Savings

Hong Kong has a single time zone, Hong Kong Time (HKT). Hong Kong is eight hours ahead of GMT (Greenwich Mean Time)/UTC (Coordinated Universal Time). It does not operate under Daylight Savings.

It is 13 hours ahead of U.S. Eastern Standard Time (12 hours ahead in Daylight Savings Time). See www.timeanddate.com/worldclock/.

To calculate Hong Kong time, add eight hours to UTC/GMT.

Telephone Country Code and Internet Suffix

The Hong Kong telephone country code is 852 and its Internet suffix is .hk.

Currency

Hong Kong currency is the Hong Kong dollar (HKD). One dollar is divided into 100 cents.

Business Culture, Etiquette, and Customs

This section covers business culture, etiquette, and customs.

Fiscal Year

The Hong Kong fiscal year is April 1 to March 31. Dates are written as day, month, year; April 1, 2020 is written 01/04/2020.

---

[17] Hong Kong Information Services Department factsheet, "Religion and Custom," October 2013, www.gov.hk/en/about/abouthk/factsheets/docs/religion.pdf (accessed November 13, 2014).

Working Week

The structure of the Hong Kong working week is outlined in Table 6.3.

Table 6.3   The Hong Kong Working Schedule

Industry	Business Hours	Days of the Week
Business and government	09:00–17:00	Monday–Friday
	09:00–13:00	Saturday (some offices)
Banks	09:30–16:00	Monday–Friday
	09:00–13:00	Saturday
Lunch	13:00–14:00	

Holidays and Festivals

Some Hong Kong holidays are determined by the lunar calendar and change from year to year. On specific holidays, an office may remain open with limited staff. Check with your embassy or trade office before planning business travel.

October through November and March through May are the best times to visit Hong Kong for business trips. Avoid making appointments during the Chinese New Year, Christmas, and Easter. Table 6.4 on page 106 contains a list of major holidays. Floating holidays are designated in Table 6.4 with an asterisk.

Business Dress/Appearance

Hong Kong has long been known as one of the world's leading destination centers for tailor-made suits, dresses, and high fashion. Business attire depends on the industry and includes tailor-made garments, luxury and designer labels, and quality leather. Men wear ties and suits in dark colors for business meetings and dinner. Ladies wear designer and tailor-made suits, dresses, and skirts. Business casual dress includes collared shirts and trousers. White and blue are funeral colors.[18]

---

[18]Dean Foster, *The Global Etiquette Guide to Asia* (New York: John Wiley & Sons, 2000); Mary M. Bosrock, *Asian Business Customs & Manners: A Country-by-Country Guide* (New York: Meadowbrook Press, 2007); and Jeanette S. Martin and Lillian H. Chaney, *Passport to Success: The Essential Guide to Business Culture and Customs in America's Largest Trading Partners* (Westport, CT: Praeger, 2009).

Table 6.4   Hong Kong Holidays and Festivals

Date	Name
January 1	New Year's Day
Late January/February	Spring Festival and Chinese New Year*
March/April	Easter*
March 8	International Women's Day
April 5	Ching Ming Festival (Tomb Sweeping Day)
May 1	Labor Day
May/June	Dragon Boat Festival*
July 1	Hong Kong Special Administrative Region Establishment Day
August	Liberation Day—Tuen Ng*
September/October	Mid-Autumnal Festival*
October 1	National Day
Autumn	Chung Yeung Festival*
December 25	Christmas Day
December 26	Boxing Day

News Sources

- *South China Morning Post*: www.scmp.com/frontpage/international
- *The Standard*: www.thestandard.com.hk

Business Cards

Business card exchanges are de rigeur. Print English on one side and Cantonese classical characters on the reverse. Rank and status matter, so include your title and any additional information including degrees and certifications.

Technology

According to Akamai Technology's *State of the Internet Report*, Hong Kong has the fourth fastest average Internet connection speed in the world and the fastest average peak connection speed.[19] Latest figures rank Hong Kong 47th

---

[19] Akamai Technologies, "State of the Internet Q4 2013," April 2014, www.akamai.com /dl/akamai/akamai-soti-q413.pdf?WT.mc_id=soti_Q413.

worldwide for the number of Internet users[20] and number 48 globally for the number of Internet hosts.[21]

Gifts

Business gift ideas for those in the private sector include high-quality pen sets, desk accessories, gifts from your home region, and domestic coffee table books. Gifts are presented from "our company" to "your company" at meetings or banquets. It is illegal to give gifts or cash to government officials.

Children's gifts from your home country may include jerseys of athletes from Hong Kong, popular sports teams, and prestigious universities. Certain gifts in Hong Kong are associated with unpleasantness: clocks (bad luck), swords, scissors, knives, sharp objects (severing of ties), white carnations or flowers (mourning), and items with red printing (mourning). Ideal wrapping paper colors are green, red (for good luck), or gold (for wealth). Avoid white and black (they represent death and tragedy).[22]

Introductions, Greetings, Personal Space, and Eye Contact

When greeting a colleague, slightly nodding your head or bowing while shaking hands is common. High-status people and elders are introduced first, and women are introduced before men. The historic honorific *Madame* is a diplomatic legacy. Most introductions include name, employer, and job description. Use the full name, which is the family name and given name or family name and title. Many Hong Kongers adopt Western names; wait for an invitation to use this name.

Physical contact other than a handshake is inappropriate, along with touching the opposite gender in public. Hong Kongers stand an arm's length close to one another and tend to make little eye contact when talking.[23]

---

[20]CIA, *The World Factbook*, "Country Comparison: Internet Users," information dated 2009, www.cia.gov/library/publications/the-world-factbook/rankorder/2153rank.html (accessed November 13, 2014).

[21]CIA, *The World Factbook*, "Country Comparison: Internet Hosts," information dated 2009, www.cia.gov/library/publications/the-world-factbook/rankorder/2184rank.html (accessed November 13, 2014).

[22]Mary M. Bosrock, *Asian Business Customs & Manners: A Country-by-Country Guide* (New York: Meadowbrook Press, 2007); and E. Devine and N. Braganti, *The Traveler's Guide to Asian Customs & Manners*, Revised Edition (New York: St. Martin's Griffin, 1998).

[23]Jeanette S. Martin and Lillian H. Chaney, *Passport to Success: The Essential Guide to Business Culture and Customs in America's Largest Trading Partners* (Westport, CT: Praeger, 2009).

Useful Phrases

Table 6.5 contains phrases that are helpful to know when you travel to Hong Kong.

Table 6.5   Useful Phrases for Hong Kong Travel

English	Chinese (Cantonese)	Pronunciation
Hello	*Nei ho*	NEE-how
Hello (on the telephone)	*Wai*	why
How are you?	*Nei hou ma*	nay HOH ma
Good morning	*Jou san*	DJOH-sun
Good afternoon	*Ngh on*	NNG ohn
Good evening	*Mahn on*	MAN ohn
Goodbye	*Joigin*	djoy-GEEN
Please	*My goi*	mm-GOY
Thank you	*Dojeh*	doh DZEH
You're welcome	*M'sai m'goi*	MM-sigh mm-goy
Yes	*Haih*	high
No	*Mh-haih*	mm-HIGH
Excuse me	*Deui mh jyuh*	der-MM-dyoo

Names

Hong Kong names are printed in order of the surname (family) name first, plus given (first) name. Use last name and courtesy titles including Mr., Mrs., Miss, and Ms. When in doubt, wait to be invited before using a first name with a colleague. Some Hong Kongers have western names. In electronic communication use the salutation *Dear* plus the courtesy or professional title, not a first name.

Meetings and Negotiations

It is best to plan meetings well in advance and arrange for an introduction to your fellow attendees before you arrive. Punctuality is important; plan to be on time, taking the heavy traffic into consideration. Although business is conducted in English, it may be helpful to send your business proposal in advance translated into Cantonese.

When communicating, Hong Kongers tend to be implicit. Note that the response "okay" means "I understand," not "I agree." The answer "yes" simply means "I have heard you" unless it's followed by a positive statement to indicate a real "yes." Oftentimes, "no" means "I have to wait" or "This may be very difficult." Avoid using jargon, slang, and figures of speech.

Presentation Styles, Conversational Topics, and Humor

Hong Kongers talk about money and business. General topics of interest are travel, family, food, sports, hobbies, and Hong Kong's natural beauty. Inappropriate topics include failure, human rights, relations with China, and Chinese politics. Be prepared for personal questions about family or salary. Contextual humor is welcomed; but not inappropriate jokes about religion, politics or minorities. For business proposals, use the good-luck numbers three (life), eight (prosperity), or nine (eternity).

Gestures

- Point with an open hand facing upward and at waist height.
- Beckon by curling four fingers under with the palm facing down.[24]

Notable Foods and Dishes

Hong Kong cuisine is known for freshness and natural flavors. Rice is a staple, along with a variety of boiled or fried noodles. Food is often parboiled, steamed, and quick-fried. Common seasonings are ginger, garlic, scallions, spring onions, soy sauce, and oyster sauce.[25]

For further insight into cross-cultural aspects of food and dining, enjoy Chapter One, 'Eating Hong Kong,' in the book *Reading Hong Kong, Reading Ourselves*.[26]

---

[24] *CultureGrams World Edition 2014: Hong Kong* (Ann Arbor, MI: ProQuest, 2014); Elizabeth Devine and Nancy L. Braganti, *The Traveler's Guide to Asian Customs & Manners* (New York: St. Martin's Griffin, 1998).
[25] Ibid.
[26] Janel Curry and Paul Hanstedt, *Reading Hong Kong, Reading Ourselves* (Kowloon: City University of Hong Kong Press, 2014).

Specialty Dishes

Some popular specialty dishes in Hong Kong include

- **Dim Sum:** Cantonese bite-sized assortments (dumplings, rice rolls) served on carts
- **Ku lao ju:** Sweet-and-sour pork
- **Sui ngoh:** Roast goose with pickled plums
- **Chin ha luk:** Fried prawns in tomato sauce
- **Si yau kai:** Steamed chicken in peanut oil with ginger
- **Jiao zi:** Ravioli stuffed with meat and served steamed or fried
- **Basal:** A dessert of toffee-covered apples
- **Dau fu fa:** Soybean custard

Dining Etiquette

A mix of Asian and Western dining customs are common in Hong Kong (refer to Chapter 3 and Chapter 5 for important U.S. and Chinese dining etiquette tips). If you are on a business visit, expect to be invited to a banquet or entertained in a restaurant, on a boat, or in a club. You may be presented with chopsticks or silverware according to the meal. Note that noises such as slurping and lip-smacking are often considered acceptable and even complimentary.[27]

Drinking and Toasting

Cocktails are often served before dinner. Beer and brandy are drunk during meals and to celebrate occasions. Hong Kong women do not consume alcohol in public.

Popular Drinks

The following are popular drinks in Hong Kong:

- **San Miguel:** Locally brewed beer
- **Zhian jing:** Rice wine served warm, like sake

---

[27] Martin and Chaney, *Passport to Success.*

- **Liang hua pei:** Plum brandy
- **Maotai:** A potent wine, like schnapps, without flavor

Cantonese toasts include *Yum bui* (yum BOO-oy, or "cheers") and *yum sing* (yum sing, or "bottoms up"). Raise your glass and make eye contact when toasting.

Tipping and Bill-Paying

Tipping is expected. Restaurant bills include a 10-percent service charge. A 15-percent additional tip is standard. Tip small change for taxi drivers, restroom attendants, coat attendants, and valets.

Smoking

Smoking is acceptable in public, and people may smoke between courses of a meal. It is polite to offer a cigarette to others nearby before lighting your own.[28]

Taboos

The following are taboo in Hong Kong:

- Displaying physical affection publicly
- Being overly loud in public
- Chewing gum or blowing your nose in public
- Colors blue and white (mourning)
- The number four (a homonym for death in Chinese)
- Winking, fidgeting, touching the top of someone's head
- Gesturing with fist up in the air[29]

---

[28] Ibid.

[29] *CultureGrams World Edition 2014: Hong Kong* (Ann Arbor, MI: ProQuest, 2014); and Elizabeth Devine and Nancy L. Braganti, *The Traveler's Guide to Asian Customs & Manners* (New York: St. Martin's Griffin, 1998).

Heroes and Sports

Knowing about another country's heroes and sports offers opportunities to incorporate culture-specific references into your conversations and presentations.

Heroes

Man Tin Cheung (1236–1283): Scholar and general. Known for his leadership in the resistance against Kublai Khan's invasion of China during the Song Dynasty. A symbol of patriotism and righteousness, his ancestors are considered one of the original founding families in the history of Hong Kong.

The Honourable Mrs. Anson Chan (1940–present): Former Chief Secretary for Administration. The first woman to hold the second-highest governmental position in Hong Kong. During her public service career, she aided the development of economic infrastructure. She is a strong supporter of democracy and full universal suffrage. Mrs. Chan received the Grand Bauhinia Medal, Hong Kong's highest honor.

The Honourable Sir Ka-shing Li (1928–present): Business magnate, investor, and philanthropist. The richest person in Asia, as of October 2013, with a net worth of U.S. $28.8 billion.[30] Known for the story of his rise from poor factory worker to "Asia's Most Powerful Man" (*Asiaweek*, 2001). In 2010, his companies were said to command about 15 percent of the capitalization of the Hong Kong Stock Exchange.[31] He is regarded as a generous philanthropist and is a recipient of the Grand Bauhinia Medal.

Sports

Sports

Due to the mixing of Chinese and British influences, a variety of sports are popular in Hong Kong: football (soccer), basketball, badminton, cricket, horse racing, rugby, table tennis, squash, golf, volleyball, tennis, swimming, and gymnastics.

---

[30]Bloomberg, "Bloomberg Billionaires: Today's Ranking of the World's Richest People," October 7, 2013, www.bloomberg.com/billionaires/2013-10-07/aaa.

[31]*Forbes* magazine, "The Miracle of Asia's Richest Man," February 24, 2010, www.forbes.com /2010/02/24/li-ka-shing-billionaire-hong-kong-richest-opinions-book-excerpt-michael-schuman.html?boxes=Homepagelighttop.

The traditional activities of martial arts and dragon boat racing have remained popular. Dragon boat racing is a traditional Chinese boat race originally held as part of the Dragon Boat Festival. It has recently gained popularity worldwide. Hong Kong draws thousands of athletes to its annual International Dragon Boat Races.

Sports Figures

Lee Wai Sze, also known as Sarah Lee (1987–present): Professional racing cyclist. Track cycling sprinter who won Hong Kong's first Olympic medal in cycling at the 2012 London Games. Received the 2011 Hong Kong Government Medal of Honor.

Fan Chun Yip (1976–present): Professional football goalkeeper and coach. Among the best Asian goalkeepers. Currently Shatin Sports Association team goalkeeper and goalkeeping coach for the Hong Kong national team. Voted Hong Kong Footballer of the Year in the 2003–2004 season. Twice voted Goalkeeper of the Tournament in the East Asian Cup.

Chan Siu Ki (1985–present): Hong Kong professional footballer. Striker currently playing for Hong Kong's South China football team. Vice-captain and the top scorer of the Hong Kong national team.

Barton Lui (1993–present): Short-track speed skater. Current Hong Kong record-holder in the 500-meter, 1000-meter, and 1500-meter events. Only Hong Kong athlete at the 2014 Olympics. The first male athlete to represent the country in the Winter Olympics.

Eight-Question Framework

This section reviews the framework to which you were introduced earlier in this book. Each of these questions addresses one or more business topics to help you attract and build the relationships upon which today's successful businesses depend.

1. How Do the Hong Kongers Prefer to Act: Individually or as a Group?

"Hong Kong has created one of the most successful societies on earth."
—*Prince Charles*

According to Jay Tang, General Manager for the Asia Pacific Region of Readen Holding Corporation, the answer to this question lies somewhere between 'I' and 'we,' adding that although company hierarchy is important, final decisions tend to be made or approved by senior management. Having said that, there is always discussion and room for an individual's thoughts to play a part:

> In Hong Kong, we emphasize team work and collaborative thinking, whereas in China, the discussion is relatively narrow, usually following the direction or plan proposed by the highest management. Management there is looking for execution by the others more than they are looking for discussion.

In order to be successful doing business in Hong Kong, Mr. Tang emphasizes the importance of listening with patience to partners' and colleagues' thoughts and ideas. You should ensure individual Hong Kongers feel recognized and respected, even during times when you think their contributions are lacking in some way. "Recognition is important to Chinese and also Hong Kongers. Even when you already have an excellent, irrefutable idea, try to bring in the alternative suggestion by discussing the possibility and asking for further comments. We hear U.S. businesspeople say, 'This is the best way you can do it.' But it is far better to reach the 'yes' together with your partners and colleagues, and let them feel they are part of the team that constructed the idea. In this way, the Western businessperson will have an easier time getting his or her idea or plan accepted and executed with the assistance of his/her Hong Kong colleagues," says Mr. Tang.

2. How Are Power and Authority Viewed in Hong Kong?

Jordan Kostelac, Project Manager for MovePlan Group, Asia Pacific, made one blunder directly related to the topics of power and authority while working on his first project at his current job: "I joined this challenging project nine months in after replacing the Chinese project manager who had resigned. Understandably, our client was ambivalent about 'the new guy' and this was compounded by the fact that I was a *laowai* or 'outsider.' My mistake was a sin of omission when the in-house team asked my background. I thought it wise to be modest and say that I had just finished school. It wasn't until a week or so before the project was completed, five months later, that we found out the client's team thought this meant that I had just graduated and was about 22 years old with little to no business experience. When my managing director explained to them that what I'd meant was that I'd just finished a MBA an M.B.A. program and was actually 30 years old with over 10 years' experience, one of the client's team gave a frank response: 'If we had known that, we would have listened to him more.'"

The next project that Mr. Kostelac undertook with the same client involved some of the same people that he had worked with previously. He says, "The level of deference with which I was treated was so much higher. It felt like I'd been instantly promoted from errand boy to subject-matter expert. There may have been other factors that influenced this, such as changes within the team and there being far less pressure at the beginning of the new project, but I sincerely believe that most of it came down to them having a clear understanding of my credentials."

3. How Do the Hong Kongers Compare Rules and Relationships?

We emphasize efficiency and like to have contracts finalized and signed as soon as possible.
—*Jay Tang, General Manager, Asia Pacific Region, Readen Holding Corp.*

Hong Kongers operate in a developed, internationally oriented country where the rules of business are taken as seriously as they are in the West. As Jay Tang of Readen Holdings pointed out, "In Hong Kong, we respect the spirit of contracts and are used to spending time negotiating terms and having them clearly outlined in written form. We emphasize efficiency and like to have contracts finalized and signed as soon as possible."

What facilitates all of this, however, are the kinds of deeper, trusting relationships that Mr. Tang says help not only to break the ice and establish credibility, but also engender confidence that a Western partner will be as result-oriented as Hong Kongers are. All of which, as Mr. Tang describes it, will "get to the Chinese heart."

In his experience, Western businesspeople—particularly those from the U.S.—could build better relationships and create a better foundation for moving forward if they avoided the temptation to *oversell* or slightly exaggerate their services and expected outcomes.

Mr. Tang points out two examples—one when his company engaged a number of marketing companies to help promote their products and services globally, and another when Readen worked with several groups of accountants and financial analysts. "In the first experience, which we had with three different U.S. marketing companies, we received proposals from each that promised us very attractive market exposure. We agreed upon the comprehensive list of duties that would be performed by these companies, entered into the requisite contracts, and paid their fees. In each case, it soon became clear that they were unable to execute on all they had promised, performing only part of the services on the agreed list. No proactive remediation was carried out in any of these cases and the results were entirely unsatisfactory.

"The same thing happened when we worked with the financial people from the States. Again, over the years, we were presented with many attractive financial deals and projects, and initially the proposals were always attractive to us. But when we tried to do more than scratch the surface and asked them to go deeper by engaging in feasibility studies, we typically had great difficulty getting them to provide all the supporting forecasting and other financials that we needed in order to feel secure enough to invest."

Despite the considerable time Mr. Tang's company spent in discussions and preparations, eventually, he said, they had to give up on most of the deals. What was promised was not what was delivered.

With respect to contractual and other business affairs, Mr. Tang suggests that Westerners tone down the "overselling" he frequently encounters. But he also underscored the importance that "heart" plays in developing the relationships that facilitate business dealings in Hong Kong. One way he uses to build relationships in Hong Kong is to invite both husband and wife to social events, bringing with him small token gifts for the whole family. These might include footballs or soccer shoes for their children and perfume for the wife.

"Don't just focus on the person you are talking business with," advises Mr. Tang. "Pay attention to the people that are important to him. This is as crucial in Hong Kong as it is in China where both cultures are family-oriented. It's no different than when someone from Europe buys something to give to a member of my family—I consider the gift much more important than whatever they might buy for me. This is how you become part of my circle. In Hong Kong, we expect Westerners who work with us to be as efficient and results-oriented as we are. What kicks off this stage and eases our journey forward, however, is showing us your heart." This shows you have a heart and can remember what was inquired about and said during the early stages of the relationship-building.

4. How Do Hong Kongers Regard Time?

The pace of Hong Kong business is high, and will never be slower than in the U.S. Time is money here as well.
   —Jay Tang, General Manager, Asia Pacific Region,
   Readen Holding Corporation

In Hong Kong, the pace is fast and punctuality is important. Appointments are made well in advance and, surprisingly, traffic is not accepted as an excuse for being late in Hong Kong, so timeliness is expected. Jay Tang explains that time is money and a valuable resource. Schedules are always tight, with meetings running continuously, so don't arrive too early for an appointment either. A previous meeting may still be in progress. Hong Kongers move fast, and still hold traditional Chinese values. They are highly motivated to be efficient, work hard, and cope well with change on an island where change is constant.

Part of the busy modern pace of Hong Kong that has differed from China is the unique position Hong Kong has held as a SAR (Special Administrative Region) of China. Hong Kong's British and international influence is layered over the core Chinese values. Hong Kong has historically played a special role as the business center of China.

Sharon's experience in Hong Kong reflects Jay's insight and she stresses that appointments are made in advance and kept. Even today, in 2015, traffic is not an excuse, and timeliness is expected.

5. How Direct Is Communication in Hong Kong?

"No" is a word which we can use, but you have to use it after listening and discussion, not right at the beginning. Otherwise you will be perceived as a dictator.
—*Jay Tang, General Manager for the Asia Pacific Region,*
Readen Holding Corporation

Given the close cultural ties between Hong Kong and China, it's easy to assume that each mirrors the other with respect to communication. But there are a number of significant differences—the first of which involves the word *no*. As you will have no doubt gleaned from Chapter 5, the Chinese operate indirectly when something isn't possible, rather than just coming out and saying "no." As Jay Tang's preceding quote highlights, saying "no" is quite acceptable in Hong Kong—as long as it's not the first word spoken. Similarly, Mr. Tang and other Hong Kong colleagues say they like it when someone uses direct eye contact when communicating because they perceive this as a form of respect and seriousness.

Perhaps not surprisingly on an island known as the Wall Street of Asia, Hong Kongers prefer that you get directly to the point in discussion because time is money and efficiency is important to them.

In Mr. Tang's experience, communicating ideas and suggestions occurs much more freely in Hong Kong than China. Here, the relatively highly educated working population is encouraged to say what they think or feel and offer dissenting comments where relevant. You will also find that lower levels of management have the freedom to present their thoughts directly to senior management rather than only communicating with the next layer above them.

Adds Mr. Tang: "In China, for the most part, only the superiors give instructions and direction; it is not really an open discussion. Management makes the decision and expects those under them to execute. In bigger companies especially, this authority level is very clear: the manager, the assistant, and then it goes step by step, every layer." In Hong Kong, however, communication occurs much more frequently between colleagues and managers at all levels within the hierarchy.

6. How Formal or Informal Do Businesspeople In Hong Kong Tend to Be?

"When I went to Hong Kong, I knew at once I wanted to write a story set there."
— *Paul Theroux*

Mr. Jay Tang offers this simple tip for using a formality that most Westerners would never think of, but that can have immeasurable effects in terms of demonstrating respect and building deep relationships.

Says Mr. Tang: "The first time you meet someone, it's important to call them Mr. or Ms., but after that, use the word "boss" in front of their surnames, especially with those people whose circle of influence you are looking to penetrate. Even if someone is not the "boss" but a lower-level manager, when his or her boss is not present, refer to them as Boss Lee or Boss Chen, for example. This is the way we do it, even between ourselves. When people meet with me, they will ask "How are you, Boss Tang?" Then, when someone superior to me comes into the room, they revert to calling me Mr. Tang.

"What does this small formality do? For a start, it makes me feel really good because when I'm with you, and in front of my subordinates, you call me Boss Tang (or Boss Jay if we are already on first-name terms), which shows you already respect me and have given me face at the beginning. It's a sign of respect. When people in Hong Kong feel that you are paying attention to them, are giving respect to them, this will gradually melt the Chinese heart."

7. How Aligned Are Hong Kong Social and Business Lives?

Hong Kong is one of the top five most densely populated places in the world. So it wasn't surprising when Jordan Kostelac pointed out that he constantly runs into people he works with, or for, on the island.

Sharon found this a useful distinction to know during her visits to Hong Kong, where the lines blur between her personal and professional lives more than is the case in the U.S. While visiting Hong Kong Sharon would remain in professional attire during evening socializing, given the likelihood that she would run into business contacts.

The size of Hong Kong has another bearing on the way people socialize. Mr. Kostelac went on to say that because apartments are relatively small compared to those in Europe or the U.S.: "We don't invite our business partners to our houses. The Chinese are also relatively conservative, so some contacts may not want to bring business connections to their homes because of privacy reasons. We will have dinner or grab a drink with our business partners where we will share experiences."

8. How Is the Concept of Women in Business Handled in Hong Kong?

In Hong Kong I don't think there is any hindrance because of being a female; here we focus on competency.
—*Jay Tang, General Manager for the Asia Pacific Region, Readen Holding Corporation*

The Women's Commission surveyed more than 3,000 Hong Kong residents in 2012 and published their results in a report called "What Do Women and Men in Hong Kong Think about the Status of Women at Work?[32] Their findings provide insight into the current thinking and what to expect in terms of the way women's participation at work is perceived:

- More than 80 percent of respondents agreed that having a job was the best way for women to become independent.
- More than 65 percent (72 percent female; 59 percent male) agreed that "an increase in the number of successful women was a positive social phenomenon."
- Nevertheless, women were commonly stereotyped as family caregivers, with just over half of respondents saying that women should focus more on family than working outside of the home.
- Eighty percent acknowledged that a homemaker's contribution is as important as that of the breadwinner.

---

[32]Hong Kong Women's Commission, *What do Women and Men in Hong Kong Think about the Status of Women at Home, Work and in Social Environments?*, "Part Three: What Do Women and Men in Hong Kong Think about the Status of Women at Work?" www.women .gov.hk/download/research/WoC_Survey_Finding_Economic_E.pdf (accessed November 13, 2014).

- Slightly more than a third of respondents thought employees preferred not to be supervised by female managers.

The good news is that the younger the age and the higher the educational attainment, the greater the shift there is against traditional gender concepts in Hong Kong. One key finding of this survey was that women who worked were happier than their nonworking peers, possibly because of increased economic independence. In another finding in *The GLOBE Study of 62 Societies*, Hong Kong's scores on gender egalitarianism ranked higher than China's, and the U.S. for that matter.[33]

According to Jay Tang, different rules apply to Western businesswomen than to their Hong Kong counterparts, which includes after-hours drinking as a key part of relationship-building: "Hong Kongers are conservative for themselves and their wives, but not for international or expat businesswomen as they understand that Americans and Europeans live in more open societies."

Mr. Tang advises women to focus on professionalism and competency in order to be seen as equals. One example is Hong Kong powerhouse businesswoman Solina Chau, a longtime confidante of Asia's richest man and billionaire, the Honorable Sir Ka-shing Li. She directs the $8.2 billion Li Ka Shing Foundation as well as high-profile deals including BitPay, the payment system for Bitcoin.

Smooth a path in Hong Kong by establishing your credentials well in advance of your arrival:

- Research and cultivate local business connections and contacts.
- Ask an intermediary to forward your business qualifications prior to introduction.
- Understand Hong Kong business culture, as the female business leader or top negotiator; request male team members enter *after* you to communicate your senior rank.
- Wear name-brand business suits and modest accessories.
- Learn a few Cantonese greetings; the effort will be appreciated and help to break the ice.

Cultural Summary

Here are some key points to remember:

---

[33]Robert J. House, et al., eds., Culture, Leadership, and Organizations: The GLOBE Study of 62 Societies (Thousand Oaks, CA: Sage Publications, 2004), 365.

- Hong Kong is different from China in pace of business, language, and communication, while providing significant market-entry through direct access to different regions in China.
- Hong Kong team members like to be consulted and to see their contributions reflected in projects.
- Being sincere and authentic is a highly prized quality.
- When dealing with multinational corporations based in Hong Kong, expect major decisions to be made quickly.

Self-Awareness Profile

This simple exercise prompts you to self-assess where you currently stand on topics related to the eight-question framework and *compare* this with the country culture. This visual will help you discover the extent to which you may need to adapt your current mindset and behavior to develop more robust business relationships. For details on how to complete this graphic, see the instructions given in the Introduction on pages xviii–xix.

Consider copying the eight-question Profile or using a pencil so that you can see, over time, how you have adjusted your cultural mindset. You might also wish to create unique graphics related to each of the businesses you work with, as these cultural positions vary depending upon geographic location, industry, generational factors, and corporate profile.

Q1: What is your preferred way of doing business?

As an individual making autonomous decisions					As a team member who seeks group consensus
1	2	3	4	**5**	6

Q2: How comfortable are you in hierarchies in which power is distributed unequally?

Very uncomfortable					Very comfortable
1	2	3	4	**5**	6

Q3: How closely do you follow rules and obey the law?

Almost always					It depends
1	2	3	4	**5**	6

Q4: What is your general attitude toward time?

| I prefer agendas, schedules, planning | | | | | I prefer flexibility, fluidity without scheduling |

1   2   3   4   **5**   6

Q5: What is your preferred way to communicate?

Very diplomatically   **Very candidly**

1   2   **3**   4   5   6

Q6: What is your interpersonal style or level of formality in business interactions?

Very formal   **Very informal**

1   2   **3**   4   5   6

Q7: What is your view on socializing within business?

A waste of time   **Essential**

1   2   3   4   5   **6**

Q8: Should a woman defer to a man as the lead, if winning business in a certain culture depended on it?

Never   **Yes, absolutely**

1   2   3   **4**   5   6

7

India

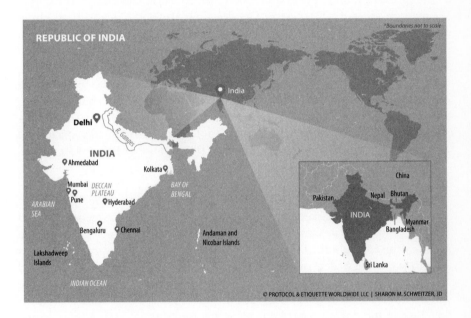

REPUBLIC OF INDIA

© PROTOCOL & ETIQUETTE WORLDWIDE LLC | SHARON M. SCHWEITZER, JD

Logic and emotion, individuality and social feeling, poverty and affluence, life and lifestyle, value and indulgence, and the past and the future simultaneously coexist in India. All these paradoxes converge to make India what it is.

—*It Happened in India,*[1] Kishore Biyani

---

[1]Kishore Biyani and Dipayan Baishya, *It Happened in India: The Story of Pantaloons, Big Bazaar, Central and the Great Indian Consumer* (New Delhi, India: Rupa & Co., 2007).

Introduction

Impressions of India, especially for those who have not yet visited the country, often come from watching movies like *Slumdog Millionaire, The Best Exotic Marigold Hotel,* and *A Passage to India.* Although each portrayal captures *some* aspects, what makes this country so fascinating is the extent to which India defies categorization.

Is India's population largely impoverished? That depends on your criteria. A quarter of the population is considered to be middle-class, according to a survey conducted by the Asian Development Bank, the majority of whom exist on $2 to $4 a day.[2] McKinsey's Global Institute projects that by 2025, India's middle class will have swollen to more than 580 million people and will represent the world's fifth-largest consumer market.

Is India successfully nurturing and keeping entrepreneurs rather than losing them to places like Silicon Valley? Yes and no. Most Indian parents still prefer to see their offspring adopt careers in engineering, the law, or medicine. In traditional families, an Indian man's marriage prospects are detrimentally impacted if he's not employed by a big-name company. But as more of India's 430 million 15 to 34 year olds[3] aspire to create, not just work for, major companies, the previous "brain drain" is slowing down.[4]

Is India a homogeneous culture? Not at all. The differences in foods, belief systems, dress, and languages among Indians can be explained by geography and history. The north faced many hostile invasions over the centuries and became a more "mixed" culture. The south—protected on three sides by water—was host to sea-faring traders, such as the Portuguese. Many interviewees expressed the view that northern Indians, historically the "guards of India," are more assertive in their business dealings than in the south.

Bear in mind these contradictions as you read through this chapter. Much of your experience in India depends on whether you are doing business in the north or the south, with a multinational or family operation, and the extent to which your contacts have been educated or have done business in the West.

---

[2] Asian Development Bank, *Framework of Inclusive Growth Indicators 2013: Key Indicators for Asia and the Pacific,* August 2013, www.adb.org/publications/framework-inclusive -growth-indicators-2013-key-indicators-asia-and-pacific-special-supp (accessed November 11, 2014).

[3] The Hindu, "India Is Set to Become the Youngest Country By 2020," April 17, 2013, www.thehindu.com/news/national/india-is-set-to-become-the-youngest-country-by -2020/article4624347.ece.

[4] PBS Newshour, "High-Tech Entrepreneurs Flock to India," June 1, 2014, www.pbs .org/newshour/bb/high-tech-entrepreneurs-flock-india/; The Economic Times, "Why Indian Middle Class Family Does Not Encourage Aspiring Entrepreneur," January 25, 2013, http://articles.economictimes.indiatimes.com/2013-01-25/news/36548273_1_young- entrepreneurs-seedfund-job.

Quiz

How much do you know about India? Answer the following questions as True or False to test your knowledge. (The Answer Key at the bottom includes page numbers that refer to the topic):

_____1. Former Prime Minister Indira Gandhi was the daughter of Mahatma Gandhi.

_____2. The date 1/5/20 signifies January 5th, 2020.

_____3. India is bounded to the east, west, and south by the Indian Ocean.

_____4. India has the greatest number of family-controlled businesses in Asia.

_____5. Some of India's biggest financial institutions are headed by female CEOs.

_____6. The highest status within the Hindu *varna*, or caste, system is given to the *Kshatriyas*, members of the armed forces and policemen.

_____7. The Indian film industry is affectionately known as *Bollywood*.

_____8. When Hindus invite people into their homes, they consider them gods.

_____9. Gujarat is one of four states in which the sale and consumption of alcohol is banned.

_____10. Buddhism was founded in India.

Answer Key: 1. F(p. 138); 2. F (p. 131); 3. F (p. 127); 4. T (p. 140); 5. T (p. 146–147); 6. F (p. 142); 7. T (p. 139); 8. T (p. 145–146); 9. T (p. 137); 10. T (p. 130).

Country Basics

This section provides information in an easy-to-read format to help you quickly grasp some of the basics necessary to navigate this culture.

Historical Timeline

A critical way to show respect for another person's culture is to have knowledge of their country's history and current affairs. Table 7.1 on page 126 outlines a few key events related to India, together with concurrent world events.

Table 7.1   Key Historical Events

Period/ Dates	Description/Events	World Events
1947	India gains independence from Great Britain. Partitioning of India and Pakistan along religious lines.	Princess Elizabeth marries Philip, Duke of Edinburgh in Westminster Abbey, London.
1948	Mohandas Gandhi assassinated by Hindu extremist Nathuram Godse.	Chiang Kai-shek becomes president of China.
1966–77	Indira Gandhi serves as India's first and only (to date) female prime minister.	First human heart transplant operation performed by Dr. Christiaan Barnard in South Africa.
1971	Bangladesh (formerly Bengal in British India, then Pakistani province) becomes independent state.	Women in Switzerland get right to vote.
1984	Indira Gandhi assassinated by one of her Sikh bodyguards, Satwant Singh Bhakar.	Brunei achieves independence from the U.K.; Desmond Tutu wins Nobel Peace Prize.
1998	India declares itself a nuclear weapons state.	Google founded.
2014	Parliament agrees to the creation of a 29th state (formerly part of Andhra Pradesh): Telangana.	The XXII Olympic Winter Games take place in Sochi, Russia.
2017	Presidential elections scheduled.	Hong Kong, South Korean, and Singaporean presidential elections scheduled.
2019	Legislative elections scheduled.	Japan to be the first Asian country to host the Rugby World Cup.[5]

---

[5]International Rugby Board, "Japan 2019 to be a World Cup for All of Asia," April 17, 2012, www.rugbyworldcup.com/rugbyworldcup2019/news/newsid=2061811 .html#japan+2019+world+cup+asia.

Full Country Name and Location

The Republic of India is the seventh largest country in the world by area, slightly larger than Argentina and roughly one-third the size of the U.S. India's neighboring countries are Bhutan, China, Nepal, Pakistan, Bangladesh, and Myanmar. India is bounded by the Arabian Sea to the west, the Indian Ocean to the south, and the Bay of Bengal to the east.

Government/Political Structure

India is the world's largest democracy. Their constitution came into effect in January 1950 and is said to be the world's longest written constitution. The Indian parliament operates similarly to the British model. National elections take place every five years. The head of government is the prime minister; the head of state is the president. The last national elections were held in April and May 2014.

Population and Economic Centers

The July 2014 *CIA World Factbook* estimates the population of India to be approximately 1.24 billion, the second largest in the world. The country has six centrally administered union territories and 29 federal states, each with its own capital. New Delhi is the country's capital. Slightly more than 31 percent of the population lives in urban areas.[6]

The main ethnic groups are Indo-Aryan (72 percent), Dravidian (25 percent), and Mongoloid and other (3 percent).[7]

The major business centers and populations (2011) are outlined in Table 7.2 on page 128.[8]

Economy

India is ranked 142nd out of 189 economies in terms of ease of doing business, according to the World Bank Group's *Doing Business 2015*

---

[6]CIA, *The World Factbook*, "India," www.cia.gov/library/publications/the-world-factbook/geos/in.html (accessed November 12, 2014).

[7]Ibid.

[8]Office of the Registrar General & Census Commissioner, India, Census of India 2011, "Urban Agglomerations/Cities Having Population 1 Lakh and Above," http://censusindia.gov.in/2011-prov-results/paper2/data_files/India2/Table_3_PR_UA_Citiees_1Lakh_and_Above.pdf (accessed November 12, 2014).

Table 7.2   Major Business Centers

Business Centers	Former (Colonial) Name	Population (Millions)
Ahmedabad	—	6.4
Bengaluru	Bangalore	8.5
Chennai	Madras	8.7
Delhi	—	16.3
Hyderabad	—	7.7
Kolkata	Calcutta	14.1
Mumbai	Bombay	18.4
Pune	—	5

report.[9] Its 2013 GDP was ranked 10th by the World Bank[10] and the composition of its GDP by sector was services (56.9 percent), industry (25.8 percent), and agriculture (17.4 percent).[11]

Corruption Perceptions Index

India ranked 94th least corrupt out of 177 countries and territories with a score of 36 out of 100.[12] This annual index, compiled by Transparency International, measures perceived levels of public sector corruption.

The Central Bureau of Investigation is the anti-corruption agency that conducts investigations in India.

---

[9]World Bank Group, *Doing Business 2015* (October 29, 2014): 4, www.doingbusiness.org/ ~/media/GIAWB/Doing%20Business/Documents/Annual-Reports/English/DB15-Full-Report. pdf (accessed November 11, 2014).

[10]The World Bank, Data, GDP Ranking, "Gross Domestic Product Ranking Table," last updated September 24, 2014, http://data.worldbank.org/data-catalog/GDP-ranking-table (accessed November 6, 2014).

[11]CIA, *The World Factbook*, "India," www.cia.gov/library/publications/the-world-factbook/geos /in.html (accessed November 11, 2014).

[12]Transparency International, "Corruption Perceptions Index 2013," www.transparency.org /cpi2013/results (accessed November 11, 2014).

Human Development Index

India ranked 135th out of 187 countries and territories.[13] The HDI, compiled by the United Nations Development Programme, is a composite index of life expectancy, education, and income statistics.

Global Gender Gap Index

India ranked 114th out of 142 countries in terms of gender equality with a score of 0.6455.[14] This annual index, compiled by the World Economic Forum, assesses gender gaps based on economic, political, educational, and health-based criteria.

Climate

The climate ranges from tropical in the south to temperate in the north, with three seasons: summer (hot)—March to May; monsoon (rainy)—June to October; winter (cool)—November to February.

Languages

Hindi is the official language, spoken by 41 percent of the population, with English the *lingua franca* of business, government, and higher education. According to 2013 People's Linguistic Survey of India,[15] there are 780 different languages and dialects in India. The most common include Bengali (8.1 percent), Telugu (7.2 percent), Marathi (7 percent), Tamil (5.9 percent), Urdu (5 percent), Gujarati (4.5 percent), Kannada (3.7 percent), and Malayalam (3.2 percent).

Hindi is not commonly spoken everywhere. For example, in Rajasthan (capital Jaipur), almost 91 percent of the population speaks Hindi. In Maharashtra (capital Mumbai), only 11 percent do; the most commonly spoken language

---

[13]United Nations Development Programme, *Human Development Report 2014*, 160–163, http://hdr.undp.org/sites/default/files/hdr14-report-en-1.pdf (accessed November 11, 2014).

[14]World Economic Forum, *The Global Gender Gap Report 2014*, 8–9, www3.weforum.org /docs/GGGR14/GGGR_CompleteReport_2014.pdf (accessed November 11, 2014).

[15]Hindustan Times, "780 Languages Spoken in India, 250 Died Out in Last 50 Years," July 17, 2013, www.hindustantimes.com/lifestyle/books/780-languages-spoken-in-india-250-died -out-in-last-50-years/article1-1093758.aspx.

in that state is Marathi. In southern states like Tamil Nadu (capital Chennai) and Karnataka (capital Bengaluru), Hindi is rarely spoken.[16]

Belief Systems, Philosophies, and Religions

Indians self-identify as Hindu (80.5 percent), Islam (13.4 percent), Christian (2.3 percent), Sikh (1.9 percent), and Buddhist (0.8 percent).[17] Note that Buddhism was founded in India.[18]

For an overview of belief systems, philosophies, and religions, please refer to Chapter 4, pages 64–65.

Time Zones/Daylight Savings

India has a single time zone, India Standard Time (IST). It is 5.5 hours ahead of GMT (Greenwich Mean Time)/UTC (Coordinated Universal Time). It does not operate under Daylight Savings.

India is 10 and a half hours ahead of U.S. Eastern Standard Time (nine and a half hours ahead in Daylight Savings Time). See www.timeanddate.com /worldclock.

To calculate time in India, add 5.5 hours to UTC/GMT.

Telephone Country Code and Internet Suffix

The Indian telephone country code is 91 and its Internet suffix is .in.

Currency

Their currency is the Indian rupee (INR). One rupee is divided into 100 paise; however, coins under 50 paise are no longer considered legal tender.

100,000 rupees equals one lakh; 10,000,000 rupees equals one crore. Be aware of the differences in how numbers are written and displayed in India.

Table 7.3 on page 131 shows a comparison between ways of writing Indian and Arabic numerals.

---

[16]Maps of India, "Languages of India," last updated October 28, 2014, www.mapsof india.com/culture/indian-languages.html (accessed November 11, 2014).
[17]Office of The Registrar General & Census Commissioner, India, "Religion," http:// censusindia.gov.in/Census_And_You/religion.aspx (accessed November 11, 2014).
[18]Encyclopedia Britannica, "Buddha," last updated July 22, 2014, www.britannica .com/EBchecked/topic/83105/Buddha (accessed November 11, 2014).

Table 7.3   Indian Numerals Compared to Arabic Numerals

Indian Numeral System	Arabic Numberal System
5,05,000	505,000
12,12,12,123	121,212,123
7,00,00,00,000	7,000,000,000

Note use of different separators for numbers.

Business Culture, Etiquette, and Customs

This section covers business culture, etiquette, and customs.

Fiscal year

The Indian fiscal year is April 1 through March 31. Dates are written as day, month, year; for example, April 1, 2020 would be written 01/04/2020.

Working Week

The structure of the Indian working week is outlined in Table 7.4. Central government offices are closed on Saturdays.

Table 7.4   The Indian Working Schedule

Industry	Business Hours	Days of the Week
Businesses	09:30–17:30	Monday–Friday
	Half day	Saturday
Banks	10:00–17:00	Monday–Friday
	10:00–12:00	Saturday
Lunch	13:00–14:00	

Holidays and Festivals

Some Indian holidays are determined by the lunar calendar and change from year to year. In Table 7.5 on page 132, floating holidays are designated with

Table 7.5   Indian Holidays and Festivals

Date	Name
January 1	New Year's Day
January 26	Republic Day
February/March	*Ramadan* (Muslim)*
March	*Holi* (Hindu)*
March 7	Hindu Fire Festival
March/April	Good Friday (Christian)*
March/April	Easter (Christian)*
May 1	Labor Day
May 5	Buddha Purnima (Buddha's birthday)
End of July	*Eid al Fitr* (Muslim)*
August 15	Independence Day
August/September	Ganesh Chaturthi*
October 2	Mahatma Gandhi's Birthday
October	Durga Puja (Hindu)*
End of October	*Muharram,* Islamic New Year*
End of October	*Diwali,* Festival of Lights (Hindu)*
December 25	Christmas Day

an asterisk. On specific holidays an office may remain open, with limited staff. Check with your embassy or trade office before planning business travel.

Given the vast number of events and celebrations associated with the different religions in India, the holiday table is limited to a few of the major festivals.

Business Dress/Appearance

Business attire for both men and women is conservative for the first meeting, and then smart casual—depending on the company culture. International organizations with a dress code encouraging suits and ties for men may relax this rule in India because of the temperature and humidity. In major metropolitan areas, Indians are likely to dress in short-sleeved shirts and pants rather than traditional Indian attire.

Women are advised to keep legs covered and avoid wearing sleeveless dresses or blouses. Indians in the south have appreciated Liz attending meetings wearing *salwar kameez* (baggy pants and a long-sleeved tunic with matching long scarf). It is less typical for Western men to dress in the long tunics (called *kurta*) commonly worn by some Indian businessmen.

News Sources

Here are some popular news sources in India:[19]

- *The Times of India*: http://timesofindia.indiatimes.com/home
- *The Hindustan Times*: www.hindustantimes.com
- *The Hindu*: www.thehindu.com

Most-read Hindi daily: *Dainik Jagran*: www.jagran.com

Business Cards

Indians tend to be innately curious and, given the hierarchical structure of their lives, look to see where you fit. Include titles and degrees (Ph.D, J.D, M.B.A) on your business card. English is the language of business, so no need to have your cards translated.

Technology

India is one of the fastest-growing global telecommunications markets. Latest figures rank India sixth for the number of Internet users[20] and number 17 globally for the number of Internet hosts.[21] Expect widespread access in major metropolitan and urban areas, but less in rural areas. Check with your hosts about the likelihood of power cuts and timings of regular power outages that affect even major cities. According to Akamai Technology's *State of the Internet Report,* India has one of the slowest average Internet connection speeds in the Asia Pacific region.[22]

---

[19]List Dose, "Top 10 Best Newspapers in India 2014," June 17, 2014, http://listdose.com/top-10-best-newspapers-in-india-2014/.

[20]CIA, *The World Factbook*, "Country Comparison: Internet Users," information dated 2009, www.cia.gov/library/publications/the-world-factbook/rankorder/2153rank.html (accessed November 12, 2014).

[21]CIA, *The World Factbook*, "Country Comparison: Internet Hosts," information dated 2009, www.cia.gov/library/publications/the-world-factbook/rankorder/2184rank.html (accessed November 12, 2014).

[22]Akamai Technologies, "State of the Internet Q4 2013," April 2014, www.akamai.com/dl/akamai/akamai-soti-q413.pdf?WT.mc_id=soti_Q413.

Gifts

Indians love giving gifts. If you stay with a business partner's family or visit their home, don't be surprised if you receive a gift, perhaps a local artisan's work, even if you only remained a few hours. Among our Indian business friends who drink alcohol, gifts of liquor have been appreciated as they can be expensive and difficult to buy locally. Other ideas are nice pens or European chocolates. Try to find an item an Indian cannot buy easily at home. Avoid black and white wrapping paper as these colors are associated with funerals and considered unlucky.

Introductions, Greetings, Personal Space, and Eye Contact

The traditional greeting in India is placing hands in a prayer-like position, chest-high, while bowing slightly and saying "*Namaste.*" You may be greeted with *Namaste* and/or a handshake; follow the lead of your host.

You may be called *auntie* (if you're a woman) or *uncle* (if you're a man) by younger people. Family relationships are important, and these titles are used as a way to allow a *stranger* to fit in. The word *ji* (gee) is an honorific used after someone's name in Hindi-speaking regions to signify respect.

At least an arm's length is considered the respectful distance to stand when meeting with Indians.

Useful Phrases

Table 7.6 on page 135 contains phrases useful to know when traveling to India.

Names

When meeting someone whose surname is Chandrasekaran, for instance or referencing former Indian Prime Minister Jawaharlal Nehru in a talk or presentation, be sure to practice the correct pronunciation beforehand. This is not just good manners, but avoids the potential for insulting your Indian counterpart, especially because many names such as Lakshmi and Ganesh are also names of Hindu gods. Several online sites offer written and verbal guidelines.[23]

---

[23]VOA Pronunciation Guide, "India," http://pronounce.voanews.com/browse-oneregion.php ?region=India (accessed November 12, 2014).

Table 7.6   Useful Phrases for Indian Travel

English	Hindi	Pronunciation
Hello/General greeting	*Namaste*	nah–mahss–TAY
How are you?	*Aap kaise hai*	AHP kay-seh HAY
Please	*Kripaya*	krip-ah–YAH
Thank you	*Dhanyavaad*	doohn yah-VAHD
You're welcome	*Aapakaa svaagat hai*	AHP-kah SWAHG-aht HAY
Yes	*Haan*	haan
No	*Nahin*	nah–HEE-n
Excuse me	*Shama kare*	shah-MAH kar-EH

Meetings and Negotiations

The higher up in business you are, the greater your status. Your family background or *class,* education level, formal title, and connections all hugely influence your standing in meetings, as well as an Indians' willingness to do deals with you. (See explanation of the caste system on page 141.) When negotiations begin, be sure not to start off with your best offer, as Indians love to bargain.

Presentation Styles, Conversational Topics, and Humor

One author, Liz, was the keynote speaker at a Rotary regional event in Coimbatore. Many speakers stood behind the lectern and used notes; others were more casual. One member, a motivational speaker, used the whole of the stage and slides to inject humor in a way that would not have been out of place at a Western conference. All had one thing in common—they demonstrated a strong command of their topic. Indians respect expertise.

You may be asked questions that are much more personal than you would expect in your own country, such as "Are you married?," "Where did you go to school?," and "Who do you know?" They are trying to figure out where you fit in the hierarchy. Avoid criticism of their infrastructure, such as trash and the state of many roads, discussions about poverty, the *dalits* or *untouchables,* and their country's relationship with Pakistan.

Gestures

The *Indian head wobble*—waving the head from side to side—is a multipurpose signal that ranges from a silent 'yes' and 'thank you' to an indication that the person you are speaking to understands what you are saying. This does not necessarily indicate agreement.

Notable Foods and Dishes

There are vast regional variations in the foods offered throughout India, depending on both geography (what can be grown) and climate. Here are just some of the specialties on offer:

South India: Rice or rice-based dishes are popular, including *idli* (steamed rice cakes, typically eaten with pickles and *sambhar*—a vegetable stew—for breakfast); *dosa* (pancakes stuffed with spiced potatoes and other vegetables); and chicken or vegetable *biriyani*.

North India: Bread is more common than rice at meals (for example, *naan*, stuffed or plain *parathas*, *roti*, or *chapatti*). Given the colder climate, meals are comprised of thick, creamy, moderately spiced gravy dishes such as *paneer* (cheese) or *daal* (lentil) *makhani*.

East India: Strong Chinese and Mongolian influences, for example, *momos* (steamed wontons). Rice-based dishes served with pickles are also popular.

West India: West India features a diverse range of highly spiced dishes. In Gujarat, *Thali*—a large number of dishes served on a round metal platter with different compartments for rice, vegetables, sweets—is popular.

Specialty Dishes

Favorite dishes in Indian cuisine include:

- **Tandoori chicken:** Chicken marinated in yogurt, seasoned with tandoori masala spices, and roasted in a clay oven
- **Rogan josh:** Gravy curry dish with braised lamb or goat and aromatic spices
- **Chole bhature:** Spicy curry chickpea dish served with fried flour bread

Dining Etiquette

The following principally applies to eating in the home, where Indians will happily invite you to cement a new relationship. This advice differs somewhat from eating in a restaurant.

Wash your hands directly before and after meals. Most globally experienced Indians will provide silverware, but you may choose to also eat with your right hand, as do many Hindus. Never use your left hand, which is considered unclean. Many dishes make up one course and serving takes place at the table. Items are passed using the left hand to avoid using the right hand that has touched food and been near the mouth. Avoid offering anyone food from your plate or taking food from someone else's.

Your host's wife may take great pride in serving you. Don't be offended or think this is demeaning for her in any way. It is common and polite for a wife to do this for guests in an Indian home.

Food is a big deal in India—never refuse an offer of food. Do not leave food on a plate or leave chai, the spiced milky tea, in a mug. When you are satisfied, say "Thank you, I've had enough for now."

When inviting business contacts to a restaurant, check everyone's dietary preferences and religious restrictions beforehand. A vegetarian who attends a meal you've arranged at a non-vegetarian restaurant may say something like "Today is a day of fasting. If you don't mind, I will just have water." It's not necessarily true, but Indians are extremely polite and restrained; they won't want to make a fuss and make you feel bad.

Drinking and Toasting

Alcohol is prohibited in four states: Gujarat, Manipur, Mizoram, and Nagaland, and the union territory of Lakshadweep. Muslims, Sikhs, and approximately 60 to 70 percent of Hindus do not drink alcohol. Women normally do not drink, especially in public.

Toasts are usually restricted to formal events—banquets and weddings—but only before dinner, not during or after the meal. A toast in English might be "To your health" or "To your prosperity."

Tipping and Bill-Paying

With taxi, or auto-rickshaw drivers, hired drivers, and hotel maids, there is no need to use a percentage of your bill to calculate a tip. We were told that in major cities, giving a hired driver even 25 rupees is too much, and that rounding up to the next even amount is appropriate. Five rupees a day is typical for hotel housekeeping. In major metropolitan areas, a 10-percent service charge is usually included at restaurants, plus 10 percent for your server.

On one occasion, a group of visiting Canadian businesspeople was taken to visit local temples and other places of interest. At the end of the day, they tipped their young guide 500 rupees, the equivalent of 10 days' wages. Although $10 did not seem like a lot to the visitors, it caused infighting among other staff members who wanted to be chosen as tour guides in the future. If you are going to be generous, be discreet and ask the recipient to do the same or to share the tip with their coworkers to avoid behind-the-scenes disturbances.

Taboos

The following are taboo in Indian culture:

- Entering someone's house or a temple wearing shoes
- Entering a temple with your head uncovered if you are a woman
- Winking and whistling in public
- Using hands or fingers to point (use your chin or eyes instead)
- Harming or disturbing cows (considered sacred to Hindus)
- Stepping over someone on the ground
- Not realizing you are being complimented

Heroes and Sports

Knowing about another country's heroes and sports offers opportunities to incorporate culture-specific references into your conversations and presentations.

Heroes

Heroes of India's history include

Mahatma Gandhi (1869–1948): No list of Indian national icons would be complete without Mohandas Karamchand Gandhi, better known as Mahatma Gandhi, who led India to independence from British rule in 1947. He was assassinated by a Hindu fanatic a year later.
   Note: Former Prime Minister Indira Gandhi and her son, Rajiv Gandhi, are not related to Mahatma Gandhi. They were the daughter and grandson, respectively, of another prominent Indian politician and prime minister, Jawaharlal Nehru.
Business leaders: Be aware of the high esteem in which Indians hold home-grown business leaders like Ratan Tata, KBE, Chairman Emeritus of the Tata Group as well as powerful female CEOs including Biocon's Kiran Mazumbar-Shaw and Chanda Kochhar, CEO of ICICI Bank.

Sports

Sports

Cricket: A national passion in India and by far the most popular sport.

Football (soccer): The second most-played and -watched sport in India.

Field hockey: A national favorite. India's successful team has won eight Olympic gold medals.

Tennis: A sport growing in popularity with the rise of internationally recognized Indian players.

Sports Figures

Sachin Tendulkar (1973–present): Former cricketer. Known as one of the greatest batsmen of all time, he retired in 2013 after playing in 200 Test matches during which he scored a record 100 centuries.

Saina Nehwal (1990–present): The first Indian to win a medal in Badminton at the Olympics, which she accomplished by earning a Bronze in the 2012 Olympics in London.

Other Cultural Icons

Bollywood—the name for the Indian film industry—is another national *treasure*. Some of the biggest stars include older actors like the distinctively white-goateed Amitabh Bachchan and Anil Kapoor, who played the game show host in *Slumdog Millionaire*. Many Indian actors have now become mainstream, thanks to movies like *Million Dollar Arm* (2014). Top movies in India include 'the greatest Bollywood movie of all time,'[24] *Mughal-e-Azam*, and the cult hit *Anand*.

Eight-Question Framework

This section reviews the framework to which you were introduced earlier in this book. Each of these questions address one or more business topics to help you attract and build the relationships upon which today's successful businesses depend.

---

[24]Times of India slideshow, "10 Must See Bollywood Movies Before You Die," http://timesofindia.indiatimes.com/entertainment/hindi/bollywood/10-Must-See-Bollywood-Movies-Before-You-Die/photostory/25816942.cms (accessed November 12, 2014).

1. How Do Indians Prefer to Act: Individually or as a Group?

But for differences in language and food, most Indians would feel quite at home within a Chinese family and vice versa. In both cultures, caring for the family (in particular, children) is paramount.
— *Anil K. Gupta and Haiyan Wang,* Getting China and India Right[25]

Family life is a major influence across all aspects of Indian culture. This includes the way businesses are run and how individual negotiations and decision making are conducted. As a report by Credit Suisse outlined, India has the highest number of family-controlled businesses in Asia, with 67 percent of all listed Indian companies falling under this category.[26] Some of India's biggest businesses are associated with a single *face,* invariably a family member or the founder such as Ratan Tata, Kishore Biyani, Nusli Wadia, and Anil Dhirubhai Ambani. The leadership styles of these patriarchs are typically described as being top–down and hands-on.

Bear two things in mind when it comes to doing business with Indians. First, Indians in senior management positions are comfortable making individual decisions and are not as consensus-seeking as many other Asian cultures. This speaks to the difference between Hinduism, which focuses more on the achievements of a single soul in this life, compared with the collectivistic nature of Confucianism. Second, in established industries and businesses, especially, a sense of paternalism permeates with employees looked upon as part of an extended family. The *Theory X* or authoritarian management style that works for many Indian businesses aligns with employees' expectations that they will be taken care of, be given clear directions (rather than expecting to show individual initiative), and provided with job security by a paternalistic organization.

Making decisions that take into account the broader social network and group loyalties was reflected by Geert Hofstede's findings on the Individualism Index (See Chapter 2, page 15). As he reported,[27] India's *intermediate score* demonstrated *both collectivistic and individualistic traits.*

---

[25] Anil K. Gupta and Haiyan Wang, *Getting China and India Right: Strategies for Leveraging the World's Fastest-Growing Economies for Global Advantage* (San Francisco: Jossey-Bass, 2009).

[26] Credit Suisse, "Asian Family Businesses Outperform Market Indices," June 10, 2011, www.credit-suisse.com/us/en/news-and-expertise/news/economy/asia-pacific.article .html/article/pwp/news-and-expertise/2011/10/en/asian-family-businesses-outperform-market -indices.html.

[27] The Hofstede Center, "What About India," http://geert-hofstede.com/india.html (accessed November 12, 2014).

2. How Are Power and Authority Viewed in India?

Consciously or subconsciously, Indians, whether in their own country or abroad, still make judgments based on caste.
— *Narendra Jadhav*[28]

This is a hierarchical, top-down society in which your various degrees, qualifications, and other accomplishments will be admired. It is quite acceptable to emphasize formal titles as Liz, one of the authors, does when she does business in India, where she is called Dr. Alexander. Nevertheless, what trumps external status symbols and titles links to what we were saying in the previous section about family mindset. Indians will do so much more for a person with whom they have developed a trusting relationship than someone merely well connected or with formal authority over them.

As Hari Ratan of Lateral Management Services in Chennai told us, "The board of directors from a large multinational bank came to India to hold a big meeting. The idea was to communicate their realization that India is the future. But they made themselves look stupid because they flew in, held their meeting, and then walked out. They failed to capitalize on their visit because they thought their presence was enough. The staff were dismayed that these high-ranking guys did not have the respect to walk across the room and say hello to them. If you think that just relying on your position to say to an Indian, "Okay, get it done," you're not necessarily going to get things done. We all appreciate good relationships; in India, especially so."

The caste system in India[29]

The Hindu *caste* or social stratification system is based on the concept of *Varnashrama,* mentioned in the religious scriptures known as the Vedas. It was the ancient way of identifying a person's *occupation* or contribution to society, loosely based on astrology. This fits the Hindu belief that each person is born with natural characteristics or inclinations that predispose them to certain societal roles. There was originally no link to class divisions or distinctions, or anything to stop people from different *varnas* from marrying each other.

---

[28]Narendra Jadhav, *Untouchables: My Family's Triumphant Journey Out of the Caste System in Modern India* (New York: Scribner, 2005).
[29]Hinduism Facts, "Hindu Caste System," http://hinduismfacts.org/hindu-caste-system (accessed November 12, 2014).

The four *varnas*, in order of status from higher to lower, are

Brahmin: Priests, teachers, scholars—*intellectuals*
Kshatriyas: Members of armed forces, keepers of law and order—
   protectors
Vaishyas: Traders, merchants, artisan, farmers—*businesspeople*
Shudras: Cleaners, cooks, laborers—the *unskilled*

3. How Do Indians Compare Rules and Relationships?

In India, what works are relationships. Once a relationship is built, things will get done, which is contrary to first focusing on a task and "here's how it needs to be."
   —*Naveen Lakkur, cofounder and director, Compassites Software*
   Solutions Pvt. Ltd.

J.B. is the owner of a mid-sized Indian company that manufactures industrial fans and cooling towers. Throughout his 30 years in business, he has had two joint venture agreements—one with a German partner, the other with a U.S. organization. J.B.'s relationship with the Germans lasted 18 years and was ratified with a two-page document. Eight years into the relationship with his U.S. partners, J.B. told us he "couldn't get out of it quick enough." Part of the problem was that the contract the U.S. Americans had insisted he sign was 120 pages long.

Trying to cover every possible contingency that *might* arise in business, while commonly practiced in many countries like the U.S., is contrary to the way Indians view the world. As Naveen Lakkur explained: "In a developed country like the U.S., many things are matured and systematized so a cookie-cutter approach is easily set in place. In a developing country like India with so much diversity, you have to be more adaptive and react in the moment. One of the reasons why Indians can travel to just about anywhere in the world and adapt to different business cultures is because of the flexibility we have learned from living in our own country."

When it comes to contracts and other legalities, V. Srinivasan, past chairman of the Indo-American Chamber of Commerce for Karnataka, summed it up this way: "Indian businessmen work from their hearts. We believe in building personal relationships and that agreements are more for formality than anything else. We never refer to them, even in the event of a dispute, unless the situation becomes hopeless. For us, anything contractual separates the heart from the purpose."

One way to think about doing business in India is to consider what happened in family banks years ago. An individual, personally known to the banker, would come in for a loan and be assessed based on the relationship. The process largely relied on the discretion and willingness of the lender to vouch for the person making the request. As Naveen Lakkur pointed out, Western systems now have systematized processes that invariably cannot be changed regardless of who is making the request. But this is not the way things are done in India. Indians prefer applying personal judgment to situations rather than follow established procedures.

4. How Do Indians Regard Time?

There are only two kinds of relationships: long-term and very long-term.
— *Rajesh Setty, cofounder and president of the cloud-based platform WittyParrot*[30]

Consider the challenges of traveling in Mumbai, whose population is more than twice that of New York. There, as in other Indian metropolitan areas, you'll see road signs clearly asking drivers to *observe lane discipline.* Yet you'll find five or even six lanes of traffic weaving in and out of highways built to accommodate only three lanes. Traffic that includes three-wheeled auto-rickshaws, entire families perched precariously on scooters, drivers ferrying businesspeople around in sedans and SUVs, not to mention the cattle, stray dogs, and wild pigs that frequently roam unchecked in city centers. The result is nothing short of chaotic and one of the reasons why punctuality in India is more theory than practice.

You may find that although you would prefer to calendar meetings well in advance, your Indian counterparts appear resistant to do so. Although this may not apply when dealing with Westernized multinationals, executives in smaller businesses will give priority to family situations that crop up during the business day. For example, while we were researching this book, several of our Indian business contacts postponed interviews because of sudden, non-emergency family commitments. As explained in an earlier section, the highly family-oriented culture of India places great importance on personal responsibilities and relationships.

Indians take a long-term perspective, which is why they place so much emphasis on relationships that stand the test of time. As one HR executive pointed out, "Work can wait. If it's not taken care of today, it will happen tomorrow. That's the attitude we have." It will help you considerably if you can adapt to that while doing business in India.

---

[30]Refer to: www.wittyparrot.com/one-voice-about-us.

5. How Direct Is Communication in India?

Author and entrepreneur Mahesh Baxi recently launched a talent acquisition and management product called TalentOjo. He reached out to his friend Raj, a senior operations manager who worked for a multinational firm in Pune. Raj recognized that Mahesh's solution would be invaluable to the company and made an introduction to the head of HR, Sameer. After receiving a demo, Sameer said he loved the product but needed to get approval from his boss in the U.S. before he could agree to launch a no-cost pilot program.

After a week of silence, Mahesh e-mailed Sameer and was told he was out of the office but would get back to him the following week. That week came and went with no news. Despite making repeated calls and sending text messages, Mahesh did not receive the response he believed would be forthcoming—even to reject the program. When Raj stepped in several months later to ask Sameer to let Mahesh know what his boss had said, those communications were also ignored.

As Mahesh, who describes himself as an Indian with a Western mindset, explained: "There are two likely explanations for Sameer's lack of follow-up. If his boss in the U.S. had nixed the idea, Sameer would have felt uncomfortable conveying this negative response to me. If he didn't make the call because he wasn't as enthusiastic about the product as he'd led me to believe, he would also have found it hard to tell me that. Most Indians make no distinction between what is being requested and the person who is making the request, which is different to the way things are done in the West. For Sameer to tell me that the company did not want my *product* would be tantamount to disrespecting or criticizing the *relationship* I already have with his colleague, Raj. The longer Sameer ignored me, the more confident he would be that I would just give up, as by now that's what most Indians would have done."

The key point being that in this culture, when a businessperson has an established reputation and is held in high regard by other colleagues, many Indians find it difficult to decline their services and avoid such confrontations by not responding at all. For additional ways that Indians communicate *no* without expressly using that word, see the article entitled *The Seven Ways an Indian Programmer Says No.*[31]

6. How Formal or Informal Do Businesspeople in India Tend to Be?

> Nobody can hurt me without my permission.
> —*Mahatma Gandhi*

---

[31] Accelerance, "The 7 Ways an Indian Programmer Says 'No,'" April 11, 2012, www.accelerance. com/blog/the-7-ways-an-indian-programmer-says-no.

One of the formalities that most Indians exemplify and therefore appreciate in others is emotional restraint. Chennai-based consultant AVIS Viswanathan recalls an occasion when the head of a California-based IT company visiting Bengaluru lost his temper in front of a group of journalists about the state of Indian infrastructure and policy-making: "His inappropriate expression of a factual state of affairs became a big PR blunder. The man was berated by the press the next morning and even the normally lethargic Indian bureaucracy joined in the clamor."

Few countries welcome outsiders discussing domestic affairs in a public forum. In India, a culture where respect and the control of one's impulses in consideration of others are highly regarded, international visitors need to be wary of speaking out without thinking through the ramifications, especially when doing so in a public forum. In this particular case, some segments within the media took offense and reported the CEO's faux pas. The company's PR machinery had to use their considerable crisis-management skills to try to contain the damage. More importantly, in terms of securing future business in the region, many Indian influencers in charge of IT and infrastructure development within that state made their discontent known to other senior officials within the company, which affected relations going forward.

7. How Aligned Are Indian Social and Business Lives?

"Can the business of business and the business of life be any different? If business becomes merely the means of living, then it loses meaning for us."
—*Debashis Chatterjee,* Timeless Leadership: 18 Leadership Sutras from the Bhagavad Gita[32]

Fifteen minutes into a drive with an Indian businessman she had just met, Liz was invited to his daughter's wedding in Bengaluru. Having attended and subsequently visited the family during her frequent visits to India, Liz is now considered an honorary member of the family. Following a presentation on thought leadership that she made to the employees of a software company in Pune, Liz accepted an invitation to dinner at the home of a senior manager. Other requests began to come in from that moment on.

It's unlikely you'll find a country where visitors are so easily and quickly integrated into your hosts' social lives than India. As Naveen Lakkur explained, in the Hindu tradition, the concept of *atithi devo Bhava,* means *the guest is God.* Most Indians take great pleasure in extending the hand of friendship by introducing you to their families. Indeed, if you don't receive an invitation to a

---

[32]Debashis Chatterjee, *Timeless Leadership: 18 Leadership Sutras from the Bhagavad Gita* (Singapore: John Wiley & Sons, 2012).

business colleague or partner's home during your stay in India, you can consider this an indication that your relationship may not progress. If you plan to build trust, inspire respect, and create long-lasting business relationships in India, our advice is to graciously accept all invitations enthusiastically. You will not regret doing so.

Dining & Drinking Etiquette in India

On one occasion, Sharon was attending a business lunch in Mumbai with a group that included a colleague named Sona who described herself as a *modern Muslim*. Sharon noticed that some members of the group, seated at one of the two designated tables, were drinking beer. Sharon and Sona sat at the table along with several other Muslims where alcohol was not being served. This dynamic was observed throughout Sharon's visit to India. During business meals, the Muslims, who did not consume alcohol and had reserved two tables in advance, sat separately from those who were drinking. Sharon noticed how drinking alcohol detrimentally impacted the development of the prospective business relationships because of the separate conversations taking place.

8. How Is the Concept of Women in Business Handled in India?

We cannot afford to follow the traditional "jobs for the boys" culture. We have to survive in a very competitive global industry. Our only criterion is to select the best people.
— *Nandan Nilekani, CEO and cofounder of Infosys*[33]

India is no stranger to strong, powerful women in business. The Forbes World's Most Powerful Women 2014 lists the following Indian businesswomen: Arundhati Bhattacharya, the chair and MD of the State Bank of India; Chanda Kochhar, CEO-MD of ICICI Bank; Kiran Muzumdar-Shaw, founder/Chair of Biocon; and Indra Nooyi, CEO of PepsiCo, who lives in the U.S. And a 2014 survey discovered that although female CEOs account for just three percent of Fortune 500 companies in the U.S., that figure jumps to 11 percent in the case of female CEOs of Indian companies.[34]

Ms. Sarada Ramani, the founder and president of Chennai-based Computers International, is a role model to younger women and is helping change the gender demographics of the Indian workplace. With respect to the challenges that international businesswomen might face when coming to India, she

[33] Edward Luce, *In Spite of the Gods: The Strange Rise of Modern India* (New York: Doubleday, 2007).
[34] Deccan Herald, "Women CEOs: India Inc Beats US Hands Down," March 9, 2010, www.deccanherald.com/content/57119/F.

said, "Although India is a patriarchal society, we also respect hierarchy. Business visitors—male or female—will be exalted because we see you as knowledgeable authorities with a global perspective. As long as you start out with a friendly approach, you will be welcomed warmly."

Ms. Ramani knows from experience how women in the IT sector have had to be assertive to make their mark and advises caution: "Men in India would take a step back if you used an assertive approach here. You will be given respect and find it more effective to take it gently and put your foot down more slowly."

When asked what advice Ms. Ramani would give to an international businesswoman visiting, she said, "In the U.S., there are some neighborhoods you know are not safe for women. This is the case in India also. While some areas are totally unsafe for all women, a word of caution for international women visitors: Don't assume a man's mental makeup has changed as fast as women's modes of dress and levels of independence." She advises it's important to dress discreetly, to be accompanied, and not go out alone late at night. Sharon's additional advice to female clients is to dine in your hotel at night unless accompanied by someone you trust.

Whereas the more conservative northern states have been slower to accept women in education and the workplace, says Ms. Ramani, the number of young women driving around on their scooters and maintaining their independence through work in major southern hubs like Bengaluru and Chennai is helping to shift long-held perceptions about women's roles in India.

Cultural Summary

Here are some key points to remember:

- Although the U.K. and India share superficial similarities in legal and banking models, significant cultural differences exist.
- Be patient with scheduling because India is relationship- and family-oriented; which may differ from your country if it is system-based.
- Check performance with courtesy; realize that environmental factors such as monsoon season impact timing.

Self-Awareness Profile

This simple exercise prompts you to self-assess where you currently stand on topics related to the eight-question framework and *compare* this with the country culture. This visual will help you discover the extent to which you may need to adapt your current mindset and behavior to develop more robust business

relationships. For details on how to complete this graphic, see the instructions given in the Introduction on pages xviii–xix.

Consider copying the eight-question Profile or using a pencil so that you can see, over time, how you have adjusted your cultural mindset. You might also wish to create unique graphics related to each of the businesses you work with, as these cultural positions vary depending upon geographic location, industry, generational factors, and corporate profile.

Q1: What is your preferred way of doing business?

As an individual making autonomous decisions					**As a team member who seeks group consensus**
1	2	3	**4**	5	6

Q2: How comfortable are you in hierarchies in which power is distributed unequally?

Very uncomfortable					**Very comfortable**
1	2	3	4	5	**6**

Q3: How closely do you follow rules and obey the law?

Almost always					**It depends**
1	2	3	4	**5**	6

Q4: What is your general attitude toward time?

I prefer agendas, schedules, planning					**I prefer flexibility, fluidity without scheduling**
1	2	3	4	5	**6**

Q5: What is your preferred way to communicate?

Very diplomatically					**Very candidly**
1	**2**	3	4	5	6

Q6: What is your interpersonal style or level of formality in business interactions?

Very formal   **Very informal**

    1   2   **3**   4   5   6

Q7: What is your view on socializing within business?

A waste of time   **Essential**

    1   2   3   4   5   **6**

Q8: Should a woman defer to a man as the lead, if winning business in a certain culture depended on it?

Never   **Yes, absolutely**

    1   2   3   4   **5**   6

8

Japan

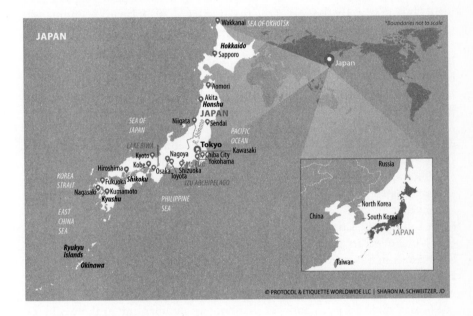

"Japan never considers time together as wasted. Rather, it is time invested."
—A Hundred Years of Japanese Film: A Concise History

Introduction

From bonsai to bullet trains, and tea ceremonies to *tanshifunin* postings, Japan is a country of contrasts in which the ancient and the ultramodern are seamlessly blended. Ancient temples are nestled among business and technology towers. Japanese concepts including emojii, kanban, kaizen and keiretsu are recognized and used worldwide. We hear about the physical and financial battering Japan endured following the March 3, 2011 Tohoku earthquake and tsunami, then marvel at the way the country's economy rebounded and surpassed expectations the following year. By the end of the first quarter of 2014, Japan's economy was growing at its fastest pace in nearly three years.[1]

According to the IMF's World Economic Outlook, Japan was the third largest world economy in 2014, behind only the U.S. and China, with a GDP of $4.8 trillion[2]—despite having only a fraction of those countries' populations. Japan has consistently been a major player in the world economy and a driving force in Asia. Indeed, it stands apart from its Asian neighbors as the only Asian member of the G7, a group of the seven most influential and wealthiest world powers and is also the only major *developed* Asian country, as recognized by the United Nations.

Undoubtedly, Japan owes its economic strength to its technological advances. Japan was second only to the U.S. in the number of patent applications filed in 2013—twice as many as those filed in China. And the largest filer of all was the Japanese company Panasonic.[3]

Why invest in Japan? JETRO, the Japan External Trade Organization lists reasons in addition to those above,[4] such as the 57 companies out of the *Fortune Global 500* headquartered in Japan and its claim to 22 Nobel Prize winners. The World Economic Forum's Global Competitiveness Report 2014-2015 ranked Japan's business environment number one in the world for 'Business Sophistication'[5] and Japan ranked first in Asia on the Global Peace Index 2014.[6]

---

[1]"Japan Posts Strong Growth Ahead of Sales Tax Rise," BBC News Business, May 14, 2014, www.bbc.com/news/business-27419848#TWEET1129127.

[2]Andrew Bergmann, "World's Largest Economies," CNN Money, http://money.cnn.com /news/economy/world_economies_gdp/ (accessed November 21, 2014).

[3]"US and China Drive International Patent Filing Growth in Record-Setting Year," World Intellectual Property Organization, March 13, 2014, www.wipo.int/pressroom/en/articles/2014 /article_0002.html.

[4]"Why Japan? '5 Reasons to Invest in Japan,'" Japan External Trade Organization, October 2014, www.jetro.go.jp/en/invest/whyjapan/pdf/5reasons-en1119.pdf (accessed November 20, 2014).

[5]"The Global Competitiveness Report 2014–2015," World Economic Forum, www3.weforum .org/docs/WEF_GlobalCompetitivenessReport_2014-15.pdf (accessed November 20, 2014).

[6]"Global Peace Index 2014," Institute for Economics and Peace, June 2014, www.visionof humanity.org/sites/default/files/2014%20Global%20Peace%20Index%20REPORT.pdf (accessed November 20, 2014).

Quiz

How much do you know about Japan? Answer the following questions as True or False to test your knowledge. (The Answer Key that follows the quiz includes page references where you can find more information.)

_____1. A conservative navy blue suit, tie, and a quality leather satchel is appropriate dress in Japan.

_____2. The Japanese prefer subtle communication and consider direct eye contact aggressive.

_____3. Japan has the second-fastest average Internet connection speed in the world.

_____4. The dominant belief system in Japan is Shinto.

_____5. Japanese bows are classified into at least three types, based on the size of the angle formed by the bend: 15, 30, or 45 degrees.

_____6. When making a business presentation in Japan, using visual aids, and allowing time afterward for questions is important.

_____7. Eating sushi with your fingers is proper.

_____8. Among Asians, the Japanese are the most individualist, and do not enjoy group-oriented activities.

_____9. In Japan, business cards are called *meishi*.

_____10. Japan is an archipelago with over 3,000 islands.

Answer Key: 1. T (p. 159–160); 2. T (p. 162); 3. F (p. 161); 4. T (p. 158); 5. T (p. 161–162); 6. T (p. 163); 7. T (p. 165); 8. F (p. 168); 9. T (p. 160–161); 10. T (p. 155).

Country Basics

This section provides key knowledge in an easy-to-read format to help you quickly grasp some of the basics necessary to navigate this culture.

Historical Timeline

A critical way to show respect for another person's culture is to have knowledge of their country's history and current affairs. Table 8.1 on page 154 outlines a few key events related to Japan, together with concurrent world events.[7]

_____

[7]Japan Timeline sources: CIA, *The World Factbook*, "Japan," www.cia.gov/library/publications /the-world-factbook/geos/ja.html (accessed November 21, 2014); *CultureGrams World Edition 2014: Japan*. (Ann Arbor, MI: ProQuest, 2014); "Japan Profile: Timeline," BBC News Asia, August 14, 2014, www.bbc.com/news/world-asia-pacific-15219730; and B. Grun, *The Timetables of History*, 4th ed. (New York: Simon & Schuster, 2005).

Table 8.1   Key Historical Events

Period/ Dates	Description/Events	World Events
ca. 660 BCE	Emperor Jimmu becomes first Emperor of Japan.	Nineveh, the capital of Assyria, is estimated the largest city in the world.
1603	Tokugawa shogunate initiates a period of isolation from foreign influence.	Founding of the Dutch East India Company (1602).
1854	Japan opens its ports after signing the Treaty of Kanagawa with the U.S.	Heinrich Goebel invents the first form of the electric light bulb.
1947	Japan adopts a new constitution and establishes a parliamentary system.	Burma is declared an independent republic.
1952	Japanese independence from post-war occupation.	China and Mongolia sign a 10-year cooperation agreement.
1975	Japan joins the Group of Seven (G7), the seven wealthiest developed nations.	Leaders of 35 nations sign the charter of Conference on Security & Cooperation.
1989	Emperor Akihito begins his current reign, the Heisei era, meaning "achievement of universal peace."	The Berlin Wall falls, reunifying East and West Germany.
2011	The Tohoku earthquake and tsunami strike; the most powerful earthquake recorded in Japan (9.0 magnitude).	The world population reaches 7 billion inhabitants according to the UN.
2014	The government approves a landmark change in Japan's security policy allowing for collective self-defense.	The XXII Olympic Winter Games take place in Sochi, Russia.
2016	National elections scheduled.	Elections scheduled in Malaysia, Taiwan, the Philippines, and U.S.
2019	Japan to be the first Asian country to host the Rugby World Cup*	Indian legislative elections scheduled.
2020	Tokyo, Japan, to host the XXXII Olympic Summer Games.	U.S. national elections scheduled.

*International Rugby Board article, "Japan 2019 to be a World Cup for all of Asia," dated April 17, 2012, http://www.rugbyworldcup.com/rugbyworldcup2019/news/newsid=2061811 .html#japan+2019+world+cup+asia (accessed November 15, 2014).

Full Country Name and Location

Japan, known domestically as *Nihon* or *Nippon,* is an archipelago extending along the eastern coast of Asia with over 3,000 populated islands. The four main islands, north to south, are Hokkaido, Honshu (mainland), Shikoku, and Kyushu. Okinawa Island is about 380 miles southwest of Kyushu. Japan is slightly larger than Germany and slightly smaller than the State of California in the U.S.

Government/Political Structure

Japan has a parliamentary government with a constitutional monarchy. The parliament, or Diet, is a bicameral legislature made up of the House of Councilors and the House of Representatives. A Prime Minister is designated from within the Diet to serve as head of government, and the Emperor, born from the ruling line, serves as symbolic head of state. Japan's 47 prefectures provide local administration.

Population and Economic Centers

Japan has a population of 127 million people, according to 2014 estimates.[8] The main ethnic group is Japanese (98.5 percent), and minorities include Korean (0.5 percent), Chinese (0.4 percent), and other (0.6 percent).[9] Approximately 91.3 percent live in urban areas.[10]

The major business centers and populations (2012) are shown in Table 8.2 on page 156.[11]

Economy

Japan is ranked 29th out of 189 economies in terms of ease of doing business, according to the World Bank Group's *Doing Business 2015* report.[12]

---

[8]CIA, *The World Factbook,* "Japan," www.cia.gov/library/publications/the-world-factbook/geos /ja.html (accessed November 21, 2014).
[9]Ibid.
[10]Ibid.
[11]Japan Statistics Bureau, *Japan Statistical Yearbook 2014,* Chapter 2: "Population and Households," Table 2-6: Population by Cities, www.stat.go.jp/english/data/nenkan/1431-02.htm (accessed November 21, 2014).
[12]World Bank Group, *Doing Business 2015* (October 29, 2014): 4, www.doingbusiness.org/~ /media/GIAWB/Doing%20Business/Documents/Annual-Reports/English/DB15-Full-Report .pdf.

Table 8.2   Major Business Centers

Business Centers	Population (millions)
Akita	0.3
Aomori	0.3
Chiba City	0.9
Fukuoka	1.4
Hiroshima	1.2
Kawasaki	1.4
Kobe	1.5
Kumamoto	0.7
Kyoto	1.4
Nagasaki	0.4
Nagoya	2.2
Niigata	0.8
Osaka	2.5
Sapporo	1.9
Sendai	1
Shizuoka	0.7
Tokyo (capital)	8.6
Toyota	0.4
Wakkanai	0.04
Yokohama	3.6

Japan's business environment is ranked number one in the world for Business Sophistication.[13].

Its 2013 GDP was ranked 3rd by the World Bank,[14] and the composition of its GDP by sector was services (73.2 percent); industry (25.6 percent); and agriculture (1.1 percent).[15]

---

[13]World Economic Forum, "Global Competitiveness Report 2014-2015," http://reports .weforum.org/global-competitiveness-report-2014-2015/economies/#economy=JPN (accessed November 21, 2014).

[14]The World Bank, Data, GDP Ranking, "Gross Domestic Product Ranking Table," last updated September 24, 2014, http://data.worldbank.org/data-catalog/GDP-ranking-table (accessed November 21, 2014).

[15]CIA, *The World Factbook*, "Japan," www.cia.gov/library/publications/the-world-factbook/geos /ja.html (accessed November 21, 2014).

Corruption Perceptions Index

Japan ranked 18th least corrupt out of 177 countries and territories with a score of 74 out of 100.[16] This annual index, compiled by Transparency International, measures perceived levels of public sector corruption. The Fair Trade Commission, National Police Agency, National Tax Administration Agency, and the Public Prosecutors Office are anti-corruption agencies that conduct investigations in Japan.

Human Development Index

Japan ranked 17th out of 187 countries and territories.[17] The HDI, compiled by the United Nations Development Programme, is a composite index of life expectancy, education, and income statistics.

Global Gender Gap Index

Japan ranked 104th out of 142 countries in terms of gender equality with a score of 0.6584.[18] This annual index, compiled by the World Economic Forum, assesses gender gaps based on economic, political, educational, and health-based criteria.

Climate

Climate in Japan varies dramatically, from tropical in the southern islands to cool in the northern islands. The summer months of June to September are hot, rainy, and humid. The winter months of December to April are mild, drier, and have less humidity. Honshu and Kyushu receive occasional snowfall at lower elevations with the mountain regions receiving significant snowfall during winter. Hokkaido's severe winters include heavy ice and snow. Japan's snow country

---

[16]Transparency International, "Corruption Perceptions Index 2013," www.transparency.org/cpi2013/results (accessed November 21, 2014).

[17]United Nations Development Programme, *Human Development Report 2014*, 160–163, http://hdr.undp.org/sites/default/files/hdr14-report-en-1.pdf (accessed November 21, 2014).

[18]World Economic Forum, *The Global Gender Gap Report 2014*, 8–9, www3.weforum.org/docs/GGGR14/GGGR_CompleteReport_2014.pdf (accessed November 21, 2014).

consistently ranks among the top 10 snowiest places on earth.[19] Okinawa and the southern islands are semi-tropical.

Languages

Nihongo or Japanese is the official language and *lingua franca*. English is a required subject in high school.

Belief Systems, Philosophies, and Religions

The country breakdown is as follows: Shintoism (83.9 percent), Buddhism (71.4 percent), Christianity (2 percent), Other (7.8 percent).[20] The total exceeds 100 percent because many Japanese practice more than one belief system.

For an overview of belief systems, philosophies, and religions, please refer to Chapter 4, pages 64–65.

Time Zones/Daylight Savings

Japan has a single standard time, Japan Standard Time (JST). To calculate time in Japan add nine hours to GMT/UTC. It does not operate under Daylight Savings Time.

It is 14 hours ahead of U.S. Eastern Standard Time (13 hours ahead in Daylight Savings Time).

For more information, see www.timeanddate.com/worldclock.

Telephone Country Code and Internet Suffix

Japan's telephone country code is 81 and the Internet suffix is .jp.

Currency

Yen (JPY). One yen is divided into 100 sen.

---

[19]Maddie Donnelly, "Ten of the Snowiest Places in the World," Condé Nast Traveler, December 14, 2013, www.cntraveler.com/galleries/2013-12-14/snowiest-places-mountain-alaska-washington/4.
[20]CIA, *The World Factbook*, "Japan," www.cia.gov/library/publications/the-world-factbook/geos/ja.html (accessed November 21, 2014).

Business Culture, Etiquette, and Customs

This section covers business culture, etiquette, and customs.

Fiscal Year

The Japanese fiscal year runs from April 1 to March 31. Dates are written month/day/year; for example, April 1, 2020 is written 04/01/2020.

Working Week

The structure of the typical Japanese working week is outlined in Table 8.3.

Table 8.3   The Japanese Working Schedule

Business Sector	Business Hours	Days of the Week
Private Sector Offices	09:00–17:00 (with long hours of overtime)	Monday–Friday
	Lunch: 12:00–13:00 (sharp)	Monday–Friday
Public Sector Offices	09:00–17:00	Monday–Friday
	Lunch: 12:00–13:00	Monday–Friday

Holidays and Festivals

When a national holiday falls on a Sunday, the following Monday is also considered a holiday. Japanese companies and government offices traditionally close during the New Year holiday season (December 29 through January 3), *Golden week* (April 29 through May 5), and O-Bon Festival (August 13 through August 15). Common Japanese holidays and festivals appear in Table 8.4 on page 160.

Business Dress/Appearance

First impressions are crucial in business circles, so it pays to look good. Wealth is admired. Men and women wearing well-made suits are seen as successful. For men, suits, white shirts, and understated ties are appropriate; avoid black ties. For women, modest suits, dresses, or skirts with low two-inch heels. Lightweight suits are appropriate during the summer and in southern regions.

Table 8.4 Japanese Holidays and Festivals

Date	Name
January 1–3	New Year's Day
January 9	Adult's Day
February 11	National Foundation Day
March 20	Vernal Equinox Day
April 29–May 5	*Golden Week*, including Showa Day, Constitution Day, Citizen's Day, Children's Day
May 3	Constitution Memorial Day
July 16	Marine Day
July or August 13–15 (depends on region)	O-Bon Festival
September 17	Respect for the Aged Day
September 22	Autumnal Equinox Day
October 8	Health and Sports Day
November 3	National Culture Day
November 23	Labor Day /Thanksgiving Day
December 23	Emperor's Birthday
December 25	Christmas Day

Wear high quality, minimal accessories to harmonize with the crowd. Wardrobe for professional men and women is tailored clothing in dark, subdued colors, including black, navy blue, and charcoal. Avoid vivid colors. Wear neutral stockings or black tights in winter. Avoid patterned or seamed stockings. Men and women both carry sleek, designer shoulder bags.

News Sources

Common news sources in Japan include the following:

- *Nikkei Asian Review:* http://asia.nikkei.com
- *The Mainichi Daily News:* http://mainichi.jp/english

Business Cards

Exchanging business cards has a specific protocol. In Japan, business cards are called *meishi*[21] and are given and received with both hands. Bring classic cards

---

[21]Boye Lafayette De Mente, *Etiquette Guide to Japan: Know the Rules that Make the Difference!*, Revised ed. (Tokyo, Japan: Tuttle Publishing, 2008).

(avoid color), printed in both English and Japanese. When exchanging, present yours with the Japanese print facing the recipient. When receiving a card, do not write on it or place it in your pocket or wallet. Examine it carefully and ask questions as a sign of respect. Place it on the table, or in a card case or portfolio.

Technology

According to Akamai Technology's *State of the Internet Report*, Japan has the second-fastest average Internet connection speed in the world.[22] Latest figures rank Japan 3rd in the world for the number of Internet users, with over 99 million Japanese online,[23] and 2nd in the world for the number of Internet hosts.[24] When riding in public transportation, or the bullet train (*shinkansen*), mobile phones must be turned to silent mode, or *manner mode*.[25] Driving while talking on a mobile phone is against the law.

Gifts

Gifts (*omiyage*, or honorable presents) are a crucial element and expected on almost all business occasions. Omiyage are an affirmative way to express appreciation to your host in anticipation of the courtesies to be extended to you during your visit. Regional gifts from government gift shops are appropriate choices. Quality is important; expense depends on the particular situation and relationship with your counterpart. Wrapping must be done professionally and the gift will not be opened in your presence unless it is elegantly packaged sweets or cookies to be shared by the group.

Introductions, Greetings, Personal Space, and Eye Contact

In Japan, the traditional greeting is the bow, which has different meanings depending on the depth of the bow—15, 30, 45, or 90 degrees—as well as

---

[22]Akamai Technologies, "State of the Internet Q4 2013," April 2014, www.akamai.com/dl/akamai/akamai-soti-q413.pdf?WT.mc_id=soti_Q413.

[23]CIA, *The World Factbook*, "Country Comparison: Internet Users," information dated 2009, www.cia.gov/library/publications/the-world-factbook/rankorder/2153rank.html (accessed November 21, 2014).

[24]CIA, *The World Factbook*, "Country Comparison: Internet Hosts," information dated 2009, www.cia.gov/library/publications/the-world-factbook/rankorder/2184rank.html (accessed November 21, 2014).

[25]"Business Manner for Phone Call," Hiwork, http://staff.hiwork.jp/eng/support/07manner.aspx (accessed November 20, 2014).

the length. In a casual *eshaku*[26] bow, for example, which is used when thanking someone or when passing someone of a higher status, the waist is bent at a 15-degree angle, and the bow is accompanied by a head nod. The *keirei* bow, used in business, involves a 30-degree waist bend, and is done when entering rooms, greeting others, and making introductions. The *saikeirei,* or most polite bow, consists of lowering the top half of the body 45 degrees; it's used to apologize or to express deep feelings of gratitude. People of equal rank bow to the same depth, and for the same length of time. If one person is of higher rank, however, the other bows deeper and longer. The Japanese avoid eye contact in crowds; direct eye contact is considered rude, aggressive by the Japanese.[27]

Useful Phrases

Useful phrases for travelers to Japan are shown in Table 8.5 on page 163.

Names

Japanese name order is last name (surname), then first name (given name).

Without regard for gender, Japanese usually add *-san* (SAHN) to the person's last name as an honorific (in place of courtesy titles such as Mr., Ms., or Mrs.).

Meetings and Negotiations

The Japanese are formal in scheduling and conducting meetings.[28] When arranging meetings in Japan, emailing the request several weeks—or even a month—in advance is recommended. Send high-quality meeting materials in advance. Last-minute changes to schedule or location are not appreciated, so be consistent with all arrangements and be prompt.

Negotiations begin with mid-ranking managers. Senior-ranked members will join later, after the relationship-building and trust begins.

---

[26]"Greetings, Etiquette, Etc.," Japan National Tourism Organization, www.jnto.go.jp/eng/indepth/exotic/lifestyle/bow.html (accessed November 20, 2014).
[27]Dean Foster, *The Global Etiquette Guide to Asia* (New York: John Wiley & Sons, 2000).
[28]Sheida Hodge, *Global Smarts: The Art of Communicating and Deal Making Anywhere in the World* (New York: John Wiley & Sons, 2000).

Table 8.5 Useful Phrases for Japanese Travel

English	Japanese	Pronunciation
Hello	*Konnichi wa*	kohn-NEE-chee-wah
Hello (on the telephone)	*Moshi-moshi*	MOH-shee MOH-shee
How are you?	*O genki desu ka*	oh-GEN-kee dess KAH
Pleased to meet you (first time)	*Hajimemashite*	hah-JEE-may-mahssh-tay
Good morning	*Ohayo gozaimasu*	oh-HAH-yoh goh-za-eye-mahs
Good afternoon	*Konnichi wa*	kohn-NEE-chee-wah
Good evening	*Konbanwa*	kohn-bahn-wuh
Good night	*Oyasumi nasai*	oh-yah-soo-mee nah-sigh
Goodbye	*Sayonara*	sigh-YOH-nah-rah
Please (when asking for something)	*Kudasai*	koo-DAH-sigh
Please (when offering something)	*Dozo*	DOH-zoh
Thank you	*Domo Arigato*	ah-ree-GAH-toe
You're welcome	*Doitashimashite*	DOH-ee-TAHSSH-mahssh-tay
I understand, I am listening	*Hai*	HIGH
Excuse me	*Gomen nasai*	goh-MEHN nah-SIGH

Presentation Styles, Conversational Topics, and Humor

When conducting presentations, present facts in an objective manner and avoid a high-energy style with overly-demonstrative gestures. Ruben A. Hernandez recommends beginning your presentation with an explanation of your business or your relationship to Japan. Explain what you know about Japan, or the enterprise you're addressing, and express your respect for Japan. In public speakers, the Japanese value composure and subdued gestures, and they prefer *systematic thinkers* who use a presentation outline and agenda. Schedule a question-and-answer session at the conclusion.[29]

---

[29]Ruben Hernandez, *Presenting Across Cultures: How to Adapt Your Business and Sales Presentations in Key Markets around the World* (Tertium Business Books, 2013).

Gestures

Common gestures in Japan include the following:

- Bows, ranging from a simple head nod to waist bends of 15, 30, 45, and 90 degrees, have a variety of meanings.
- A single clap of the hands in front of the face expresses thanks for a meal, asks for forgiveness, or requests a favor.
- Nodding acknowledges that someone is speaking (and does not mean agreement).
- Waving the hand back and forth with the palm out in front of the face means 'no.'
- A smile may indicate or mask sadness, confusion, embarrassment, happiness, or anger.
- A surprised expression can be used as a form of flattery and courtesy.
- A blank, know-nothing expression (a poker face) may be worn to avoid involvement.
- Extended eye closing, as if in a short nap (means concentration).

Notable Foods and Dishes

Main dishes may include seafood, beef, chicken, pork, or tofu. Rice is a staple with every meal. Popular noodles include *udon, soba,* and *somen,* which are common in soups with protein, vegetables, and spices.

Specialty Dishes

Favorite dishes in Japanese cuisine include the following:

- **Tempura:** Lightly battered seafood or vegetables fried in sesame oil
- **Ramen:** Traditional noodle dish of Chinese origin served in a flavorful broth
- **Sushi:** Rice, raw fish, seaweed, and various fillings, served with sliced ginger and soy sauce
- **Sashimi:** Slices of raw fish served various ways
- **Uni:** Sea urchin, a Japanese delicacy, served as sushi
- **Sukiyaki:** Hot-pot–style beef, with vegetables and a flavorful broth
- **Teriyaki:** Protein and vegetables, broiled or grilled with a glaze of soy sauce, mirin, and sugar

Dining Etiquette

Itadaki-masu ("enjoy your meal") is said at the beginning of a business meal,[30] and *Gochisou-samadeshita* (which shows appreciation and says "thanks for the meal") is said at the end. Chopsticks are used to dine; if you are not proficient, however, you may be a source of amusement. Sip soups out of the bowl; noodles and vegetables may be enjoyed with chopsticks. Use both hands simultaneously to pass or receive items, and to present your glass for refills.

Sushi

When eating sushi, keep these tips in mind:

- Use your fingers to eat sushi and/or sashimi in one bite.
- Shaved ginger is eaten as a palate cleanser. Avoid combining sushi and ginger or ginger and soy sauce.
- Dip sushi fish-side down into soy sauce. To avoid embarrassment, don't shake off the soy sauce after dipping.

Drinking and Toasting

A popular drink is sake, or *nihonshu,* which can be served hot, chilled, or at room temperature. Each person receives a carafe and small cup. The custom is to refill your neighbor's cup, never your own. A helpful phrase when you have had enough to drink is *kekko desu* meaning "I have had enough."

During a meal, after all attendees have been served, the host may offer the first of many toasts. Sometimes the toast is said by all in unison. Honored guests reciprocate toasts. *Kampai* means "cheers."

Tipping and Bill-Paying

Tipping is not customary, and may be considered an insult or a loss of face and refused. A gratuity is included in most restaurants. International hotels may add a 10- to 15-percent service charge to your bill, in which case no additional gratuity is required. If you must tip—say, to reward special service—place the yen in an envelope; do not hand currency to the server directly.

---

[30]Saiko Motonaga, Hitachi High Tech, Tokyo, Japan.

Taboos

Cultural taboos in Japan include:

- Yawning, winking, or whistling in public
- Laughing without a hand vertically placed to cover the mouth and teeth (women only)
- Crossing legs at the ankle or knee (women only) (Instead, keep your feet flat on the floor.)
- Public nose-blowing or throat-clearing
- Using a linen handkerchief (use privately)
- Sticking both chopsticks upright in rice
- Even numbers and the numbers 4, 9, 14, and 44
- Openly displaying currency (Use an envelope instead.)
- Interrupting silence or finishing someone else's sentence
- Using a mobile phone in hotel lobbies, restaurants, trains, or crowded places
- Pouring a drink for yourself, and not your dining companion

Heroes and Sports

Knowing about another country's heroes and sports offers opportunities to incorporate culture-specific references into your conversations and presentations.

Heroes

Some examples of Japanese heroes include the following:

Oda Nobunaga (1534–1582): Samurai, military leader, and warlord. Japanese warrior known for ending the Warring States period. Restored stability in the government, which led his successors to unify all of Japan.

Sakamoto Ryoma (1836–1867): A "founding father" of the modern age in Japan. One of the most famous and influential people in Japanese history, Ryoma played a critical role in the movement to overthrow the Tokugawa shogunate, leading to the restoration of imperial rule and a new era of modernization.

Sports

Sports

Baseball: A national game in Japan with two major leagues, Central and National, each with six teams.

Golf: In Japan, the "king of sports" is astronomically expensive with initiation fees of $1 million U.S. or more, and annual dues of U.S. for a club membership.

Volleyball: A popular national women's sport that provides accolades to participants.

Sumo: A 2,000-year-old practice and the most popular spectator sport in Japan. Six major tournaments occur annually in Tokyo.

Judo: A modern martial art whose objective is to take down the opponent with hands, feet, or weapons.

Kendo: Japanese fencing.

Kyudo: Japanese archery.

Sports Figures

Kōhei Uchimura (1989–present): Artistic gymnast. Often considered the greatest gymnast of all time. Uchimura is a five-time Olympic medalist and a 13-time World Championships medalist.

Mao Asada (1990–present): Competitive figure skater and Olympic silver medalist. Only female figure skater to land three triple axels in one competition. Three-time winner of the World Figure Skating Championship.

Ichiro Suzuki (1973–present): Professional Baseball Outfielder. Former Nippon Professional Baseball player who currently plays for the New York Yankees. He holds Major League Baseball's single-season hit record (262 hits) and has the longest streak of 200-hit seasons in history (10). He's a 10-time All Star and won the 2007 All-Star Game MVP Award.

Eight-Question Framework

This section reviews the framework to which you were introduced earlier in this book. Each of these questions addresses one or more business topics to help you attract and build the relationships upon which today's successful businesses depend.

1. How Do the Japanese Prefer to Act: Individually or as a Group?

A single arrow is easily broken, but not 10 in a bundle.
> The stake that sticks out gets hammered down.
> —*Japanese proverbs*

Spend time in the financial or technology districts of Tokyo or any other major city in Japan, and you are likely to get a sense of déjà vu. This is not Groundhog Day but Salaryman Day! During her most recent visit, Sharon saw many Japanese men identically dressed in dark suits, white shirts, subdued ties, and black shoes, each carrying leather shoulder bags. If ever there was a classic example of group harmony in Japan, it is the way the Japanese dress for business.

The same emphasis on harmony and team spirit—in Japanese, the concept of *wa*—pervades business dealings. Discussing the importance of group consensus in Japanese business, Yuki Ochiai, the vice-consul general of Japan in Houston, explained the concept of *nemawashi* or advance planning. This gardening phrase refers to the importance of pruning and transplanting trees so they don't go into shock.

When applied in a business context, Mr. Ochiai said this process involves explaining a project or idea in a *pre-meeting* with any office colleagues who will be attending the full meeting or later negotiations. *Nemawashi* provides an opportunity for the *roots* of any challenge to surface, be discussed, and watered or smoothed over. The goal of this prior consultation is to achieve group consensus in order to avoid friction, disagreement, and confrontation in the actual meeting. Ever attended a meeting with Japanese businessmen and wondered why you have the sense that their decision has already been made? These preliminary discussions help explain how the Japanese reach consensus before a meeting starts.

Japanese society reflects many of the characteristics of a collectivist society, including placing harmony of the group above the expression of personal opinion. People have a strong sense of shame for losing face. However, Japan is not as collectivistic as most of her Asian neighbors (See Chapter 2, page 15) with an individualism score of 46.

2. How Are Power and Authority Viewed in Japan?

The highest goal is not distinctions, but synthesis and harmony
> —*Alan MacFarlane*

Japan is an *ascription-oriented* culture, meaning that status is based on gender, age, and connections, as well as the universities attended.[31] Most prestigious

---

[31] Foster, *The Global Etiquette Guide to Asia.*

Japanese companies recruit candidates from the best universities, as U.S. American companies do, but according to more than just academic credentials—the Japanese also consider a candidate's social and interpersonal skills. The reason why this is important is two-fold.

First, until relatively recently, joining a Japanese company was seen as a lifetime commitment. Prospective employees were judged on how quickly and easily they were likely to fit into this new social group—the Japanese company or *kaisha*,[32] as opposed to their family group.

Second, Japanese organizations are hierarchical, and maintaining order and structure is crucially important to their management style. *Kaisha*[33] decision-making is a *bottom-up* process in which approval is sought in layers, each a stepping stone to the final decision maker.

As Jerald Wrightsil, CEO of Eco-Merge USA, with 11 years of experience living and working in Japan, advised: "Your direct superior in traditional Japanese companies gives you direction, because they are answering to someone else; the chain of command is mission-critical—don't break the chain of command. You don't really go above your direct supervisor's head. That is just taboo. And you don't try and cozy up with the president before the vice president or before the *kacho* or the *bucho* or the *honbucho*. You've got to work step-by-step."

In some ascription-oriented cultures, power is held *over* people. In others, including many of the Asian countries included in this book, power is *participative*.

For example, as Michael DeCaro, a former Dell executive who lived in Japan, explains: "Western leaders that arrive on the scene and simply announce decisions without getting everyone involved have a much greater likelihood of finding it difficult to achieve their objectives in Asia. For example, in Japan, a position of authority customarily empowers a leader to take the initiative for developing and gaining consensus as to what the ultimate decision will be."

This means that Westerners should have patience.

3. How Do the Japanese Compare Rules and Relationships?

I believe most international business executives would agree that, with the Japanese model, there is no contract agreement without a relationship, and that it may take years to develop.

— *Thomas Conry, International Advisor in Public Affairs, Communications & Protocol*

---

[32] Noboru Yoshimura and Philip Anderson, *Inside the Kaisha: Demystifying Japanese Business Behavior* (Boston: Harvard Business School Press, 1997).
[33] Ibid.

On March 11, 2011, Japan experienced the most powerful earthquake in its history, followed by a tsunami that damaged several nuclear reactors, devastated millions of homes, and killed almost 16,000 people.[34] Although it represents only 1/400th of the world's land mass, the Japanese archipelago includes a full tenth of the world's active volcanoes (including the spectacular Mt. Fuji).[35] Some 1,500 seismic events—each with the potential to result in earthquakes, tsunamis, and typhoons—occur there every year.[36]

When you consider this in light of the fact that Japan's population density (337 people per square mile) is ten times that of the U.S. (32 people per square mile) and that 91 percent of people in Japan live in urban areas, you begin to get a sense of the mindset that shapes Japanese lives—including business. Indeed, you cannot truly understand how people think and behave until you consider the environment in which they live. The concept of group harmony is so important in Japan largely because of the natural instabilities with which the Japanese live every day.

This also helps explain why establishing trust in long-term relationships is crucial for the Japanese—that trust reduces business risk, and there are few business risks the Japanese *can* control. As formal and rule-oriented as the Japanese tend to be, trusted relationships built over a long period of time are valued. Japan is 'one of the most uncertainty-avoiding countries on earth[37]' with a high ranking of 92 in uncertainty avoidance, and is a culture that tries to avoid risks.[38]

Failing to appreciate this Japanese aversion to risk while seeking a quick return on an investment is one of the biggest mistakes Westerners make.

Jerald Wrightsil offers this advice: "Developing a relationship, whether it's at the entry level or mid-level, may mean years of not doing anything. I've gone back and forth sometimes with no return on my investment, at least from a travel perspective, just to visit my colleagues—not necessarily for karaoke but maybe yakitori and always bringing an *omiyage* (honored gift) with me. I'll stop by just to say, 'Good to see you. If you guys ever need . . .'

"Then, when I do call and ask 'What do you think about this?' they will be prepared to talk further. They trust me because I have made the effort to understand their practices. Most of the time you don't get to develop a relationship at the senior level until you can gain their trust by your performance."

---

[34] "2011 Japan Earthquake—Tsunami Fast Facts," CNN World, July 11, 2014, www.cnn.com /2013/07/17/world/asia/japan-earthquake---tsunami-fast-facts (accessed November 21, 2014).
[35] "Japan's Geography," AsianInfo.org, www.asianinfo.org/asianinfo/japan/geography.htm #SVOLCANOES%20AND%20EARTHQUAKE (accessed November 21, 2014).
[36] CIA, *The World Factbook*, "Japan," www.cia.gov/library/publications/the-world-factbook /geos/ja.html (accessed November 21, 2014).
[37] The Hofstede Center, "What About Japan," http://geert-hofstede.com/japan.html (accessed November 20, 2014).
[38] Milena Bočánková, *Intercultural Communication: Typical Features of the Czech, British, American, Japanese, Chinese and Arab Cultures* (Praha: Oeconomica, 2010).

He adds, "Even if you miss the mark, if you have the right prior relationship you will still have the relationship and may get a second opportunity. But without that foundation, you don't get a second chance most of the time."

This may mean taking on a small project for your Japanese customers or partners *without* having a contract in place beforehand. This can seem counter-intuitive to the Western mindset, which tends to believe that relationship-building should occur only during the course of making money. Certainly the Japanese are conscious of the fact that Westerners are seeking to make money, just as the Japanese themselves are when operating overseas, but, from a Japanese perspective, this doesn't constitute relationship-building—it's superficial.

Jinji-ido

Jinji-ido (jeen-jee-e-doe). Another key factor to be aware of when developing business relationships in Japan is the concept of *jinji-ido*. In order to help their employees gain broader experience, most Japanese organizations transfer people from one area of the business to another every few years. This practice encourages relationship-building among employees, who can expect at some point to be working with a different group of colleagues. But it also means being prepared to meet and develop deep bonds of trust and respect for western counterparts, so that successful alliances may continue to flourish.

4. How Do Japanese Business People Regard Time?

Decision making may seem slow due to the time involved with consensus building; implementation occurs rapidly.

—*Joel Momberger*

Arriving 30 minutes early for her appointment to interview an executive at a high-tech company in Tokyo, Sharon sat in the lobby—without being announced—in order to observe and listen. She and Thomas Conry, a 23-year veteran of JETRO, the Japan External Trade Organization, had recently had a discussion about the ways the Japanese view time. Thomas had pointed out the tendency of Japanese management to wait until the exact time of an appointment to receive a guest, regardless of whether they were free to meet earlier.

At 11:50, the floodgates opened: For the next 10 minutes, workers began departing the company elevator in a steady stream. Sharon's meeting began promptly at noon and lasted exactly 60 minutes (possibly allowing her interviewee a half hour nap at her desk before resuming work). This kind of routine and punctuality occurs on a daily basis in the Japanese business environment.

The Japanese put a tremendous amount of effort into meetings, negotiations, and long-term planning; this is perhaps not surprising in a country where time is considered a crucial part of the smooth running of everyday life.[39]

As the senior business development manager of a Fortune 500 manufacturer in Tokyo explained, "The Japanese are highly structured on their budgets. Their fiscal year runs April through March. I can't forecast anything for my company in Japan until roughly mid-February to March, which is when they start talking to you. Other than that, if it's not in the budget, there is unlikely to be any more business unless you come in with something revolutionary that gives them a huge ROI and saves them a ton of money."

He illustrated the relationship between time and commitment in Japan by relating how he and his manager tried to give the purchasing director of an electronics company some disappointing news. The Japanese director was unequivocal: "This is what you've committed to do on these tools. If they're not delivered, you're going to impact my revenue." The director's underlying message was that if the supplier didn't meet the deadlines, future orders would go to another company.

His strategy? "If I can't commit to that, I don't open my mouth. I just say, 'We'll work on it.' But the minute I say, 'I commit to giving you these systems by this date. You will have them,' my word is considered my bond. Unless some major catastrophe justifies missing that date, the Japanese are not going to be willing to do business with you in the future unless they absolutely have to. When you commit to something with the Japanese, unless an act of God delays it, you have to meet your commitments."

Time, commitment, and planning are important here. The Japanese prepare well in advance, and their relationship to time is another example of their risk-averse mindset. If you commit to delivery at a certain time and don't meet your obligations, the impact on their fiscal year may be felt throughout their organization.

Punctuality, lateness, and shame

When asked about the Japanese attitude toward punctuality, Mr. Motokatsu Sunagawa, CEO of Eco-Merge Philippines, said: "We have been taught to respect punctuality since childhood. Teachers were always telling us, 'It is shame to be late.' Then, when we become adults, we know that time is money. The reason why most Japanese businesspeople stress the importance of punctuality is because we associate being late with shame."

---

[39] Hodge, *Global Smarts*.

5. How Direct Is Communication in Japan?

"It is frequently the most obvious and taken for granted and therefore least studied aspects of culture that influence behavior in the deepest and most subtle ways."
—*Edward T. Hall*, Beyond Culture

A.L., who is experienced in negotiating business in Japan, recently accompanied a client on a trip to Tokyo to lay out a potential business deal with a major Japanese organization. Prior to the trip, A.L. outlined for his client some of the basic cultural differences between the U.S. and Japan, such as the fact that the Japanese observe business etiquette and prefer long-term business relationships. A.L. also emphasized the importance of seating in meetings, in addition to other, more general advice on the Japanese concept of *kao tateru* or *saving face*. In the U.S., in a traditional corporate structure, A.L.'s client could expect to sit at the head of the table to emphasize his position of power as CEO, but A.L. encouraged him to sit elsewhere on their trip to Japan. During the meeting, A.L. advised, the client should sit in the middle of the table so as to facilitate communication with his Japanese counterpart, who would be seated across from him.

At the meeting, after business cards were exchanged, the U.S. client, ignoring A.L.'s advice, sat down at the head of the table.

This was strikes one through three in a single move. Luckily A.L., who is fluent in Japanese, gave the necessary apologies for this inappropriate behavior. The meeting continued, with A.L. seated in the position his client should have taken. All went well—until the next blooper.

As A.L. explained: "In Japanese culture, if your direct contact invites you to dinner after the meeting that is a good sign. It signals that the Japanese are willing to take business dealings to the next level, to 'consummate the relationship,' so to speak."

When the Japanese president extended a dinner invitation, then, the U.S. CEO should have been excited. Instead, he impolitely declined the offer, saying that he was jet-lagged and in any case wanted to go to dinner with other Japanese business associates. A.L.'s reaction was unequivocal: "I thought, wow, I can't fix that one!"

From that point, the deal was dead in the water, despite the fact that the U.S. company had something the Japanese wanted, *and* the Japanese knew it would mean an 80-percent return on their investment.

A.L. was not able to help his client recover from that cultural faux pas because the CEO stubbornly focused on what *he* wanted and gave no consideration to the concepts of face, respect, and honor that are so important to Japanese communication.

The Japanese consider saying *no* to be impolite, preferring instead to use words like *chaigau* or *chigau masu,* which mean *not quite* or *not exactly.* If you ever hear your Japanese counterpart say *kangaete okimasu*[40] ("I'll think about it") during negotiations, you can be almost certain he is saying *no*.

In A.L.'s case, his U.S. CEO client was never told directly that his proposal was unsuccessful. But A.L.'s strong ties with his Japanese counterpart, achieved over many years, enabled him to read between the lines during their post-meeting one-on-one dinner and drinks. The CEO's plan did not move forward.

6. How Formal or Informal Do Business People in Japan Tend to Be?

"My demeanor is always formal in approaching Japanese individuals, and I am reluctant to respond informally until the relationship has developed."
— *Thomas Conry, International Advisor in Public Affairs, Communications & Protocol*

In Japan, the focus on *Wa*, means harmonious, good feelings; the Japanese are formal yet warm. If you've ever been in a Japanese taxi, you may have noticed that the seating of passengers was different than the seating in a western taxi. In Japan, the customer is seated directly behind the driver because it is the safest position in the event of an accident. With groups, the most important visitor (the VIP) sits behind the driver, the second most important sits next to the VIP, and the host sits closest to the driver so he can more easily pay. This exemplifies the formality of Japanese culture, especially where the comfort and safety of customers are concerned.

Formality and the strong emphasis on respect ensures the ongoing homogeneity of Japanese culture. For example, as Ms. Saiko Motonaga of Hitachi High-Tech in Tokyo pointed out, after beginning her employment, she and the other new recruits participated in a business manners course to ensure they could always deliver a high level of service and comfort to customers. The Japanese are the ultimate diplomats, speaking with others in neutral terms (*tatemae*), regardless of whether they hold a different opinion privately (*honne*).[41]

Be aware that the Japanese will take your business manners into consideration *before* they will do business with you. This includes your abilities to listen with focus during discussions, to take copious notes, and to accept silences with reflection rather than trying to fill them. Demonstrating gracious social skills

---

[40]Boye Lafayette De Mente, *Japanese Etiquette & Ethics in Business* 6th ed. (Lincolnwood, IL: NTC Publishing Group, 1994).
[41]Sue Shinomiya and Brian Szepkouski, *Business Passport to Japan*, Revised and updated edition (Berkeley, CA: Stone Bridge Press, 2008).

and humility are highly valued. These skills include diplomatically cooperating with colleagues, observing silence, and referring to *our company* instead of *my company me* or *I*.

As Thomas Conry pointed out: "My demeanor is always formal in approaching Japanese individuals and I am reluctant to respond informally until the relationship has developed. For example, I would never presume to use the first name of a Japanese contact unless I was specifically invited to do so, and it's often when the individual has acquired a Western name to use, like 'Ken,' or has abbreviated his or her name to a nickname status. Initial introductions are usually kept formal. Socialization can be the path to an informal context."

7. *How Aligned Are Japanese Social and Business Lives?*

We do not work together with anyone we cannot trust as a *person*.
— *Mr. Motokatsu Sunagawa, CEO, Eco-Merge Philippines*

Japanese social and business lives reflect strict rules of etiquette and behavior. Their deeply ingrained social system prevents colleagues from showing individuality or developing personal relationships during office hours. To offset this, the Japanese allow for short *rule-breaking* times known as *bureiko* (*without etiquette* or *informal parties*). These times include New Year's celebrations, athletic events, and after-hours drinking sessions.

After-hours socializing can be especially important for Western or international business people, who can be viewed as *gaijin* (a somewhat derogatory word meaning *outsiders* or *non-Japanese*) or *gaijin-no kata* (a more polite term meaning *foreign-person*). The Japanese phrase *hame wo hazusu* means to 'pull out all of the stops' by 'letting one's hair down' or in other words to take part in unrestrained nighttime drinking with work colleagues. If you cannot *hame wo hazusu*, you may be thought of as untrustworthy, arrogant, inauthentic, or lacking in sincerity.

This presented a challenge for one senior development manager who was traveling to Japan with an associate. His story highlights the importance of socializing in developing deep business relationships:

"I was working with a Japanese conglomerate. There were fifteen Japanese and the two of us at dinner. My colleague was sitting next to me with hot tea due to an alcohol allergy; his face would flush and he'd pass out. Everybody else was drinking, toasting, and smoking cigarettes. My colleague was just sitting there like a bump on a log; he didn't want to be there. So, my customer gravitated toward me and I created a relationship. But they didn't talk to my colleague, who's a Ph.D. and a hundred times smarter than me in this technology."

The difference in approach had a significant impact. The senior business development manager's Japanese colleagues later greeted him with a huge smile "Oh, we had a great time at the steakhouse. Oh, I remember that. Great to see you again!" One night out was all it took to get the relationship started. His colleague, on the other hand, was greeted with a brief "Hello."

When socializing, however, remember to consider what level in the organization you're working with. CEOs are unlikely to join in on *hame wo hazusu*. "If you're traveling to Japan and interact at the director level with decision makers, you have to be aware of what you're getting into because lack of discretion could impede your customer relationship. It could be a simple dinner with a nice bottle of wine when you talk about your family life and social structure and then you go back to your hotel. Or, you could be dragged out later where it gets a little more crazy and rowdy. You need to know what you can expect, because lack of foresight could impede your success," the senior development manager told us.

8. How Is the Concept of Women in Business Handled in Japan?

When visiting Japan as a female business executive or lead negotiator, emphasize your standing within your own company hierarchy by asking your male team members to follow your lead, stand back and wait to enter the room after you have done so.
—*Reina Sawada*

Japanese women are increasingly making their mark in the workforce, a sign that government efforts to help working mothers have been successful.[42] Indeed, Prime Minister Shinzo Abe has said he is determined to make better use of Japan's potential female workforce. Additionally, the U.S. Ambassador to Japan, Caroline Kennedy, is known as a strong supporter of women's rights.

Through welcome changes like these, international businesswomen can expect to succeed in Japan and to enjoy the experience. Reina Sawada of Showcase-tv in Tokyo emphasizes the importance of research in smoothing your path to success: "An awareness of the past and current status of women in Japanese business culture is important. It is essential to research your Japanese business contacts' background before trying to cultivate those connections. Knowing about the people you may be asking to act as intermediaries and accompany you to meetings and negotiations is a mark of respect. Learning a few Japanese greetings will be appreciated and helps break the ice."

---

[42]"More Women Staying on the Job in Japan," Nikkei Asian Review, January 21, 2014, http://asia.nikkei.com/Politics-Economy/Economy/More-women-staying-on-the-job-in-Japan.

Another key point women travelers should be aware of is the Japanese culture's adherence to certain protocols and etiquette. Says Arii Aoi: "When visiting Japan as a female business executive or lead negotiator, emphasize your standing within your own company hierarchy by asking your male team members to follow your lead, stand back and wait to enter the room after you have done so. This will communicate your elevated position to your Japanese hosts. Be sure that you maintain that status by avoiding actions associated with a lower status, such as passing out materials or serving coffee."

Finally, as Ms. Aoi and Ms. Sawada both reiterated, women in Japan visibly signal credibility through their attire, and also maintain harmony among their peers. Saiko Motonaga of Hitachi High-Tech in Tokyo, told Sharon that professional appearance in Japan is all about harmonizing. High, thin, or stiletto heels are *not appreciated* in the Japanese business world and vivid colors are *too surprising* for the Japanese. Be sure to read and follow the advice given in the Business Dress/Appearance section of this chapter for ways to make a good first impression.

Cultural Summary

Here are some key points to remember:

- Japanese communication is subtle, almost an art form. It is what cultural anthropologists describe as *high context,* meaning that it asks you to 'read between the lines' of speech and body language. The Japanese tend to dislike the straightforward, direct communication style of U.S. Americans and other Westerners.
- Silence is equated with wisdom, judgment, and self-control. When the Japanese counterpart is silent and leaning back with their eyes closed, they are deeply contemplating.
- The Japanese in larger *kaisha* will walk away from desirable business deals, even those guaranteeing huge returns on investment, if they believe the relationship is not respectful or long-term.

Self-Awareness Profile

This simple exercise prompts you to self-assess where you currently stand on topics related to the eight-question framework and *compare* this with the country culture. This visual will help you discover the extent to which you may need to adapt your current mindset and behavior to develop more robust business

relationships. For details on how to complete this graphic, see the instructions given in the Introduction on pages xviii–xix.

Consider copying the eight-question Profile or using a pencil so that you can see, over time, how you have adjusted your cultural mindset. You might also wish to create unique graphics related to each of the businesses you work with, as these cultural positions vary depending upon geographic location, industry, generational factors, and corporate profile.

Q1: What is your preferred way of doing business?

As an individual making autonomous decisions   **As a team member who seeks group consensus**

      1   2   3   4   **5**   6

Q2: How comfortable are you in hierarchies in which power is distributed unequally?

Very uncomfortable   **Very comfortable**

      1   2   **3**   4   5   6

Q3: How closely do you follow rules and obey the law?

Almost always   **It depends**

      1   **2**   3   4   5   6

Q4: What is your general attitude toward time?

I prefer agendas, schedules, planning   **I prefer flexibility, fluidity without scheduling**

      1   2   3   4   5   6

Q5: What is your preferred way to communicate?

Very diplomatically   **Very candidly**

    1   2   3   4   5   6

Q6: What is your interpersonal style or level of formality in business interactions?

Very formal   **Very informal**

    1   2   3   4   5   6

Q7: What is your view on socializing within business?

A waste of time   **Essential**

    1   2   3   4   5   **6**

Q8: Should a woman defer to a man as the lead, if winning business in a certain culture depended on it?

Never   **Yes, absolutely**

    1   2   3   4   5   **6**

9 | Malaysia

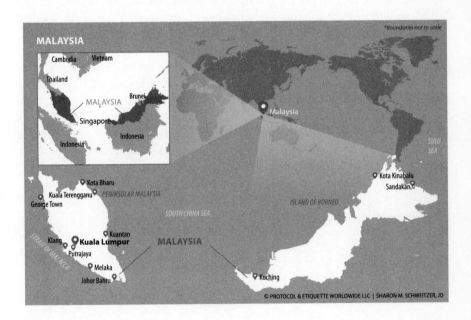

Every one of us must respect each other's rights and feelings, be tolerant of each other's religions, customs, and habits.

—Tunku Abdul Rahman Putra, First Prime Minister of Malaysia

Introduction

Malaysia has many unique competitive advantages in Southeast Asia, with its land mass and capacity for the expansion of corporate and manufacturing projects. The magnificent dual Petronas Towers in Kuala Lumpur were an important project of former Prime Minister Dr. Mahathir bin Mohamad and are Malaysia's signature landmark worldwide.

During the 20 years after independence from Britain in 1957, Malaysia was one of the early *Asian Tigers*, and its economy developed into one of the fastest-growing in the region. The population comprises some of the world's oldest civilizations: the Bumiputra (including Malays, Dayaks, Ibans, Kadazans and Muruts), Chinese, and Indians.[1] Although the constitution generally allows for religious freedom, more than 60 percent of the country's population practices the Islamic religion. Malays are Muslim by definition, and the official religion of Malaysia is Islam.[2]

For those in the oil and gas business, A.T. Kearney's Global Services Location Index, which ranks the top 50 countries worldwide in their attractiveness as potential locations for offshore services, has placed Malaysia as number three since the inception of the index in 2004.[3]

In the Economist Intelligence Unit's 2012 report, *Hot Spots: Benchmarking Global City Competitiveness*, Kuala Lumpur was noted as the top-ranked emerging-market city.[4]

Malaysia has also become a destination for wealthy Asians to retire and vacation in summer, acquiring a *second home*, according to the Malaysian Investment Development Authority.[5]

Quiz

How much do you know about Malaysia? Answer the following questions as True or False to test your knowledge. (The Answer Key at the bottom includes page numbers that refer to the topic.)

---

[1] Cultural Detective, www.culturaldetective.com (accessed January 16, 2015).
[2] Ibid.
[3] A.T. Kearney, *Global Services Location Index 2014*, www.atkearney.com/research-studies/global-services-location-index (accessed November 17, 2014).
[4] Economist Intelligence Unit, *Hot Spots: Benchmarking Global City Competitiveness*, January 2012, www.citigroup.com/citi/citiforcities/pdfs/eiu_hotspots_2012.pdf (accessed November 17, 2014).
[5] Malaysian Investment Development Authority, www.mida.gov.my/home (accessed November 17, 2014).

_____1. One of Malaysia's financial systems follows Islamic or *Sharī'ah*[6] law to provide financial services to Muslims worldwide.

_____2. During Ramadan Muslims are expected to fast from dawn to dusk.

_____3. During Ramadan, Muslims break their fast after sunset with a meal called *Iftar*.

_____4. The official religion or belief system is Islam.

_____5. Culturally, it is acceptable to eat and pass food with the left hand; the right is considered unclean.

_____6. Malaysians value personal contact and building a relationship before negotiating a deal.

_____7. In 2015, Malaysia will chair ASEAN.

_____8. *Halal* foods are those prepared according to Islamic law.

_____9. The constitution generally allows for religious freedom.

_____10. Suitable gifts include money, liquor, and frangipani flowers.

Answer Key: 1. T (p. 200); **2. T (p.** 201); **3. T (p.** 201); **4. T (p.** 187); **5. F (p.** 196–197); **6. T (p.** 194); **7. T (p.** 184); **8. T (p.** 196); **9. T (p.** 182); **10. F (p.** 192).

Country Basics

This section provides key knowledge in an easy-to-read format to help you quickly grasp some of the basics necessary to navigate this culture.

Historical Timeline

A critical way to show respect for another person's culture is to have knowledge of their country's history and current affairs. Table 9.1 on page 184 outlines a few key events related to Malaysia, together with concurrent world events.[7]

---

[6]Encyclopedia Britannica, "Shari'ah," last updated November 3, 2014, www.britannica.com/EBchecked/topic/538793/Shariah (accessed November 17, 2014).

[7]Malaysia Timeline Sources: Bernard Grun, *The Timetables of History*, (New York: Touchstone Press, 2005); BBC News Asia, "Malaysia Profile: Timeline," 4th ed. last updated November 13, 2014, www.bbc.com/news/world-asia-pacific-15391762 (accessed November 17, 2014); People's Information Center, Government of Malaysia, "Summary of the History of Malaysia," last updated November 17, 2014, pmr.penerangan.gov.my/index.php/profil-malaysia/7954-ringkasan-sejarah-malaysia.html (accessed November 17, 2014); and Craig A. Lockard, "Malaysia," Encyclopedia Britannica, November 4, 2013, www.britannica.com/EBchecked/topic/359754/Malaysia/279192/Malaysia-from-independence-to-c-2000 (accessed November 17, 2014).

Table 9.1   Key Historical Events

Period/ Dates	Description/Events	World Events
ca. 1400	Foundation of Malacca Sultanate brings golden age for the Malay people.	Timurid dynasty founded in Asia by the Turko-Mongol, Timur.
1948	British–ruled Malayan territories unify.	World Health Organization established by the UN.
1957	Federation of Malaya achieves independence from Britain.	U.S.S.R. launches Sputnik I and II, the first satellites.
2002	New immigration laws prompt exodus of foreign workers.	Taiwan officially joins the World Trade Organization, as Chinese Taipei.
2007	Malaysia, Indonesia, and Brunei sign rainforest protection agreement.	Global stock markets plummet.
2009	Malaysia limits foreign workers and unveils a $16 billion stimulus plan.	China adopts Hanyu Pinyin as its official Chinese Romanization.
2011	Construction of mass rapid transit system begins in Kuala Lumpur.	The world population reaches 7 billion inhabitants according to the United Nations.
2012	Official coronation of King Tuanku Abdul Halim Mu'adzam Shah.	NASA's *Curiosity* rover successfully lands on Mars.
2013	The ruling National Front coalition retains power in national elections.	Cardinal Bergoglio of Argentina elected pope, the first from the Americas.
2014	Malaysia and Turkey sign Free Trade Agreement.	The XXII Olympic Winter Games take place in Sochi, Russia.
2015	Malaysia is scheduled to be ASEAN chair.	Myanmar's presidential elections scheduled.
2016	Selection of king scheduled.	Japan's legislative elections and the presidential elections of Taiwan, the Philippines, and the U.S. are scheduled.
2018	Legislative elections scheduled.	China's presidential elections and PyeongChang, South Korea, to host the XXIII Olympic Winter Games.

Full Country Name and Location

Malaysia is approximately the size of Norway or the State of New Mexico in the U.S. It is divided into two distinct regions. Peninsular Malaysia shares a land border with Thailand, with the Strait of Malacca to the west, and the South China Sea to the east. East Malaysia is located on the northern one-third of the island of Borneo, sharing land borders with Indonesia and Brunei. It is surrounded by the South China Sea, the Sulu Sea, and the Celebes Sea.

Government/Political Structure

Malaysia is a constitutional monarchy. The latest constitution became effective after 1957 independence from British colonial rule. Parliament meets in Kuala Lumpur, the capital city. The King serves as head of state and is elected from a pool of hereditary rulers every five years. The head of government is the Prime Minister, elected from the House of Representatives. The last national elections were held on May 5, 2013; the next elections are scheduled for 2018.

Population and Economic Centers

The population of Malaysia is approximately 30.1 million, according to the *CIA World Factbook*. The country is divided into 13 states and three federal territories (Kuala Lumpur, Labuan, and Putrajaya), with 72.8 percent living in urban areas.[8]

The population percentages are: Malays (Bumiputeras) (50.1 percent), Chinese (22.6 percent), Indigenous (11.8 percent), Indian (6.7 percent), and small numbers of other groups (0.7 percent). About 8.2 percent of the population is made up of noncitizens.[9]

The business centers and populations are outlined in Table 9.2 on page 186.[10]

---

[8]CIA, *The World Factbook*, "Malaysia," www.cia.gov/library/publications/the-world-factbook /geos/my.html (accessed November 15, 2014).
[9]Ibid.
[10]Department of Statistics Malaysia, "Population Distribution by Local Authority Areas and Mukims, 2010," http://statistics.gov.my/portal/index.php?option=com_content&view=article &id=1354&Itemid=111&lang=en (accessed November 17, 2014).

Table 9.2   Major Business Centers

Business Centers	Population (millions)
George Town	0.2
Johor Bahru	1.3
Klang	0.8
Kota Bharu	0.5
Kota Kinabalu	0.5
Kuala Lumpur (capital)	1.6
Kuala Terengganu	0.3
Kuantan	0.4
Kuching	0.6
Melaka	0.5
Putrajaya	0.07
Sandakan	0.4

Economy

Malaysia is ranked 18th out of 189 economies in terms of ease of doing business, according to the World Bank Group's *Doing Business 2015* report.[11] Its 2013 GDP was ranked 35th by the World Bank,[12] and the composition of its GDP by sector was services (48.1 percent), industry (40.6 percent), and agriculture (11.2 percent).[13]

Corruption Perceptions Index

Malaysia ranked 53rd least corrupt out of 177 countries and territories with a score of 50 out of 100.[14] This annual index, compiled by Transparency International, measures perceived levels of public sector corruption. The

[11]World Bank Group, *Doing Business 2015* (October 29, 2014): 4, www.doingbusiness.org/~/media/GIAWB/Doing%20Business/Documents/Annual-Reports/English/DB15-Full-Report.pdf.

[12]The World Bank, Data, GDP Ranking, "Gross Domestic Product Ranking Table," last updated September 24, 2014, http://data.worldbank.org/data-catalog/GDP-ranking-table (accessed November 15, 2014).

[13]CIA, *The World Factbook*, "Malaysia," www.cia.gov/library/publications/the-world-factbook/geos/my.html (accessed November 15, 2014).

[14]Transparency International, "Corruption Perceptions Index 2013," www.transparency.org/cpi2013/results (accessed November 11, 2014).

Malaysian Anti-Corruption Commission is the anti-corruption agency that conducts investigations in Malaysia.

Human Development Index

Malaysia ranked 62nd out of 187 countries and territories.[15] The HDI, compiled by the United Nations Development Programme, is a composite index of life expectancy, education, and income statistics.

Global Gender Gap Index

Malaysia ranked 107th out of 142 countries in terms of gender equality with a score of 0.6520.[16] This annual index, compiled by the World Economic Forum, assesses gender gaps based on economic, political, educational, and health-based criteria.

Climate

The climate is tropical, with no distinct seasons. Weather is hot and humid throughout the year, with two monsoon seasons: May to September and November to March.

Languages

Bahasa Melayu, or Bahasa Malaysia, is the official language. English is widely spoken. Other languages include Chinese (Mandarin, Cantonese, Hokkien, Hakka, Hainan, and Foochow), Tamil, Hindi, Telugu, Malayalam, Panjabi, Thai, and indigenous languages (Iban, Kadazan).

Belief Systems, Philosophies, and Religions

The country breakdown is as follows: Islam (61.3 percent), Buddhist (19.8 percent), Christian (9.2 percent), Hindu (6.3 percent), Chinese

[15]United Nations Development Programme, *Human Development Report 2014*, 160–163, http://hdr.undp.org/sites/default/files/hdr14-report-en-1.pdf, (accessed November 11, 2014).
[16]World Economic Forum, *The Global Gender Gap Report 2014*, 8–9, www3.weforum.org/docs/GGGR14/GGGR_CompleteReport_2014.pdf (accessed November 11, 2014).

traditional (1.3 percent), other (0.4 percent), none (0.8 percent), unspecified (1 percent) (2010 est.).[17]

For an overview of belief systems, philosophies, and religions, please refer to Chapter 4, pages 64–65.

Time Zones/Daylight Savings

Malaysia has a single time zone, Malaysia Time (MYT). Malaysia is eight hours ahead of GMT (Greenwich Mean Time)/UTC (Coordinated Universal Time). It does not operate under Daylight Savings.

It is 13 hours ahead of U.S. Eastern Standard Time (12 hours ahead in Daylight Savings Time). See www.timeanddate.com/worldclock.

To calculate time in Malaysia, add eight hours to UTC/GMT.

Telephone Country Code and Internet Suffix

The Malaysian telephone country code is 60, and the Internet suffix is .my.

Currency

The currency in Malaysia is the ringgit (MYR). One ringgit is divided into 100 sen.

Business Culture, Etiquette, and Customs

This section covers business culture, etiquette, and customs.

Malaysia has significant Chinese and Indian populations. Please refer to Chapter 5 (China) and Chapter 7 (India).

Fiscal Year

The Malaysian fiscal year runs from January 1 to December 31. Dates are written day, month, year; April 10, 2020 is 10/4/2020.

---

[17]CIA, *The World Factbook*, "Malaysia," www.cia.gov/library/publications/the-world-factbook/geos/my.html (accessed November 15, 2014).

Working Week

General business hours are observed in most regions, including the capital, Kuala Lumpur. The structure of the Malaysian work week is outlined in Table 9.3.

Some businesses, most government offices, and many banks are open Saturday mornings from 8:30 to 12:00. Muslims working in these regions take a two-hour break on Fridays to attend a mosque.

Table 9.3   The Malaysian Working Schedule

Industry	Business Hours	Days of the Week
Businesses	08:00–17:00	Monday–Friday
Government	08:30–16:45	Monday–Friday
Banks	09:00–15:00	Monday–Friday

Traditional Islamic Working Week

The traditional Islamic work schedule in Table 9.4 is observed in the Malaysian states of Perlis, Kedah, Kelantan, Terengganu, and Johor (all on the peninsula) in order to preserve Friday as the Islamic Holy Day.

Some businesses, most government offices, and many banks are open a half-day on Thursday from 8:30 to 12:00.

Table 9.4   The Traditional Islamic Working Schedule

Industry	Business Hours	Days of the Week
Businesses	08:00–17:00	Saturday–Wednesday
Government	08:30–16:45	Saturday–Wednesday
Banks	09:00–15:00	Saturday–Wednesday

Holidays and Festivals

Some Malaysian holidays are determined by the lunar calendar, and therefore change from year to year. Floating holidays are designated in Table 9.5 on page 190 with an asterisk. On specific holidays, an office may remain open with

Table 9.5   Malaysian Holidays and Festivals

Date	Name
January 1	New Year's Day
12th day, 3rd month of the Islamic calendar	*Maulidur Rasul* (The Prophet Muhammad's Birthday)*
January/February	Chinese New Year*
February 1	Kuala Lumpur City Day
May 1	Labor Day
May	*Wesak* Day (celebration of the birth of Buddha)*
First Saturday in June	Birthday of Monarch Agong
June 5	King's Birthday
9th month of the Islamic calendar	Ramadan*
1st day, 10th month of the Islamic calendar	*Hari Raya Puasa* (Feast of Breaking the Fast)*
August 31	National Day
10th day, 5th month of the Islamic calendar	*Hari Raya Haji* (Feast of the Sacrifice)*
1st day of the Islamic calendar	*Awal Muharram* (Islamic New Year)*
October/November	*Deepavali* (Hindu festival)*
December 25	Christmas Day

limited staff. Check with your embassy or trade office before you plan your travel.

   March through July is the best time for business trips. Avoid making appointments for dates during Ramadan, Chinese New Year, and Christmas.

Business Dress/Appearance

Lightweight cotton and linen fabrics are recommended for the year-round hot, humid weather. Attire is conservative and formal. Men wear suits and ties or light-colored shirts with a tie and dress trousers for less formal events. Women wear suits or business dresses, or blouses and skirts or slacks for less-formal events. Revealing clothing such as sleeveless blouses, skirts above the knee, and shorts are never worn. Acceptable casual clothing includes jeans, open collar or golf shirts with slacks for men, and blouses with pants or skirts for women.

Avoid yellow colors reserved for royalty.[18] The *hijab*, a Muslim head covering or scarf representing modesty, purity, humility, and piety, is not required for non–Muslim women in business meetings.

News Sources

Popular news sources in Malaysia include:

- *New Straits Times*: www.nst.com.my
- *The Star*: www.thestar.com.my
- *The Sun*: www.thesundaily.my
- *The Malay Mail*: www.themalaymailonline.com
- *The Malaysian Insider*: www.themalaysianinsider.com

Business Cards

The government uses business cards printed with *Bahasa Melayu*, the official language of Malaysia. When conducting business with Malaysian Chinese, print Mandarin on your card. An exchange of cards occurs upon introduction. The formal custom is to give and receive cards with both hands, or the right hand but not the left. Study the card and place it on the table, in a portfolio, or card case.

Technology

According to Akamai Technology's *State of the Internet Report*, Malaysia has the 74th fastest average Internet connection speed in the world.[19] Latest figures

---

[18]Mary Bosrock, *Asian Business Customs & Manners: A Country-by-Country Guide* (New York: Meadowbrook Press, 2007); Ann Marie Sabath, *International Business Etiquette: Asia & The Pacific Rim* (Lincoln, NE: ASJA Press, 1999, 2002); Jeanette S. Martin and Lillian H. Chaney, *Passport to Success: The Essential Guide to Business Culture and Customs in America's Largest Trading Partners* (Westport, CT: Praeger, 2009).

[19]Akamai Technologies, "State of the Internet Q4 2013," April 2014, www.akamai.com/dl/akamai/akamai-soti-q413.pdf?WT.mc_id=soti_Q413 (accessed November 17, 2014).

rank Malaysia 26th in the world for the number of Internet users,[20] and 53rd globally for the number of Internet hosts.[21]

Gifts

Gifts are appreciated and exchanged after a relationship has been established, not at first meetings. Give and receive gifts with both hands or the right hand only. Send a thank-you note and reciprocate with an equal gift.

Ideas for business gifts include company logo items, pens, desk accessories, and books. If invited to a home, bring boxed fruit or sweets. Avoid money; sharp objects (these indicate a severing of ties); liquor; gifts that depict pigs or canines (these are Muslim taboos); leather gifts (Indians consider cows sacred); and local frangipani flowers (they represent death). Wrap gifts in pink or red (these colors indicate good luck) or bright colors (they represent happiness). Avoid white or black (they symbolize mourning) and yellow (it is reserved for royalty).

"Corporate gift-giving with the international company's logo is common. The gift should be simple and not high-value so it will not be viewed as a bribe—for example, Apple iPhones and branded watches are a no-no," one Malaysian Airlines executive said.

Introductions, Greetings, Personal Space, and Eye Contact

Malaysia's ethnic groups include Chinese (see also Chapter 5 on China), and Indians (see also Chapter 7 on India). See the respective chapters for further greeting information regarding these groups.

Malaysian males greet each other by shaking hands and bowing slightly. In the Muslim world, physical contact with the opposite sex is avoided, including inter-gender hand shaking. Younger or international Muslims may shake hands with everyone, saying "*Selamat.*" Greetings to someone of the opposite sex may include a head bow (*salaam*) with placement of the right hand on the left side of the chest (signifying "I greet you from my heart") while saying *Selamat.*

---

[20]CIA, *The World Factbook*, "Country Comparison: Internet Users," information dated 2009, www.cia.gov/library/publications/the-world-factbook/rankorder/2153rank.html (accessed November 17, 2014).

[21]CIA, *The World Factbook*, "Country Comparison: Internet Hosts," information dated 2009, www.cia.gov/library/publications/the-world-factbook/rankorder/2184rank.html (accessed November 17, 2014).

A Muslim woman wearing the *hijab* may show her hand to shake hands with another woman.

Useful Phrases

See Table 9.6 for helpful phrases when traveling in Malaysia.

Table 9.6   Useful Phrases for Malaysian Travel

English	Bahasa Melayu	Pronunciation
Good morning	*Selamat pagi*	seh–LAH–maht PAH–ghee
Good afternoon	*Selamat tengah hari*	seh–LAH–maht teng–AH hah–REE
Good evening	*Selamat petang*	seh–LAH–maht peh–TAHNG
How are you?	*Apa khabar*	AH–pah kah–BAR
Please	*Tolong*	TOH–long
Thank you	*Terima kasih*	TEHR–ee–mah KAH–see
You're welcome	*Sama sama*	SAH–mah sah–MAH
Yes	*Ya*	ee–AH
Excuse me	*Minta maaf*	MEEN–tah mah–AHF

Names

For Chinese and Indian naming conventions, please refer to Chapter 5 and Chapter 7, respectively. Muslim naming conventions (see Table 9.7 on page 194) include the following:

- Historically, the Muslim name order has been given (or first) name, followed by *bin* (male) or *binti* (female), followed by the father's given name.
- Today, some Muslims don't use *bin* or *binti;* just the given name and the father's given name.
- Some Muslims add a tribal or family name with the prefix *−al* to the name.
- Professionals use their professional title (such as Dr. or Engineer) or courtesy title (Mr., Mrs., Ms.) plus their given name.
- After marriage, females retain their maiden names.

Table 9.7   **Muslim Naming Conventions**

Bahasa Melayu	Male or Female	English Honorific or Title
Encik	Male	Mr.
Puan	Female	Mrs.
Cik	Female	Miss
Tuan haji	Male	Completed the hajj or pilgrimage to Mecca
Puan hajjah	Female	Completed the hajj or pilgrimage to Mecca
Sayyed	Male	Descendent of the Prophet Mohammed
Sharifah	Female	Descendent of the Prophet Mohammed

Meetings and Negotiations

The company's ethnic makeup will have a significant impact on your approach to doing business. Dennis Unkovic recommends identifying good local advisors to help understand ethnic dynamics.[22] In general, Malaysians value personal contact and building a relationship before negotiating a deal. They tend to focus more on harmony than competition and are more impressed with people of greater seniority and experience.

To initiate a business relationship, request a meeting by sending a letter of introduction. Be prepared for a much slower pace of doing business, which may require several trips to Malaysia over many months. Malaysians take their time in decision-making. Although negotiations may be lengthy, Malaysians tend to concede more and more over time. Written contracts are considered open to further negotiation and escape clauses are common.

Presentation Styles, Conversational Topics, and Humor

After the third or fourth visit, as the relationship and comfort level develops, Malaysians may ask you questions about income or marital status, which are culturally acceptable. Appropriate conversational topics include ASEAN,

[22]Dennis Unkovic, *Understanding Asia: Winning Strategies for Business Success* (Chicago: ABA Publishing, 2011).

Malaysian culture, cuisine, sports, future plans, and company success. Inappropriate topics include personal success, sex, religion, and controversial current events.

Gestures

Be aware of these points when interacting with Malaysians:

- Understand that smiling may signify embarrassment, shyness, or unhappiness, as well as happiness.
- Bow slightly when passing people, entering, or leaving.
- Point with the entire right hand or with the thumb (not with the index finger).
- Beckon with right hand palm down by making scooping motion with fingers a few times.

Notable Foods and Dishes

Cuisine is spicy and flavorful, with regional spices and herbs. Rice is a staple. Barbecued meat, beef or fish curry, vegetables (spinach and cabbage), chili paste, salted eggs, fried dried fish, and fruit (mangoes, papayas, and pineapple) are popular. Fruit juice, tea, or coffee with sweetened condensed milk may be offered. *Peranakan* or *Nonya* cuisine, a unique blend of mild, flavorful spices and sauces, is popular.[23]

Specialty Dishes

Favorite Malaysian dishes include:[24]

- **Satay**: National dish; grilled protein kabobs in spicy marinade, with peanut sauce
- **Nasi lemak**: Spicy breakfast rice dish cooked with coconut milk and fish
- **Soto ayam**: Chicken stew with rice, bean sprouts
- **Laksa**: Spicy fish soup with noodles

---

[23]Dean Foster, *The Global Etiquette Guide to Asia* (Hoboken, NJ: John Wiley & Sons, 2002).
[24]Elizabeth Devine and Nancy L. Braganti, *The Traveler's Guide to Asian Customs & Manners*, Revised Edition (New York: St. Martin's Griffin, 1998).

- **Panggang golek**: Spiced duck with cashews and coconut cream
- **Rojak**: Stir-fried fruits and vegetables in shrimp-based sweet-and-sour sauce
- **Mee rebus**: Boiled noodles in a rich beef gravy
- **Gula Malacca**: A sago pudding
- **Roti canon**: Fried flatbread
- **Char kway teow**: Stir-fried rice noodles with soy, chili, and prawns

Dining Etiquette

The guest of honor sits to the host's right or at the head of the table. When sitting on floor mats, men sit cross-legged and women fold their legs and feet under. The host provides towels and a bowl of water to wash hands before dinner. Men may eat before women. Taste a bite of every dish. Use only the right hand to eat and pass food; the left is used for personal hygiene and considered unclean.

Dining customs vary by ethnic group. Malaysians eat with their hands or with spoons, often using a fork in the left hand to push food onto the spoon in the right hand. Indians usually eat with their hands, but may give Westerners a fork and spoon. Many Indians are vegetarians. The Chinese use chopsticks and soup spoons. Muslims do not eat pork or consume alcohol and eat *halal* foods, prepared according to Islamic law. Hindus and Buddhists do not eat beef because cows are considered sacred.

Drinking and Toasting

Alcohol may be served after a meal; however, it is not the custom because Muslims abstain from alcohol. Chinese Malaysians drink beer. *Minum* (MEE–noom) or *cheers* is a common toast.

Tipping and Bill-Paying

Restaurants include a service charge; an additional 10-percent tip is customary. Tip small change or round up to the nearest *ringgit* for taxi drivers, maids, and restroom attendants. Tip valets two *ringgits* per bag.

Taboos

The following are taboos in Malaysian culture:

- Touching or handling the Qur'an
- Standing or sitting on prayer rugs
- Smoking in front of the elderly or royalty
- Entering a mosque wearing a hat, shoes, or sunglasses
- Pounding one fist into the other hand
- Public displays of affection
- Touching anyone on the head
- Using feet to move objects or point at anyone
- Showing the soles of the feet
- Using left hand to shake, gift, point, eat, or pass items
- Whistling, hissing, or shouting
- Standing with hands in pockets or on hips
- Crossing legs or resting an ankle on the knee
- Littering
- Nose-blowing and throat-clearing

Heroes and Sports

Knowing about another country's heroes and sports offers opportunities to incorporate culture-specific references into your conversations and presentations.

Heroes

Some heroes from Malaysia's history are:

Tunku Abdul Rahman Putra (1903–1990): First prime minister (1957–1970) of Malaysia and the "Father of Independence." Former president of the United Malays National Organization (UMNO). Best known for negotiations that achieved Malaysian independence from Britain in 1957, after which he became the first prime minister of the newly established Federation of Malaysia.

Tun Abdul Razak Hussein (1922–1976): Second prime minister (1970–1976) and the "Father of Development." Politician who played key role in gaining national independence; he is best known for his New Economic Policy, a plan to reduce poverty and racial antagonism. Established the National Front (Barisan Nasional), a coalition of ethnically based parties, to increase political stability.

Tun Abdullah Ahmad Badawi (1939–present): Malaysia's fifth prime minister (2003–2009). Prolific politician with 30 years of government service, focused on cultivating an ethical society, combating corruption, modernizing agriculture, developing economic centers, and improving public-sector services.

Sports

Sports

Football (soccer) is the most popular sport in Malaysia. Badminton follows as a close second; others include cricket, track and field, rugby, golf, field hockey, and squash. The traditions of top-spinning and kite flying remain popular, as well as *sepak takraw* (kick volleyball), a traditional ball game adapted from the Myanmar sport of *chinlone*. Players use their heads, knees, and feet to hit a rattan ball over a net. The game has expanded to international competition, with top-ranked Malaysian teams.

Sports Figures

Datuk Lee Chong Wei (1982–present): Professional badminton player. Currently Malaysia's number one player, ranked number one worldwide for 199 consecutive weeks, 2008–2012. First Malaysian to reach the men's singles finals in the Olympics, in the 2008 games in Beijing. His accomplishments earned him the honorary title *Datuk*. Prime Minister Najib Tun Razak described him as a national hero.

Pandelela Rinong anak Pamg (1993–present): Olympic diver. First female Malaysian to win an Olympic medal; winning bronze in 10, meter diving at the 2012 London Games. It was Malaysia's first Olympic medal in a sport other than badminton.

Datuk Nicol Ann David (1983–present): Professional squash player. First Asian to be ranked number one worldwide in women's squash. Won the British Open title five times, the World Open title a record seven times, and the Asian Squash Championships a record eight times. Considered one of the greatest women's squash players of all time.

Mohd Safee Mohd Sali (1984–present), Norshahrul Idlan Talaha (1986–present): Footballers. Two Malaysian national football team players who are often considered by Malaysians to be their best striker pair.

Eight-Question Framework

This section reviews the framework to which you were introduced earlier in this book. Each of these questions addresses one or more business topics to help you attract and build the relationships upon which today's successful businesses depend.

1. How Do Malaysians Prefer to Act: Individually or as a Group?

The multi-religious and multi-cultural differences play different roles in business relationships. There is not a uniform approach fitting all the business situations or relationships in Malaysia. Being sensitive to views, feelings, and saving face is important.

—*Executive, Malaysia Airlines*

A strong sense of belonging, *gotong royong*, or cooperation and a spirit of collectivism that requires one to seek the views of challenges before making significant decisions, encourages Malaysians to give priority to group over individual interests.[25]

The Malaysian business environment includes at least three diverse cultures: Malaysian, Chinese, and Indian, each with their own approach to individual and group dynamics. In that respect, it may be useful to refer to Chapter 5 (China) and Chapter 7 (India) to supplement this information.

"Malaysians are group-oriented and make collective decisions. Group consensus extends to a willingness to prioritize multiple interests over individual concerns; it is a team environment with a sense of belonging," shares Dr. Amin Osman, Director of Taman Bijaya Pte. Ltd. Consensus seeking is known as *Mesyuwarah*.

The holy month of Ramadan impacts group as well as individual decision making, especially within large companies, government, and public sector organizations. During Ramadan, when key principals are out of the office and hours are reduced, the decision-making process slows considerably.

2. How Are Power and Authority Viewed in Malaysia?

Status is inherited, not earned, and is confirmed by demonstrating leadership and a caring attitude. Malays feel comfortable in a hierarchical structure in which they have a definite role.

—*Richard D. Lewis,* When Cultures Collide: Leading Across Cultures[23]

In Malaysia, people born in high positions are expected to demonstrate leadership capabilities. A good leader is seen as religiously devout, sincere, humble, and tactful. The Malaysians are comfortable in a hierarchical structure,

---

[25]Cultural Detective, www.culturaldetective.com (accessed January 15, 2015.)

[26]Richard D. Lewis, *When Cultures Collide: Leading Across Cultures* (Boston: Nicholas Brealey International, 2006).

showing deference to seniors, elders, and authority. They are also comfortable in structures where they have a definite role to play. They tend to be modest and will resist asking for promotion because they expect this to occur naturally.

Ethnic Malaysians, known as *Bumiputeras*, comprising more than 60 percent of Malaysian citizens, hold the political power in Malaysia. Various states have hereditary rulers who have political influence within the borders. The Chinese are active in business and economic affairs, and Indians are well represented in the professional arenas, including law and medicine. The administrators of the country are predominately Muslim.

Another source of power and authority is MIDA, the Malaysian Investment Development Authority, which evaluates and approves applications for manufacturing, tax, and investment.[27] MIDA is a quasi-governmental group working with the ministries and prime minister.

According to Ms. Yeo Lam of Johnson Medical, working with the government and the proper contacts is crucial. She goes on to add, "Many people will tell you they are the key; but you still need to check references; bankers and lawyers are helpful references."

3. How Do Malaysians Compare Rules and Relationships?

"Together we must bear the responsibility, whether big or small."
 —*Ringan sama dijinjng, berat sama dipikul*

A group affiliation, or *Kawan*, is a "system of relationships among colleagues and associates that contributes to a spirit of togetherness, founded on unwritten rules of trust and understanding, [which] takes precedence over a task. More often this value stems from common interests and background based on family affiliation and ethnicity."[28]

In addition, Islamic law impacts more than 60 percent of the population in Malaysia, so rules and relationships are intertwined. What is important to know is that Malaysia is one of the world's top Islamic finance centers, providing *Sharī'ah*-compliant financial services to Muslims worldwide—a market estimated to reach $3.4 trillion by 2018.

Under the Qur'an, which sets forth Islamic law, compliant financial services organizations may not charge interest on loans and *riba* is a term that

---

[27] Malaysian Investment Development Authority, www.mida.gov.my/home (accessed November 17, 2014).
[28] "Malaysian Values Lens," www.culturaldetective.com (accessed January 11, 2015).

prohibits this practice.[29] Financial activities must be socially responsible with profits and losses shared by the community to avoid violating the Qur'an. After a financial agreement or any type of contract is negotiated, it is still considered open to further negotiation and escape clauses are common. It is always best to consult an attorney and a certified public accountant for country-specific legal advice.

4. How Do Malaysians Regard Time?

For most government organizations and government linked companies, time for Muslim prayer will have a bearing on meeting time. In addition, during the fasting month of Ramadan, they tend to dislike a meeting in the afternoon.
— *Executive, Malaysian Airlines*

At one of Sharon's international protocol training sessions, a senior project manager for a U.S. tech company was concerned about whether his two-month implementation schedule should be modified to accommodate the holy month of Ramadan. Concerned with potential delay, his VP decided to proceed with "business as usual" and scheduled meetings regardless. The project team faced not only absent team members, but questions about their disrespect for Islam. The implementation was subsequently delayed six months.

Spending time virtuously and respecting Islamic law is particularly important during Ramadan when work hours are significantly reduced, employees take holidays, telecommuting increases, and colleagues are likely to decline business travel. Some organizations offer an *Iftar* for their employees, both Muslim and non-Muslim, to get into the spirit of Ramadan. During Ramadan, Muslims are expected to fast from dawn to dusk. *Iftar* is the meal eaten by Muslims to break their fast after sunset during Ramadan.[30]

Meetings should be scheduled around prayer times and the holy month of Ramadan. Islamic law impacts time as it relates to holidays and the traditional Muslim workweek, with the weekend falling on Thursday and Friday.[31]

---

[29]James R. Silknet, Jeffrey M. Aresty, and Jacqueline Klosek, *The ABA Guide to International Business Negotiations: A Comparison of Cross-Cultural Issues and Successful Approaches,* 3rd Edition (Chicago: ABA Publishing, 2009).

[30]Catherine England and Lee Mozena, 2014 SIETAR-USA Conference presentation, "Ramadan Basics for Savvy Managers," October 22-25, 2014, Portland, Oregon, www.zenaconsulting .com/EVENTS.html.

[31]CIA, *The World Factbook,* "Malaysia," www.cia.gov/library/publications/the-world-factbook /geos/my.html (accessed November 17, 2014).

In locations where Friday remains a workday, many offices close at noon as Muslims take a two-hour break for prayers at a local mosque. Malaysians feel the past and future rest in God's hands. You are likely to frequently hear the phrase *Inshallah*, which means, "God willing."[32]

On a daily basis, time in Malaysia is fluid. As one airline executive explained, "Companies and the management team are becoming more punctual when it comes to meetings in the office. Lunch and dinner meetings may be viewed as more relaxed with an allowance for some delay because of traffic, which is an acceptable social excuse."

He added, "International visitors should also realize that time is money and it is important to Malaysians that they shift their paradigm to concentrate on 'us' rather than on 'I.' However, the slight wait that occurs at local companies and government offices is to send the subtle message that they are busy and important people and definitely worth waiting for."

Malaysians enjoy long-range planning and routinely make future plans, as evidenced by the government's completed long-term projects (the airport, Petronas towers, Putrajaya, a planned city). Former Prime Minister Mahathir Mohamad's 1998 *Vision 20/20* program for developing Malaysia into an industrialized country is scheduled for completion in 2020.[33]

5. How Direct Is Communication in Malaysia?

Communication may be formal and indirect to start because Malaysians are expert at indirect references to avoid offense and save face. It is rare to hear the word "no," which is considered impolite. Listen closely to tone of voice when you hear terms such as "I agree," "yes," "possibly," or "maybe" for insight into whether the answer is positive or negative. Sucking air in through the teeth is a nonverbal signal of difficulty with your request.

When conducting business, pay attention to unique ways the scope or impact of the message may change. For example:

"You are wrong" (inappropriate) is direct, specific, without room for mis-interpretation.

"You are wrong lah." The message is softened and acknowledgment is given that you are only human, may have made a mistake, and can be forgiven.

Accordingly:

---

[32]Lewis, *When Cultures Collide.*

[33]Office of the Prime Minister, www.pmo.gov.my (accessed November 17, 2014).

"No" is strong and final.

"No lah" is not as harsh and the impact is lessened; but it is still a no.

Communicating "no" may also occur in the following ways: "Oh, very difficult lah" (*susah lah*), or "Cannot lah" (*tak boleh lah*).

As these examples illustrate, calm and harmonious communication during business negotiation is preferred; listening carefully is valued, and interruptions are to be avoided. Compromise is respected.

Malaysian Values

The Malaysians value gentleness, respect, courtesy, silence, modesty, trust, formality, God's will, humility, and virtue.

6. How Formal or Informal Do Businesspeople in Malaysia Tend to Be?

Read about Islamic ways . . . it is preferred, as you know we are an Islamic country. It is advisable to be courteous and formal. Respect accorded is not in vain.

Ms. Yeo Eng Lam, Managing Director, Johnson Medical International

When beginning a business relationship, a letter of introduction or a formal, personal introduction is required; a written response to an invitation from a business associate is expected. One Malaysian Airlines executive was emphatic: "Malaysia has one of the highest 'power distances' in the world, with a score of 104, meaning that formality, respect, and courtesy are expected. Be formal in addressing people by name and titles."[34]

In meetings, he suggests, "Let the host direct the guest where to be seated, and be formal in wardrobe. However, more companies are now practical in attire, and removing a coat if others is is appropriate. Ladies should be businesslike. Humor is generally welcomed, especially as an ice-breaker, but no one wants a clown in the meeting room. Gestures should be controlled and below the American norm. Understand that others many find it difficult to comprehend the American accent, so speak slower and do not be too loud. Maintain personal space and a glass bubble. A man should not offer his hand or a handshake to a Muslim lady."

---

[34] Geert Hofstede, Gert Jan Hofstede, and Michael Minkov, *Cultures and Organizations: Software of the Mind—Intercultural Cooperation and Its Importance for Survival,* 3rd Edition (New York: McGraw Hill, 2010).

7. *How Aligned Are Malaysian Social and Business Lives?*

There are many opportunities for international visitors to socialize in ways that cement deep, long-lasting relationships. "Malaysians are friendly people, and often welcome guests into their life, especially during festive seasons such as the *Hari Raya, Deepavali,* or *Chinese New Year;* the New Year celebrations for each of the three cultures in our country," said Ms. Lam. "Guests are expected to attend and advised to wear Malaysian dress such as *baju,* which shows interest and respect to the host. Men can also wear *batik,* which is very popular for formal functions, although not required. An example of this was when the wife of the Chinese premier visited and wore Malaysian *baju*, not Chinese *cheong sum*. I think the Chinese researched our culture to display their respect."

During social events, religious customs and restrictions must be observed. If you are hosting a meal, do not order or offer pork or alcohol to your Muslim guests and avoid ordering beef for Hindus and Sikhs. Cows are considered sacred in both of these belief systems.

As a Malaysian Airlines executive shared, "Golfers will find opportunities at the CEO and senior management level to socialize during a round of golf. An invitation for dinner that takes note of Muslim restrictions is acceptable, especially to a small group of three to four people. For private and international companies, invitations to drinks are welcome, although not if you are working with government organizations and Muslims who do not drink alcohol."

8. *How Is the Concept of Women in Business Handled in Malaysia?*

As a woman in business, I do not find it particularly constrained. We have a female governor of the National Bank, female heads of the stock exchange, corporations, and business enterprises.
—*Ms. Yeo Eng Lam*

According to the *Randstad World of Work Report* 58 percent of Malaysian business leaders believe women will play a critical role in ensuring the success of Malaysian organizations in an innovative economy.[35] Indeed, many already do, including inspiring female leaders such as Tan Sri Zeti Akhtar Aziz, the governor of the Malaysian Central Bank (BNM), who was named a candidate for president of the International Monetary Fund (IMF). She was also the first woman to be ranked within the top ten central bank governors

---

[35]Randstad, *2013/14 Randstad World of Work Report: Talent Strategy Game-changer Series,* http://cdn2.hubspot.net/hub/258995/file-568002761-pdf/WOWR_GC_4.pdf?t=1394173772000 (accessed November 17, 2014).

of the world, helping to place Malaysia at the leading edge of the Islamic money market.

The Randstad report surveyed more than 14,000 employers in Asia Pacific and found Malaysia to be more advanced than some of its neighbors. According to their Malaysian director, Ms. Jasmin Kaur: "Female leaders are often known for possessing important people skills; such as the ability to foster strong teams, build trusted relationships, leverage emotional intelligence, and pick up on non-verbal cues."[36]

Nevertheless, said one Malaysian Airlines executive: "Although about 60 percent of the local university undergraduates are comprised of females, women make up (only) 46 percent of the working population. The number of women in senior management, boardrooms, and the Cabinet is slowly but surely increasing. However, this success is still behind the norm for Western nations."

He offered in-the-trenches advice to incoming businesswomen: "Conduct business dealings professionally and at arms' length. Behavior, dress, and mannerisms must be conservative, modest, and ladylike."

Cultural Summary

Here are some key points to remember:

- Research the organization and ethnicity of owners and founders. A company owned by Malaysians will operate differently than one owned by Chinese or Indians. Also research your Malaysian counterpart's belief system and respect their cultural values before ordering pork or beef, or drinking alcohol. Develop a relationship with a local contact for advice regarding the numerous cultural layers, ethnic dynamics, and Malaysian finance.
- Develop an understanding of Islamic finance as some financial dealings must be Sharī'ah-compliant. Financial responsibilities under the Qur'an prohibit *riba* (loan interest payments), and activities must be socially responsible, with the community sharing profits and losses.
- During the holy month of Ramadan, work hours are reduced; telecommuting increases; public eating and drinking is strongly discouraged; and business colleagues may decline travel, resulting in a slow-down of decision making and project progress.

---

[36]Staffing Industry Analysts, "Malaysia—Female Leaders Are Critical in the Workplace," December 12, 2013, www.staffingindustry.com/row/Research-Publications/Daily-News/Malaysia-Female-leaders-are-critical-in-the-workplace-28318#sthash.O75VYTXN.dpuf.

Self-Awareness Profile

This simple exercise prompts you to self-assess where you currently stand on topics related to the eight-question framework and *compare* this with the country culture. This visual will help you discover the extent to which you may need to adapt your current mindset and behavior to develop more robust business relationships. For details on how to complete this graphic, see the instructions given in the Introduction on pages xviii–xix.

Consider copying the eight-question Profile or using a pencil so that you can see, over time, how you have adjusted your cultural mindset. You might also wish to create unique graphics related to each of the businesses you work with, as these cultural positions vary depending upon geographic location, industry, generational factors, and corporate profile.

Q1: What is your preferred way of doing business?

As an individual making autonomous decisions

As a team member who seeks group consensus

1	2	3	4	5	**6**

Q2: How comfortable are you in hierarchies in which power is distributed unequally?

Very uncomfortable

Very comfortable

1	2	3	4	5	**6**

Q3: How closely do you follow rules and obey the law?

Almost always

It depends

1	2	3	**4**	5	6

Q4: What is your general attitude toward time?

I prefer agendas, schedules, planning

I prefer flexibility, fluidity without scheduling

1	2	3	4	**5**	6

Q5: What is your preferred way to communicate?

Very diplomatically   **Very candidly**

1   **2**   3   4   5   6

Q6: What is your interpersonal style or level of formality in business interactions?

Very formal   **Very informal**

1   2   **3**   4   5   6

Q7: What is your view on socializing within business?

A waste of time   **Essential**

1   2   3   4   **5**   6

Q8: Should a woman defer to a man as the lead, if winning business in a certain culture depended on it?

Never   **Yes, absolutely**

1   2   3   4   **5**   6

10 | Myanmar

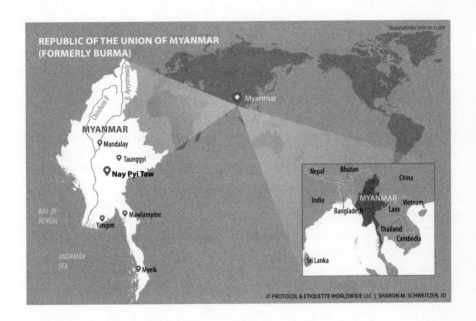

"*Citizens of Burma/Myanmar have ample justification for pride in the history of their country. The three major dynasties that have controlled what we know today as Myanmar have contributed much to world culture.*"

—David I. Steinberg, Burma/Myanmar: What Everyone
Needs to Know

Introduction

First, the good news:

Consulting group McKinsey describes Myanmar, formerly known as Burma, as "one of the few remaining largely untapped markets in the world."[1] "By 2025, over half the world's consuming class ... will live within a five-hour flight of Myanmar." It is neighbor to the enormous markets of China and India, as well as Bangladesh, Laos, and Thailand. Ecologically diverse and resource rich, Myanmar was once considered to be the richest country in southeast Asia and many hope it will be so again. This "land of pagodas" is one of the most fascinating nations worldwide and a mystery to most visitors, including some of its Asian neighbors.

Change is occurring at a rapid pace as Myanmar opens its borders to global trade. The European Union and U.S. have eased long-held bans on foreign investment there, which has created a blossoming entrepreneurial environment. Westerners are currently flooding the country with all the enthusiasm of prospectors during the Klondike gold rush, attracted by Myanmar's *greenfield advantage*.[2]

One political figure with whom people may be familiar is Daw Aung San Suu Kyi.[3] If she wins the 2015 presidential election, this pro-democracy icon and Nobel Peace Prize laureate is expected to herald in many changes that undoubtedly will be good for business.

Now, for the challenges: Myanmar is ranked number 182 out of 189 economies by the World Bank's *Doing Business 2014* report. As McKinsey points out, the country will require an investment of $650 billion ($320 billion to cover infrastructure alone) in order to support potential growth. Its local, largely agricultural workforce currently receives an average schooling of only four years. Nevertheless, there are considerable opportunities and potential rewards for those prepared for the challenge.

It is in that spirit of adventure that we share our interview material from mysterious Myanmar. As the McKinsey Global Institute report concluded: "International companies must move fast, be prepared to commit to Myanmar for the long term, and consider partnerships with local firms."

How to Pronounce Myanmar

If you are wondering how to pronounce *Myanmar*, the BBC Pronunciation Unit recommends myan-MAR—with main emphasis placed on the

---

[1] The McKinsey Global Institute's report: *Myanmar's Moment: Unique Opportunities, Major Challenges*
[2] Greenfield Advantage is defined as beginning with bare ground and building or investing in a new venture from the foundation. www.investopedia.com/terms/g/greenfield/asp (accessed November 9, 2014)
[3] Clements, Alan. The Voice of Hope: Aung San Suu Kyi Conversations with Alan Clements. World Dharma Publications, 2012. Kindle edition.
[4] BBC News Magazine Monitor, article *How to Say: Myanmar*, September 26, 2007 www.bbc.co.uk/blogs/legacy/magazinemonitor/2007/09/how_to_say_myanmar.shtml.

last syllable, based on the advice of native Burmese speakers in the BBC Burmese Section.[2]

Quiz

How much do you know about Myanmar? Answer the following questions as True or False to test your knowledge. (The Answer Key at the bottom includes page numbers that refer to the topic):

_____1. Myanmar is one of three countries using the imperial system of measurement instead of the metric system.

_____2. Until recently, it was illegal for international visitors to be invited into Myanmar homes.

_____3. Today the country is referred to as Myanmar by its government and people, but as Burma by the U.S. and the U.K.

_____4. Myanmar has 135 ethnic groups divided into eight national races.

_____5. A Western man should greet a Myanmar woman by shaking her hand.

_____6. It is customary to buy gifts to celebrate the Chinese New Year in Myanmar.

_____7. Myanmar tends to be an individualistic culture rather than collectivist.

_____8. *Ahnarde* means "Hello, how are you?" in Burmese.

_____9. The sport of Chinlone is focused not on winning or losing but on how beautifully the game is played.

_____10. English is the *lingua franca* in Myanmar.

Answer Key: 1. T (p. 215); 2. T (p. 222); 3. T (p. 213); 4. T (p. 214); 5. F (p. 219); 6. F (p. 219); 7. T (p. 225–226); 8. F (p. 220); 9. T (p. 224); 10. F (p. 215–216).

Country Basics

This section provides key knowledge in an easy-to-read format to help you quickly grasp some of the basics necessary to navigate this culture.

Historical Timeline

A critical way to show respect for another person's culture is to have knowledge of their country's history and current affairs. Table 10.1 on pages 212–213 outlines a few key events related to Burma/Myanmar, together with concurrent world events.

Table 10.1   Key Historical Events

Period/Dates	Description/Events	World Events
40 million years ago	World's earliest prehistoric primate, Pondaung Man, believed to live in area of northern Burma. Some claim modern-day Myanmar is "the land of human origin."[3]	*Basilosaurus*, one of the first of the giant whales, appears in the fossil record.
850 B.C.	Kingdom of Tagaung established north of Mandalay.	Homer composes the *Iliad* and *Odyssey* (circa 850 B.C.).
1287	Kingdom conquered by the Mongols under Kublai Khan; country divided into separate city states.	Spectacles believed to be invented (1290).
1885–1886	Burma becomes a British colony. Burmese royal family exiled to India.	John M. Fox popularizes golf outside Scotland.
1942	Japan invades and occupies Burma, with help of Aung San's Thirty Comrades Group.	World War II (1939–1945)
1948	Burma achieves independence. U Nu becomes prime minister.	World Health Organization established by the UN.
1974	New constitution creates the Socialist Republic of the Union of Burma.	Yugoslavia adopts one of the longest constitutions in the world.
1988	Ruling military junta forms the State Law and Order Restoration Council (SLORC). Economy opened to investment.	Benazir Bhutto elected first female prime minister of Pakistan.

[5]Embassy of the Republic of the Union of Myanmar, "Myanmar," www.metelaviv.co.il /myanmar.htm (accessed November 19, 2014).

Table 10.1 (*Continued*)

Period/Dates	Description/Events	World Events
1989	Burma renamed Myanmar. The capital, Rangoon, becomes Yangon. Aung San Suu Kyi first placed under house arrest.	Crown Prince Akihito becomes Emperor of Japan.
2007	"Saffron Revolution" demonstrations by monks and laypeople.	Apple debuts iPhone.
2011	New quasi-civilian government eases restrictions on international investment and global market participation.	The world population reaches 7 billion according to the UN.
2012	Aung San Suu Kyi released after 20 on and off years of house arrest.	U.S. president Barack Obama extends the "hand of friendship" in exchange for more reform in Myanmar.
2014	First national population census conducted since 1983. Myanmar chairs ASEAN (Association of South Eastern Asian Nations).	The XXII Olympic Winter Games take place in Sochi, Russia.
2015	National elections scheduled.	Malaysia is scheduled to be ASEAN chair.

Full Country Name and Location

The Republic of the Union of Myanmar (still known as Burma in the U.S. and U.K.) is slightly smaller than the State of Texas in the U.S. It shares land borders with Bangladesh, China, India, Laos, and Thailand. The Bay of Bengal lies to the west and the Andaman Sea to the south.

Government/Political Structure

Myanmar has a parliamentary government. The president of the country is both head of state and head of government. The first elections in two decades were held in November of 2010.

Population and Economic Centers

In 2014, Myanmar's Department of Population[6] conducted its first census since 1983 and estimated the country's population to be approximately 51.4 million.[7] The country is divided into seven states and seven divisions. Myanmar is a rural nation, with 34 percent of the population living in urban areas.[8]

The Myanmar government lists 135 ethnic groups divided into eight national races: Burman/Myanmar (approximately 70 percent), Kachin, Kayah, Karen, Chin, Mon, Rakhine, and Shan. Other groups include Chinese and Indian.

The major business centers and populations (2014) are outlined in Table 10.2.[9]

Table 10.2   Major Business Centers

Business Centers	Population (Millions)
Mandalay	1.2
Mawlamyine	0.3
Myeik	0.3
Naypyidaw (capital)	1.2
Taunggyi	0.4
Yangon	5.2

Economy

Myanmar is ranked 177th out of 189 economies in terms of ease of doing business, according to the World Bank Group's *Doing Business 2015* report.[10] The composition of its 2013 GDP by sector was services (41.7 percent), industry (20.3 percent), and agriculture (38 percent).[11]

---

[6]Myanmar Department of Population, www.dop.gov.mm (accessed November 19, 2014).

[7]Myanmar Department of Population, "Population and Housing Census of Myanmar, 2014," August 2014, www.dop.gov.mm/wp-content/uploads/2012/12/Census_Provisional_Results _2014_ENG1.pdf (accessed November 19, 2014).

[8]CIA, *The World Factbook*, "Burma," www.cia.gov/library/publications/the-world-factbook/geos /bm.html (accessed November 19, 2014).

[9]Myanmar Department of Population, "Population and Housing Census of Myanmar, 2014," August 2014, www.dop.gov.mm/wp-content/uploads/2012/12/Census_Provisional_Results _2014_ENG1.pdf (accessed November 19, 2014).

[10]World Bank Group, *Doing Business 2015* (October 29 2014): 4, www .doingbusiness.org/~/media/GIAWB/Doing%20Business/Documents/Annual-Reports/English /DB15-Full-Report.pdf.

[11]CIA, *The World Factbook*, "Burma," www.cia.gov/library/publications/the-world-factbook/geos /bm.html (accessed November 19, 2014).

Corruption Perceptions Index

Myanmar ranked 157th least corrupt out of 177 countries and territories with a score of 21 out of 100.[12] This annual index, compiled by Transparency International, measures perceived levels of public sector corruption.

The Bureau of Special Investigation, Ministry of Home Affairs is the anti-corruption agency that conducts investigations in Myanmar.

Human Development Index

Myanmar ranked 150th out of 187 countries and territories.[13] The HDI, compiled by the United Nations Development Programme, is a composite index of life expectancy, education, and income statistics.

Global Gender Gap Index

Myanmar is not included in the Global Gender Gap Index.

System of Measurement

When shipping or transporting materials to and from Myanmar, be aware that it is one of only three countries in the world that uses the imperial system of measurement instead of the internationally popular metric system (the other two being the U.S. and Liberia).

Climate

Myanmar has three seasons: relatively cool (November–February), hot (March–May), monsoon or rainy (June–October). The highest humidity is during the hot season; the lowest is in cooler months.

Languages

Burmese is the official language of Myanmar, with more than 100 different dialects and languages spoken by ethnic minorities. Although businesspeople

[12] Transparency International, "Corruption Perceptions Index 2013," www.transparency.org /cpi2013/results (accessed November 19, 2014).
[13] United Nations Development Programme, *Human Development Report 2014*, http://hdr.undp .org/sites/default/files/hdr14-report-en-1.pdf, p. 160-63 (accessed November 19, 2014).

in Mandalay and Yangon speak English, it is not commonly spoken outside major cities. Chinese is spoken in Mandalay, Yangon, and major trade zones near the China–Myanmar border. Thai is widely spoken in major trade zones near the Thai–Myanmar border.

Belief Systems, Philosophies, and Religions

The country breakdown is as follows: Buddhist (89 percent), Christian (4 percent), Baptist (3 percent), Roman Catholic (1 percent), Islam (4 percent), Animist (1 percent), and Other (2 percent).[14]

For an overview of belief systems, philosophies, and religions, please refer to Chapter 4, pages 64–65.

Time Zones/Daylight Savings

Myanmar has a single time zone, Myanmar Time (MMT). Myanmar is 6.5 hours ahead of GMT (Greenwich Mean Time)/UTC (Coordinated Universal Time). It does not operate under Daylight Savings.

It is 11 and a half hours ahead of U.S. Eastern Standard Time (10 and a half hours ahead in Daylight Savings Time). See www.timeanddate.com /worldclock.

To calculate time in Myanmar, add 6.5 hours to UTC/GMT.

Telephone Country Code and Internet Suffix

The Myanmar telephone country code is 95, and the Internet suffix is .mm.

Currency

The unit of currency in Myanmar is the Kyat (MMK, pronounced *chart*), which is divided into 100 *pyas* (rarely used due to inflation). Myanmar is still a heavily cash-based economy. Use only bills that are freshly minted. Small tears or folds in U.S. dollars are just some of the reasons why cash may come under close scrutiny or be refused. Bring larger bills such as $50 and $100 for both purchases and exchange.

---

[14]CIA, *The World Factbook*, "Burma," www.cia.gov/library/publications/the-world-factbook /geos/bm.html (accessed November 19, 2014).

Business Culture, Etiquette, and Customs

This section covers business culture, etiquette, and customs.

Fiscal Year

Myanmar's fiscal year is April 1 to March 31. Dates are written day, month, year; April 1, 2020 is written 01/04/2020.

Working Week

Business hours are not uniform. Most private/government offices are closed on Saturday and Sunday. The working schedule is detailed in Table 10.3.

Table 10.3   The Myanmar Working Schedule

Business Sector	Business Hours	Days of the Week
Public sector offices	08:30–16:30 (35-hour workweek)	Monday–Friday
Private sector offices	08:00–17:00 (44-hour workweek)	Monday–Friday
Lunch	12:00–13:00	Monday–Friday
Annual leave	Practices vary	

Holidays and Festivals

Some Myanmar holidays are determined by the lunar calendar and change from year to year. Floating holidays are designated with an asterisk. On specific holidays, an office may remain open with limited staff. Check with your embassy or trade office before planning business travel. Table 10.4 on page 218 outlines common Myanmar holidays and festivals.

Business Dress/Appearance

Despite heat and humidity, professional business dress is expected for first meetings, contract signings, and official events. In less-formal situations, many businessmen wear an open collar, light-colored shirt, and dark slacks. Women should dress modestly, covering arms, legs, and décolleté. Wear dresses or

Table 10.4   Myanmar Holidays and Festivals

Date	Name
January 4	Independence Day
January/February	*Thingyan* Holiday*
February 12	Union Day
March 2	Peasants' Day (anniversary of 1962 coup d'état)
March	*Tabaung* Full Moon Day*
March 27	Armed Forces Day
April	Burmese New Year and Water Festival*
May (Full Moon)	Kason Festival*
May 1	Workers' Day or May Day (Labor Day)
July 19	Martyrs' Day
July/August	Full moon of Waso/Beginning of Buddhist Lent*
September/October	*Thadingyut* Full Moon Day (End of Buddhist Lent)*
October	Greater *Eid**
October	*Depawali**
November	*Tasaung Taing* Full Moon Day*
December	National Day*
December 25	Christmas Day

skirts at any length below the knee. Depending on the office, it is common to remove shoes, so choose socks accordingly. Expect local businessmen to wear *longyi* (a long skirt–like garment) and Mandarin collar shirts.

News Sources

Following are some of the most popular news sources in Myanmar:

- *Myanmar Times:* www.mmtimes.com
- *Myanmar Business Journal:* http://mmbiztoday.com

Business Cards

Although few people think of translating their cards into Burmese on the reverse, this is appreciated by local business people.

Technology

The latest figures rank Myanmar 158th in the world for the number of Internet users[15] and 172nd globally for the number of Internet hosts.[16] Expect limited access in major metropolitan and urban areas, mainly in hotels and costly Internet cafés, and none in rural areas. Expect your browsing history to be reported: The government currently requires café owners to submit customer records. Power cuts and outages regularly affect major cities.

Gifts

Appropriate business gifts include pens, golf balls, and liquor, especially whisky. Business visitors to Myanmar have received ties, inexpensive watches, and small flags. Never give cash or gifts to government officials. Consult the latest Myanmar import/export rules prior to departure.

It is not customary to buy gifts for the Chinese New Year in Myanmar. Office colleagues expect gifts on three occasions: leaving employment, getting married, or having a baby. Your gift may be declined with "You should not have gone to so much trouble". Reply that it is your honor to present the gift.

Introductions, Greetings, Personal Space, and Eye Contact

Men greet each other by shaking hands. Women may be greeted with a smile and a nod. If a Myanmar businesswoman offers her hand, it is acceptable to shake it, but Western men should not offer their hand to a Myanmar woman first. Businesswomen typically shake hands with each other. Refrain from hugging. An arm's length of personal space is most common between men, more than an arm's length distance with women. Ensure no physical contact unless it is invited. Direct eye contact is fine.

Due to the strong respect for elders, Myanmar stand up when an older person enters a room or business meeting. Younger, more junior members of staff bow extremely low as others pass, as if to avoid being seen.

---

[15] CIA, *The World Factbook*, "Country Comparison: Internet Users," information dated 2009, www.cia.gov/library/publications/the-world-factbook/rankorder/2153rank.html (accessed November 19, 2014).

[16] CIA, *The World Factbook*, "Country Comparison: Internet Hosts," information dated 2009, www.cia.gov/library/publications/the-world-factbook/rankorder/2184rank.html (accessed November 19, 2014).

Useful Phrases

The phrases in Table 10.5 can be helpful when traveling in Myanmar.

Table 10.5   Useful Phrases for Myanmar Travel

English	Burmese
Hello	*Hello* or *Mingalaba*
How are you? (to men)	*A ko ne-kaun-yeh-la*
How are you? (to women)	*A ma ne-kaun-yeh-la*
Good afternoon	*Kaung Thaw nae.* Or *lal khinn par*
Good evening	*Kaung Thaw nya.* Or *nay khinn par*
Goodbye	*Ta tar*
Please (when asking for something)	*Kyay zoo pyoot pee*
Thank you	*Kyei zu tin baðe*
You're welcome	*Ya par tal*
Excuse me, just a minute	*Kha na lay naw*

Names

Naming conventions in Myanmar are a fascinating topic and worth familiarizing yourself with. Myanmar have no surnames; therefore, women have no need to change their names after marriage. Female names frequently contain a double syllable such as Mi Mi Aung. Names are a combination of a virtue and the weekday the person is born in the Myanmar lunar calendar. For example, a Sunday-born person's name will start with "A" like Aung.

Names composed of two, three, or four words are common, and all are spoken when greeting. For example, the name "Aung" means "succeed" as used in three and four word names—Aung San Suu Kyi or Aung Ko Ko. Note, too, the use of honorifics in front of someone's name. The 'U' (pronounced Oo) is the honorific used to denote a mature man holding a senior position. In Myanmar, names are preceded by a title as shown in Table 10.6 on page 221.

Meetings and Negotiations

First and second meetings are the time for introductions with ministry officials and for building trust. Myanmar place strong emphasis on chemistry between business partners. It is important to be patient during these early meetings:

Table 10.6   Naming Conventions in Myanmar

Meaning	Male Form	Female Form
Child	Maung (may be first name)	Ma
Under 30	Ko (younger brother)	Ma (younger sister)
Over 30	U (uncle)	Daw (aunt)

This is when general administrative and paperwork matters are handled. More in-depth business is discussed in later meetings. Myanmar may consult with astrologers or others before making decisions, or they may conclude business quickly.

Presentation Styles, Conversational Topics, and Humor

Slide decks like PowerPoint are used during formal presentations in business offices, but not in casual meetings, where personal interaction is preferred. Culture-specific jokes and humor used as introductory icebreakers do not translate well. Although the Myanmar are lighthearted, be aware that political dissidents and Myanmar comedians The Moustache Brothers were jailed for making government and military leaders the subjects of their jokes.[17]

Gestures

- Removing shoes when entering a business office and placing them with other shoes near the entrance to show respect
- Rising when an elder enters a room or business meeting
- Younger, more junior members of staff bowing extremely low as others pass, as if to avoid being seen

Notable Foods and Dishes

Traditional dishes blend Burmese, Indian, Thai, and Chinese influences. Rice is the basis of almost every meal. Curry and rice are always eaten together.

---

[17] James Menendez and Katharine Hodgson, "Burma: Moustache Brothers Keep on Telling Jokes," BBC News Magazine, January 4, 2013, www.bbc.com/news/magazine-20528893.

Hindu and Buddhist influences prohibit eating beef and pork; however, fish, chicken, duck, and lamb may be served. All dishes, including rice, are served as one meal, not as separate courses. Tea is the national drink, specifically Burmese and Chinese green tea. Ginger tea is a favorite, with fresh root steeped in boiled water. Strong black tea with sweetened condensed milk is also popular. Beer, water, and juice may also be served with meals.

Specialty Dishes

Favorite dishes in Myanmar cuisine include:[18]

- **Mohinga:** The unofficial national dish; a thick fish-based soup flavored with lemongrass, garlic, onion, and spices, often served with thin rice noodles
- **Nangyi thoke:** A "salad" of thick rice noodles with chicken, egg, bean sprouts, chickpea flour, turmeric, and chilies, served with broth on the side
- **Mondhi:** Noodles served with chicken or fish
- **Laphet:** Pickled green tea leaves with sesame seeds, fried peas, dried shrimp, and nuts
- **Jaggery:** Burmese chocolate

Dining Etiquette

Most business entertaining takes place in hotels and restaurants. Until recently, it was illegal for international visitors to be invited into a Myanmar home. At business meals, the most junior host will begin serving the guests first. Forks, spoons, or chopsticks may be provided, but knives are not. Serving spoons are provided with each dish.

Drinking and Toasting

Beer, rum, and whisky are popular drinks for businesspeople. Locally brewed Myanmar beers include Irrawaddy, Mandalay, Myanmar, and Tiger. At

---

[18]Austin Bush, "10 Meals Every Myanmar Traveler Should Try," CNN Travel, August, 14, 2013, http://travel.cnn.com/myanmar-food-669416; and Lonely Planet, "Eating in Myanmar (Burma): An Intro to Burmese Food," January 10, 2013, www.lonelyplanet.com/asia/travel-tips-and-articles/77618.

business events, whisky is commonly drunk neat (unchilled without mixers or ice). In some areas, a drink called *toddy* made from fermented palm juice is popular.

The toast for "cheers" is *Aung myin par say,* pronounced 'Au-ng my-in par say' in Burmese.

Tipping and Bill-Paying

At dinner, your guest will likely insist on paying. You must insist at least three times to pay the full bill before you are allowed to pay. Tip 10 percent at major hotels and restaurants in the larger cities, although most restaurant servers will be pleased with $2 per guest or 5 percent of the total bill.

Smoking

Smoking is not prevalent during meetings, in government offices, in restaurants, and during meals. If asked, the Burmese/Myanmar will put out their cigarettes.

Taboos

The following are taboo in Myanmar culture:

- Crossing legs by men or women (keep feet flat on floor)
- Wearing shoes in an office when others have removed theirs (observe entryway)
- Placing feet on a desk or table
- Indicating direction with your foot or shoe
- Passing objects or reaching over the head of anyone, especially a monk
- Touching a statute of Buddha
- Touching a monk's robes or body (if female)

Heroes and Sports

Knowing about another country's heroes and sports offers opportunities to incorporate culture-specific references into your conversations and presentations.

Heroes

The most prominent Myanmar heroes are associated with the country's fight
for political independence and unity:

Aung San (1915–1947): "Father of modern day Burma;" father of Aung
San Suu Kyi. Politician and nationalist leader who played a key role
in freeing Burma from British rule. Anti-British before World War II,
his group the Thirty Comrades allied with the Japanese to fight for
Burmese independence. After experiencing Japanese oppression, Aung
San switched allegiance to the Allies. He was assassinated in the executive chambers in Rangoon, along with other cabinet ministers, on July
19, 1947, while serving as prime minister. Political rival U Saw was later
executed for his part in the killings.

U Thant (1909–1975): Secretary-General of the United Nations,
1961–1971. Formerly a Burmese educator and civil servant, he facilitated discussions between former U.S. President John F. Kennedy and
former General Secretary of the Communist Party of the Soviet Union
Nikita Khrushchev during the Cuban Missile Crisis. His body is buried
at the foot of the Shwedagon Pagoda in Yangon, where Buddha's hair
and other holy relics are enshrined.

Daw Aung San Suu Kyi (1945–present): Politician and winner of the
Nobel Peace Prize (1991). Daughter of nationalist leader Aung San.
Mother was a career diplomat who was appointed Ambassador to India
in 1960. Married British scholar Michael Aris (deceased). Became secretary general of the National League for Democracy (NLD) in 1988.
Placed under house arrest in 1989 because of her opposition to military
rule. House arrest lasted on and off until November 13, 2010. Ran for
political office and was elected spring 2012. Made her first speech to
parliament in July of 2012.

Sports

Sports

Chinlone: Chinlone is a ball game comprising two teams of six people
each. It is less about winning or losing and more about how beautifully
the game is played. Using a combination of sports and dance, the teams
delicately control a wicker ball using their feet and knees in a way said
to be almost meditative.

Football: Football (soccer in the U.S.) is hugely popular, with fans watching games from the English Premier League and European Champions
League in bars and restaurants. The U.K.'s Manchester United is the
most-watched team.

Golf: The love of golf dates back years. Courses are located throughout the country. Many are considered to be world-class.

Lethwei (pronounced "la-way"): Myanmar's favorite martial art, similar to kickboxing. Traditionally, the winner was the first person to draw blood. In the modern version, a points system is used instead.

Sports Figures

Aung Ngeain (1985–present): Archer. Won three gold medals in the 2011 Southeast Asian Games and one gold medal in the 2013 Games. Accumulated 52 medals in international tournaments. One of 12 Myanmar individuals who received a 2013 President's State Excellence Award.

Thet Zaw Win (1991–present): Sprinter. Myanmar flag-bearer at the 2012 London Olympic Games Opening Ceremony. He finished in eighth place in the 400-meter event. His personal bests are 22 seconds for the 200-meter and 49 seconds for the 400-meter.

Aye Aye Aung (1984–present): Judoka. Star Myanmar judo athlete in 78 kg event. Won gold in both 2013 Southeast Asian Games and International Invitational Judo Tournament.

Eight-Question Framework

This section reviews the framework to which you were introduced earlier in this book. Each of these questions addresses one or more business topics to help you attract and build the relationships upon which today's successful businesses depend.

1. How Do the Myanmar Prefer to Act: Individually or as a Group?

In terms of individualism . . . Myanmar is closer to Spain in this dimension than any of the Southeast Asian nations[19]
  — *Professor Charles Rarick, Purdue University*

Myanmar's surprising trend toward individualism may stem from two sources. The first concerns the way families are formed. In Myanmar, "sons and daughters make personal bonds to relatives on both sides of the family instead of being limited to the father's side."[20] Also, the predominant religion

---

[19]C. Rarick and I. Nickerson, "An Exploratory Study of Myanmar Culture Using Hofstede's Value Dimension," February 20, 2006, doi:10.2139/ssrn.1114625.
[20]Jean A. Blake, "Helping Hands in Myanmar," October 2005, www.yale.edu/seas/helpinghands.doc

is Buddhism, which emphasizes the individual, unlike the collectivist values of countries influenced by Confucianism. That is why organizational loyalty is to an individual or *personal leader* in Myanmar rather than the entity as a whole.

One board member of a Japanese semiconductor company who visits Myanmar frequently pointed out that in the current political climate, "Any entity trying to do constructive business in Myanmar absolutely must have a strong relationship with the government. In my experience, decisions are based on a few people collectively agreeing to allow you, the company, to move forward and succeed—usually someone in the Ministry governing that industry sector."

Nevertheless, travelers who come to Myanmar with an individualistic mindset, thinking their way is the only way, are unlikely to succeed. Robert Easson, CEO of Imagino Group, pointed out that "Unlike Thailand, Cambodia, or Vietnam, the Myanmar don't put foreigners on as high a pedestal. They will be treated with respect, but that will quickly disappear if you appear arrogant."

Jonathan Nichols of Nicho Ventures echoed this: "Americans are used to coming in loud and proud and expecting the world to take heed. The Myanmar people seem to have missed this memo and really don't get the whole concept of USA dominance. When a business approach is focused more on *me*, the response is typically less than positive."

2. How Are Power and Authority Viewed in Myanmar?

The only way to get anything done in Myanmar is to have boots on the ground in the country. Do not trust brokers . . . always try to work directly with Myanmar government contacts.
—*Jerald Wrightsil, CEO, Eco-Merge USA*

In Myanmar, the word *power* has different forms, resulting in many subtleties in the way business is conducted. *Ana* represents coercive power, whereas *awza* is influence based on personal characteristics or charisma. For example, pro-democracy leader and Nobel Laureate Aung San Suu Kyi has *awza,* whereas the military exhibits *ana.*

As David I. Steinberg points out in *Burma/Myanmar: What Everyone Needs to Know,*[21] power here is a *zero-sum game.* The analysis is that because it is seen as a finite resource, authority is diminished if power is shared. This helps to explain why government ministries, mostly run by former military officers, control business in Myanmar.

---

[21]David I. Steinberg, *Burma/Myanmar: What Everyone Needs To Know* (New York: Oxford University Press, 2010).

According to Jonathan Nichols, "Business in Myanmar is far from a level playing field. This is definitely not a place to be betting on the underdog. Anybody who wants to make progress will take my late grandfather's advice to me on my first day at school. 'Find the biggest, strongest kid in the playground and make him your best friend.'"[22]

The country is currently in a state of flux after decades of military rule and economic sanctions. Many Myanmar government departments are experiencing considerable churn. If one minister is ousted, his entire team may follow. It's therefore inadvisable to spend *too* much time tapping into the influence of one particular individual or group because you could find yourself without any allies at all. The political climate may change after the 2015 elections.

With respect to personal authority, your educational qualifications will be highly valued here. Having letters like M.B.A, Ph.D, or J.D. after your name is considered so important that the Myanmar will include them not only on business cards, but also wedding invitations.

Myanmar Man of Influence

The term *big face* is used in Myanmar in reference to people who, having done favors for the rich and powerful, receive preferential treatment in return. One Myanmar proverb states: "All pieces of meat in the dish go to the 'big face,'" meaning "man of influence."[21]

3. How Do the People of Myanmar Compare Rules and Relationships?

Invest in Burma and do it responsibly; be an agent of change.
— *Hillary Clinton, former U.S. Secretary of State*

Myanmar was a military dictatorship until recently. Although this may suggest that the nation's culture is more oriented toward processes than people, the opposite is true. Myanmar culture is heavily focused on a complex web of relationships that can appear confusing unless you take the time to understand their importance.

For example, CEO Errol Flynn of business advisory and consulting firm KPC & G International Australia arrived in Myanmar in 1995 with his wife, who was assigned the task of opening a representative office for the ING Bank. While in Myanmar and during his two-year stay, Mr. Flynn nurtured

---

[22]Jonathan Nichols, *Myanmar for Foreign Dummies: The Businessman's 18 Point Guide to Myanmar* (Hong Kong: Asia Business Books, 2013).
[23]U. Nyi, *Practical Aspects of Buddhist Ideals* (UK: AuthorHouse, 2010).

an influential circle of personal connections in both government and in the business community. On one occasion, after meeting a Thai sugar exporter who had traveled 15 times to Myanmar to establish joint ventures without success, Mr. Flynn introduced him and his company to the state minister and cabinet members of Myanmar's Kayin Ministry. Other business entities from the mining and agriculture sectors followed and were introduced to several other relevant state ministries in Myanmar.

Errol Flynn is an example of how you can establish valuable relationships without resorting to bribery and corruption. The most expensive gift he and his senior staff ever gave ministers were several bottles of branded whisky. What has helped KPC & G International Australia and Thailand, together with companies like them, become so influential when introducing clients to high-ranking Myanmar government decision makers is patience, respect, and a sincere approach toward the country and its people. Speaking and understanding the Burmese language also helps. This hugely benefited Mr. Flynn's organization, as Myanmar officials made sure his Australian representatives and sponsored organizations were safe while traveling to remote mining sites in the country.

One of the most challenging things visiting professionals need to learn is that they cannot achieve their business goals in terms of weeks or even months. As one Texas-based CEO pointed out: "You will likely need to invest in relationships over a period of several years before expecting anything to be signed, sealed, or delivered." We address this further in the next section.

Specially Designated Nationals List and Foreign Corrupt Practices Act

Become familiar with and learn to navigate the Specially Designated Nationals List, or SDN list, issued by the Office of Foreign Assets Control, U.S. Department of Treasury[24] (also known as the Blocked Persons list). Those on the Blocked Persons list may be involved in activities prohibited by the U.S. U.S. Americans are prohibited from doing business with a person or company on the list. Be aware, too, of the Foreign Corrupt Practices Act (FCPA).[25] Designed to discourage corrupt business practices and encourage free and fair trade, this Act imposes severe penalties on companies and individuals, who promise, offer, or give anything of value to foreign government officials in order to secure business.

---

[24]U.S. Department of the Treasury, "Specially Designated Nationals List (SDN)," last updated November 19, 2014, www.treasury.gov/resource-center/sanctions/SDN-List/Pages/default.aspx (accessed November 19, 2014).
[25]Foreign Corrupt Practices Act of 1977 (FCPA) (15 U.S.C. 78dd-1 et seq.), http://www.justice.gov/criminal/fraud/fcpa/

4. How Do the Myanmar Regard Time?

> If the Myanmar don't see each other today, they can always meet another
> day. Both sides will attach the same non–importance to time.
> —*Dominique Savariau*, French consultant

Burmese Standard Time is a fluid concept, so you'll need to manage your expectations about scheduling, punctuality, and any notion that time is money. Deadlines may not be taken as seriously as you are accustomed to in your culture, and written reports may come in late. Meetings and conferences may not stay on schedule because politeness requires that others are not cut short or interrupted.

As Imagino Group CEO Robert Easson advises, "If the people you are connecting with are used to dealing with 'foreigners,' they will undoubtedly understand how important punctuality is and make adjustments. The point is to ensure that all appointments are confirmed in advance, especially if you are going to drive long distances. Punctuality is not particularly high on the average Myanmar's list of priorities because of the traffic and public transport challenges."

Also bear in mind the effects of continuing superstition in Myanmar. Your meetings may get cancelled or contracts delayed because an astrologer consulted by a Myanmar businessperson has said the time, day, or month is not fortuitous. Western perspectives on time are unfamiliar to many Myanmar government ministers and businesspeople. Until relatively recently, the Myanmar lived and worked under a regime where extreme caution was rewarded and the smallest mistakes were punished.

5. How Direct Is Communication in Myanmar?

> Myanmar are very courteous and direct. However, when a Myanmar com-
> municates that he can deliver, you need to get confirmation from a gov-
> ernment or ministry source. This is your best guarantee.
> —*U.S. American engineer*

Even if you don't hear the word *ah-nar-de* spoken, this concept will undoubtedly influence your business communications in Myanmar. It is considered a deeply ingrained national trait in a country where there is an unspoken aversion to interfering in someone else's life or business.

Ah-nar-de means saving face in the sense of not wanting to do anything that would provoke strong negative emotions in another person. When a Myanmar exhibits *ah-nar-de,* they are helping to defuse the potential anger or disappointment experienced when someone demands something of them that they don't want to give or cannot provide. The closest English phrases are: "I don't want to bother you, however . . . " or "I feel kind of bad, but. . . . "

For example, a subordinate may accept a bigger job assignment than they are able to handle because they feel *ah-nar-de*. The project may be completed on schedule, but staff could feel overworked or the final result might not be up to par. Make sure that your written and verbal communications are explicit and that you're regularly checking progress with local partners. Learning to ask nonjudgmental questions helps save face.

At times, an eagerness to please may result in your Myanmar contacts over-selling their capabilities or exaggerating their influence. Because people here do not want to disappoint a superior by telling them they can't meet a dead-line, many avoid saying no, saying instead, "I would like to, but . . . " This all depends on the seniority and international experience of the person with whom you are communicating. Some businesspeople in Myanmar will happily say no.

Here is one area in which U.S. Americans and Myanmar are similar: Getting directly to the point. The Myanmar dislike beating around the bush.

6. How Formal or Informal Do Businesspeople in Myanmar Tend to Be?

This is Burma, and it will be quite unlike any land you know about.
— *Rudyard Kipling (1865–1936)*

In Myanmar a distrust of international visitors, especially after many years of being a closed society, reinforces the need to handle all formal introductions correctly. Your attitude, conversation style, behavior, and small details in your appearance will be observed. Naming conventions are worth familiarizing yourself with (Table 10.6 on page 221) and are especially important in a culture where people believe that the way you act and think writes the "story of your life." Your handling of introductions lays the foundation for how closely your business acumen and credentials will be scrutinized. You are responsible for your business story, and respect from the Myanmar will begin from that point.

Respect from the Myanmar begins with a formal introduction through another Myanmar business professional. This introduction is considered a local responsibility and will not be undertaken without professional certainty that you are to be trusted. If you have asked for an introduction, be prepared for a number of responses. First, a Myanmar may hesitate before responding because they must think before committing – as they are cautious and a mistake is costly. Second, a Myanmar may agree too readily and quickly. Be prepared for delay, excuses to arise, and a failure of the introductions to materialize.

As an example of the right way to be introduced, one U.S. CEO, who had been doing business in Myanmar for many years, was invited by a Malaysian board member to get involved in a natural resources transaction in Myanmar. Formal introductions to Myanmar counterparts were facilitated by the Malaysian, and the U.S. CEO was well received.

Be prepared for your formal introduction and the process by having business credentials, banking, and funding documentation in hand.

7. How Aligned Are Myanmar Social and Business Lives?

U.S. businesspeople will most likely not be invited for Sunday lunch at a business associate's home; a nice restaurant is more likely in the cards.

—*Robert Easson, Imagino Group CEO*

Although the Myanmar are sociable among themselves and with close friends, this is not yet a completely open country. A number of restrictions remain below the surface, often impacting business–social events. Until recently, it was illegal for international visitors to be invited into a Myanmar home. Don't take it personally if you're not invited to a business associate's home.

Most entertaining outside of office hours takes place in hotel restaurants and private dining areas. When executives go to dinner, the most junior Myanmar executive will serve the food and alcohol, first to you or other guests. Expect the senior Myanmar executive to offer a toast when drinking. Unlike many parts of Asia where drinking liquor often seems mandatory, in Myanmar, you will be asked if you want to take part in after-hours business socializing. There is no need to feel awkward about declining alcohol; the Myanmar will not hold this against you.

When socializing outside of a formal business environment, watch for unwittingly directing conversations into territory that could be tricky for your Myanmar hosts, such as discussions about politics. According to one source, "There are still one million people in the country who receive small amounts of money to be active as part of the secret police in the country."[26] The secret police may be listening at any gathering. Discussions of sensitive issues involving the military junta or country politics may jeopardize your Myanmar hosts or colleagues after your departure. This is such a concern that one anonymous 'aging general' concluded the foreword to Jonathan Nichols's latest book by writing: "The names of the characters and some of the circumstances in *My My*

[26]VNG International, "Day 6 & 7—A Visit to Myanmar," www.vng-international.nl /communication/blog/blog-single/Day_6_7_A_visit_to_Myanmar.html (accessed November 19, 2014).

Myanmar are fictitious to prevent recognition and preserve reputations—and possibly a life or two."

The other reason why the Myanmar may appear reticent to discuss certain topics with you during business-social gatherings concerns their fear of foreigners. After nearly 50 years under a military regime, the average Myanmar is still trying to come to terms with the fact that people from the outside may actually provide some benefit for their country.

The challenge Myanmar now face in learning to socialize with international colleagues is illustrated by an energy CEO who went drinking with ministers after a long day of business meetings and dinner and told us, "Myanmar business leaders are just beginning to accept their new freedoms and think about how to phrase questions. As we socialize, we can literally see the wheels turning and watch them formulate how to phrase a query."

8. How Is the Concept of Women in Business Handled in Myanmar?

In some parts of this society, men's clothes must be hung higher (on racks) than women's, and losing face to a woman is considered by many men to be the ultimate insult. Yet there are those in Myanmar who don't concern themselves with many of these traditions.
    —*Robert Easson, Imagino Group CEO*

Businesswomen in Myanmar still face many challenges. As Robert Easson revealed, "Should you decide to host an evening dinner, you might find that a female member of the Myanmar group asks you to speak to her mother beforehand, to confirm that it really is a company event. Make the call: Many adult women in Myanmar still have a 6 p.m. curfew set for them by their parents."

Business in Myanmar is largely influenced, if not controlled, by the various government ministries, whose decision makers tend to be former members of the military. It was only in late 2013 that women were allowed to join the army. Depending on the success of the proposed amendments to Myanmar's constitution, it may be years before women hold positions of power in the country. However, this wasn't always the case as, historically, women in Myanmar enjoyed much higher status and freedom than in some other Asian countries. This prompted Sir James George Scott (1851–1935) to say, "A Burmese woman going about her business is more than a match for any man."

Currently, Myanmar is not ranked on the World Economic Forum's Global Gender Gap Index, a measure of gender-based disparities across four criteria: economic participation, educational attainment, political empowerment, and health for 136 countries. It will be interesting to see a future ranking.

Nevertheless, national heroine Aung San Suu Kyi is a highly respected role model across generations.[27] As legal consultant Moe Lwin shared, "I show my daughter the speeches of Madam Aung San Suu Kyi on YouTube, whose example of confidence, professionalism, and grace can help women in Myanmar achieve positions of prominence in almost all walks of life and industries. This is how you become admired by your counterparts in our culture." Mr. Lwin pointed out that the grace and humility with which Myanmar women exert their influence in many smaller, family operations provides a useful hint to Western businesswomen visiting the country. Or, as human resources development manager Aung Ko Ko advises, "If you follow the values our nation stands for, you will have no problem working as a female executive here."

As Pam Reed, CEO of Texas Climate and Carbon Exchange shared, "While in Myanmar on business, Gay Gillen and I dressed conservatively and were very mindful of the local culture and customs. The Burmese were very polite and respectful to us. We observed that while much in Myanmar is in flux since the 'opening' of the country, their society continues to be built on order, respect of elders, and to be centered on their Buddhist faith."

Aung Ko Ko's advice for businesswoman traveling to Myanmar: Dress conservatively, carry yourself with grace and elegance, show respect for seniority, and use diplomacy when you cannot back down from the terms of the deal.

Cultural Summary

Here are some key points to remember:

- Refer to the country and its people as *Myanmar*. Avoid using the colonial name Burma, especially when conducting business with the government (for example, the ministries).
- The ministries and government control and approve business, so develop these crucial relationships first.
- Even though the country is open for global trade, business professionals are apprehensive about doing business with international visitors, for fear of becoming too *Westernized*. They greatly appreciate your knowledge and respect for their unique culture and customs.

Self-Awareness Profile

This simple exercise prompts you to self-assess where you currently stand on topics related to the eight-question framework and *compare* this with the country

---

[27] Alan Clements, *The Voice of Hope: Aung San Suu Kyi Conversations with Alan Clements* (World Dharma Publications, 2012), Kindle edition.

culture. This visual will help you discover the extent to which you may need to adapt your current mindset and behavior to develop more robust business relationships. For details on how to complete this graphic, see the instructions given in the Introduction on pages xviii–xix.

Consider copying the eight-question Profile or using a pencil so that you can see, over time, how you have adjusted your cultural mindset. You might also wish to create unique graphics related to each of the businesses you work with, as these cultural positions vary depending upon geographic location, industry, generational factors, and corporate profile.

Q1: What is your preferred way of doing business?

As an individual   **As a team**
making   **member who**
autonomous   **seeks group**
decisions   **consensus**

     1   2   3   4   5   **6**

Q2: How comfortable are you in hierarchies in which power is distributed unequally?

Very uncomfortable   **Very comfortable**

     1   2   3   4   5   **6**

Q3: How closely do you follow rules and obey the law?

Almost always   **It depends**

     1   2   3   4   **5**   6

Q4: What is your general attitude toward time?

I prefer   **I prefer flexibility,**
agendas, schedules,   **fluidity without**
planning   **scheduling**

     1   2   3   4   5   **6**

Q5: What is your preferred way to communicate?

Very diplomatically   **Very candidly**

  1   **2**   3   4   5   6

Q6: What is your interpersonal style or level of formality in business interactions?

Very formal   **Very informal**

  1   **2**   3   4   5   6

Q7: What is your view on socializing within business?

A waste of time   **Essential**

  1   2   3   4   5   **6**

Q8: Should a woman defer to a man as the lead, if winning business in a certain culture depended on it?

Never   **Yes, absolutely**

  1   2   3   **4**   5   6

11 | The Philippines

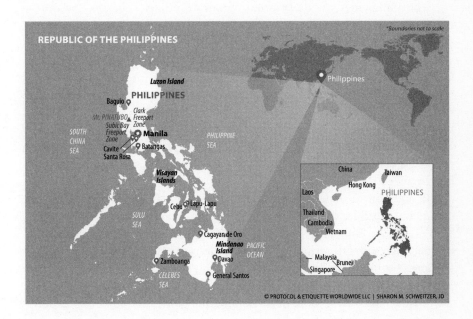

Our country has the social and economic momentum to go from success to success, and truly make waves throughout our archipelago, in the international community, and in the vast, immeasurable ocean of history.

> —Benigno Simeon Aquino, President of the Philippines

Introduction

The Philippines, otherwise known as the *Pearl of the Orient Seas*, is a unique archipelago that has the third largest English-speaking population in the world, after the U.S. and India.[1] It is Asia's largest Catholic country and the highest birth rate in Asia, and one-third of its population is under the age of 35. Predictions are that the population may double in 30 years. Not surprisingly, it has been known as the *text capital of the world* and now as the *selfie capital of the planet*.[2]

The Philippines has unwavering optimism, positive outlook toward the future, and *bahala na*—meaning that life is to be enjoyed to its fullest every day, without worry (literal translation is *leave it up to God*). Similarly, business confidence remains high, and its growth outlook is robust. President Benigno C. Aquino III's administration is focused on five areas for job generation and economic development: outsourcing, tourism, infrastructure, agriculture and fisheries, and semiconductors and electronics. The national budget is aligned to provide massive support. Indeed, Deloitte's *Doing Business in the Philippines 2014* report[3] revealed that the country's GDP expansion in 2013 was among the fastest across Asia and it is ranked as one of the most promising recently industrialized countries.

In addition to their technical skills and English proficiency, Filipinos are culturally adaptable, dependable, and dedicated world-class service providers. This places the Philippines at the forefront of the manufacturing, electronics, outsourcing, and offshoring industries. Filipino culture began with tropical farming, fishing, and Spanish Catholic church doctrine. Filipinos are also renowned in the medical and healthcare industries for top-quality service worldwide—providing more nurses around the globe than any other nation.

On A.T. Kearney's *Global Services Location Index 2014*,[4] the country currently sits at number seven on the list of the top 50 countries worldwide that are attractive potential locations for offshore services. It is the Index's largest destination for call centers outside of India. Newer industries are expanding, including higher-value voice services, IT, and business process outsourcing (BPO).

---

[1] Maps of World, "Top Ten English Speaking Countries," www.mapsofworld.com/world-top-ten /countries-with-most-english-language-speaker-map.html (accessed November 17, 2014).
[2] http://time.com/selfies-cities-world-rankings/
[3] Deloitte, "Doing Business in the Philippines: Seizing Opportunities," January 2014, www.deloitte.com/assets/Dcom-Philippines/Local%20Assets/Documents/Doing%20Business% 20in%20the%20Philippines%20(Jan2014).pdf.
[4] A.T. Kearney, *Global Services Location Index 2014*, www.atkearney.com/research-studies/global -services-location-index (accessed November 17, 2014).

Quiz

How much do you know about the Philippines? Answer the following questions as True or False to test your knowledge. (The Answer Key at the bottom includes page numbers that refer to the topic):

_____1. A bow is an appropriate greeting in the Philippines.

_____2. The Philippines is the text capital of the world.

_____3. Asia's first female head of state was Philippine President Maria Corazon Aquino.

_____4. Filipino culture began with tropical farming, fishing, and Spanish Catholic church doctrine.

_____5. The Philippines is the third-largest English-speaking nation in the world.

_____6. There are two official languages: Filipino (Tagalog) is the native language, and English is the *lingua franca* of business, government, and education.

_____7. Spain's King Philip II is the country's namesake after Captain Ferdinand Magellan claimed the islands while circumnavigating the globe.

_____8. The Philippine's is Asia's largest Catholic country.

_____9. The Philippine archipelago comprises more than 7,100 islands.

_____10. Reciprocating a business lunch, dinner, or drinks invitation is crucial.

Answer Key: 1. F (p. 247–248); 2. T (p. 238); 3. T (p. 258); 4. T (p. 254–257); 5. T (p. 238); 6. T (p. 244); 7. T (p. 240); 8. T (p. 238); 9. T (p. 239); 10. T (p. 257).

Country Basics

This section provides key knowledge in an easy-to-read format to help you quickly grasp some of the basics necessary to navigate this culture.

Historical Timeline

A critical way to show respect for another person's culture is to have knowledge of their country's history and current affairs. Table 11.1 on pages 240–241 outlines a few key events related to the Philippines, together with concurrent world events.

Table 11.1   Key Historical Events

Period/ Dates	Description/Events	World Events
1542	Ferdinand Magellan claims the islands on behalf of Spain, naming them after King Philip II.	Andreas Vesalius authors influential book on human anatomy.
1898	After Spanish–American War, Spain cedes the Philippines to the U.S.	Russia obtains the lease of Port Arthur, China.
1935	The Philippines is established as a self-governing commonwealth, with Manuel Quezon as the first president.	Chiang Kai-shek named president of China.
1942–1945	Filipinos and U.S. forces fight to regain control of the Islands.	World War II (1939–1945).
1946	The islands are granted full independence and renamed the Republic of the Philippines.	The U.N. General Assembly holds its first session.
1965	Ferdinand Marcos becomes president.	Martin Luther King, Jr. heads civil rights procession in Alabama.
1972	Marcos declares martial law, which suspends parliament and remains in place for nine years.	India and Bangladesh sign friendship treaty.
1973	A new constitution gives President Marcos absolute powers.	Concorde makes its first non-stop flight crossing the Atlantic (Washington DC to Paris) in record-breaking time (3h 33m).
1986	Mrs. Corazon Aquino is sworn in as president.	Japanese probe Suisei observes Halley's Comet during its journey through the inner solar system.
1996	Peace agreement reached with Moro National Liberation Front.	Russia's first president, Boris Yeltsin, begins second term.

Table 11.1   (*Continued*)

Period/ Dates	Description/Events	World Events
2001	President Joseph Estrada stands down due to trial and mass protests.	First draft of the complete Human Genome is published in *Nature*.
2013	Typhoon Haiyan devastates the country, prompting international aid.	Cardinal Bergoglio of Argentina elected pope, the first from the Americas.
2014	A peace deal is reached with the Moro Islamic Liberation Front, ending a 40-year conflict.	The XXII Olympic Winter Games take place in Sochi, Russia.
2016	Presidential and legislative elections scheduled.	Japan's legislative elections, Malaysia's selection of king, and presidential elections for Taiwan, the Philippines, and the U.S. scheduled.
2019	Legislative elections scheduled.	India's legislative elections scheduled.

Full Country Name and Location

The Republic of the Philippines is an archipelago in Southeastern Asia comprising more than 7,100 islands. Luzon and Mindanao are the largest of the 11 main islands with the highest populations. The total land area is approximately the size of Italy or the State of Arizona in the U.S. Taiwan lies to the north, Indonesia to the south, and Vietnam to the west. Surrounding waters include the South China Sea, Sulu Sea, Celebes Sea, and the Philippine Sea.

Government/Political Structure

The Philippines is a republic with a representative bicameral legislature and a president who serves as both the head of state and head of government. The president and vice president both hold office for a single six-year term. The last elections held in May 2010 were the country's first nationwide automated elections. Next elections are scheduled May of 2016.

Population and Economic Centers

The population is approximately 107.7 million, according to *CIA World Factbook* estimates (July of 2014). The country consists of 80 provinces and

39 chartered cities, including the capital Manila, with 48.8 percent of the population living in urban areas.[5]

The ethnic makeup of the Philippines is Tagalog (28.1 percent), Cebuano (13.1 percent), Ilocano (9 percent), Bisaya/Binisaya (7.6 percent), Hiligaynon Ilonggo (7.5 percent), Bikol (6 percent), Waray (3.4 percent), and other (25.3 percent).[6]

The major business centers and populations (2010) are outlined in Table 11.2.[7]

Table 11.2   Major Business Centers

Business Centers	Population (Millions)
Baguio City	0.3
Batangas City	0.3
Cagayan de Oro	0.6
Cavite	0.1
Cebu City	0.9
Clark Freeport Zone	*
Davao	1.4
General Santos	0.5
Lapu–Lapu	0.4
Manila (capital)	1.7
Santa Rosa	0.3
Subic Bay Freeport Zone	*
Zamboanga	0.8

*The 2010 Census of Population and Housing does not cover all cities/towns, only main districts. See the Philippine Statistics Authority website for more information.[8]

Economy

The Philippines is ranked 95th out of 189 economies in terms of ease of doing business, according to the World Bank Group's *Doing Business 2015* report.[9]

[5]CIA, *The World Factbook*, "Philippines," www.cia.gov/library/publications/the-world-factbook /geos/rp.html (accessed November 17, 2014).
[6]Ibid.
[7]Philippine Statistics Authority, "Population and Housing," www.census.gov.ph/statistics/census /population-and-housing (accessed November 17, 2014).
[8]Ibid.
[9]World Bank Group, *Doing Business 2015* (October 29, 2014): 4, www.doingbusiness.org/~ /media/GIAWB/Doing%20Business/Documents/Annual-Reports/English/DB15-Full-Report .pdf.

Its 2013 GDP was ranked 40th by the World Bank[10] and the composition of its GDP by sector was services (57.2 percent), industry (31.6 percent), and agriculture (11.2 percent).[11]

Corruption Perceptions Index

The Philippines ranked 94th least corrupt out of 177 countries and territories with a score of 36 out of 100.[12] This annual index, compiled by Transparency International, measures perceived levels of public sector corruption.

The Office of the Ombudsman is the anti-corruption agency that conducts investigations in the Philippines.

Human Development Index

The Philippines ranked 117th out of 187 countries and territories.[13] The HDI, compiled by the United Nations Development Programme, is a composite index of life expectancy, education, and income statistics.

Global Gender Gap Index

The Philippines ranked 9th out of 142 countries in terms of gender equality with a score of 0.7814.[14] This annual index, compiled by the World Economic Forum, assesses gender gaps based on economic, political, educational, and health-based criteria.

Climate

The Philippines has a tropical, humid climate with three seasons. The rainy season occurs June through November, with frequent typhoons. March through

---

[10]The World Bank, Data, GDP Ranking, "Gross Domestic Product Ranking Table," last updated September 24, 2014, http://data.worldbank.org/data-catalog/GDP-ranking-table (accessed November 17, 2014).

[11]CIA, *The World Factbook*, "Philippines," www.cia.gov/library/publications/the-world-factbook /geos/rp.html (accessed November 17, 2014).

[12]Transparency International, "Corruption Perceptions Index 2013," www.transparency.org /cpi2013/results (accessed November 17, 2014).

[13]United Nations Development Programme, *Human Development Report 2014*, 160–163, http://hdr.undp.org/sites/default/files/hdr14-report-en-1.pdf (accessed November 17, 2014).

[14]World Economic Forum, *The Global Gender Gap Report 2014*, 8–9, www3.weforum.org/docs /GGGR14/GGGR_CompleteReport_2014.pdf (accessed November 17, 2014).

May is the hot dry season, whereas December through February is cool and dry.

Languages

The native language of the Philippines is Filipino (Tagalog), and English is the *lingua franca* of business, government, and education. Approximately 172 languages are acknowledged, including Arabic and Spanish. It is insulting to assume Spanish is the native language in the country. Major dialects include Cebuano, Ilocano, Hiligaynon or Ilonggo, Bicol, Waray, Kapampangan, and Pangasinan.

Belief Systems, Philosophies, and Religions

The country breakdown is as follows: Catholic (82.9 percent: Roman Catholic 80.9 percent; Aglipayan 2 percent), Islam (5 percent), Evangelical (2.8 percent), Iglesia ni Kristo (2.3 percent), other Christian (4.5 percent), Other (1.8 percent), Unspecified (0.6 percent), None (0.1 percent) (2000 census).[15]

The Philippines is predominantly Catholic after four hundred years of Spanish rule, although the base layer of animism is never far from the surface.[16]

For an overview of belief systems, philosophies, and religions please refer to Chapter 4, pages 64–65.

Time Zones/Daylight Savings

The Philippines has a single time zone, Philippine Time (PHT). The Philippines is eight hours ahead of GMT (Greenwich Mean Time)/UTC (Coordinated Universal Time). It does not operate under Daylight Savings.

It is 13 hours ahead of U.S. Eastern Standard Time (12 hours ahead in Daylight Savings Time). See www.timeanddate.com/worldclock.

To calculate time in the Philippines, add eight hours to UTC/GMT.

Telephone Country Code and Internet Suffix

The Philippine telephone country code is 63, and the Internet suffix is .ph.

---

[15] CIA, *The World Factbook*, "Philippines," www.cia.gov/library/publications/the-world-factbook/geos/rp.html (accessed November 17, 2014).
[16] Alan M. Rugman, ed., *The Oxford Handbook of International Business* (New York: Oxford University Press, 2009), 689.

Currency

The Philippine currency is the Philippine Peso (PHP). One peso is divided into 100 centavos.

Business Culture, Etiquette, and Customs

This section covers business culture, etiquette, and customs.

Fiscal Year

The fiscal year in the Philippines is January 1 to December 31. Dates are written as day, month, year; April 1, 2020 is written 01/04/20.

Working Week

The typical work schedule is outlined in Table 11.3. Some private offices are open Saturdays 9:00–12:00.

Table 11.3 The Filipino Working Schedule

Industry	Business Hours	Days of the Week
Private and Government Offices	08:00–17:00 or 09:00–18:00	Monday–Friday
Banks	09:00–15:00	Monday–Friday
Shops	Variable hours	Open daily

Holidays and Festivals

Some Philippine holidays change from year to year. Floating holidays are designated with an asterisk. On specific holidays, an office may remain open with limited staff. Check with your embassy or trade office before planning business travel. Common holidays and festivals are outlined in Table 11.4 on page 246.

Business Dress/Appearance

Personal appearance and grooming is crucial; some Filipinos shower three or four times daily. Over- or underdressing may cause a loss of face. Dress well to

Table 11.4   Holidays and Festivals

Date	Name
January 1	New Year's Day
March/April	Easter/Holy Week*
April 9	Day of Valor (*Araw ng Kagitingan*)
May 1	Labor Day
May 6	National Heroes Day
June 12	Independence Day
August 21	Ninoy Aquino Day
August 27	National Heroes Day
November 1	All Saint's Day
November 30	Bonifacio Day
December 25	Christmas Day
December 30	José Rizal Day (national independence hero)

leave a good impression. Some professional Filipino men wear the traditional *barong*, a lightweight, embroidered shirt that your host may encourage you to wear. Women's traditional costume is the *terno*, a long dress with puffy sleeves and a scoop neckline.

For business, men should wear a two-piece suit, especially for initial meetings. Shirts and ties with or without a coat are acceptable for subsequent meetings and less formal occasions. Follow your Filipino colleague's lead.

Women wear pantsuits, dresses, or skirts for business, and pants or a skirt when casual. When visiting Muslim areas, women dress modestly with long sleeves, pants, or skirts knee-length or longer. Suits and cocktail dresses are worn to formal dinners.

News Sources

Some of the most popular news sources in the Philippines include the following:

- *Philippine Star:* www.philstar.com
- *Philippine Daily Inquirer:* www.inquirer.net
- *The Manila Times:* www.manilatimes.net
- *Philippines News Agency:* www.pna.gov.ph/index.php
- *Business World:* www.bworldonline.com
- *Malaya Business Insight:* www.malaya.com.ph

Business Cards

Business cards may be printed in English. Include your position or title because status and rank within the hierarchy are valued.[17]

Technology

According to Akamai Technology's *State of the Internet Report*, the Philippines ranked 108th globally for average Internet connection speed and 36th for average peak connection speed.[18] The country was commended in the report for high improvement rates year-over-year. Latest figures rank the Philippines 34th worldwide for the number of Internet users[19] and 52nd globally for the number of Internet hosts.[20]

Gifts

Gifts are given at first meetings; bring gifts for everyone or give a group gift. Business gifts include company logo items, domestic crafts, office desk sets, pen sets, whisky, or other liquor. Never give cash or gifts to government officials.

In the Philippines, a gift from a male to a female should come with a card stating the gift is also from his wife, sister, or mother to avoid the appearance of impropriety. Send a gift or thank-you card the day after attending a dinner or social gathering. Wrap gifts in pastels; avoid black, chrysanthemums and white lilies.[21]

Introductions, Greetings, Personal Space, and Eye Contact

A handshake is the most common greeting; intergender handshaking is acceptable because men and women are considered business equals. Men greet with a pat on the back; however, avoid touching beyond a handshake until

---

[17] David Clive Price, *The Master Key to Asia: A 6-Step Guide to Unlocking New Markets* (CreateSpace 2013), 116.

[18] Akamai Technologies, "State of the Internet Q4 2013," April 2014, www.akamai.com /dl/akamai/akamai-soti-q413.pdf?WT.mc_id=soti_Q413 (accessed November 17, 2014).

[19] CIA, *The World Factbook*, "Country Comparison: Internet Users," information dated 2009, www.cia.gov/library/publications/the-world-factbook/rankorder/2153rank.html (accessed November 17, 2014).

[20] CIA, *The World Factbook*, "Country Comparison: Internet Hosts," information dated 2009, www.cia.gov/library/publications/the-world-factbook/rankorder/2184rank.html (accessed November 17, 2014).

[21] Ibid, 117.

a relationship is established. Moderate eye contact is acceptable. *Mano po* is a sign of respect to elders by bringing the back of their hand to your forehead.

Useful Phrases

Table 11.5 covers phrases that may be useful for travel in the Philippines.

Table 11.5　Useful Phrases for Philippine Travel

English	Filipino	Pronunciation
Hello	*Mabuhay*	Mah–BOO–high
Pleased to meet you	*Ikinagagalak kong makilala kayo*	Ihn–ahg–AHL–ak kong mahk–ee–LA–la kye–OH
How are you?	*Kumusta ka*	Kuh–MOO–stah kah
Good morning	*Magandang umaga*	Mahg–NDAHNG oo–MAH–ga
Good afternoon	*Magandang tanghali*	Mahg–NDAHNG than–GAL–ay
Good evening	*Magandang gabi*	Mmahg–NDAHNG ga–BEE
Goodbye	*Paalam*	Pah–AH–lahm
Please	*Pakisuyo*	Pah–kee–SU–yo
Thank you	*Salamat*	Sah–LAH–maht
You're welcome	*Walang anuman*	Wah–LAHNG ah–noo–MAHN
Yes	*Oo*	Oh oh
Excuse me	*Patawad po*	Pat–OW–ahd POH

Meetings and Negotiations

Due to the focus on hierarchy and group–oriented thinking, meetings usually involve little problem solving or decision making, unless you are with the top decision maker. The pace of business negotiations is slower than in the West. Filipinos negotiate formally with a high value on precision, respect, and harmony.[22]

Presentation Styles, Conversational Topics, and Humor

Filipinos appreciate innovation and current technology. Appropriate topics include travel, hobbies, food, music, language, sports, especially basketball, and

---

[22]David Clive Price, *The Master Key to Asia: A 6-Step Guide to Unlocking New Markets* (CreateSpace 2013), 119.

culture. Inappropriate topics include politics, U.S. relations, family, sex, risqué jokes, and complaints.

Gestures

Here are some important points to remember about gestures in the Philippines:

- Laughing or smiling may indicate embarrassment.
- Raising the eyebrows may indicate hello.
- Jerking the head upward is an affirmative gesture.
- A downward jerk of the head indicates no.
- Point by gesturing with eyes toward object.
- Point by puckering lips and gesture with the mouth.
- Point by motioning with the whole hand.

Notable Foods and Dishes

Cuisine stems from a mix of South Asian, Chinese, Spanish, and American influences. Soups contain meat, vegetables, and noodles. Rice is popular. Lemon, *kalamansi* (lime) vinegar, fish sauce, shrimp paste, garlic, and onions are popular ingredients.

Specialty Dishes

Here are some well-known dishes from the Philippines:

- **Adobo:** National dish of the Philippines, a meat stew marinated in palm vinegar, bay leaf, garlic, and black pepper
- **Pochero:** Beef, sausage, pork in a sauce with sweet potatoes, tomatoes, cabbage, and chickpeas
- **Sinigang:** Soup with a variety of meats or fish, vegetables, and fruits
- **Afritada:** Beef in olive oil and tomato paste with olives and vegetables
- **Kari-kari:** Beef or seafood in spicy peanut sauce with vegetables
- **Lechon:** Barbequed whole pig stuffed with tamarind leaves
- **Pancit Palabok:** Rice noodles with shrimp-based sauce

Dining Etiquette

In the Philippines, three meals a day, with two snacks, or *meriendas*, between meals is common. Forks and spoons are used; knives are not. The fork is used in the left hand to push food onto the spoon in the right hand. Hosts often wait for the honored guest to start eating. Depending on the dish, it may be acceptable to eat with your hands. Be sure to clean your plate.[23]

Drinking and Toasting

Cold beer, Scotch, gin, and liquor including brandy are popular. Drunkenness is frowned upon, and women rarely drink alcohol in public. Popular drinks include:

- Ginebra San Miguel: Locally brewed gin; world bestseller
- High-quality Scotch
- Lambanog: Potent (80- to 90-proof) Philippine liquor made of coconut

Toast to health or business prosperity in English or *"Mabuhay"* (mah-BOO-high) meaning 'long life.'

Tipping and Bill-Paying

Tipping is expected from international travelers. Hotels and restaurants usually include a service charge of 10 percent. Tip porters and bellhops 50 to 100 pesos per bag. Tip maids, taxi drivers, and valets small change. Agree on a taxi fare before departing.

Taboos

The following are taboo in Filipino culture:

- Lack of personal hygiene (Filipinos shower several times a day.)
- Chewing gum
- Hands in pockets
- Public nose-blowing
- Publicly using a handkerchief
- Physical displays of affection
- Poor posture or slouching
- Speaking in a loud voice
- Drunkenness
- Standing with hands on hips
- Extended middle finger (considered an obscene gesture)

---

[23] *CultureGrams World Edition 2014: Philippines* (Ann Arbor, MI: ProQuest, 2014).

Heroes and Sports

Knowing about another country's heroes and sports offers opportunities to incorporate culture-specific references into your conversations and presentations.

Heroes

The following are heroes from Philippine history:

Dr. José P. Rizal (1861–1896): Filipino nationalist, novelist, and revolutionary. Often considered the greatest Filipino hero, he was a leader in the reform movement against Spain's colonial rule. The novels he wrote inspired the people of his country, as he exposed discrimination and called for equality in the Philippines. Although he promoted peaceful reform, his execution in 1896 sparked the Filipinos to revolt against Spain.

Andrés Bonifacio (1863–1897): Father of the Philippine Revolution. Born to a poor family in Manila, he rose to become a great revolutionary leader in the movement for independence from Spain. In 1892, he founded the nationalist society Katipunan, which consisted mainly of workers and peasants and grew by the thousands over the next few years. Bonifacio led this group in the revolt of 1896 against Spanish troops, initiating the Philippine Revolution.

Benigno "Ninoy" Aquino, Jr. (1932–1983): Filipino senator (1967–1972) and hero of democracy. The youngest senator elected to office in the Philippines and former governor of Tarlac Province. He was a candidate for presidency in 1972. However, President Marcos declared martial law and jailed all of his political opponents, including Aquino. Aquino's assassination in 1983 sparked the People Power Revolution and prompted his wife Corazon Aquino to run for president, eventually leading to Marcos' downfall.

Sports

Sports

Currently the most popular sports in the Philippines are boxing and basketball (the PBA is the Philippine Basketball Association).

Sports Figures

Emmanuel "Manny" Dapidran Pacquiao (1978–present): Professional boxer. Named the "Fighter of the Decade" for 2000–2009, he has won world titles in eight weight divisions and has been noted as the 14th highest paid athlete in the world.[24] He is the current WBO welterweight champion and was long rated as the best pound-for-pound boxer in the world. Pacquiao was elected to the House of Representatives in the 15th Congress of the Philippines and reelected in 2013 to the 16th Congress.

Rubilen Amit (1981–present): Female professional pocket billiards player. A Filipino billiards legend who won three different titles in 2013; the first Filipino woman to become a world pool champion. Helped Team Asia win the inaugural Queens Cup and capped her year with a gold medal in 10-ball.

Wesley So (1993–present): Chess grandmaster. Became chess grandmaster when just 14 years old, the eighth youngest in history. In 2013, he broke into the Top 30 World Chess Federation rankings, placing in the juniors list and finishing first place in five different competitions.

James Carlos Agravante Yap, Sr. (1982–present): Professional basketball player. Won seven PBA championships and was chosen as a PBA All-Star team starter 11 times. Won the All-Star MVP award in 2012 and is currently one of the most popular players in the league.

Eight-Question Framework

This section reviews the framework to which you were introduced earlier in this book. Each of these questions addresses one or more business topics to help you attract and build the relationships upon which today's successful businesses depend.

1. How Do Filipinos Prefer to Act: Individually or as a Group?

I want our people to be like a molave tree, strong and resilient, standing on the hillsides, unafraid of the rising tide, lighting and the storm, confident of its strength.

—*Manuel L. Quezon, president of the Commonwealth of the Philippines (1935–1944)*

---

[24] *Forbes* magazine, "The World's Highest-Paid Athletes 2013: Behind the Numbers," June 5, 2013, www.forbes.com/sites/kurtbadenhausen/2013/06/05/the-worlds-highest-paid-athletes-2013-behind-the-numbers/.

When asked this question, Mr. Michael Ozaeta, Chairman of the Board, All Medica Global Corporation, based in Manila, responded that the degree of consensus-seeking in the Philippines varies on a case-by-case basis. "More often than not, a group will be involved in making a business decision, but there are occasions when one individual will overrule them or make a decision on his or her own," he says. "Decision making within large, family-owned conglomerates and big corporations occurs within a hierarchy. For example, the patriarch, chairman, or owner will have the last say, after considering the opinions and insights from those at the director level. Similarly, in smaller businesses run by entrepreneurs, decisions will tend to be made by a single individual."

Making decisions that take into account group loyalties is reflected by Geert Hofstede's findings on the Individualism index (See Chapter 2, page 15) As he reported, the Philippines "collectivist" score of 32 reflects close long-term commitment to the member 'group.'[25]

Given the strong family group orientation within this Latin-based culture, directors may want to ensure that every Filipino impacted or involved in a decision is consulted. However, unless asked to do so, managers may not wish to take a position, share their opinion, or take action until an agreement is reached. In the Philippines, there is an element of self-esteem or self-pride involved known as *hiya*, somewhat similar to *face*. It is important for each person to hold high *hiya* and be seen to make beneficial contributions, which affords him *amor-propio,* or the sense of being a good team player.

2. How Are Power and Authority Viewed in the Philippines?

In the Philippines, power and authority are all about trust and track record, not seniority.
— *Mr. Michael Ozaeta*, AU Medica Global Corporation

Mr. Ozaeta says: "Someone at the director level who has the ear of those at the highest levels or the 'big boss' will have considerable long-term influence if they've made a couple of successful past decisions and made the company money."

Mr. Ozaeta shared this story to illustrate: "The chairman of a Philippines telecommunications company, a very successful and prominent businessman in his sixties, acquired a new technology from a company whose founder was probably in his early thirties. They decided to retain the younger man who, like many Silicon Valley-style founders, came to work wearing flip-flops and shorts, in contrast to the chairman, who is always in a coat and tie. The younger man has a degree from Harvard, but it wasn't that which caused the chairman to

---

[25] The Hofstede Center, "What About the Philippines," http://geert-hofstede.com /philippines.html (accessed November 17, 2014).

respect his opinion and listen to him. It's because of his track record of having built a company that was acquired, as well as several other successful ventures. It is for these reasons that the chairman really respects him."

It's a surprise to many business travelers to learn that although structure and hierarchy are present in all Filipino organizations, as well as educational, religious, and military institutions, one's stature may be improved. The difference in the Philippines is that while your rank and status are important for Filipinos to determine where you fit, your status may change based on trust and your track record, as mentioned earlier. This is a crucial distinction from other vertical or hierarchical-based Asian cultures where your seniority, class, or caste may be the primary or only factor that determines your status.

3. How Do Filipinos Compare Rules and Relationships?

Relationship-building is central to the Filipino culture.
— *Ms. Jamie Nanquil, Austin branch manager, Social Media Delivered*

Not surprisingly, in a country more reliant on human resources than agricultural or manufacturing products, and as one of the world's biggest service providers, relationships are key to doing business here. *Pakikipagkapwa-tao* is shared identity or interconnectedness with others in an ongoing relationship that demonstrates respect, concern and recognition of dignity. If pakikipagkapwa-tao is abused or compromised, trust is irreversibly lost.[26,27] As Mr. Ozaeta explains, "One of the fastest growing industries in the Philippines is the business process outsourcing industry (BPO). Within the BPOs, the back-office work is done mainly for the U.S. and some European countries, given our historical ties with the U.S. and the fact that people here speak English."

He adds that in the Philippines it is relatively easy to be introduced to one or two people who will then connect you to everyone else you need to know. "There is a tight-knit top business club in the city of Makati, which is part of metro Manila, and once you break into that, you'll get to know the key people from the big conglomerates and business groups. Join the American Chamber of Commerce and the European Chamber of Commerce and you'll get to know all these people immediately. Developing relationships with key people in our country is pretty efficient."

According to Ms. Jamie Nanquil of Social Media Delivered, "You shouldn't expect a contract to be signed without first building rapport. There will be definite roadblocks to progressing through business deals if you are not actively meeting with your Filipino partner in person." The nurturing

---

[26]Cultural Detective, www.culturaldetective.com (accessed January 11, 2015).
[27]Ibid.

of relationships with regular trips overseas to manage the process is a part of meeting expectations.[28]

Unlike in some Asian cultures where contracts are considered to be guidelines, after a contract is negotiated and signed in the Philippines, Filipinos stick to the contract.

It is people and circumstances, not universal laws or abstract rules, that determine how a Filipino decides to act. *Utang (debt)na loob* refers to the building and fulfilling of lifelong obligations among Filipinos and goes well beyond direct contractual obligations.[29] Do not confuse this with the direct, equivalent release of an obligation, which is a different concept relating to a single occurrence. These enduring obligations are the glue that bind Filipino society together and keep relationships flowing smoothly.

4. How Do Filipinos Regard Time?

We operate under the belief that "good things come to those who wait."
—*Ms. Jamie Nanquil*, Austin Branch Manager, Social Media Delivered

"In big corporations, being late has become unacceptable. People are more punctual because we recognize that time is money," says Mr. Ozaeta. "Even though traffic here is bad, it really shouldn't be an excuse. However, punctuality here is not as strict as you'll find in New York, Hong Kong, or Singapore, so new visitors need to keep a flexible attitude. Generally speaking, showing up 20 to 30 minutes late to a meeting is sometimes acceptable. At least with cell phones, you can call or text that you're running late.

"Filipinos who have been educated abroad are very particular about time. Everyone else has what we call a colonial mentality. This means that for an average Filipino, if my meeting is with an American, I'm going to show up on time. If I'm in the U.S., I follow the rules of the road. But if I'm in the Philippines and I'm meeting a Filipino, I can be 15 minutes late. It's rather like driving in the Philippines, where I don't have to stay in my lane. We all make a joke about how, in our own country we don't follow the rules, but the minute we land in America, we follow them to the letter."

The dimensions of time are changing in the sense that, historically, the Philippines have been a polychronic culture. This means that numerous things happen simultaneously and Filipinos are able to multitask. Filipinos look toward the future, not the past, and appreciate it when today's actions show results.

---

[28]Barry Tomalin and Mike Nicks, *World Business Cultures: A Handbook*, 3rd ed. (London: Thorogood Publishing, 2014), 53.
[29]Cultural Detective, www.culturaldetective.com (accessed January 11, 2015).

Time in the Philippines

According to Richard Lewis in *When Cultures Collide: Leading Across Cultures:* "A *manãna* tendency has also been inherited from the Spanish. When making appointments, it is advisable to ask if they are on 'American time' or 'Filipino time.' In the case of the latter, being one or two hours late is not unusual."[30]

5. How Direct Is Communication in the Philippines?

Some people will communicate "no" directly, but some will not. Listen carefully.
— *Mr. Motokatsu Sunagawa*, CEO, Eco-Merge

The advice that Mr. Motokatsu Sunagawa, chairman and CEO of Eco-Merge Philippines, Inc., offers about communicating in the Philippines is to pay attention to what is *really* being said. Mr. Sunagawa is originally from Japan and is based in Manila, having lived in the Philippines for five years: "Some people will communicate 'no' directly, but some will not. Listen carefully for expressions that are politely communicating 'no,' such as, 'I would like to, but I can't;' 'Let me see;' 'I would like to, but it's very difficult.' The unique phrase that Filipinos use a lot is, 'I will try, and will let you know.'"

Similarly, according to Mr. Michael Ozaeta, avoid saying you cannot meet a deadline or offering an unequivocal 'no,' especially when a relationship is new. "Try not to make your answers too direct because Filipinos tend to be sensitive to those who just state, 'This is what we want; this is what we don't want.' They will think of you as cocky and arrogant, especially if they don't know you that well.

"If your first contact in a company or industry is with someone who has worked in the U.S. or places like Hong Kong that are more international, they'll be more used to direct communication. But as a rule of thumb, try to soften your language by saying something like: "I'll try, and I'll let you know." Although, when you are dealing with someone in your own company or you have known for years, sometimes a direct 'no' is more appropriate."

Communication during business meetings and negotiations is high-context, meaning it occurs indirectly through body language and other non-verbal signals. There is a word for smooth, harmonious interaction: *pakikisama*.

6. How Formal or Informal Do Business People in the Philippines Tend to Be?

This is another area in which paying attention will reap benefits in terms of nurturing relationships with your Filipino colleagues and partners. According to Mr.

---

[30]Richard D. Lewis, *When Cultures Collide: Leading Across Cultures*, 3rd ed. (Boston: Nicholas Brealey International, 2006).

Michael Ozaeta, "At the beginning of a relationship, the business environment is formal. Once it is established and more relaxed, it's okay to use first names. For people who are senior in rank, status, or age, for example, you would address them by Mr. or Ms. and allow them to say, 'Oh, call me John,' or 'Call me Jill.'"

Adds Mr. Ozaeta: "The only titles we use are with people who are doctors, attorneys, ambassadors, and government officials' titles like senator or vice president: for example, 'Dr. Schweitzer,' although most people prefer to be referred to by their first or last names. We do not use *architect* or *banker*."

Mr. Sunagawa has found that using first names is a common practice in the Philippines. Many people do not consider that to be an informality, but a way of making the relationship friendlier than using family names. This is perhaps not surprising in a country where a great majority of the population is under the age of 35, resulting in generational differences in the workplace.

However, as Ms. Jamie Nanquil points out, "Although Filipinos are friendly and hospitable, you should always show professionalism and respect. Filipinos are big on respect."

7. *How Aligned Are Filipino Social and Business Lives?*

Socializing is very important for solidifying business relationships in the Philippines.
— *Ms. Jamie Nanquil*, Austin Branch Manager, Social Media Delivered

Visitors are thought of as guests (*dayuan*), not outsiders, and are often impressed by the friendliness and hospitality extended to them.[31] However, the art of reciprocity is often seen as a surprising part of relationship building in the Philippines. Mr. Ozaeta explained how this is played out.

"If you're dealing with government officials, definitely it is the international business professional that needs to extend an invitation to have drinks. However, the government officials may not reciprocate. In the private sector, it depends. If a Filipino group is looking for business from the international visitor, then they would definitely extend an invitation from the start. But if the international visitor seeks information from the Filipino or wants to get to know them better, it would be nice if they extended the invitation first. Depending on their status, the Filipino may insist on paying the bill. When they do insist, it's okay to let them pay. In fact, they may have already done so before you know it. In which case, you should just say, "It's my turn next time," advises Mr. Ozaeta. It is crucial to remember to extend another invitation and to make sure you do pay the bill on that occasion.

With respect to culture, Mr. Sunagawa shares that, "Most Filipinos respect their time with family. It is not common practice to socialize outside of office

---

[31] Cultural Detective, www.culturaldetective.com (accessed January 10, 2015).

hours as it is in, say, my own country. In Japan, I was used to establishing business relationships and personal relationships frequently after office hours, for dinner or drinks. But this is not as common in the Philippines, where you may choose to take an alternative approach and join them in a church activity or sports."

As Ms. Nanquil pointed out: "Filipinos tend to love singing and engage in a lot of karaoke, so if you are vocally blessed, you will be well-appreciated."

8. How Is the Concept of Women in Business Handled in the Philippines?

With Western businesswomen, there is no difference at all between how men and women are treated in business. You can behave like you're behaving in the West.

—*Mr. Michael Ozaeta*, AU Medica Global Corporation

"In a country where two women have already been elected president— Ms. Maria Corazon Aquino (1986–1992) and Ms. Gloria Macapagal-Arroyo (2001–2010)—women can do exceptionally well in the business world," says Ms. Jamie Nanquil. Ms. Aquino was also Asia's first female head of state. Although the Filipino culture values machismo, women here are considered equal to men in most business situations. Mr. Michael Ozaeta agrees, saying that women hold many prominent positions in government and in the private sector, and more of them are rising in professional occupations.

Ms. Nanquil's advice to successful international businesswomen women is, "Don't try to be too assertive or overzealous as it may be construed poorly."

"There are no rules preventing women going for after-work drinks at a hotel bar, or being invited to dinner and then perhaps going on to a nice club with music," advises Mr. Ozaeta. "The only exception to this would be going to a hostess bar. You only ever find businessmen attending them."

He adds that: "In terms of after-work entertaining, an international woman will feel very much at home in Manila. If she is here to set up a business, the advice is the same as I would give to a man: Get well connected within the business community, with people who can introduce you to the key players in your industry and who can give you sound advice."

Cultural Summary

Here are some key points to remember about the Filipino culture:

- The Philippines is different from other vertical Asian cultures where seniority, class, and caste are important considerations. Here, trust and track record take priority and status may change and improve based on these factors.

- Developing close relationships with local knowledge is essential in this culturally diverse nation with a mix of eastern and western characteristics.
- Progress moves slowly at times and quickly at other times. Demographically, the country is young, with a great majority of the population under the age of 30, leading to generational differences in the workplace.

Self-Awareness Profile

This simple exercise prompts you to self-assess where you currently stand on topics related to the eight-question framework and *compare* this with the country culture. This visual will help you discover the extent to which you may need to adapt your current mindset and behavior to develop more robust business relationships. For details on how to complete this graphic, see the instructions given in the Introduction on pages xviii–xix.

Consider copying the eight-question Profile or using a pencil so that you can see, over time, how you have adjusted your cultural mindset. You might also wish to create unique graphics related to each of the businesses you work with, as these cultural positions vary depending upon geographic location, industry, generational factors, and corporate profile.

Q1: What is your preferred way of doing business?

As an individual making autonomous decisions					As a team member who seeks group consensus
1	2	3	4	**5**	6

Q2: How comfortable are you in hierarchies in which power is distributed unequally?

Very uncomfortable					Very comfortable
1	2	3	4	5	**6**

Q3: How closely do you follow rules and obey the law?

Almost always					It depends
1	2	3	4	**5**	6

Q4: What is your general attitude toward time?

**I prefer
agendas, schedules,
planning**

**I prefer flexibility,
fluidity without
scheduling**

1   2   3   **4**   5   6

Q5: What is your preferred way to communicate?

Very diplomatically   **Very candidly**

1   2   **3**   4   5   6

Q6: What is your interpersonal style or level of formality in business interactions?

Very formal   **Very informal**

1   2   **3**   4   5   6

Q7: What is your view on socializing within business?

A waste of time   **Essential**

1   2   3   4   **5**   6

Q8: Should a woman defer to a man as the lead, if winning business in a certain culture depended on it?

Never   **Yes, absolutely**

1   2   3   **4**   5   6

12 | Singapore

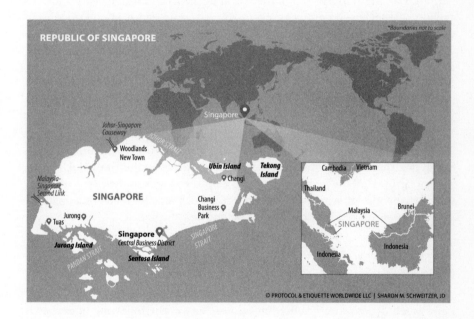

Introduction

As an article in *The Economist* proposed, if there was to be one 'world capital,' what better choice could there be than Singapore?[1] In light of how often this city-state appears at the top of various world rankings and best-of lists, it's easy to see why the writer made this choice. Singapore boasts the world's healthiest people, the lowest crime rate, the lowest level of drug abuse, and the shortest average time needed to become a millionaire. Populated by high achievers, Singapore is also number one in the world for math and science education. In a report that reviewed creative problem-solving competence among students in OECD countries, Singapore came out at the top. And for eight consecutive years, the World Bank has recognized Singapore as the world's easiest place to do business.[2]

Secular Confucian values of hard work, thrift, honesty, and integrity find their place within a state-of-the-art infrastructure that has made Singapore so attractive to foreign trade and investment.

As an independent republic, Singapore is barely 50 years old. The country is a rich ethnic mix of Chinese, Malay, and Indian cultures. When traveling to Singapore, then, you'd do well to take into consideration the cultural dynamics and background of the people there with whom you seek to develop a relationship. Review the information in this chapter, but then also review the material in the chapter devoted to that ethnic background.

Quiz

How much do you know about Singapore? Answer the following questions as True or False to test your knowledge. (The Answer Key that follows the quiz includes page references where you can find more information.):

_____1. Singapore is one of only three city-states in the world.

_____2. Over 1.5 million of Singapore's 5.5 million total population are non-residents.

_____3. The island of Singapore lies just south of the equator.

---

[1] *Intelligent Life*, "Singapore, Capital of the World," September/October 2011, http://moreintelligentlife.com/content/ideas/edward-carr/singapore-capital-world.

[2] World Bank Group, "Ease of Doing Business in Singapore," www.doingbusiness.org/data/exploreeconomies/singapore (accessed November 10, 2014).

_____4. Singapore is the only Asian country assigned an AAA credit rating by all three major agencies.

_____5. According to the World Bank, it is easier to do business in Singapore than in any other country in the world..

_____6. English is the most widely spoken official language in Singapore.

_____7. Singapore's head of state is the prime minister.

_____8. Singapore is an informal culture, with use of first names in business common at first meetings.

_____9. Adding the "Singlish" *lah* to the end of many words and sentences helps visitors from the West fit in.

_____10. Singaporeans point with their thumbs rather than their index fingers. (Pointing with an index finger is considered rude).

Answer Key: 1. T (p. 266); 2. T (p. 266); 3. F (p. 268); 4. T (p. 267); 5. T (p. 262); 6. F (p. 268); 7. F (p. 266); 8. F (p. 272); 9. F (p. 280); 10. T (p. 273).

Country Basics

This section provides key knowledge in an easy-to-read format to help you quickly grasp some of the basics necessary to navigate this culture.

Historical Timeline

A critical way to show respect for another person's culture is to have knowledge of their country's history and current affairs. Table 12.1 on pages 264–265 outlines a few key events related to Singapore, together with concurrent world events.

Full Country Name and Location

The Republic of Singapore consists of the main island plus 63 smaller islets. It is separated from the southern tip of the Malay Peninsula by the Johor Straits and Indonesia's Riau Islands by the Singapore Strait. It has no land borders, but part of its 193 miles of coastline is connected to Malaysia by a causeway and bridge, offering road and rail access. At 697 square kilometers, Singapore is slightly smaller than Bahrain (765 square kilometers) and almost four times the size of the U.S. capital, Washington, D.C. (177 square kilometers).

Table 12.1 Key Historical Events

Period/Dates	Description/Events	World Events
Third-century A.D.	Early Chinese records refer to 'Pu-loo-chung' or 'island at the end of a peninsula.'	248 A.D. is the year Rome celebrates its 1,000th anniversary.
Late thirteenth century A.D.	Legend says the fishing village of Temasek ('Sea Town' in Malay) is renamed Singapora ('Lion City') when a Srivijayan prince mistakes a tiger for lion.	Marco Polo begins an expedition to China (1271).
1819	Modern Singapore is founded when Sir Thomas Stanford Raffles of the East India Company buys land for a trading station.	The U.S. buys Florida from Spain.
1821	First Chinese immigrants arrive (Hokkiens from Fujian).	Mexico gains independence from Spain.
1869	After the opening of the Suez Canal, Singapore finds itself in a strategic location—linking the East and the West—and enjoys a period of prosperity.	Dmitri Mendeleev presents the first periodic table to the Russian Chemical Society.
Feb. 1942–Sept. 1945	Occupied by Japan during WWII and renamed Syonan ('Light of the South').	Penicillin successfully used in the treatment of chronic diseases (1942).
1946	Becomes separate crown colony of the British Empire.	The UN General Assembly holds its first session.
1959	First general elections won by People's Action Party (PAP). Mr. Lee Kuan Yew becomes first Prime Minister.	Fidel Castro becomes Prime Minister of Cuba.

Table 12.1 (*Continued*)

Period/Dates	Description/Events	World Events
1963	Joins the Federation of Malaysia.	Valentina Tereshkova (USSR) is first woman in space.
August 9, 1965	Becomes an independent republic and joins the U.N.	First ground station–to–aircraft radio communication via satellite.
1967	Founding member of ASEAN.	Mohammed Reza Shah Pahlavi and his wife are crowned Emperor and Empress of Iran.
1990	Prime Minister Lee Kuan Yew stands down after 31 years.	Ireland elects its first female President (Mary Robinson).
2003	First Asian nation to sign free trade agreement with U.S.	The Federal Republic of Yugoslavia is renamed as Serbia and Montenegro.
2011	Tony Tan elected President after recount.	The world population reaches 7 billion according to the United Nations.
2013	Land-strapped public universities explore the possibility of expanding underground.	Cardinal Jorge Mario Bergoglio of Argentina is elected pope of the Catholic Church, the first from the Americas.
2014	Singapore is ranked the most transparent real-estate market in Asia.	The XXII Olympic Winter Games take place in Sochi, Russia.
2017	National elections scheduled.	Hong Kong, Indian, South Korean, and Singaporean elections scheduled.

Government/Political Structure

Singapore is a parliamentary republic with a president voted in as head of state and a prime minister selected by parliamentary majority (as in the U.K.) as the head of government. Elections for the unicameral legislature are held every six years, most recently in May, 2011, when the People's Action Party (PAP) took just over 60 percent of the votes. The next presidential and legislative elections are scheduled for 2017. Voting is compulsory for eligible citizens. Nonvoters are struck off the electoral register and cannot stand as a candidate for presidential or parliamentary elections. Singapore is one of only three city-states in the world.

Population and Economic Centers

Singapore's total population is 5.5 million, of which just over 1.5 million are non-residents (June 2014 estimates).[3] It is the second most densely populated country in the world after Monaco,[4] and 100 percent of its population lives in urban areas.[5]

The main ethnic groups are Chinese (74.2 percent), Malay (13.3 percent), Indian (9.2 percent); the remainder (3.3 percent),[6] includes Arabs, Jews, and Armenians.

The major business centers and populations (2014) are shown in Table 12.2 on page 267.[7]

Economy

Singapore ranks second in the world for foreign trade and investment, according to the Globalization Index 2012.[8]

Due to its historical geostrategic position, it has long been an *entrepot* trading center, meaning that goods can be imported and exported without incurring duties. The city-state's economic growth is driven by exports—

[3]City Population, "Singapore," www.citypopulation.de/Singapore-Regions.html (accessed November 17, 2014).

[4]Maps of World, "Top Ten Most Densely Populated Countries," www.mapsofworld.com/world-top-ten/world-top-ten-most-densely-populated-countries-map.html (accessed November 10, 2014).

[5]CIA, *The World Factbook*, "Singapore," www.cia.gov/library/publications/the-world-factbook/geos/sn.html (accessed November 10, 2014).

[6]Ibid.

[7]City Population, "Singapore," www.citypopulation.de/Singapore-Regions.html (accessed November 17, 2014).

[8]The Globalization Index, http://ww.ey.com/GL/en/Issues/Driving-growth/Globalization—Looking-byond-the-obvious—2012-Index (accessed January 15, 2015)

Table 12.2 Major Business Centers

Business Centers	Population
Changi	2,530
Jurong East	86,570
Singapore (Central Region)	946,240

mainly in manufacturing (principally biomedical, chemicals, and electronics); financial and insurance services; wholesale and retail; and transportation and storage sectors.

Singapore's mixed economy (free market combined with government intervention) is known as the Singapore Model. It's the only Asian country to be designated with an AAA credit rating by all three major agencies.[9]

Its biggest export partners are Malaysia, Hong Kong, China, and Indonesia, followed by the U.S., Japan, Australia, and South Korea.[10]

Singapore is ranked first out of 189 economies in terms of ease of doing business according to the World Bank Group's *Doing Business 2015* report.[11] Its 2013 GDP was ranked 36th by the World Bank[12] and the composition of its GDP by sector was services (70.6 percent) and industry (29.4 percent).[13]

Corruption Perceptions Index

Singapore ranked 5th least corrupt out of 177 countries and territories with a score of 86 out of 100.[14] This annual index, compiled by Transparency International, measures perceived levels of public sector corruption.

The Corrupt Practices Investigation Bureau is the anti-corruption agency that conducts investigations in Singapore.

---

[9]Economy Watch, "Singapore Economy," March 18, 2010, www.economywatch .com/world_economy/singapore/?page=full.

[10]CIA, *The World Factbook*, "Singapore," www.cia.gov/library/publications/the-world-factbook /geos/sn.html (accessed November 10, 2014).

[11]World Bank Group, *Doing Business 2015* (October 29, 2014): 4, www.doingbusiness .org/~/media/GIAWB/Doing%20Business/Documents/Annual-Reports/English/DB15-Full –Report.pdf, p. 4.

[12]The World Bank, Data, GDP Ranking, "Gross Domestic Product Ranking Table," last updated September 24, 2014, http://data.worldbank.org/data-catalog/GDP-ranking-table (accessed November 10, 2014).

[13]CIA, *The World Factbook*, "Singapore," www.cia.gov/library/publications/the-world-factbook /geos/sn.html (accessed November 10, 2014).

[14]Transparency International, "Corruption Perceptions Index 2013," www.transparency.org /cpi2013/results (accessed November 11, 2014).

Human Development Index

Singapore ranked 9th out of 187 countries and territories.[15] The HDI, compiled by the United Nations Development Programme, is a composite index of life expectancy, education, and income statistics.

Global Gender Gap Index

Singapore ranked 59th out of 142 countries in terms of gender equality with a score of 0.7046.[16] This annual index, compiled by the World Economic Forum, assesses gender gaps based on economic, political, educational, and health-based criteria.

Climate

Positioned 137 kilometers (approximately 85 miles) north of the Equator, Singapore experiences a year-round tropical climate. Temperatures remain consistently high (75–85 degrees during the day, 70–80 degrees at night), with high humidity and frequent rain. The island's average annual precipitation is 95 inches and rain is said to fall somewhere on the island every day of the year.

There are two monsoon periods: December to March, and June to September.

Languages

Singapore has four official languages, reflecting the diversity of the population: Mandarin Chinese (36.3 percent); English (29.8 percent); Tamil (4.4 percent); and Malay (1.2 percent). Other languages spoken are: Hokkien (8.1 percent); Cantonese (4.1 percent); Teochew (3.2 percent); and other Chinese dialects (2.8 percent).

English, which is widely spoken, is the language of business and government, and is used for instruction in schools and by the media. Singaporean students are encouraged to learn at least one of the other official languages.

The Singapore government promotes the use of Mandarin and seeks to stamp out the prevalence of what is called *Singlish,* a mix of English, Chinese, and Malay.[17]

---

[15]United Nations Development Programme, *Human Development Report 2014*, 160–163, http://hdr.undp.org/sites/default/files/hdr14-report-en-1.pdf (accessed November 11, 2014).

[16]World Economic Forum, *The Global Gender Gap Report 2014*, 8–9, www3.weforum.org/docs/GGGR14/GGGR_CompleteReport_2014.pdf (accessed November 11, 2014).

[17]National University of Singapore, International Business Law program, "A Quick Guide to 'Singlish,'" www.nusiblalumni.com/basic-singlish.html (accessed November 10, 2014).

Belief Systems, Philosophies, and Religions

The country breakdown is as follows: Buddhist (33.9 percent), Islam (14.3 percent), Taoist (11.3 percent), Catholic (7.1 percent), Hindu (5.2 percent), Other Christian (11.0 percent), None (16.4 percent), Other (0.7 percent).[18]

For an overview of belief systems, philosophies, and religions, please refer to Chapter 4, pages 64–65.

Time Zones/Daylight Savings

Singapore has a single time zone, Singapore Time (SGT). To calculate time in Singapore, add eight hours to GMT/UTC. It does not operate under Daylight Savings.

It is 13 hours ahead of U.S. Eastern Standard Time (12 hours ahead in Daylight Savings Time).

For more information, see www.timeanddate.com/worldclock.

Telephone Country Code and Internet Suffix

The Singaporean telephone country code is 65 and the Internet suffix is .sg.

Currency

The currency in Singapore is the Singapore Dollar (SGD). One dollar is divided into 100 cents.

Business Culture, Etiquette, and Customs

This section covers business culture, etiquette, and customs.

Fiscal Year

The Singaporean fiscal years runs from April 1 through March 31. Dates are written as day, month, year; for example, April 1, 2020 would be written 01/04/2020.

---

[18]CIA, *The World Factbook*, "Singapore," www.cia.gov/library/publications/the-world-factbook /geos/sn.html (accessed November 10, 2014).

Working Week

The structure of the typical Singaporean working week is outlined in Table 12.3.

Table 12.3   The Singapore Working Schedule

Business Sector	Business Hours	Days of the Week
Private sector and government offices	08:30–17:00	Monday–Friday
Private sector	09:00–13:00	Saturday
Shops	10:00–21:00	Daily

Holidays and Festivals

Some Singapore holidays are determined by the lunar calendar and change from year to year. On some holidays, offices may remain open with limited staff. Check with your embassy or trade office before planning business travel. Common Singaporean holidays and festivals appear in Table 12.4. Floating holidays are designated with an asterisk.

Table 12.4   Singaporean Holidays and Festivals[19]

Date	Name
January 1	New Year's Day
Jan/Feb	Chinese New Year*
March/April	Good Friday (Christian)*
May 1	Labor Day
May	*Vesak* Day (Buddhist: Buddha's birthday)*
July/August	*Hari Raya Puasa* (Muslim: Feast of Fast Breaking)*
August 9	National Day
October	*Hari Raya Haji* (Muslim: Feast of Sacrifice)*
Oct/Nov	*Deepavali* (Hindu: Festival of Lights)*
December 25	Christmas Day

[19]Singapore Ministry of Manpower, "Singapore Public Holidays 2014," April 10, 2013, www.mom.gov.sg/newsroom/Pages/PressReleasesDetail.aspx?listid=493 (accessed November 10, 2014).

Business Dress/Appearance

Clothing of lightweight material is common among Singaporean business people. Men wear dress shirts, ties, and trousers for business meetings and at restaurants. Jackets are suggested for more formal initial meetings and meetings with government officials. On most occasions, women wear modest pantsuits or skirts and blouses with sleeves. Pay attention to cultural nuances concerning modesty when doing business with different ethnicities.

News Sources

Common news sources in Singapore include:

- *The Straits Times:* www.straitstimes.com
- *Business Times:* www.businesstimes.com.sg
- *Today:* www.todayonline.com

Business Cards

When exchanging business cards in Singapore, offer your card with both hands and with the print facing the recipient. It's acceptable for information on the card to be in English, as it is the language of business. During a meeting, business professionals may arrange cards on the table in front of them in order to remember names and titles. Avoid taking a business card without looking at it properly first; when possible, ask questions or make a reference to the information given.

Technology

With both 3G and 4G networks available, Singapore enjoys excellent telecommunications services. Mobile population penetration rate stands at 152 percent, and household broadband penetration is 85 percent. A wireless broadband service with speeds of up to 2MBp can be accessed free with Wireless@SG. The government is close to completing an island-wide roll out of a high-speed fiber-optic broadband network.

According to Akamai Technology's *State of the Internet Report*, Singapore has the third-fastest average peak connection speed in the world, and the 20th-fastest average connection speed.[20] Latest figures rank Singapore 65th in

---

[20] Akamai Technologies, "State of the Internet Q4 2013," April 2014, www.akamai.com/dl/akamai/akamai-soti-q413.pdf?WT.mc_id=soti_Q413.

the world for the number of Internet users,[21] and 39th globally for the number of Internet hosts.[22]

Gifts

Business-related gift-giving is not a common practice. See the respective chapters for Malaysia (Chapter 9), India (Chapter 7), and China (Chapter 5) gift-giving tips.

However, if you are invited to someone's home (such offers tend to be rare), by all means bring your hosts a small gift, as you would at home. The same applies if your host has been especially generous with their time, taking you on tours or for meals; giving your host a gift in appreciation would be seen as good manners.

Use both hands to present the recipient with your gift, but do not expect them to open it in your presence. Due to the ethnic diversity in Singapore, gift-giving customs vary. Do your research on culture specific customs.

Never give any gift, no matter how small, to government officials.

Introductions, Greetings, Personal Space, and Eye Contact

Err on the side of formality here. Especially at a first meeting, use the appropriate honorific before a person's name. Read the Malaysia, India, and China chapters for more culture-specific information. Watch what others do and follow their lead. Sometimes Singaporeans will bow as they shake your hand, and it is considered polite for you to do the same. This is especially true for those originating from China. With Singaporeans it is best to practice intermittent eye contact, making sure not to stare. Avoid touching or patting someone, as they are likely to see it as disrespectful.

Names

For the order of names, refer to the respective country chapters for China, India, and Malaysia.

---

[21] CIA, *The World Factbook*, "Country Comparison: Internet Users," information dated 2009, www.cia.gov/library/publications/the-world-factbook/rankorder/2153rank.html (accessed November 10, 2014).

[22] CIA, *The World Factbook*, "Country Comparison: Internet Hosts," information dated 2009, www.cia.gov/library/publications/the-world-factbook/rankorder/2184rank.html (accessed November 10, 2014).

Meetings and Negotiations

The tendency in Singapore is to get straight to business. Singaporeans are regarded as astute, honest, and highly skilled; as a result, they exercise precision in their business dealings and have high expectations of others. It is best to come prepared to the negotiating table, as Singaporeans are tough negotiators. They focus on costs and deadlines, are keen to make decisions quickly, and tend to hold to contracts more strictly than business professionals do elsewhere in Asia. Also, be mindful of demands for transparency by the Singaporean government, which may draw out the negotiation process.

Presentation Styles, Conversational Topics, and Humor

The protocol for giving presentations can vary depending on your audience. Ask in advance what the protocol is for your presentation, and always take the advice of someone who is known and trusted by the attendees.

If there is a Q&A session at the end of your presentation, precede your answers with a respectful silence. Although westerners often feel uncomfortable with silence, Asians can see it as appropriate or respectful. Responding too quickly to a question indicates that you haven't given it sufficient thought.

Because of their access to U.S. television and other programming, Singaporeans are familiar with western humor. Acceptable topics of conversation are food, travel, art, and the economy.

Gestures

Common gestures in Singapore include:

- Pointing with your thumb, not your index finger: making a fist with the thumb on top and point with the thumb (signs show this).
- smiling or laughing to hide embarrassment.
- Holding open doors, giving up a seat, and, when elders enter a room, rising.
- Bowing when passing people and when entering or leaving a room.

Notable Foods and Dishes

The Singaporean cuisine is truly a melting pot, influenced by a variety of cultures including Malay, Chinese, Indian, Indonesian, Thai, and English. These foreign cuisines are well represented in restaurants throughout Singapore and also in the unique blends of flavors and ingredients found in popular dishes.

Specialty Dishes

Favorite dishes in Singaporean cuisine include:

- **Hainanese chicken rice:** Considered a national dish; chicken steeped in broth, rice, cucumber, and a dipping sauce of chili, garlic, and soy
- **Chili crab:** Considered the national seafood dish; crabs stir-fried in a sweet-and-savory, chili-tomato sauce

Dining Etiquette

Due to the ethnic diversity in Singapore, it is best to follow the dining customs appropriate to the background of your host. See the respective chapters for Malaysia, China, and India.

Some general points to note: Food is a spiritual thing—never refuse an offer of food. In dining, chopsticks are commonly used, but Western-style utensils are usually also available. When dining with Malays or Indians, never use your left hand when eating or passing items. It is customary for the host to select and order all of the dishes for the group when dining at a restaurant.

Drinking and Toasting

For drinking and toasting customs, see the respective chapters for Malaysia, China, and India.

Beer and ale are the favorite drinks in Singapore, although wine and whisky are also popular.

Though toasting is not commonplace, Singaporeans generally stand to offer and receive a toast. The person giving the toast holds his/her glass with both hands and makes eye contact while speaking. The recipient holds his/her glass with the right hand and thanks the person who gave the toast.

Tipping and Bill-Paying

Tipping is not customary and is actively discouraged by the Singaporean government. Restaurants add a 10 percent service charge and 7 percent goods and services tax (GST) to the bill. Although it's not expected, rounding up a taxi fare to the nearest dollar is common.

Smoking

The Singaporean government has prohibited smoking in virtually all indoor places and in most public places, with the exception of designated smoking areas. Offenses are punishable by fines from $200 to $1,000 Singapore.[23]

Taboos

Cultural taboos in Singapore include:

- Public displays of affection
- Touching someone on the head
- Pointing or facing the sole of your foot toward someone
- Pointing with your index finger
- Jaywalking
- Possessing, packing in a suitcase, or carrying chewing gum
- Smoking in public
- Littering or spitting

Heroes and sports

Knowing about another country's heroes and sports offers opportunities to incorporate culture-specific references into your conversations and presentations.

Heroes

Some examples of Singaporean heroes include the following:

Adnan bin Saidi (1915–1942): Malaysian soldier. Regarded as a hero for leading the defense of Singapore against the invading Japanese in the Battle of Pasir Panjang (1942). He refused to surrender and held off the Japanese until he was wounded, captured, and executed. Remembered for his bravery, his story was portrayed in the 1999 film, *Leftenan Adnan*.

Lim Bo Seng (1909–1944): Chinese resistance fighter and major-general. Regarded as a war hero in Singapore for his leadership in anti-Japanese activities during World War II, he is best known for blasting the causeway as Japanese troops descended upon Singapore. He was posthumously awarded the rank of major-general.

---

[23]National Environment Agency of Singapore, "Smoking Prohibition," last updated August 5, 2014, http://app2.nea.gov.sg/public-health/smoking/smoking-prohibition (accessed November 10, 2014).

Sports

Sports

Popular sports include cricket, rugby, badminton, basketball, table tennis, supercar motorsports, and football (the most popular spectator sport).

Sports Figures

Fandi Ahmad (1962–present): Retired Singaporean football striker, considered a national legend. Captain of the national team (1993–1997) and first Singaporean millionaire sportsperson. Current head coach of Lions XII in the Malaysian Super League.

Feng Tianwei (1986–present): Table tennis player, ranked as the number 4 singles player in the world; member of Singapore's 2008 Beijing Olympics team, which won the silver medal.

Eight-Question Framework

This section reviews the framework to which you were introduced earlier in this book. Each of these questions address one or more business topics to help you attract and build the relationships upon which today's successful businesses depend.

1. How Do Singaporeans Prefer to Act: Individually or as a Group?

My experience with people in Singapore is that they prefer to act as individuals first.

—*Allan Smith, foreign exchange trader, GMC*

Singaporeans love to have individual choice. Their early-bird mentality even has its own word, *kiasu,* which literally means 'fear to lose.' That said, this is a hierarchical and collectivist culture in which the government exerts considerable influence. The stringent laws and rules that apply to everyone ensure high efficiency and the almost nonexistent levels of corruption in the country—but they also govern behaviors ranging from smoking and littering to chewing gum and jaywalking, and they prevent Singaporeans from enjoying the freedom to criticize or joke about their government, as people do in the West.

As an example, consider the experience of one of our interviewees, a senior business development manager for a Fortune 500 manufacturer. Among all the

Asian countries in which he operates, he found the *value sell,* selling a customer on value over price, the most difficult to make in Singapore:

"You have to create relationships with each person in the decision-making chain in a way that makes them all look successful. You might think an agreement has already been reached but then discover that their boss won't sign off unless you have something in reserve, such as an additional discount. Unlike many other Asian cultures, a Singaporean VP can be pretty aggressive and direct in telling you that he won't take the deal to his CEO unless there is something else you can put on the table."

As one Singapore-based consultant told us, when it comes to establishing business relationships, in Singapore, you are "guilty until proven innocent"—meaning that each individual in a chain of command will want to be sure of you before granting you access to the next-highest person in the hierarchy.

The bottom line? You don't start at the top when building relationships in Singapore: You work your way up, one individual at a time.

2. How Are Power and Authority Viewed in Singapore?

This is a country that has a very high expectation of quality. Once Singaporeans regard you as someone they can potentially do business with, it settles on merit very quickly.
—*Fermin Diez, human resources executive*

Singapore is a meritocracy. It is also a highly network-based culture. What this means is that you have to earn your right to be part of the circle—you're an outsider until you prove yourself worthy of being an insider. According to Dr. Tanvi Gautam of Global People Tree, who has lived in Singapore for close to four years, Singaporeans judge others according to a number of *status markers,* which signal an individual's competence and credibility. One of the most salient is education, and graduate degrees are especially highly regarded. Others include a number of personal attributes, such as high integrity, as well as global connections with respected business organizations, including think tanks, institutes, and professional associations.

As Dr. Gautam explained, "You need to be mindful of the fact that Singapore runs largely on its human capital and services rather than agriculture or manufacturing products. And human capital is strongly based on social capital, which is all about networks. The people who succeed most in this country are boundary spanners. Demonstrating that you have strong connections with the global network *matters* in Singapore, as that signals your higher social capital."

As an outsider, you can demonstrate added value in Singapore business circles by emphasizing your existing networks. As Dr. Gautam pointed out: "When you are talking to someone in Singapore it's never just about that person, you are talking to their entire network."

3. How Do Singaporeans Compare Rules and Relationships?

The relative emphasis on people and processes in Singapore is illustrated by two disruptions that occurred a few years ago. Human resources executive Fermin Diez related two stories to us that were in the press. First, the country's largest bank, DBS, and its sister bank, POSB, endured a technical glitch that caused their ATMs to be out of service for seven hours. Customers were up in arms and CEO Piyush Gupta appeared on TV and radio to apologize. He also sent out a personal letter that has since been held up as an exemplar of excellent crisis management. Gupta remains the CEO.

The second incident occurred in late December of 2011, when Singapore rail operator SMRT shut down one of its subway lines twice within 36 hours because of damage that was said to be due to lack of maintenance. The service disruption affected almost 250,000 commuters. CEO Saw Phaik Hwa resigned the following month.

According to Mr. Diez, "Singaporeans are not used to things breaking down. But whereas the transport operator's initial reaction was to hunker down to fix the problem and made no public statements until it was seen as too late, the bank CEO made himself immediately available to the media and was hugely apologetic about the grief this disruption had caused his customers."

Although both executives managed the problems in the way they thought right, the degree to which each CEO was forgiven by the public differed greatly. In the case of the bank, public perception was that the bank valued the relationship with their customers. This may well have been the case with the transport operator, also, but by largely ignoring the public outcry and by focusing instead on their maintenance issues, the transport operator left the public with a quite different perception. There is a lesson here for anyone conducting business in Singapore to put people and relationships ahead of processes and rules.

4. How Do Singaporeans Regard Time?

Singaporeans value time and don't like to waste it. They are punctual and honor time to the minute. To illustrate Singapore's attitudes about time and the ways these attitudes affect matters like developing trust, inspiring respect, and focusing on relationships, consider Dr. Tanvi Gautam's experiences during her first meeting with some Singaporean Chinese clients:

"A couple of months before I moved to the country I had arranged a meeting with a group of Singaporean businessmen. In my preliminary e-mail I had explained that we needed to have a hard stop at 7 p.m. and this was mutually agreed upon in advance. When the meeting took place we must have drunk about 16 cups of green tea and were chatting about everything under the sun other than business. And I'm looking at my watch thinking, 'Okay it's now 6.30 p.m., then 6:40 p.m. Maybe they forgot my email to say we needed to stop at 7 p.m.' But I didn't want to be rude and just come out and say, 'Can we stick to the agenda?' Then, at five minutes to seven one of the businessmen turned to me and said the group would like us to work together.

"What I have learned since is that if you think you can come to Singapore to get a piece of paper signed and then walk out, it's not going to happen. It's going to take more time. Of course, even in Singapore you will find people whose viewpoint on time is governed more by a professional code than the cultural code. But either way you need to be prepared and realize that here people are interested in understanding who you are and want to get to know you before they enter into any long-term deals."

5. How Direct Is Communication in Singapore?

Singaporeans are a little bit more thick-skinned than the others (Asians). You have to second guess the Japanese, right? With Singaporeans, if it's no, he will tell you it's no.
— *Yu-Jin Chua, Panther Capital*

When doing business in Singapore, then, a good approach is to think in terms of the culture of the people with whom you would be meeting. For example, lawyer Looi Teck Kheong pointed out how the Singaporean government effectively uses officials from each ethnic group to communicate and liaise: "It does not make sense to send a Chinese representative to communicate with the Indians, who have their own specific and unique Indian culture. So we had a minister that I believe was originally from the south of India, who was sent to handle things. The same approach is used with the Chinese, where a Chinese minister from a similar background will be engaged because they have a firm understanding of the Chinese culture. The same holds true for the Muslims, and we have what they call a Minister of Muslim Affairs."

Mr. Kheong recommended that visiting businesspeople find out in advance the culture of origin of the people with whom they'll be working. Our advice is to review the other country chapters—China, Malaysia, and India—to familiarize yourself with the cultural nuances that play a part in all communications in Singapore.

Also, know that when a Singaporean prefaces communication with, "In my humble opinion," or "In my modest opinion," they are giving you a firm directive.

SINGLISH

One aspect of communication unique to Singapore is the custom of speaking *Singlish*. Indeed, the Singaporean government has attempted to encourage its citizens to write and speak Standard English with their Speak Good English Movement.[24] Although the National University of Singapore suggests[25] that it's a good idea for visitors to know a few Singlish phrases, it is unlikely you will come across Singlish spoken in business contexts. If you encounter it, it will be only in informal contexts—perhaps when visiting a bar or club.

A few examples: If someone tells you they've been *saboed,* they're expressing the view that they've been intentionally harmed or had their failings shown up by a third party (as in the English word *sabotage*). *Can can* means the speaker believes something is possible. *So how?* is the Singlish short form for "What do we do now?" and *Catch no ball?* indicates the other person doesn't understand you!

Avoid speaking Singlish yourself, especially to business contacts. It is said to be a *nod* to the speaker's Singaporean or Malaysian roots and some Singaporeans may find your use of it condescending.

6. How Formal or Informal Do Business People in Singapore Tend to Be?

There is high regard for seniority and a certain code of conduct in Singapore, a culture in which restraint is considered to be a personal virtue. Although Mr. Looi Teck Kheong invited Liz to call him by his first name, he also pointed out that this was the exception rather than the norm. Holding a senior position within the law firm that bears his name, he finds that people in Singapore prefer to address him as Mr. Looi. Likewise, you should err on the side of formality and use a courtesy title or an honorific until invited otherwise.

---

[24]Speak Good English Movement website, www.goodenglish.org.sg/site/index.html (accessed November 10, 2014).
[25]National University of Singapore, International Business Law program, "A Quick Guide to 'Singlish,'" www.nusiblalumni.com/basic-singlish.html (accessed November 10, 2014).

On the one hand, Singapore's cosmopolitan nature makes visitors feel at home because road signs are in English and a rich mix of cultures is represented. On the other hand, as Mr. Yu-Jin Chua pointed out, this leads to the expectation that international visitors already understand the high standards to which Singaporeans naturally conform:

"Everyone should have read about Singapore or spoken with people who know the country well so that they know the formalities and ways of treating people that are expected. If someone demonstrates bad manners—like walking into a bar and saying, 'Hey, baby, get me a table' to the waitress, or who breaks the law by chewing gum in public, we don't consider them to be ignorant—we think they are doing it on purpose."

7. *How Aligned Are Singaporean Social and Business Lives?*

As with other Asian countries, trust begins before you arrive in the country. This is why the formality emphasized in the previous section is important for e-mail, Skype, phone calls, and other preliminary communication.

As Mr. Yu-Jin Chua of Panther Capital pointed out: "If you go for a three-day business meeting elsewhere in Asia, there may be no business discussion on days one and two. On day three, perhaps even on the way to the airport, you will hear that the contract has been signed. In Singapore, if you have planned a three-day business trip it's likely that the job will be done on the very first day because Singaporeans will not invite you here unless there's business already. They will discuss specifics and get down to signing the deal right at the outset."

Assuming your good reputation has preceded you, Singaporeans will definitely want to entertain you. But here, again, there are differences in approach. In Singapore, the home is sacrosanct. Space on the island is at a premium and Singaporeans, most of whom take their family obligations seriously, will either be rushing off after work to be with their partners and children or to look after their parents. Business entertaining, then, is more likely to take place over lunch than dinner.

You may find that you are taken to some of the many excellent places to eat in Singapore or offered a guided tour of the island. Most socializing of this kind takes place during the working day. As Mr. Chua added: "In Singapore, a lunch or maybe dinner, is the time when someone will ask questions that they wouldn't ask you in a group meeting because they don't want to say something 'stupid' that might make them look weaker than their colleagues. It's the time for informal discussions that they feel are less intimidating."

8. *How Is the Concept of Women in Business Handled in Singapore?*

The women here that take on any position are there because they are good.
—*Looi Teck Kheong, lawyer*

According to Dr. Tanvi Gautam, "I have not experienced that being a woman has got in the way of anyone accepting my authority or credibility or competence. I think the professional space is available for women to do whatever they need to do. If women want to come to Singapore to set up a business, they will find it's as good, if not better, than a lot of other places when it comes to the professional respect and courtesy they expect. Gender is not the first filter with which you would be evaluated."

While working at her company's foreign exchange trading office in Singapore, KPMG executive Ms. Elizabeth Hay always felt comfortable. Certainly there were differences to working in her native Australia, but nothing related to gender. "I always felt welcome when joining a group of Singaporean professionals for a meal or drinks after work, as we used to go out twice a week on a regular basis. Singaporeans are Western-minded and don't have any sort of complex speaking to western women. I'll always have good things to say about Singapore and still maintain solid friendships there with both men and women."

Even so, a woman may be judged by her wardrobe—with respect to style. Dr. Gautam highlighted this by saying: "The Singaporean style of dressing in the workplace is quite unique and stylish, almost like dressing for a meeting in New York. In fact, I have never seen as many branded purses anywhere else in the world as I have in Singapore. They are always very much in line with the latest trends. Singaporeans enjoy their brands!"

International businesswomen are therefore advised to wear brand-name, high-fashion suits with designer shoes and leather bags.

Cultural Summary

Key points to remember:

- Research the Singaporean organization and ethnicity of owners and founders. A company owned by Chinese operates differently than one owned by Indians, Malays, or another ethnic group.
- Develop a relationship with a local Singaporean contact for insight and advice regarding Singapore's numerous cultural layers and ethnic dynamics.
- Familiarize yourself with the nuances of Chinese, Indian, and Malaysian cross-cultural communication.

Self-Awareness Profile

This simple exercise prompts you to self-assess where you currently stand on topics related to the eight-question framework and *compare* this with the country culture. This visual will help you discover the extent to which you may need to adapt your current mindset and behavior to develop more robust business relationships. For details on how to complete this graphic, see the instructions given in the Introduction on pages xviii–xix.

Consider copying the eight-question Profile or using a pencil so that you can see, over time, how you have adjusted your cultural mindset. You might also wish to create unique graphics related to each of the businesses you work with, as these cultural positions vary depending upon geographic location, industry, generational factors, and corporate profile.

Q1: What is your preferred way of doing business?

As an individual making autonomous decisions					As a team member who seeks group consensus
1	2	3	4	**5**	6

Q2: How comfortable are you in hierarchies in which power is distributed unequally?

Very uncomfortable					Very comfortable
1	2	3	4	5	**6**

Q3: How closely do you follow rules and obey the law?

Almost always					It depends
1	2	3	**4**	5	6

Q4: What is your general attitude toward time?

I prefer agendas, schedules, planning					I prefer flexibility, fluidity without scheduling
1	2	3	**4**	5	6

Q5: What is your preferred way to communicate?

Very diplomatically   **Very candidly**

       1   2   **3**   4   5   6

Q6: What is your interpersonal style or level of formality in business interactions?

Very formal   **Very informal**

     1   **2**   3   4   5   6

Q7: What is your view on socializing within business?

A waste of time   **Essential**

      1   2   3   **4**   5   6

Q8: Should a woman defer to a man as the lead, if winning business in a certain culture depended on it?

Never   **Yes, absolutely**

     1   2   **3**   4   5   6

13 | South Korea

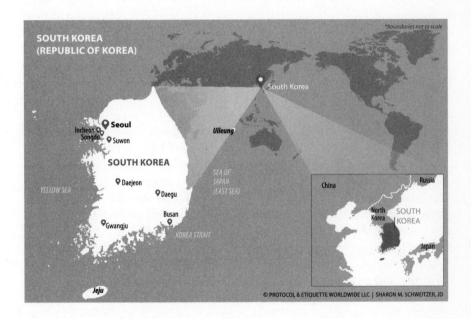

My father's biggest achievement was to motivate the South Korean people, to show them we could become prosperous if we worked hard. He taught me to love my country, and serve my country.

—Park Geun-hye

Introduction

Although South Korea[1] is known as the "land of the morning calm," you might question the calm of this Asian Tiger, one of four, along with Hong Kong, Singapore, and Taiwan, considering how rapidly the country has globalized and grown economically. Many interviewees made reference to the fact that things happen fast in Korea, as expressed in the phrase *palli palli* or "faster, faster." This is "the most wired country in the world," and has led the digital revolution as a pioneer of TV on mobile devices. K-dramas evolved into the "Korean Wave" as Korean pop (*K-Pop*) culture spreads across the globe. Korea tweets at twice the world average and the blogging community places second behind China worldwide.[2]

Korea's rise technologically and economically has been remarkable, and the country holds some surprises for the business traveler. First, as far as belief systems and practices are concerned, Korea is a predominately Christian country. It is one of only seven countries with a population of 50 million-plus to have a GDP of $20,000 per capita. Korea is the 12th-largest economy in the world.[3]

One observation from author and founder of CEO International, Dr. Eun Young Kim is that "Most people outside of Korea have held the myth that Korea is a deeply Confucian country, while Koreans have been challenging traditional Confucian values for decades."[4] Indeed, Koreans have also been strongly influenced by Buddhism and Shamanism and, more recently, by belief systems from the international community. This international blend is also showing up in relation to the generational differences that are impacting Korean business life. Working with someone aged 50 or older in Korea, who may hold to greater formality and established ways of relating, will be a different experience than working with those considerably younger.

Another fascinating, yet complicating factor when doing business in Korea concerns the country's external facing economy that overlays the internal domestic Korean economy. For example, most international business is driven through conglomerates called *chaebols*. *Chaebol* is a government-sponsored corporate arrangement that was designed to encourage the growth of

---

[1] Within business circles, South Korea is referred to as Korea and we do the same within this chapter.

[2] Office of the United States Trade Representative, "New Opportunities for U.S. Exporters Under the U.S.-Korea Trade Agreement," www.ustr.gov/trade-agreements/free-trade-agreements/korus-fta (accessed November 19, 2014).

[3] CIA, *The World Factbook*, "Country Comparison: GDP (Purchasing Power Parity)," 2013, www.cia.gov/library/publications/the-world-factbook/rankorder/2001rank.html (accessed November 19, 2014).

[4] Eun Young Kim, *A Cross-Cultural Reference of Business Practices in a New Korea*, (Westport, CT: Quorum Books, 1996).

family-owned industrial conglomerates. Currently, there are approximately thirteen of these vast business groups that hold privately owned or publicly traded companies, involved in industries ranging from automobiles, construction, and shipping, to consumer electronics. Change is occurring quickly with the *chaebols*, the economy, and the varying generational attitudes; this magnificent tiger is moving fast!

Quiz

How much do you know about Korea? Answer the following questions as True or False to test your knowledge. (The Answer Key at the bottom includes page numbers that refer to the topic):

_____1. The population of Korea is considered nearly homogenous; almost all people are of Korean ethnicity.

_____2. *Chaebol* is a government-sponsored corporate arrangement that was designed to encourage the growth of family-owned industrial conglomerates.

_____3. The U.S. does not currently trade freely with Korea.

_____4. English is widely taught in schools and commonly used in business.

_____5. The Korean form of government is an electoral democracy.

_____6. Eye contact between Koreans is commonly direct and prolonged.

_____7. Korea is one of Asia's most affluent countries.

_____8. Business entertainment commonly takes the form of dinner at a restaurant followed by socializing at a bar or nightclub.

_____9. Korea has the fastest average Internet connection speed in the world.

_____10. Korean names are usually in the order of family name plus given generational name plus given name.

Answer Key: 1. T (p. 290); 2. T (p. 286–287; 305); 3. F (p. 289); 4. T (p. 292); 5. T (p. 288); 6. F (p. 296); 7. T (p. 286); 8. T (p. 300–301); 9. T (p. 295); 10. T (p. 298).

Country Basics

This section provides key knowledge in an easy-to-read format to help you quickly grasp some of the basics necessary to navigate this culture.

Historical Timeline

A critical way to show respect for another person's culture is to have knowledge of their country's history and current affairs. Table 13.1 on pages 289–290 outlines events related to Korea, together with concurrent world events.[5]

Full Country Name and Location

The Republic of Korea occupies the southern half of the Korean peninsula. It comprises more than 3,300 islands, is slightly smaller than Iceland, and slightly larger than the State of Indiana in the U.S. It shares its only land border with North Korea. The Yellow Sea lies to the west and the Sea of Japan to the east. The DMZ (demilitarized zone) wall is the most heavily fortified worldwide.

Government/Political Structure

Korea has been a democratic republic since 1948 when the first general elections were held and the current constitution became effective. The capital city, Seoul, is considered a 'special city,' meaning it has the status of a province; however, it is still directly controlled by the federal government. A president elected by popular vote serves a single five-year term as head of state. The heads of government are the prime minister and deputy prime minister, both appointed by the president. The National Assembly is a single legislative body of 300 seats. National elections were last held December 19, 2012.

Population and Economic Centers

The population is approximately 49.5 million, with 83 percent living in urban areas. The country is divided into nine provinces, six metropolitan cities, one special city (Seoul), and one special self-governing city (Sejong).[6]

---

[5]Korea Timeline Sources: Bernard Grun, *The Timetables of History*, 4th ed. (New York: Touchstone Press, 2005); CIA, *The World Factbook*, "Korea, South," www.cia.gov/library/publications/the-world-factbook/geos/ks.html (accessed November 19, 2014); and BBC News Asia, "South Korea Profile: Timeline," last updated November 11, 2014, www.bbc.com/news/world-asia-pacific-15292674 (accessed November 19, 2014).

[6]CIA, *The World Factbook*, "Korea, South," www.cia.gov/library/publications/the-world-factbook/geos/ks.html (accessed November 19, 2014).

Table 13.1 Key Historical Events

Period/Dates	Description/Events	World Events
1905	Japan occupies Korea following the Russo-Japanese War.	Revolution throughout the Russian Empire.
1910	Japan annexes the entire Korean Peninsula.	Start of the Mexican Revolution.
1945	Korea regains independence.	End of World War II.
1948	Republic of Korea (ROK) set up in the south, Democratic People's Republic of Korea (DPRK) in the north.	World Health Organization established by the UN.
1950	Korean War begins with northern forces invading the south.	Rajendra Prasad elected the first president of the Republic of India.
1953	The peninsula is officially split into North and South Korea.	Scientific paper published in *Nature* first describes the double helix structure of DNA.
1961	General Park Chung-hee takes over government in a military coup.	Dag Hammarskjöld, Secretary-General of the UN, awarded Nobel Peace Prize.
1987	First free election under revised democratic constitution.	U.S. President Reagan announces the nation's first trillion-dollar budget.
1993	Kim Young-sam becomes first civilian president.	The European Economic Community creates a unified European market.
2010	North and South Korea break off all trade and diplomatic ties.	The Burj Khalifa in Dubai, the world's tallest building, is officially opened.
2011	U.S.-South Korea Free Trade Agreement is ratified.	The world population reaches 7 billion inhabitants according to the United Nations.

(Continued)

Table 13.1 *(Continued)*

Period/Dates	Description/Events	World Events
2012	Park Geun-hye elected as first female president for five-year term.	The 2012 World Expo takes place in Yeosu, South Korea.
2013	South Korea successfully launches first satellite into orbit.	Cardinal Bergoglio of Argentina elected pope, the first from the Americas.
2014	President Park Geun-hye receives World Telecommunication and Information Society Award.	The XXII Olympic Winter Games take place in Sochi, Russia.
2016	Legislative elections scheduled.	Laos is scheduled to be ASEAN chair.
2017	Presidential elections scheduled.	Hong Kong chief executive elections scheduled; Indian, Korean, and Singaporean presidential elections scheduled.

The main ethnic group is Korean. The country is considered homogenous, except for a minority of about 20,000 Chinese.[7] The major business centers and populations (2010) are shown in Table 13.2 on page 291.[8]

Economy

Korea is ranked fifth out of 189 economies in terms of ease of doing business, according to the World Bank Group's *Doing Business 2015* report.[9] Its 2013 GDP was ranked 14th by the World Bank,[10] and the composition of its GDP

---

[7]Ibid.; Mary M. Bosrock, *Asian Business Customs & Manners: A Country-by-Country Guide* (New York: Meadowbrook Press, 2007).

[8]Statistics Korea, Statistical Database, "Population, Households and Housing Units," http://kosis.kr/eng/statisticsList/statisticsList_01List.jsp?vwcd=MT_ETITLE&parentId=A#SubCont (accessed November 19, 2014).

[9]World Bank Group, *Doing Business 2015* (October 29, 2014): 4, www.doingbusiness.org/~/media/GIAWB/Doing%20Business/Documents/Annual-Reports/English/DB15-Full-Report.pdf.

[10]The World Bank, Data, GDP Ranking, "Gross Domestic Product Ranking Table," last updated September 24, 2014, http://data.worldbank.org/data-catalog/GDP-ranking-table (accessed November 19, 2014).

Table 13.2 Major Business Centers

Business Centers	CIA World Factbook/Google Maps	Encyclopedia Britannica	Population (Millions)
Busan	Busan	Pusan	3.4
Daegu	Daegu	Taegu	2.4
Daejeon	Daejeon	Taejon	1.5
Gwangju	Gwangju	Kwangju	1.5
Incheon	Incheon	Inch'on	2.7
Seoul (capital)	Seoul	Seoul	9.8
Songdo	Songdo	Songdo	*
Suwon	Suwon	Suwon	1.1

*The 2010 Census does not cover all cities/towns, only main districts. See the Statistics Korea website for more information.[11]

by sector was services (58.2 percent), industry (39.2 percent), and agriculture (2.6 percent).[12]

Corruption Perceptions Index

Korea ranked 46th least corrupt out of 177 countries and territories with a score of 55 out of 100.[13] This annual index, compiled by Transparency International, measures perceived levels of public sector corruption.

The Anti-Corruption and Civil Rights Commission of Korea is the anti-corruption agency that conducts investigations in Korea.

Human Development Index

Korea ranked 15th out of 187 countries and territories.[14] The HDI, compiled by the United Nations Development Programme, is a composite index of life expectancy, education, and income statistics.

---

[11]Statistics Korea, http://kostat.go.kr/portal/english/index.action (accessed November 19, 2014).
[12]CIA, *The World Factbook*, "Korea, South," www.cia.gov/library/publications/the-world -factbook/geos/ks.html (accessed November 19, 2014).
[13]Transparency International, "Corruption Perceptions Index 2013," www.transparency.org /cpi2013/results (accessed November 18, 2014).
[14]United Nations Development Programme, *Human Development Report 2014*, 160–163, http:// hdr.undp.org/sites/default/files/hdr14-report-en-1.pdf (accessed November 18, 2014).

Global Gender Gap Index

Korea ranked 117th out of 142 countries in terms of gender equality with a score of 0.6403.[15] This annual index, compiled by the World Economic Forum, assesses gender gaps based on economic, political, educational, and health-based criteria.

Climate

Korea has a temperate climate with four seasons: spring (April to May) is pleasant with temperatures in the mid-50-degrees Fahrenheit; summer (June to August) is hot and humid and contains the monsoon season with its heavy rainfall; fall (September to October) is cool and pleasant, and winter (November to March) is cold with temperatures between the teens and 30 degrees F.

Languages

Korean is the official language, with the Seoul dialect as the standard. English is widely taught in schools, along with Japanese and Chinese.

Belief Systems, Philosophies, and Religions

The country breakdown is as follows: Christian (31.6 percent: Protestant 24 percent, Roman Catholic 7.6 percent), Buddhist (24.2 percent), Other or Unknown (0.9 percent), and None (43.3 percent).[16]

For an overview of belief systems, philosophies, and religions, please refer to Chapter 4, pages 64–65.

Time Zones/Daylight Savings

Korea has one time zone, Korea Standard Time (KST), which is nine hours ahead of GMT (Greenwich Mean Time)/UTC (Coordinated Universal Time). It does not operate under Daylight Savings.

---

[15] World Economic Forum, *The Global Gender Gap Report 2014*, 8–9, www3.weforum.org/docs /GGGR14/GGGR_CompleteReport_2014.pdf (accessed November 18, 2014).
[16] CIA, *The World Factbook*, "Korea, South," www.cia.gov/library/publications/the-world -factbook/geos/ks.html (accessed November 19, 2014).

It is 14 hours ahead of U.S. Eastern Standard Time (13 hours ahead in Daylight Savings Time). See www.timeanddate.com/worldclock.

To calculate time in Korea, add nine hours to UTC/GMT.

Telephone Country Code and Internet Suffix

The Korean telephone country code is 82, and the Internet suffix is .kr.

Currency

The Korean currency is the won (KRW). One won is divided into 100 jeon.

Business Culture, Etiquette, and Customs

This section covers business culture, etiquette, and customs.

Fiscal Year

The Korean fiscal year is January 1 to December 31. Dates are written as year, month, day; for example, April 1, 2020 is 20/04/01.

Working Week

Koreans have long working weeks and work long hours, as shown in Table 13.3.

Table 13.3   The Korean Working Schedule

Industry	Business Hours	Days of the Week
Businesses	09:00–17:00	Monday–Friday
	09:00–13:00	Saturday
Banks	09:00–16:30	Monday–Friday
	09:00–13:00	Saturday
Government Offices	09:00–17:00	Monday–Friday
	09:00–12:00	Saturday
Lunch	12:00–13:00	

Holidays and Festivals

Some Korean holidays are determined by the lunar calendar and change from year to year. Floating holidays are designated with an asterisk. On specific holidays, an office may remain open with limited staff. Check with your embassy or trade office before planning business travel.

During the Lunar New Year and Harvest Moon Festival, all businesses and government offices are closed. It is best to schedule business meetings February through June. Common Korean holidays and festivals are outlined in Table 13.4.

Table 13.4   Common Holidays and Festivals

Date	Name
January 1–3	New Year's Day
January/February	Lunar New Year (*Seollal*)*
March 1	Independence Movement Day
April 5	Arbor Day (unofficial)
May 5	Children's Day
May	Buddha's Birthday*
June 6	Memorial Day
July 17	Constitution Day
August 15	Liberation Day
September/October	Harvest Moon Festival/Thanksgiving (*Ch'usok*)*
October 3	National Foundation Day
October 9	Korean Language Day (unofficial)
December 25	Christmas Day

Business Dress/Appearance

Koreans say clothing is *a wing,* meaning your image can change depending on your wardrobe selection. In Seoul and urban areas, appearance is crucial, with an emphasis on fashionable, conservative, and brand-name suits and dresses. Both men and women should select black, white, gray, and neutral colors, a brand-name watch, and the best-quality shoes and bags they can afford. Wear natural fabrics and avoid synthetic suits and dresses for humid summer weather. Women can opt for short-sleeve (not sleeveless) dresses and blouses and go without stockings in the summer.

Select understated, quality jewelry such as a pendant necklace and stud earrings. Pearls are appropriate for business dinners and cocktail parties, but not at the office. Wear two- to three-inch closed-toe heels or flats, nude stockings, and neutral make-up. Avoid collarless shirts, jeans, sleeveless items, high or stiletto heels, blue or green eye make-up, lash extensions, neon or bright-colored clothing, colored stockings, statement or inexpensive jewelry, and colored nail polish, according to Ms. Young Lee, Financial Manager, YERICO Manufacturing, Inc.

News Sources

Some of the most popular news sources in Korea are

- *Chosun Ilbo*: http://english.chosun.com
- *Dong-a-Ilbo*: http://english.donga.com
- *Korea Herald*: www.koreaherald.com
- *Korea Times*: www.koreatimes.co.kr

Business Cards

Follow your host's lead; cards are usually exchanged after a head bow and proper introductions. Present your card and accept the other person's with both hands. Print your information in English on one side and Korean on the reverse. Koreans highly value education; include degrees.

Technology

Korea is a trailblazer for high-speed and wireless Internet. It led the digital revolution as a pioneer of TV on mobile devices (IPTV), and it tweets at twice the world average. The country is close to reaching universal broadband connectivity. According to Akamai Technology's *State of the Internet Report*, Korea has the fastest average Internet connection speed in the world.[17] The latest figures rank Korea 11th worldwide for the number of Internet users[18] and number 62 globally for the number of Internet hosts.[19] Korea's online gaming

---

[17]Akamai Technologies, "State of the Internet Q4 2013," April 2014, www.akamai .com/dl/akamai/akamai-soti-q413.pdf?WT.mc_id=soti_Q413.

[18]CIA, *The World Factbook*, "Country Comparison: Internet Users," information dated 2009, www.cia.gov/library/publications/the-world-factbook/rankorder/2153rank.html (accessed November 19, 2014).

[19]CIA, *The World Factbook*, "Country Comparison: Internet Hosts," information dated 2009, www.cia.gov/library/publications/the-world-factbook/rankorder/2184rank.html (accessed November 19, 2014).

is a national obsession, and the blogging community places second behind China worldwide.

Gifts

Gifts are presented with both hands. At first, decline a gift, and then graciously accept it. When meeting with a group, bring gifts for everyone. The highest ranked receives a slightly more valuable gift. As the recipient of a gift, reciprocate with a similar value gift.

Business gift ideas include USB flash drives, high-quality pens, lanyards, desk accessories, and clocks, which symbolize good luck in Korea. Gifts should be moderately priced. Do not give liquor to a woman. Gifts to avoid include sharp items (symbolize severing of ties), green headwear (associated with infidelity), red ink (represents mourning), shoes (signify running away), and handkerchiefs (also represent mourning). Wrapping gifts neatly with attention is important. Gold is considered a royal color. Avoid red (represents communism) and green, black, white, and blue because they are associated with funerals and mourning.

Introductions, Greetings, Personal Space, and Eye Contact

The Korean greeting is, "Are you in peace?" The teaching of Confucianism is that the sense of well-being in other people should not be disturbed. The Korean custom for greeting is a slight bow at the waist with head and eyes down, hands at the sides. A handshake may be used when greeting Westerners. Greetings depend on rank, seniority, gender, and age. Younger or lower-ranking people bow first to older or higher-ranking people and often give a deeper bow. The senior person usually offers the handshake first. Men may shake hands with men, and women give a slight nod. As a Westerner, shake hands with a Korean woman only if she extends her hand first. After bowing, Western women may extend their hand first to men. Elders prefer indirect eye contact and not direct, while the younger generation is comfortable with both.

Useful Phrases

Table 13.5 on page 297 covers phrases that may be useful for travel in Korea.

Table 13.5   Useful Phrases for Korean Travel

English	Korean	Pronunciation
Hello/good morning/ good afternoon/good evening (formal)	*Annyeong hasimnika*	AHN-yohng hah-SHEEM-nee-kah
How are you? ("Are you at peace?")	*Annyeong haseyo?*	AHN-yohng HAH-say-oh
Goodbye (said by person leaving, meaning, "Go in peace")	*Annyonghi kesipsiyo*	AHN-yohng-hee kah-SIP-sih-yoh
Goodbye (said by person staying, meaning "Go in peace")	*Annyonghi kasipsiyo*	AHN-yohng-hee kay-SIP-sih-yoh
Pleased to meet you	*Man-na-so pan-kap-sum-ni-da*	MAHN-nah-so pahn-gop-SOOM-nee-dah
Please	*Yo*	Yoh
Thank you	*Kamsa hamnida*	KAHM-sah HAHM-nee-dah
You're welcome	*Chon-man-e Mal-sum-im-ni-da*	CHON-mahn-AH-yo mahl-SOOM-eem-nee-DAH
Yes	*Ye*	YEE-eh
Excuse me	*Che-song-ham-ni-da*	CHAY-song hahm-NEE-dah

Names

Korean names are usually on the order of family name (surname or last name) plus given generational name plus given name.

Use courtesy titles and family name. Once a relationship is established, use of the family name may be followed by *ssi* (Mr., Mrs., or Miss), pronounced *shee*. Females retain their maiden names after marriage. Using a professional title and a family name such as Attorney Kim, President Lee, or Chairman Min is common.[20]

---

[20]Norine Dresser, *Multicultural Manners: Essential Rules of Etiquette for the 21st Century* (Hoboken, NJ: John Wiley & Sons, Inc., 1996, 2005).

International Blunder: Korean Naming Conventions

After leaving Japan, President Bill Clinton traveled to Korea to meet with then President Kim Young Sam. Clinton repeatedly referred to President Kim's wife as 'Mrs. Kim.' The South Korean officials were embarrassed. The U.S. president had been erroneously advised that the Koreans had the same naming conventions as the Japanese and was not informed that Korean wives retain their maiden names. In Korea, the family name precedes the given name. President Kim's wife Sohn Myong Suk should have been addressed as Mrs. Sohn.[21] The failure to follow Korean protocol left the impression that Korea was not as important as Japan.

Meetings and Negotiations

Koreans penalize those who are late. Punctuality is important, however, high-level Korean executives may arrive late for meetings.

Meetings begin with beverages and small talk and may extend past office hours. At first meetings, be prepared to match the level of formality set by the Koreans—wait to be invited to sit down. Listen more and speak less. In a group meeting, the seating arrangement will closely reflect status. When departing, show respect by bowing to everyone present.

Koreans are competitive, efficient negotiators wanting success for their company and Korea. During negotiations, a calm, persistent approach works best.

Presentation Styles, Conversational Topics, and Humor

When giving a presentation, share as much detail as possible about your company and your status within it to establish credibility and trust. If using Slide Share or PowerPoint, start with a purpose statement and an agenda. Koreans prefer background context before the main objective is presented, with data and facts to support a position. Pictures and charts are helpful because Korean culture emphasizes symbols. Major concepts should be summarized. Koreans are solutions-focused, group-oriented, and tend to be deductive thinkers who appreciate rational explanations with examples and analogies. Because Koreans tend to be hesitant to interrupt and reluctant to ask questions, reserve time for a question-and-answer period.[22]

---

[21] Ibid.

[22] Ruben Hernandez, *Presenting Across Cultures: How to Adapt Your Business and Sales Presentations in Key Markets Around the World* (Tertium Business Books, 2013); Dean Foster, *The Global Etiquette Guide to Asia* (New York: John Wiley & Sons, 2000); and Farid Elashmawi, Ph.D., *Competing Globally: Mastering Multicultural Management and Negotiations* (Woburn, MA: Butterworth-Heinemann, 2001).

Gestures

The following are noteworthy gestures in Korea:

- Sucking in air between the teeth usually means 'no' or 'difficult.'
- To beckon someone, extend your hand, palm down and curl your four fingers together several times.
- Spitting on the street is an act of hygiene in Korea.[23]

Notable Foods and Dishes

Ms. Young Lee of YERICO Manufacturing advises, "If you did not eat rice today, then you did not have food." Rice is a dish of honor in Korean cuisine, so always accept this national favorite. Korean cuisine includes vegetables, soups, meats, and seafood. Korean food is steamed, stir-fried, or boiled. Unique teas may include cinnamon, ginger, or ginseng. Korean barbecue is a popular and interactive experience where guests order ingredients from the menu and observe as they are prepared at a grill built into the table.

Specialty Dishes

Here are some well-known dishes from Korea:[24]

- **Bi bim bap:** Hot stone bowl of rice mixed with meat, vegetables, egg, and spices
- **Kimchi:** Spicy fermented condiment made of daikon (a type of east-Asian radish)
- **Juk:** Rice porridge; the basis for many dishes
- **Bulgogi:** Strips of marinated and barbecued beef
- **Gimbap:** Steamed rice, vegetables, and meat or seafood rolled in dried seaweed
- **Samgyae-tang:** Chicken and ginseng stew with rice
- **Kim:** Dried seaweed heated in sesame oil and cut in squares
- **Shinsollo:** Meat, fish, vegetables, eggs, and nuts cooked in a hotpot

---

[23] *CultureGrams World Edition 2014: South Korea.* (Ann Arbor, MI: ProQuest, 2014); and Roger E. Axtell, et al., *Do's and Taboos Around the World for Women in Business* (New York: John Wiley & Sons, 1997).

[24] *CultureGrams World Edition 2014: South Korea* (Ann Arbor, MI: ProQuest, 2014); and Elizabeth Devine and Nancy L. Braganti, *The Traveler's Guide to Asian Customs & Manners*, 2nd ed. (New York: St. Martin's Griffin, 1998).

- **Mul-man-du:** Soup with dumplings filled with onion, egg, meat, sesame seeds, and chives
- **Tteok:** Pounded rice cake
- **Chunkwa:** Candy-coated thinly sliced fruit

Dining Etiquette

'Eating from the same pot' is a Korean way of purposefully bonding relationships. Be sure to respect the host as the highest in rank or age to begin the meal, and others join in later. Business dinners are more common than lunches. Dishes are simultaneously served with round metal chopsticks; sometimes spoons are provided as utensils. Individuals serve themselves and place food from the serving platter into their own bowl before eating it; they do not place food from the serving bowl into their mouth. Items are passed or poured with the right hand. Table seatmates fill each other's glasses; it is impolite to refill your own glass because an empty glass shows more is needed. It is acceptable to slurp soup, but avoid picking up food with your hands or raising a dish to your face. Leave food on your plate or the host may lose face because it may appear they did not serve enough.

Drinking and Toasting

After-hours drinking is part of the relationship building in the business lives of Korean men. White wine, *soju,* is served during meals. After dinner, it is popular to move to a club. Here is where the paths may change directions: a group of men may continue to talk separately, whereas a mixed group of men and women may go to a bar for drinks and singing. Drinking is inappropriate for Korean women. However, moderate drinking is acceptable for international businesswomen.

Popular Drinks

Some popular drinks in Korea are:[25]

- Scotch and beer
- Soju: Distilled rice wine

---

[25] *CultureGrams World Edition 2014: South Korea* (Ann Arbor, MI: ProQuest, 2014); Elizabeth Devine and Nancy L. Braganti, *The Traveler's Guide to Asian Customs & Manners,* 2nd ed. (New York: St. Martin's Griffin, 1998); and Dean Foster, *The Global Etiquette Guide to Asia* (New York: John Wiley & Sons, 2000).

- Makgeolli: Rice-based alcoholic drink
- Takchu and yakchu: Made from grain or potatoes, similar to vodka
- Chong-jong: A rice wine similar to sake, usually served hot

Toasting is common in Korea. The host offers the first toast and the guest of honor returns the gesture. At formal occasions, proper etiquette is to lift the glass in your right hand while using the left to support the forearm. A common toast is *gonbae* (GOHN-beh) or "bottoms up." A formal occasion toast is *wihayo* (wee-hah-yoh) or "for health and prosperity."

Tipping and Bill-Paying

Historically, tipping has not occurred in Korean culture. Today, the expectation is that business travelers will tip. International hotels and restaurants may include a 10- to 15-percent service charge automatically, so examine the bill. Taxi drivers and bellman may expect a small tip. As the host, the person extending the lunch or dinner invitation pays the bill. Offer to pay three times, and then graciously accept the rejection.

Taboos

The following are cultural taboos in Korea:

- Confusing Koreans with the Chinese, Japanese, or other Asians
- Blowing your nose in public
- Placing chopsticks sticking upright in rice or parallel on top of bowl
- Touching other people with your feet or shoes
- Printing or writing in red ink
- The numbers 4 and 9 and even numbers (bad luck); 3 and 7 are good luck.
- Standing with your hands in your trouser pockets
- Laughing, yawning, or using a toothpick without covering mouth
- Winking or whistling

Heroes and Sports

Knowing about another country's heroes and sports offers opportunities to incorporate culture-specific references into your conversations and presentations.

Heroes

The following are heroes from Korean history:

Kim Gu (1876–1949): Political leader and "Father of the Nation." A leading figure of the independence movement against Japanese colonial rule. He served twice as president of the Provisional Government of the Republic of Korea, organized the Korea Independence Army, and carried out crucial insurgencies against the Japanese.

Kim Dae-Jung (1925–2009): President and the so-called "Nelson Mandela of Asia." A prominent political figure and president known for his efforts to restore democracy and economic stability. In the year 2000, he became the first Korean awarded the Nobel Peace Prize for these efforts and the success of his Sunshine Policy, which broke ground in restoring relations and political contact with North Korea.

Sports

Sports

The most popular professional sports are football (soccer), baseball, basketball, and volleyball. Other common sports include badminton, bowling, tennis, golf, table tennis, swimming, figure skating, skiing, and snowboarding.

Two traditional sports that remain popular today are:

Taekwondo: A traditional martial art originating as a form of self-defense. Movements use the entire body, especially the hands and feet, as the name translates to "the way of punching and kicking." Practiced to strengthen physical and mental well-being, along with cultivating character and discipline.

Ssireum (Korean wrestling): A traditional form of wrestling with ancient roots. Two contenders each wearing a *satba*, or sash around the waist and thigh, try to throw their opponent to the ground in a sandy ring to win points. Today it is a popular sport, and professional teams exist.

Sports Figures

Hyun-jin Ryu (1987–present): Professional baseball pitcher. One of the most famous baseball players in Korea and the first Korean to be a starting pitcher in U.S. Major League Baseball, playing for the L.A. Dodgers. In

2005, while playing in Korea, he was the first to win Rookie of the Year and MVP in the same season. At the Beijing Olympics, he pitched for the Korean team and took the gold. In 2009, he became the first pitcher in history to strike out 17 batters in nine innings.

K.J. Choi (1970–present): Professional golfer. Asia's most prolific and successful golfer. First Korean to play on the PGA tour, starting in 1994. Has won 20 Pro golf tournaments worldwide, including eight on the PGA.

Michelle Wie (1989–present): Professional golfer. Born to Korean-American parents, was the youngest player to qualify for the USGA Amateur Championship at 10, turned pro at 16. In 2006, she became the second woman to make the cut on the Asian pro golf tour.

Kim Yuna (1990–present): Retired figure skater. First Korean figure skater to medal at the Olympics—a gold at 2010 Games and a silver in 2014. Two-time world champion (2009, 2013). Six-time Korean national champion who has broken 11 world records.

Park Tae-Hwan (1989–present): Korean national team swimmer. First Korean to win a medal in swimming. First Asian to win a gold in the 400-meter freestyle at the 2008 Olympics. He began his career at seven and has won numerous titles, including two silvers at the 2012 Olympics.

Hwang Kyung-seon (1986–present): Taekwondo practitioner. Two-time Olympic champion in the 2008 and 2012 Games. First woman to win three consecutive Olympic taekwondo medals.

Eight-Question Framework

This section reviews the framework to which you were introduced earlier in this book. Each of these questions address one or more business topics to help you attract and build the relationships upon which today's successful businesses depend.

1. How Do Koreans Prefer to Act: Individually or as a Group?

Korea, with an Individualism score of 18 on the Hofstede dimension,[26] is considered a collectivist society (See Chapter 2, page 15). However, not all businesspeople there are consensus decision makers. After 20 years living and

---

[26]The Hofstede Center, "What About South Korea?" http://geert-hofstede.com/south-korea .html (accessed November 19, 2014).

working in Korea, Joel Momberger, the former director of the Korea Tech Innovation Program at The University of Texas at Austin found that within multinationals and groups, such as SK or LG, groups are hierarchical. Usually one high-ranking person makes the go-or-don't-go decision. That decision maker may take into account the opinion of others and factor that in, but, at the end of the day, it's their decision.

This means that although Koreans may work in groups and teams to accomplish projects, team members at lower levels in an organization won't make a decision without prior approval from their superior. Even if a team has been following a certain protocol for some time, when a superior says, "No, you need to do it this way," everything changes. Indeed, as Soraya Kim of The University of Texas' Global Commercialization Group says, she can't think of a situation in which a subordinate or junior has ever openly disagreed with the highest-ranking person.

2. How Are Power and Authority Viewed in Korea?

In Korea, it's who you know, not what you know.
—*Anonymous*

In Korea's ancient Confucian society, there were four classes of people representing vertical relationships. The *Sa,* the scholars, were the literate class, and wielded the most power and authority. Below them came the farmers *(Nong),* the manufacturers *(Kong),* and the merchant class *(Sang).* High world rankings in educational attainment reflect the value that Koreans place on scholarship. The country consistently places in the top five with Singapore, Hong Kong, and Taiwan. Mr. Ih Min, CEO of YERICO Manufacturing, Inc., said that Korean children learn to focus on education and prepare for exams, and that this is ingrained from kindergarten through high school, to compete for college. Education plays strongly into who holds power and authority in Korea.

The crowning achievement of this education-based upbringing is graduating from one of Korea's three prestigious universities (Seoul National University, Korea University, and Yeunsei University). Korea's premier graduates join conglomerates known as *chaebols* (pronounced *jay-bol*), comprising many different companies across various industries held under the umbrella of a single, family-owned holding company.

Koreans will be interested in where you went to school. As Trompenaars and Hampden-Turner say in *Riding the Waves of Culture,*[27] in

---

[27] Trompenaars, Fons and Charles Hampden-Turner. *Riding the Waves of Culture: Understanding Diversity in Global Business.* 3rd ed. New York: McGraw-Hill, 2012.

achievement-oriented societies such as the U.S., U.K., and Canada, you are likely to be asked "What did you study?" whereas in ascriptive cultures like Korea, the question is, "*Where* did you study?"

In Korean organizations, the power and authority is at the top, and business works top-down.

However, who has the power to make decision varies depending on geographic location. One professional advised "In the province in which we did a lot of work, it was the chairman of the small and medium business center that made the major decisions, then above him was the governor. So when the governor says, 'This is what I want,' it gets done. When the chairman says, 'This is what I want,' it all gets done."

If you want to get a deal done, you must have a comparable-level person attend the negotiations. High-ranking Korean businesspeople will normally not discuss anything with someone who is lower ranking.

Korea has a score of 60 on Hofstede's power distance dimension, which means it is a slightly hierarchical society. Everyone in the organization has a place, and subordinates expect to be given orders.[28]

3. How Do Koreans Compare Rules and Relationships?

As Joel Momberger pointed out, one of the most important things to remember is that Korea is a 50-million member family, with 60 percent of Koreans sharing one of three names: Park, Kim, or Lee. The entire network relies on relating to each other, alongside a set of common values that are more like familial values.

For the past six years, Mr. Momberger has asked Korean innovators: Why are you in this business? "Number one reason is to promote Korean culture worldwide, then to help their family, then to build a legacy. Money is usually fifth or sixth on the list. And that's shocking to Westerners, Americans in particular. In the U.S., we tend to rely on contracts and litigation because we don't have that common cultural grounding that goes back centuries to say 'this is how we do things.' Contracts are so important because the contract isn't about the relationship."

Not surprisingly, the idea of a binding commercial contract that solidifies all the details of the relationship is not the Korean way.[29] Koreans look at contracts as flexible documents or guidelines, not to be strictly construed or enforced.[30] This is an important distinction to appreciate when negotiating with Koreans.

---

[28] Ibid.

[29] Dennis Unkovic, *Understanding Asia: Winning Strategies for Business Success* (Chicago: ABA Publishing, 2001), 105.

[30] James R. Silkenat, Jeffrey M. Aresty, and Jacqueline Klosek, *The ABA Guide to International Business Negotiations: A Comparison of Cross-Cultural Issues and Successful Approaches*, 3rd Edition (Chicago: ABA Publishing, 2009), 683.

4. How Do Koreans Regard Time?

Whatever you think you know about Korea is going to change within three weeks. It's a place that evolves so fast.
—*Joel Momberger*

The Koreans have an expression that pervades business and their approach to life generally: *palli palli,* meaning 'faster, faster' or 'always in a hurry.' People we interviewed for this book repeatedly pointed out the high speed at which deals are done after a relationship has been established.

For example, the moment contracts had been signed with a Korean institute, another professional said that, "It was as if the floodgates had opened. Koreans are known to work very quickly. They want something done—like now. In fact, I think they get frustrated when an agreement is sent over to the U.S. and attorneys take time to review it."

To help shorten the length of time it takes to finalize a deal you should bear in mind what was addressed in the first two questions: Wherever possible, locate and work with the highest-ranking decision maker from the beginning. Also bear in mind the concept known in Korea as *chung,* which Ms. Kim defines as the bond between people and also speaks to loyalty. Face-to-face meetings between equals in the hierarchy help establish a bond that otherwise might take years to develop when exchanging email. International business negotiations may appear to be more efficient through email, but Koreans prefer Skype calls and face-to-face meetings so they can read body language and other nonverbal cues.

5. How Direct Is Communication in Korea?

The goal (of face) is to guarantee that everyone is in a constant state of *anshim* (ahn-sheem) which means "peace of mind" or "at perfect ease."
—The Korean Mind: Understanding Contemporary Korean Culture[31]

Poor communication and manners can detrimentally impact business negotiations. Due to the Korean preference for harmony, international business travelers should be clear and firm about their positions, while avoiding adversarial and aggressive approaches. Koreans may respond to questions with a question

---

[31]Boye Lafayette De Mente, *The Korean Mind: Understanding Contemporary Korean Culture* (Tokyo, Japan: Tuttle Publishing, 2012).

of their own in an attempt to determine how much you know, and the point of your questions.

Be prepared to listen carefully for phrases that mean "no" such as "I am not sure," "I will consider it," and "I would like to, however . . ."

Professionals who fail to observe subtle communication cues unwittingly violate what is known in Korea as *myongye* or 'the need for honor.' As Boyé Lafayette De Mente explains, "To succeed in Korea, both foreign businesspeople and diplomats must understand the nature and role of honor in Korean life. . . . This requires a substantial degree of knowledge about Korean values, expectations, and behavior."[32]

6. How Formal or Informal Do Businesspeople in Korea Tend to Be?

It is becoming more informal here, especially within smaller, start-up companies. But it's not there yet with larger corporations where relationships are usually quite formal, especially with outsiders.
— *Senior Scientific Advisor, Fortune 50 Company*

If you think figuring out how formal to be during introductions in Korea is difficult, be aware that your hosts probably find it just as challenging. Says Soraya Kim, "We are still in the process of trying to figure out how to address each other. On the one hand, you find Westerners trying to accommodate Koreans by referring to people formally, as Governor Kim, Chairman Hong, and President Lee. The Koreans are trying to accommodate Westerners, and will say Joel, Sid, Bob, and Susan."

One thing to bear in mind is that, as Joel Momberger explains: "Koreans live within a distinct hierarchy, and the degree of formality used in Korean speech is largely dependent on who you are in relation to everyone else. It's not just level of speech, it's a total mindset. If you're older, then I owe you respect; I owe you deference. If you ask me to do something, it is incumbent on me to do that. If you're younger than me, I can tell you what to do; I can instruct you. This is not necessarily a conscious Korean thought process; it's something automatic. Everybody knows where they fit in the society and where everybody else fits and what they are supposed to do."

That is why when a Korean asks questions regarding your age that may seem personal in a Western context, they're trying to assess where you fit in the hierarchy in relation to them, so they know how formal or informal to be.

In the meantime, things are changing rapidly. As a general rule, you are likely to find smaller organizations populated with younger people to be more

---

[32]Ibid., 265–266.

informal in their dealings than larger, more established organizations whose senior managers are more formal.

7. How Aligned Are Korean Social and Business Lives?

"Make a friend first, and a client second."
— *Local Korean saying*

Ms. Donna Lipman of the Korea Tech Innovation Program at The University of Texas shared that, "I find business and social to be intertwined when I conduct business in Korea. After my presentations training, the group has taken me out every time. The male-to-female ratio of the group is roughly 7:3. We enjoy drinking *soju*, a white wine, sometimes until 3:00 a.m. This is how to nurture business relationships. We all take our turns at karaoke, and I offer some John Denver songs I sang with him in Colorado."

One of the differences in business socializing today is that both men and international women dine and drink together. Drinking and singing into the early hours of the morning is part of relationship building in Korea, so accept invitations. It's the way deals are sealed and business relationships cemented. Mr. Min confirms that much of the decision making and relationship-building in Korea is conducted after dinner. Music is also a major way to find favor because Koreans love music. As Ms. Lipman emphasized, it's invaluable to have an authentic musical talent or ability, whether it's singing or playing an instrument.

8. How Is the Concept of Women in Business Handled in Korea?

Mr. Min says international businesswomen with expertise, specialization, seniority, and rank will encounter *less* resistance in Korea from male counterparts, although challenges remain. Ms. Soraya Kim offered three key insights for international businesswomen visiting Korea:

1. "First, you need to understand our history and culture. Korea is predominantly a Confucian-based society, and Koreans ask questions to understand where in the hierarchy to place you. In the past, they asked: 'How old are you?', 'Are you married?', 'Do you have children?' But Koreans are beginning to understand these are inappropriate to ask Westerners. Now they will ask, 'What is your position in the company?', 'How long have you been with the company?', 'Are you the

manager?', 'Are you the assistant manager?', or 'Are you the team manager?' In that way, everybody knows how to talk to people based on their position. In Korean culture, everyone is in the hierarchy."

2. The second point is that this hierarchy of relationships can play to your benefit, especially if you're an older professional. Says Ms. Kim: "Oftentimes, when I am in meetings, I'm older than most people, except perhaps for the CEO. Koreans want to accommodate Westerners and not offend, depending on who you are talking to." She pointed out generational differences in the country and that you are less likely to be slighted when working with more progressive, younger companies and team members.

3. Ms. Kim's third point highlights that this is a country where women may still be viewed as second-class citizens. While Ms. Kim was in a reception line with Caucasian men, a Korean female went down the line shaking hands but turned away, didn't make eye contact, and walked off before reaching Ms. Kim, "because she assumed that I was support staff." Although this may be an unsettling experience for an international businesswoman, know that leaders like Cho Sun-hae, founder and CEO of Geo Young, who began her career as a pharmacist and is now one of Korea's most well-known female executives, are paving the way for the next generation of powerful females in the nation,[33] as are entrepreneurs like Romi Haan, CEO and founder of Haan Corporation,[34] and as Korea's first female president, Guen-hye Park, who is eleventh on Forbes' *The World's 100 Most Powerful Women 2014* list.[35]

Cultural Summary

Here are some key points to remember about the Korean culture:

- Study and understand the *chaebol* system in Korea, where relationships are a high priority.
- Match the formality, rank, and status of your Korean counterparts in negotiations—hierarchy is highly valued. Wherever possible, send senior representatives to conduct business. Age and seniority may no

[33] *Forbes* magazine, "Asia Power Women 2014: Cho Sun-hae 60 (South Korea)," www.forbes.com /pictures/fdgk45ggee/cho-sun-hae-60-south-korea (accessed November 19, 2014).
[34] HAAN Corporation, "HAAN History," www.haanusa.com/ABUS.html#history (accessed November 19, 2014).
[35] *Forbes* magazine, "The World's 100 Most Powerful Women," www.forbes.com/power-women /list/#tab:overall (accessed November 19, 2014).

longer automatically equal respect with the younger generation, who are more likely to respect specialization and expertise. In a group setting, the seating arrangement will closely reflect status. Koreans often arrange one-on-one meetings. It is customary upon leaving a meeting to show respect by bowing to everyone present and walking guests to the exit, waiting until they are out of sight.

- Given the importance of understanding relationships within a hierarchical structure, expect to be asked questions about your title, position, and status within the company. Ask open-ended questions or rephrase statements to avoid yes or no answers. Face and honor are important and Koreans will politely avoid giving a "no" response.

Self-Awareness Profile

This simple exercise prompts you to self-assess where you currently stand on topics related to the eight-question framework and *compare* this with the country culture. This visual will help you discover the extent to which you may need to adapt your current mindset and behavior to develop more robust business relationships. For details on how to complete this graphic, see the instructions given in the Introduction on pages xviii–xix.

Consider copying the eight-question Profile or using a pencil so that you can see, over time, how you have adjusted your cultural mindset. You might also wish to create unique graphics related to each of the businesses you work with, as these cultural positions vary depending upon geographic location, industry, generational factors, and corporate profile.

Q1: What is your preferred way of doing business?

As an individual making autonomous decisions					As a team member who seeks group consensus
1	2	3	4	5	**6**

Q2: How comfortable are you in hierarchies in which power is distributed unequally?

Very uncomfortable					Very comfortable
1	2	3	4	**5**	6

Q3: How closely do you follow rules and obey the law?

Almost always   **It depends**

   1   2   3   **4**   5   6

Q4: What is your general attitude toward time?

I prefer   **I prefer flexibility,**
agendas, schedules,   **fluidity without**
planning   **scheduling**

    1   **2**   3   4   5   6

Q5: What is your preferred way to communicate?

Very diplomatically   **Very candidly**

    1   2   **3**   4   5   6

Q6: What is your interpersonal style or level of formality in business interactions?

Very formal   **Very informal**

   1   **2**   3   4   5   6

Q7: What is your view on socializing within business?

A waste of time   **Essential**

   1   2   3   4   5   **6**

Q8: Should a woman defer to a man as the lead, if winning business in a certain culture depended on it?

Never   **Yes, absolutely**

   1   2   3   4   **5**   6

14 | Taiwan

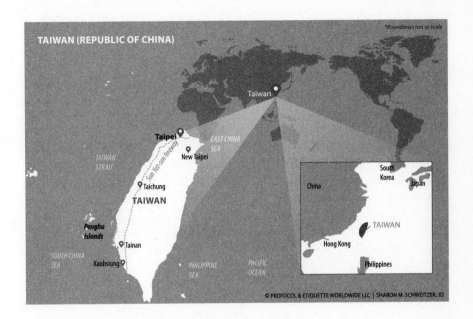

"I am Taiwanese as well as Chinese."

—Ma Ying-jeou

Introduction

One adjective we heard many times in connection with Taiwanese business was *hypercompetitive*. Some of the people we interviewed for this book said this cultural tendency begins in school. Others believed it is historical, stemming from the time when earning *jinshi,* the modern-day equivalent of the Ph.D., by passing the system of imperial examinations established by the Chinese emperors, led to prestigious positions and land ownership. The drive to study hard and earn a degree, preferably in an engineering discipline, is commonly found across many Asian countries. However, this drive to compete, at least as it was explained to us, seems to have been inculcated in Taiwan through a centuries-old system in which many competed but few received the highest rewards.

Such drive and ambition has served Taiwan well. In the early 1980s, the combination of well-educated talent, progressive government policies, and investment in areas such as Hsinchu Science Park, helped to establish Taiwan's economic focus as a global high-tech powerhouse. As one BBC article pointed out, "You may not have heard of the companies Quanta Computer, Compal Electronics, Pegatron, Wistron, and Inventec, but together they make more than 90 percent of the laptops sold worldwide, including those sold by brands such as Apple and Dell."[1] Today, Taiwan boasts the second-highest density of high-tech companies in the world behind the U.S., according to Bloomberg's list of the Most Innovative Countries in the World 2014.[2] Its "innovation district" of Keelung Road in Taipei is also the location of many start-up companies. Perhaps not surprisingly, while Taiwan is ranked 10th overall in the same Bloomberg list (South Korea ranked number one; the U.S. number three), the island received the highest ranking for patent activity, meaning the number of patents granted as a percentage of the world total.

Innovation is often associated with the sort of individualistic characteristics found in places like Silicon Valley and Austin's Silicon Hills. Yet it is important to remember that familial relationships and core values central to Confucianism remain strongly influential here. As Taiwan's former President of the Industrial Technology Research Institute (ITRI), Mr. Chintay Shih, said in one interview,

---

[1]BBC Future, "Taiwan's Struggle to Become an Innovation Leader," September 18, 2013, www.bbc.com/future/story/20130918-taiwans-rocky-road-to-innovation.
[2]Bloomberg slideshow, "30 Most Innovative Countries," January 22, 2014, www.bloomberg .com/slideshow/2014-01-22/30-most-innovative-countries.html#slide22; and Bloomberg, "In Global Innovation Race, Taiwan Is Tops in Patents, Israel Leads in R&D," January 23, 2014, www.bloomberg.com/news/2014-01-22/in-global-innovation-race-taiwan-is-tops-in-patents -israel-leads-in-r-d.html.

after graduating from Princeton University and hearing about his country's desire to be pioneers in semiconducting, "I really had no idea what was waiting for me in Taiwan. I only knew that serving the country was the right thing to do."[3] It is worth remembering that sentiment as you navigate this fascinating collectivist culture.

Quiz

How much do you know about Taiwan? Answer the following questions as True or False to test your knowledge. (The Answer Key at the bottom includes page numbers that refer to the topic):

_____1. Taiwan was once connected by a land bridge to mainland China.

_____2. The island lies in the southern hemisphere, bisected by the Tropic of Capricorn.

_____3. Taiwan was originally known as the island of Formosa.

_____4. Taiwanese inventors hold the greatest number of patents in the world.

_____5. The national sport of Taiwan is baseball.

_____6. The leading religion in the country is Confucianism.

_____7. Taiwan is a "high-context" culture in terms of communication style.

_____8. You can smoke anywhere in Taiwan.

_____9. It is perfectly acceptable to joke about the country's political situation with China, as the Taiwanese do not take offense.

_____10. Parts of the movie *Life of Pi* were filmed on the island.

Answer Key: 1. T (p. 316); 2. F (p. 318); 3. T (p. 316); 4. T (p. 314); 5. F (p. 329); 6. F (p. 321); 7. T (p. 333); 8. F (p. 328); 9. F (p. 326); 10. T (p. 317).

Country Basics

This section provides key knowledge in an easy-to-read format to help you quickly grasp some of the basics necessary to navigate this culture.

---

[3]Taiwan *Today*, "Veterans Tell Story of Taiwan's Semiconductor Industry," dated June 18, 2010, http://taiwantoday.tw/ct.asp?xItem=107417&ctNode=1743.

Historical Timeline

A critical way to show respect for another person's culture is to have knowledge of their country's history and current affairs. Table 14.1 outlines a few key events related to Taiwan, together with concurrent world events.

Table 14.1   Key Historical Events

Period/Dates	Description/Events	World Events
Stone Age (10,000–12,000 years ago)	The land bridge between Taiwan and mainland China is covered by water.	Introduction of the first boats and bows and arrows.
3,000 BC	Earliest inhabitants of Taiwan arrive from Pacific islands.	Phoenicians settle in Crete.
1400s	Chinese arrive from Fujian province.	Louis XI establishes French royal mail service.
Early 1500s	Portuguese sailors name the island Ilha Formosa, or "Beautiful Island."	Proposal of the construction of the Suez Canal.
1624	The island is colonized by the Dutch.	Dutch settle in New Amsterdam (later New York).
1661–1662	Ming Dynasty loyalist Zheng Cheng-gong and Han followers expel Dutch.	Death of Shun Chih, first Qing Dynasty Emperor.
1683	Qing Dynasty declares Taiwan a prefecture of mainland China.	Sir Isaac Newton proposes his Tidal Theory.
April 17th, 1885	Taiwan becomes a separate Chinese province.	Louis Pasteur develops rabies vaccine.
1895	Taiwan and Penghu ceded to Japan following Qing defeat in first Sino-Japan war.	Alfred Nobel's will establishes the Nobel Prizes.
September 1945	China establishes Taiwan Provincial Government following Japanese defeat in World War II.	The Federal People's Republic of Yugoslavia is formed.

Table 14.1 (*Continued*)

Period/Dates	Description/Events	World Events
1949	Chiang Kai-shek's KMT party (1.5 million Chinese) flees Mao's communist regime. Martial law is declared.	Nehru becomes Prime Minister of India.
1980s	Democratic reforms by Chiang Chingkuo and lifting of martial law.	The compact disc is launched.
1996	First direct presidential elections.	Russia's first president, Boris Yeltsin, begins second term.
2000	Chen Shi-ban becomes first non-KMT president.	Australia hosts "the most popular ever" Olympic Games in Sydney.[4]
2009	Ang Lee's award-winning movie *Life of Pi* partially filmed in Taichung and Kenting.	Barack Obama inaugurated as U.S. American president, the first African-American to be elected.
2010	Taiwan and China sign a landmark free trade agreement.	The Burj Khalifa in Dubai, the world's tallest building, is officially opened.
2012	Ma Ying-jeou is reelected President for his second term.	NASA's *Curiosity* rover successfully lands on Mars.
2016	National elections scheduled.	Laos is scheduled to be ASEAN chair.
2017	Taipei to host the XXIX Summer Universiade for the International University Sports Federation.	Hong Kong chief executive elections and Indian, South Korean, and Singaporean presidential elections scheduled.

---

[4]BBC News Asia, "Australia Profile," last updated September 18, 2014, www.bbc.com/news/world-asia-15675556 (accessed November 10, 2014).

Full Country Name and Location

Taiwan is officially known as Taiwan, Republic of China, differentiated from the People's Republic of China. It is located 100 miles east, across the Taiwan Strait. The island is 245 miles long and 89.5 miles wide. Roughly the size of Denmark, its shape might be described as a vertically leaning sweet potato. The capital, Taipei, is positioned at the northern tip. The country is situated in the northern hemisphere. The Tropic of Cancer bisects the island horizontally.

Government/Political Structure

Taiwan is a constitutional republic with a president who is voted in every four years as head of state. In addition to the office of the president, the central government comprises five branches or *Yuan*: the Executive Yuan, the Legislative Yuan, the Judicial Yuan, the Examination Yuan, and the Control Yuan.[5] A premier appointed by the president serves as the head of government and president of the Executive Yuan. Next elections are scheduled for January 2016.

Population and Economic Centers

The population of Taiwan is approximately 23.4 million.[6] The country is divided into two provinces, consisting of 14 counties and three provincial municipalities, and five special municipalities (which have the same rank as a province). According to U.N. statistics, approximately 75 percent of the population lives in urban areas.[7]

The main ethnicities are Taiwanese, including Hakka (84 percent), mainland Chinese (14 percent), and indigenous (Polynesian/Malay descent, 2 percent).[8]

---

[5]Ministry of Foreign Affairs, Republic of China (Taiwan), "Government Structure," last updated November 11, 2014, www.taiwan.gov.tw/ct.asp?xItem=27177&ctNode=1920&mp=1001 (accessed November 10, 2014).

[6]CIA, *The World Factbook*, "Taiwan," www.cia.gov/library/publications/the-world-factbook/geos/tw.html (accessed November 10, 2014).

[7]United Nations, Department of Economic and Social Affairs, Population Division, "Country Profile: Taiwan, Province of China," *World Urbanization Prospects, 2014 revision*, http://esa.un.org/unpd/wup/Country-Profiles/Default.aspx (accessed November 10, 2014).

[8]CIA, *The World Factbook*, "Taiwan," www.cia.gov/library/publications/the-world-factbook/geos/tw.html (accessed November 10, 2014).

The major business centers and populations (2013) are outlined in Table 14.2.[9]

Table 14.2 Major Business Centers

Business Centers	Population (Millions)
Kaohsiung	2.8
New Taipei	4.0
Taichung	2.7
Tainan	1.9
Taipei (capital)	2.7

Economy

Taiwan is ranked 19th out of 189 economies in terms of ease of doing business according to the World Bank Group's *Doing Business 2015* report.[10] The composition of its 2013 GDP by sector was services (68.6 percent), industry (29.4 percent), and agriculture (2 percent).[11] Almost 60 percent of the labor force is involved in service industries, while just more than a third of laborers (36.2 percent) work in industry. Agriculture contributes little to the GDP from products including rice, tea, pigs, poultry, and fish.

Taiwan's strategic position as a gateway between East and West has historically underscored its importance globally to traders including the Dutch, Portuguese, Spanish, as well as to Japan. Although the Taiwanese government used to be directly involved in investment and foreign trade, this has eased over the years, and the economy is now described in the *CIA World Factbook* as *a dynamic capitalist economy*.[12] In 2012, Taiwan was the U.S.'s 11th largest trade partner and the 16th largest U.S. export market. Economic development has been achieved largely through the export of electronics, machinery, and

---

[9]Department of Statistics, Ministry of the Interior, Republic of China (Taiwan), *Statistical Yearbook of Interior*, "2.12 Number of Townships & Districts, Villages, Neighborhoods, and Presdent Population," http://sowf.moi.gov.tw/stat/year/elist.htm (accessed November 10, 2014).

[10]World Bank Group, *Doing Business 2015* (October 29, 2014): 4, www.doingbusiness.org/~/media/GIAWB/Doing%20Business/Documents/Annual-Reports/English/DB15-Full-Report.pdf.

[11]CIA, *The World Factbook*, "Taiwan," www.cia.gov/library/publications/the-world-factbook/geos/tw.html (accessed November 10, 2014).

[12]Ibid.

petrochemicals. Additional key industries include communications and IT products, consumer products, and pharmaceuticals.

Corruption Perceptions Index

Taiwan ranked 36th least corrupt out of 177 countries and territories with a score of 61 out of 100.[13] This annual index, compiled by Transparency International, measures perceived levels of public sector corruption.

Several anticorruption agencies conduct investigations in Taiwan: the Investigation Bureau of the Ministry of Justice; the Department of Government Employee Ethics of the Ministry of Justice; and the Special Investigation Division of the Supreme Prosecutors Office.

Human Development Index

Taiwan was not included in the HDI report.

Global Gender Gap Index

Taiwan was not included in the Global Gender Gap Index.

Climate

Temperatures in Taiwan average in the low to mid-70s Fahrenheit year round. In the coldest months (January to March), the temperature is unlikely to drop below 50 degrees F. The hottest months are June to August, when temperatures may reach 100 degrees in extreme cases, although more typically the highs are in the high 80s. Humidity is high everywhere with May through June being the rainiest months. From June to October, typhoons resulting in heavy rainstorms occasionally occur.

Languages

Mandarin is the official language, although many words and idioms used in Taiwan would not be familiar to Mandarin speakers in China. More than 20 other

---

[13]Transparency International, "Corruption Perceptions Index 2013," www.transparency.org /cpi2013/results (accessed November 11, 2014).

languages are in existence throughout the country, including Taiwanese or Hokkien. English is widely spoken for business. Not all taxi drivers understand English, so be sure to have addresses written in Mandarin to show them.

Belief Systems, Philosophies, and Religions

The country breakdown is as follows: Mixture of Buddhist and Taoist (93 percent), Christian (4.5 percent), and Other (2.5 percent).[14]

Religious freedom is constitutionally protected in Taiwan. There are more than 20 officially recognized religions/belief systems.

For an overview of belief systems, philosophies, and religions, please refer to Chapter 4, pages 64–65.

Time Zones/Daylight Savings

Taiwan has a single time zone, China Standard Time (CST). It is eight hours ahead of GMT (Greenwich Mean Time)/UTC (Coordinated Universal Time). It does not operate under Daylight Savings.

It is 13 hours ahead of U.S. Eastern Standard Time (12 hours ahead in Daylight Savings Time). See www.timeanddate.com/worldclock.

To calculate time in Taiwan, add eight hours to UTC/GMT.

Telephone Country Code and Internet Suffix

The Taiwanese telephone country code is 886, and the Internet suffix is .tw.

Currency

The unit of currency in Taiwan is the New Taiwan Dollar (TWD), or yuan. One dollar, or yuan, is divided into 100 cents.

Business Culture, Etiquette, and Customs

This section covers business culture, etiquette, and customs.

---

[14]CIA, *The World Factbook*, "Taiwan,"www.cia.gov/library/publications/the-world-factbook /geos/tw.html (accessed November 10, 2014).

Fiscal Year

The Taiwanese fiscal year is January 1 through December 31. Dates commonly used in business and everyday life are written as year, month, day; for example, April 1, 2020 would be written 2020/04/01. However, dates on official documents use the Republic of China (ROC) calendar, which starts from the year 1911 when the People's Republic of China was formed. Therefore, April 1, 2020 would be the 105th year of the Republic, written as 105/04/01.

Working Week

Office hours are said to be 9:00 to 17:30 (factory workers' hours, 8:00 to 17:00) with one hour for lunch, but in many cases, employees arrive slightly later in the morning and work throughout the evening. The structure of the typical Taiwanese working week is outlined in Table 14.3.

Table 14.3   Typical Taiwanese Work Week

Business Sector	Business Hours	Days of the Week
Businesses	09:00–17:30	Monday–Friday
Banks	09:00–15:30	Monday–Friday
Shops and restaurants	11:00–22:00	Daily

Table 14.4   Taiwanese Holidays and Festivals

Date	Name
January 1	National Founding Day (Republic of China)
January/February	Chinese New Year*
February 28	Memorial Day
April	Tomb Sweeping Day*
June	Dragon Boat Festival*
September	Mid-autumn Moon Festival*
October 10	Double Tenth National Day
October 25	Taiwan Restoration Day
October 31	Birthday of President Chiang Kai-shek
December 25	Constitution Day

Holidays and Festivals

Some Taiwanese holidays are determined by the lunar calendar and change from year to year. Common Taiwanese holidays and festivals appear in Table 14.4. Floating holidays are designated with an asterisk. On specific holidays, an office may remain open with limited staff. Check with your embassy or trade office before planning business travel.

Business Dress/Appearance

Business dress in Taiwan should err on the formal and modest side. Men should wear a high-quality lightweight suit because of the humidity, and a tie is expected when visiting northern Taiwan, especially for first meetings. Short-sleeved shirts are acceptable when visiting clients or customers in southern or central Taiwan, where the weather tends to be hotter. Depending on the industry, a blazer and khakis are acceptable.

For Western women, a skirt, blouse, and jacket are recommended. Pants are considered *smart casual*, and dresses tend to be reserved for more formal occasions. Necklines and hemlines need to conform to the Asian preference for modesty. Avoid bright colors to prevent negative perceptions.

News Sources

Some popular news sources in Taiwan include:
- *The China Post*: www.chinapost.com.tw
- *Taipei Times*: www.taipeitimes.com
- *Taiwan News*: www.etaiwannews.com/etn/index_en.php
- *Focus Taiwan*: http://focustaiwan.tw

Business Cards

Show respect by honoring the presentation of a person's card. Take time to review the cards you are given. Do not place them in your pockets or write on them. Present your card with the print facing the recipient, held out with both hands. Have your information translated into Mandarin on the reverse. Ensure you bring plenty of cards to distribute: Not doing so is considered rude and unprofessional.

Technology

According to Akamai Technology's *State of the Internet Report*, Taiwan has the 6th fastest average peak Internet connection speed in the world and the 18th fastest average connection speed.[15] The latest figures rank Taiwan 24th in the world for the number of Internet users[16] and 18th globally for the number of Internet hosts.[17]

Gifts

The Taiwanese are enthusiastic and generous gift-givers and receivers. What's important is the story behind the gift, not its value. Something handcrafted selected to represent your city or region is appreciated because it shows you have spent time choosing the gift. Avoid having things inscribed or personalized. The Taiwanese are big on regifting, which is a positive activity here. For example, we might bring a cowboy hat from Texas to a client, who then passes it on to a customer of theirs with the message that it's a genuine Texas hat similar to one worn by a famous actor in a well-known movie.

Food is another safe gift-giving staple. The Taiwanese may have Costco, where they can buy Canadian maple syrup or Australian macadamia cookies for themselves, but the fact that you carried the gifts over thousands of miles and can tell a story about them ("CEO Wang, I hope you like these cookies—my wife picked them out because they remind her of the ones her grandmother used to make,"), makes a big impression here and helps with bonding.

When receiving gifts, do so with both hands, palms facing up. Do not open a gift in front of someone, in case what you have given them is considered of higher value or quality than their gift to you.

Introductions, Greetings, Personal Space, and Eye Contact

A handshake is the common greeting among business acquaintances, though you may notice the Taiwanese nod and smile when introduced. A slight bow is a sign of respect. There is generally a lack of personal contact among the Taiwanese, and standing two arms' length distance when speaking to someone is a good rule of thumb. As a sign of respect, avoid a direct gaze, especially with elders.

---

[15]Akamai Technologies, "State of the Internet Q4 2013," April 2014, www.akamai .com/dl/akamai/akamai-soti-q413.pdf?WT.mc_id=soti_Q413.

[16]CIA, *The World Factbook*, "Country Comparison: Internet Users," information dated 2009, www.cia.gov/library/publications/the-world-factbook/rankorder/2153rank.html (accessed November 10, 2014).

[17]CIA, *The World Factbook*, "Country Comparison: Internet Hosts," information dated 2009, www.cia.gov/library/publications/the-world-factbook/rankorder/2184rank.html (accessed November 10, 2014).

Useful Phrases

Tables 14.5 and 14.6 contain useful travel phrases in both Taiwanese and Mandarin.

Table 14.5   Useful Phrases for Taiwanese

English	Taiwanese
Hello (singular)	*Li-ho*
Hello (plural)	*Lin-ho*
Good morning	*Gau-cha*
Good afternoon	*Go-an*
Good evening	*Am-an*
Goodbye	*Chai-kian*
Please	*Chhia*
Thank you	*To-sia, Kam-sia* or *Lo lat*

Table 14.6   Useful Madarin Phrases for Taiwanese Travel

English	Chinese (Mandarin)	Pronunciation
Hello	*Ni hao*	NEE-how
Good morning	*Zao shang hao*	zhow-shang HOW
Good afternoon	*Xia wu hao*	she-ah-woo HOW
Good evening	*Wanshang hao*	wahn-shang HOW
Goodbye	*Zaijian*	dzeye zhee-EHN
Please	*Qing*	Cheen
Thank you	*Xie xie*	See-EH see-EH
You're welcome	*Bu yong xie*	boo yohn see-EH
Yes	*Shi*	Shih
Excuse me	*Qing rang/Qing rang yi xia*	shing ree-AH/ EE-SHAH

Meetings and Negotiations

As age and status are highly revered, it is wise to make sure your team includes at least a few senior-level executives. At meetings, seating arrangements will reflect the importance of status: The highest-ranked members from each team sit in the middle on each side of the table and the next highest-ranked members sit to their sides accordingly. Because business is highly competitive in Taiwan, you will need to emphasize profits and thoroughly present the fine details of your proposal. However, keep in mind that greater emphasis is placed on personal relationships and reputation than profits alone. The Taiwanese are excellent bargainers, so pay attention to the subtleties of indirect communication. Although the pace of doing business is slow, avoid pressing too hard to reach an agreement and allow your Taiwanese host to set the pace of negotiations.

Presentation Styles, Conversational Topics, and Humor

When giving presentations it is beneficial to emphasize key points at the beginning and end. Allow for lengthy question and answer periods: The Taiwanese appreciate detailed information in proposals. Remember to remain composed and avoid using too many distracting hand gestures.

In conversation, avoid political references, especially about mainland China, and anything that might be considered a cultural criticism. Idioms and references used in your own country, including jokes, are unlikely to be clearly understood because they lack context. Praising sports stars such as Jeremy Lin, the Los Angeles Lakers basketball player, is appreciated.

Gestures

The Taiwanese are polite and fairly formal in their posture and gestures:

- Opening doors and offer seats to elders.
- Removing shoes before entering a home.
- Using both hands when passing or receiving items, including business cards.
- Sitting with both feet flat on the floor with hands in your laps.
- Using the whole hand to indicate or point.
- Using the V-sign (victory) is common when posing for photographs.

Notable Foods and Dishes

Taiwanese cuisine is heavily influenced by dishes originating in China, especially the adjacent Fujian province. Seafood is prevalent in this island nation's cuisine and the subtropical climate allows for a wide variety of fruits to be grown. Common ingredients include pork, chicken, rice, and soy, and typical seasonings are soy sauce, rice wine, sesame oil, pickled mustard greens, peanuts, chili peppers, cilantro, and basil. An important part of the cuisine in Taiwan is *xiaochi*, a variety of snack-like dishes similar to Spanish *tapas*, which may be served with entrées or by themselves.

Specialty Dishes

The following are some specialty dishes popular in Taiwan:[18]

Niu rou mian: Beef noodle soup with beef, thick noodles, vegetables, and pickled greens in a dark broth (the Beef Noodle Festival is held annually in Taipei)

Lu rou fan: Chopped braised pork belly in soy sauce and spices

You fan: Sticky rice with mushrooms, dried shrimp, shallots, and pork slices

Milkfish: Fish, pan-fried, braised, or served as a fish-ball soup

Ba wan: Dumplings stuffed with minced meat, vegetables, and often eggs

Oya misua: A thickened soup with thin vermicelli rice noodles and oysters

Cuttlefish: A squid-like sea animal typically in a soup with herbs and vegetables during winter

Bao bing: Shaved ice with fruit and flavorings such as juice and sweet condensed milk

Dining Etiquette

Breakfast meetings are not common because many Taiwanese tend to work late into the evening. Lunch or dinner is preferred. Allow your host to indicate where you should sit. Do not begin serving yourself until invited to do so. Do not refuse food. For utensils, be prepared to use chopsticks and a ceramic spoon. Leave something at the end of a meal to show you have had enough to eat.

Drinking and Toasting

Taiwanese are not big drinkers of alcohol and many prefer tea with their meals. Often you see people make a small glass of beer last a whole evening. When going out for a drink with coworkers, you may see Taiwanese buy one large bottle of beer. Everyone shares this by pouring small amounts into their own glasses.

---

[18]CNN Travel, "45 Taiwanese Foods We Can't Live Without," January 29, 2014, http://travel.cnn.com/explorations/eat/40-taiwanese-food-296093.

Toasting is common and may take place frequently during a meal. The glass is raised with both hands, one supporting the bottom, and eye contact is maintained. *Ganbei*, pronounced *ghan-bay*, means *bottoms up*. The group is expected to *do a shot* or empty the glass all at once. If you do not want to continue the bottoms-up approach, politely say "*suei yi*" (sway-yee), which roughly translates as *drink to your liking.*

Tipping and Bill-Paying

Tipping is not expected; however, a tip for exceptional service is always appreciated. A 10-percent service charge is usually added to hotel and restaurant bills. Round up to the nearest dollar for taxi drivers.

Smoking

There is a countrywide ban on smoking in all public places, both indoors and outdoors.[19] E-cigarettes are considered controversial and designated as medicines rather than tobacco products.

Taboos

The following behaviors are taboo:

- Winking
- Pointing or beckoning to someone with the index finger
- Loud or rowdy behavior
- Placing your arm around someone's shoulders; placing your feet on a table; moving or touching objects with your feet
- Leaving chopsticks sticking up in a bowl of rice
- Crossing legs at the knee or ankle

Heroes and Sports

Knowing about another country's heroes and sports offers opportunities to incorporate culture-specific references into your conversations and presentations.

---

[19]Americans for Nonsmokers' Rights, "Taiwan," last updated April 4, 2014, www.no-smoke.org /goingsmokefree.php?id=521 (accessed November 10, 2014).

Heroes

The following figures are heroes in Taiwan:

Zheng Chenggong (1624–1662): Chinese military leader, also known as Koxinga.

A Ming Dynasty loyalist credited for seizing control of Taiwan from Dutch colonialists and establishing the Han Chinese government. A temple built to honor him and his mother stands in Tainan City.

Mona Rudao (1882–1930): Influential aboriginal chieftain.

A Seediq tribal leader known for carrying out the revolt of Wushe in 1930 against Japanese authorities. He is featured on the New Taiwan Dollar coins and his story has been immortalized in the 2011 Taiwanese film, *Warriors of the Rainbow: Seediq Bale*.

Yuan Tseh Lee (1936–present): Taiwanese Nobel Laureate.

First Taiwanese citizen to win the Nobel Prize in Chemistry in 1986 for contributions to the development of chemical-reaction dynamics.

Sports

Sports

Basketball is considered to be the national sport of Taiwan. Also popular are football (soccer), softball, tennis, and golf.

Sports Figures

Yani Tseng (1989–present): Professional golfer. Taiwan's top-ranked women's golfer. She is the youngest person ever to win five major tournaments and ranked number one in the Women's World Golf Rankings from February 2011 to March 2013.

Jeremy Shu-how Lin (1988–present): Professional basketball player. A point guard for the NBA's Los Angeles Lakers and the first U.S. American of Taiwanese descent to play in the league.

Eight-Question Framework

This section reviews the framework to which you were introduced earlier in this book. Each of these questions addresses one or more business topics to help you attract and build the relationships upon which today's successful businesses depend.

1. How Do the Taiwanese Prefer to Act: Individually or as a Group?

Finding the right people with the power to make decisions, especially in local companies, can be a source of frustration in Taiwan, as Gabe Higham, a former hardware development manager with Dell Taiwan, discovered while based on the island for three years. Much of this had to do with the low initiative expected of subordinates, also illustrated by Taiwan's low individualism score in Geert Hofstede's findings.

As Mr. Higham pointed out, "In fast-paced Western-style companies, you expect to find more empowerment at lower levels where, even if you make a decision and it's wrong, there is a lesson to be learned. This is preferable to waiting around being told what to do, especially if you have the experience."

When working alongside some of the Taiwanese original design manufacturers (ODMs), for example, Mr. Higham found there was a hierarchical form of decision making. At times, it was not possible to make progress on something, whether making changes to a design, scheduling, or spending money, without his boss having to meet with whomever *he* reported to further up the chain. What helped to circumvent a lot of wasted time, Mr. Higham found, was the nature of the relationships he had developed within the company. Having already had dinner or drinks with a senior-level decision maker, or having spent time on the golf course together, Mr. Higham discovered that it was much easier just to pick up the phone and have some kinds of decisions made directly.

What Mr. Higham and others have found is that although the Taiwanese operate as a group through hierarchical decision maker, this can be bypassed at higher levels within a company when strong relationships are already in place.

2. How Are Power and Authority Viewed in Taiwan?

> People here judge you by two things: how much influence you have on other people, and money.
> — *Taiwanese senior executive, global management consulting firm*

We were told that there are three kinds of Taiwanese company cultures you are most likely to come across, each of which regards status somewhat differently, and should be borne in mind as you navigate businesses and industries.

For business cultures adopting a Taiwanese style of leadership—including small- and medium-sized businesses that represent 97 percent of the island's enterprises[20]—think *Jerry McGuire*: "Show me the money!" As one leading

---

[20]*Jakarta Post*, "Government Support Plays Key Role in SME Development," September 9, 2013, www.thejakartapost.com/news/2013/09/09/government-support-plays-key-role-sme-development.html.

consultant pointed out: "What is considered status is less where you come from or the school you went to—although these things matter—but the ability to bring them a big order. If you work for HP or Intel, that's what makes you powerful because that's where the real money is."

Many long-established Taiwanese companies are influenced by the Japanese style of leadership, where seniority is paramount. For more on this, please refer to Chapter 8, which covers Japan.

The U.S. American-style business culture is more typical of the newer industries including high-tech, as well as companies whose owners or senior management may have lived or studied in the West. Demonstrating achievement is the number one way to establish power and authority in these structures. This means emphasizing your international connections, the deals you have done with major global organizations, and your position in your company's hierarchy.

3. How Do the Taiwanese Compare Rules and Relationships?

It's not that you can't do anything without a relationship, but it definitely helps.

— *Taiwanese management consultant*

One example where it is not advisable to take a rule-bound here's how it needs to be approach in Taiwan is the year-end bonus party.

"The fiscal year is based on the Chinese New Year, which usually falls somewhere between mid-January and mid-February.[21] That's when there is a huge 'end of year' party, and everyone gets bonuses," explained Jaime Melanson, who worked as an engineering manager in Dell's Taipei office from 2009 to 2012. "The Taiwanese get their monthly salary every month as we do, but the last month—around Chinese New Year—they get double: their monthly pay plus the bonus.

"All employees expect this party, and if you don't have one, people might not work for you. This was awkward for us at a time when in the U.S. there were no parties and we were having layoffs, but were having this huge celebration for Taiwanese employees. What people didn't understand was how this is an important part of the culture and you could lose your best people if you don't do something at the end of the year."

Employers in Taiwan know to carve out time for preparations for this event. In this example, Ms. Melanson shared that the dancing entertainment was put on by the employees who, "probably spent two months before the party, every day during lunch, going to practice and working with

---

[21]China Travel, "Chinese New Year Dates from 2013 to 2024," www.chinatravel.com/focus /chinese-new-year/new-year-calendar.htm (accessed November 10, 2014).

a professional choreographer." This illustrates the importance of cultural tradition in Taiwanese workplaces. Even though it encroached on company time and took place during a time of recession, this year-end party still needed to be celebrated.

4. How Do the Taiwanese Regard Time?

The Taiwanese work long hours: an average of 2,200 hours a year, 20 percent higher than in Japan or the U.S.[22]

David Kuo, director of operations for Taiwan and China for Adexa Inc., confirmed that subordinates are expected to stay later and arrive sooner than their bosses. In the semiconductor industry, which he services, it is typical for people in the industry to leave the office at 1:00 a.m. or 2:00 a.m. and be expected back again by 8:30 a.m..

One of the ways that workplace culture in Taiwan allows for people to catch up on their sleep is during what is referred to here as *nap time*. As Ms. Jaime Melanson of Dell explained: "At noon, in the ODMs (original design manufacturers), the lights will dim and they play soothing music. This is when everyone lays face down with their jackets over their heads to sleep at their desks. Nap time can last for half an hour to an hour, sometimes an hour and a half, so it's advisable not to schedule meetings or make calls that will run into the time between 12 noon and 1:30 p.m."

Another time that doesn't work well for arranging important meetings or trying to finalize negotiations is the period known as the Hungry Ghost Festival, sometimes referred to as Ghost Month. Most Taiwanese are unlikely to make important decisions and purchases, both professional and personal, at this time. These range from not starting a new business to deferring buying a house or car. This annually observed period varies according to the Chinese New Year. In 2015, the festival will begin on August 28.[23] Visitors to Taiwan during this period see imitation money burned in the streets and banquet tables of food prepared to appease the hungry spirits. If you find that responses are slow from your Taiwanese counterparts during Ghost Month, it could be because they are taking part in one of the many rituals and ceremonies that honor the spirits of their ancestors. Such respect is hugely important in this culture.

---

[22]BBC News Asia, "Deaths Spotlight Taiwan's 'Overwork' Culture," March 19, 2012, www.bbc.com/news/world-asia-16834258.

[23]Time and Date AS, "Ghost Festival in Taiwan," www.timeanddate.com/holidays/taiwan/spirit-festival (accessed November 10, 2014); and Albatros Travels, "Hungry Ghost Festival," http://chinatoursandholidays.com/hungry-ghost-festival (accessed November 10, 2014).

5. How Direct Is Communication in Taiwan?

On the streets, the most common greeting heard (in Taiwan) "Have you eaten?"[24]

—Common Taiwanese Greeting

In many respects, Taiwan is a hybrid of East and West. Some people are quite comfortable saying 'no' to a request they cannot accommodate, whereas others avoid that word at all cost. As this story from a Taiwanese consultant who works for a global management consulting firm illustrates, there is a simple way to *read between the lines*.

"We were hired by a very large electronics company to do an organization design. Halfway through the project, the CEO was let go. When our senior partners spoke with the new CEO about whether they should continue, they were told: 'Why don't we think about this?' which, of course, is fairly ambiguous. All our partners were foreigners and interpreted this as meaning we should keep going. What we discovered later was that the CEO was really saying, 'Why don't you guys just leave?' This became obvious when no one was interested in hearing our recommendations.

"What we should have done—to avoid this kind of costly misunderstanding—was to have undergone a debrief with a trusted ally, who was not the decision maker, but could have helped to ensure we correctly understood what was being said, or clarify what the decision maker is thinking."

When you are dealing with individuals whose responses may not be directly understood, make sure you speak separately with an insider to confirm you have read the situation correctly. Taiwan is a "high context" culture in terms of communication style.

6. How Formal or Informal Do Businesspeople in Taiwan Tend to Be?

It takes sweat to work on things, but only saliva to criticize things.
— *Taiwanese proverb*[25]

For companies that can afford their services, market intelligence firms provide valuable insights into industry trends. That kind of financial outlay is not

---

[24] *Taiwan* Today, "Have You Eaten Yet?" May 1, 2008, http://taiwantoday.tw/ct.asp?xitem =35883&ctnode=1346&mp=9.
[25] One Hour Translation, "Interesting Taiwanese Proverbs," www.onehourtranslation.com /translation/blog/interesting-taiwanese-proverbs (accessed November 10, 2014).

always feasible for small and medium-sized enterprises in Taiwan, whose management is still hungry for in-the-trenches information. David Kuo, who works in the semiconductor industry, uses the informal chatting that tends to take place at the beginning of meetings to share insightful stories. This helps him build trust, inspire respect, and nurture long-lasting relationships with his clients—a practice well worth emulating.

"Obviously it's unethical to reveal anything secret or that violates a non-disclosure agreement, but there are many things you can share about a client's competitors that are hugely appreciated here. For example, at a first meeting when I'm getting to know the CEO, I might start by saying, 'CEO Lee, I happen to do business with your competitor and they have a new VP of sales with whom I played golf last week. Do you play golf?' Golf is a popular sport for business executives in Taiwan, so that tends to be a universal topic of discussion. You might then mention that the new guy has a 10 handicap and likes to play at a particular club. Asian people appreciate conversations about positive things. They don't want you bashing the competitor because they'll assume you would do the same about them. The CEO might then say, 'Tell me more about this guy; I hear he's really good.' That allows you to elaborate in a way that could be useful to your client or prospect.

"It's the gesture that counts, not the story itself—the fact that you're willing to share information with your client. It shows that you know your stuff and you know it ahead of everyone else. Taiwanese businesspeople will then consider you to be someone they want to get closer to. Most people in Taiwan don't really know much about, or tend to use, the professional networking sites like LinkedIn. You can use this to your advantage by becoming a trusted source of insights and industry information."

7. How Aligned Are Taiwanese Social and Business Lives?

Many Westerners are trapped by the "9 to 5" work model, while many Asians work to the "Beyond 5" model. This is the time when true feelings are expressed, when people's characters are genuinely assessed, and when deals are struck.

    —Business Journey to the East, *Chow-HouWee and Fred Combe*[26]

One unexpected fact about Taiwan in relation to the crossover between social and business life is the use of social media, especially Facebook. Taiwan boasts the highest penetration rate (65 percent) of Facebook users in Asia,

---

[26] Chow Hou Wee and Fred Combe, *Business Journey to the East: An East-West Perspective of Global-is-Asian* (McGraw-Hill, Singapore, 2008).

indeed, "in any other market in the world."[27] Although many of us in the West might not use Facebook to send business emails, David Kuo does this all the time:

> "Facebook is my customer relationship system (CRM) and where I can get to know people socially to gain their trust. For example, a customer of mine might share something about their dog or their kids. I'll go to their page, leave a comment, and bring that up when we meet physically."

> "A lot of senior management in my industry (semiconductors) use Facebook because they are working 18 hours and need some down-time when they can vent and share their emotions. I see it as part of my job to be on there two or three hours a day. It's part of the way we do business here in Taiwan. If you want to be seen as an influencer, to keep people informed, and to offer value, using social media to share articles and insights is one way that social and business come together in Taiwan."

8. How Is the Concept of Women in Business Handled in Taiwan?

In Taiwan . . . where family and matriarchal-oriented societies are common—women often help run companies alongside a husband or brother in a family business.
—Do's and Taboos Around the World for Women in Business[28]

Women decision makers used to be less common in Taiwanese business, but in industries such as high-tech, especially companies run by younger, Western-educated people, few are going to be surprised to be working with or taking instructions from a female these days.

Certainly there are plenty of high-powered Taiwanese businesswomen and prominent female politicians who are role models, their numbers supported by the Executive Yuan's Commission of Women's Rights Promotion established in 1997.[29] Examples include Nita Ing, the chair of Continental Holdings, and Judy Lee, the founder and chair of Test Rite International, both of whom were

[27] *Taipei* Times, "Taiwan Likes Facebook, Has Highest Penetration," February 28, 2014, www.taipeitimes.com/News/biz/archives/2014/02/28/2003584495.
[28] Roger E. Axtell, et al. *Do's and Taboos Around the World for Women in Business* (New York: John Wiley & Sons, 1997), 50.
[29] *Taipei* Times, "Taiwan's Most Powerful Women," March 6, 2005, www.taipeitimes .com/News/feat/archives/2005/03/06/2003225760.

cited by Forbes in their Top 50 Asian Power Women list of 2014.[30] In addition, Cher Wang has been called *the pride of Taiwan* for her standing within the high-tech industry, having cofounded two companies, as well as being featured in *Forbes'* The World's 100 Most Powerful Women list.[31]

Having said that, this is still a country where men outnumber women in the workplace. When Jaime Melanson worked for Dell in Taiwan, she noticed how businessmen would make personal comments to her that would be considered inappropriate in the West. For example, "One time, I was in a meeting to make a presentation to 15 people and one of the engineers, right in the middle of the meeting, said, 'Jaime is the most beautiful engineer I've ever worked with.'"

Rather than be offended by this, Ms. Melanson says that it's something she misses now that she's back in the U.S. You may choose to use such admiration to your advantage.

Cultural Summary

Here are some key points to remember:

- Be aware of the three different company cultures operating in Taiwan: Taiwanese, Japanese, and U.S., and adopt the appropriate business practices accordingly.
- Time has a different meaning here, including the practice of nap time during lunch, as well as adherence to major festivals such as Hungry Ghost month.
- The Taiwanese are big users of social media and this plays a part in relationship-building and maintaining networks professionally as well as personally.

Self-Awareness Profile

This simple exercise prompts you to self-assess where you currently stand on topics related to the eight-question framework and *compare* this with the country culture. This visual will help you discover the extent to which you may need to adapt your current mindset and behavior to develop more robust business

---

[30] *Forbes* magazine, "Asia Power Women 2014: Judy Lee 63 (Taiwan)," www.forbes.com /pictures/fdgk45ggee/judy-lee-63-taiwan/ (accessed November 10, 2014).
[31] *Times of India*, "10 Most Powerful Women in Tech," January 31, 2014, http://timesofindia .indiatimes.com/tech/slideshow/10-most-powerful-women-in-tech/itslideshowviewall /29666641.cms.

relationships. For details on how to complete this graphic, see the instructions given in the Introduction on pages xviii–xix.

Consider copying the eight-question Profile or using a pencil so that you can see, over time, how you have adjusted your cultural mindset. You might also wish to create unique graphics related to each of the businesses you work with, as these cultural positions vary depending upon geographic location, industry, generational factors, and corporate profile.

Q1: What is your preferred way of doing business?

As an individual making autonomous decisions					**As a team member who seeks group consensus**
1	2	3	4	**5**	6

Q2: How comfortable are you in hierarchies in which power is distributed unequally?

Very uncomfortable					**Very comfortable**
1	2	3	4	5	**6**

Q3: How closely do you follow rules and obey the law?

Almost always					**It depends**
1	2	3	4	5	**6**

Q4: What is your general attitude toward time?

I prefer agendas, schedules, planning					**I prefer flexibility, fluidity without scheduling**
1	**2**	3	4	5	6

Q5: What is your preferred way to communicate?

Very diplomatically					**Very candidly**
1	2	3	4	5	6

Q6: What is your interpersonal style or level of formality in business interactions?

Very formal   **Very informal**

     1   2   **3**   4   5   6

Q7: What is your view on socializing within business?

A waste of time   **Essential**

     1   2   3   4   5   **6**

Q8: Should a woman defer to a man as the lead, if winning business in a certain culture depended on it?

Never   **Yes, absolutely**

     1   2   3   4   **5**   6

15 | Summary

John Lennon once said: "Life is what happens to you while you're busy making other plans." That couldn't be more true with respect to the experience we've had writing this book.

What began as an idea to capture Sharon's insights and experience about global etiquette gradually transformed into a deeper look at the differences between business relationships in Asia and the West. Rather than rely on a single expert voice, we broadened our scope in order to collaborate with over 100 professionals and executives who so generously shared their in-the-trenches experience. Certainly we recognize that their stories are personal anecdotes, and are therefore subjective; however, this book is not a scientific treatise and was never meant to be the final word on the topic of intercultural exchanges. Instead, we hope the insights in this book give you a sense of the nuances found among diverse cultures, a desire to embrace new concepts, and the curiosity to learn more.

In developing what we hoped would be an essential guide to building trust, inspiring respect and creating long-lasting business relationships in Asia, we've learned a few things ourselves. After all, didn't the Roman philosopher Seneca say, "While we teach, we learn"? And, in that respect, we'd like to leave you with three of the most surprising findings we gained from speaking with our Asian and Western interviewees. These were glimpses into the natures of these cultures that might not have surfaced if we'd merely engaged in online or desk research.

The first concerns a theme dear to both our hearts: the topic of women across cultures. We often wonder if women in Asia are more disadvantaged than women in our own culture, but a review of *Forbes*'s lists of Asia's rising stars and female power brokers shows just how much women across this continent have achieved. We wanted to illuminate such successes within our overarching framework, which is why we added the eighth question, *How is the concept of women in business handled?*

Certainly our focus in each of these sections in the country-specific chapters was to offer practical advice to international businesswomen traveling to the ten Asian countries included in this book. We suspected that the treatment of international businesswomen would be different, at least in some respects, than that of their Asian female counterparts. We all know how important inspiring role models can be and so we also wanted to acknowledge the achievements of the many CEOs, entrepreneurs, founders, politicians, and other female leading lights in Asia.

Consider, for example, that although the U.S. has never had a female president or vice president—at least not *yet*—Asia has already achieved this milestone. Corazon Aquino served as president of the Philippines from 1986 to 1992, the first female in Asia to be so elected. A few years later, Gloria Macapagal-Arroyo served first as that country's vice president, and then as president from 2001 to 2010. In 2012, Park Geun-hye was elected as the first female president of Korea.

Malaysia's first female cabinet minister, Fatimah Hashim, took office in 1969. Before then, Indira Gandhi's first term as prime minister of India ran from 1966 to 1977, and the second from 1980 until her assassination in 1984.

Long before these achievements, of course, China's Lü Zhi[1] had amassed considerable political influence as the wife of the founder of the Han Dynasty, and became Empress Regent in 202 BC. In Japan, also, Suiko Tennö became the country's first reigning empress in the sixth century A.D.[2]

Although we naturally applaud the business or political achievements of women like Chew Gek Khim of Singapore, Cho Sun-hae of Korea, and Aung San Suu Kyi of Myanmar, let us not forget that Asian woman have been forging paths in political and business arenas for considerably longer than many of us realize. And they have done so while navigating the expectations of females in their respective cultures, which included marrying young, having large families, maintaining a home, and looking after in-laws as well as children.

[1] Ulrich Theobald, "Persons in Chinese History," ChinaKnowledge, March 8, 2011, www.chinaknowledge.de/History/Han/personslvhou.html.
[2] "Suiko," Encyclopedia Britannica, www.britannica.com/EBchecked/topic/572155/Suiko (accessed November 21, 2014).

This segues nicely to the second of our three findings: generational differences.

We wanted our book to offer salient, practical advice on vast and diverse business cultures, and so we tried to find interviewees representative of different regions within a country—such as those familiar with the way business is done in Shanghai as opposed to Beijing, for example. One of the key differences we became aware of while researching this book was how long-held cultural expectations are changing, however glacially, as younger people take on leadership positions in Asian businesses.

One important piece of advice is to be mindful of the age range of your Asian counterparts when applying the guidance offered in this book. India is a prime example of how the millennial generation, and even a few that preceded it, are gently breaking from tradition and adopting different approaches both to business and life. As pointed out in the India chapter, young Indian women ride motorcycles, expect to choose their own career paths, start entrepreneurial businesses, and adopt leadership positions within the corporate world as much as their male counterparts, especially in high-tech cities like Bangalore and Chennai.

Bear in mind that your experiences across Asia will differ depending on the generation to which your Asian counterparts and decision makers belong. While we have only scratched the surface of this increasingly important topic, it is as important to understand how to engage different generational cohorts as it is to know the differences inherent in dealing with high-tech start-ups compared with traditional multinational companies.

Our third finding has been a central influence throughout the two years we took to research and write this book: relationships. Certainly, we both feel honored to have met and interviewed so many new business colleagues and friends while embarking on this project, from the gracious and warm hosts of Sharon's most recent trips to China, Hong Kong, Japan, Myanmar, and Vietnam, to the incredibly hospitable Indians who invited Liz into their homes and made her feel like a part of their families.

For leaders everywhere, placing emphasis on building strong, authentic, *human* relationships is of fundamental importance. As more people consider themselves to be global citizens, intercultural communication and awareness becomes more important. The most effective way to cope with change is to create it. Although it's important to adopt a greater understanding of and respect for cultural differences, we should never lose sight of the ways in which we are—all of us—fundamentally alike.

Finally, we would like to leave you with a favorite quotation: "Life is a journey, not a destination." Sharon invites you to think of this book as the beginning of an ongoing conversation and hopes you will contact her at info@sharonschweitzer.com to share your thoughts and experiences.

What helped you? What could be done better? What new understanding have you come to appreciate from working with your Asian counterparts?

Recently, Sharon received an email from a young entrepreneur she had coached regarding his first business trip to Japan: "I was a huge hit with my host family and made my first international friends in Tokyo. I truly felt assimilated in a foreign land when my host family would remark on how I looked like a salaryman headed out the door. I would be dishonest if I didn't say that a part of me didn't want to come home. It's as if my heart was left in Tokyo. I can't wait to learn the language and return for an even more fulfilling experience. I can't thank you enough for your instruction. Approaching people using the proper protocol simply made them far more open to me and the ideas I would go on to present to them. I don't think I would have had such a wonderful trip without you."

It is our fervent wish that Sharon's passion for intercultural awareness, along with the wit and wisdom of our interviewees, will produce similar successes for you.

Bibliography

Books

Armstrong, Nancy, and Melissa Wagner. *Field Guide to Gestures*. Philadelphia: Quirk Books, 2003.

Asitimbay, Diane. *What's Up, America?: A Foreigner's Guide to Understanding Americans*. 2nd ed. San Diego: Culturelink Press, 2009.

Axtell, Roger E., Tami Briggs, Margaret Corcoran, and Mary Beth Lamb. *Do's and Taboos Around the World for Women in Business*. New York: John Wiley & Sons, 1997.

Axtell, Roger E. *Gestures: The Do's and Taboos of Body Language around the World*. 2nd ed. New York: John Wiley & Sons, 1998.

Biyani, Kishore, and Dipayan Baishya. *It Happened in India: The Story of Pantaloons, Big Bazaar, Central and the Great Indian Consumer*. New Delhi, India: Rupa & Co, 2007.

Bočánková, Milena. *Intercultural Communication: Typical Features of the Czech, British, American, Japanese, Chinese and Arab Cultures*. Praha: Oeconomica, 2010.

Bosrock, Mary M. *Asian Business Customs & Manners: A Country-by-Country Guide*. New York: Meadowbrook Press, 2007.

Bosrock, Mary M. *Asian Business Customs & Manners: A Country-by-Country Guide*. New York: Meadowbrook Press, 2010. Kindle edition.

Bosrock, Mary M. *Put Your Best Foot Forward USA: A Fearless Guide to Understanding the United States of America*. St. Paul, MN: International Education Systems, 1999.

Brislin, Richard. *Cross-Cultural Encounters: Face to Face Interaction*. New York: Pergamon Press, 1981.

Chai, May-lee, and Winberg Chai. *China A to Z: Everything You Need to Know to Understand Chinese Customs and Culture*. New York: Plume Books, 2007.

343

Chaney, Lillian Hunt, and Jeanette St. Clair Martin. *The Essential Guide to Business Etiquette*. Westport, CT: Praeger, 2007.

Chatterjee, Debashis. *Timeless Leadership: 18 Leadership Sutras from the Bhagavad Gita*. Singapore: John Wiley & Sons, 2012.

Clements, Alan. The Voice of Hope: Aung San Suu Kyi Conversations with Alan Clements. World Dharma Publications, 2012. Kindle edition.

Curry, Janel and Paul Hanstedt. *Reading Hong Kong, Reading Ourselves*. Kowloon: City University of Hong Kong Press, 2014.

De Mente, Boye Lafayette. *Etiquette Guide to Japan: Know the Rules that Make the Difference!* Revised ed. Tokyo, Japan: Tuttle Publishing, 2008.

De Mente, Boye Lafayette. *Japanese Etiquette & Ethics in Business*. 6th ed. Lincolnwood, IL: NTC Publishing Group, 1994.

De Mente, Boye Lafayette. *Japan: Understanding & Dealing with the New Japanese Way of Doing Business!* Scottsdale, AZ: Phoenix Books, 2012.

De Mente, Boye Lafayette. *The Korean Mind: Understanding Contemporary Korean Culture*. Tokyo, Japan: Tuttle Publishing, 2012.

Denison, Daniel, Robert Hooijberg, Nancy Lane, and Colleen Lief. *Leading Cultural Change in Global Organizations: Aligning Culture and Strategy*. San Francisco: Jossey Bass, 2012.

Devine, Elizabeth, and Nancy L. Braganti. *The Traveler's Guide to Asian Customs & Manners*. 2nd ed. New York: St. Martin's Griffin, 1998.

Devonshire-Ellis, Chris, ed. *India Briefing: Doing Business in India*. 3rd ed. New York: Springer, 2012.

Doniger, Wendy. *Hindu Myths*. London: Penguin Books, 1975.

Dresser, Norine. *Multicultural Manners: Essential Rules of Etiquette for the 21st Century*. 2nd ed. Hoboken, NJ: John Wiley & Sons, 2005.

Elashmawi, Farid. *Competing Globally: Mastering Multicultural Management and Negotiations*. Woburn, MA: Butterworth-Heinemann, 2001.

Elashmawi, Farid and Philip R. Harris. *Multicultural Management 2000: Essential Cultural Insights for Global Business Success*. 2d ed. Houston, TX: Gulf Publishing Company, 1998.

Flower, Kathy. *Culture Smart! China: The Essential Guide to Customs & Culture*. 2nd ed. London: Kuperard, 2010.

Foster, Dean. *The Global Etiquette Guide to Asia*. New York: John Wiley & Sons, 2000.

French, Carole and Reg Butler. *Tips on Tipping: A Global Guide to Gratuity Etiquette*. Buckinghamshire, England: Bradt Travel Guides, Ltd., 2011.

Friedman, George. *The Next 100 Years: A Forecast for the 21st Century*. New York: Doubleday, 2009.

Friedman, George. *The Next Decade: Where We've Been . . . And Where We're Going*. New York: Doubleday, 2011.

Gannon, Martin J. and Rajnandini Pillai. *Understanding Global Cultures: Metaphorical Journeys Through 31 Nations, Clusters of Nations, Continents, and Diversity.* 5th ed. Los Angeles: Sage Publications, 2013.

Garnaut, Anthony. *Mandarin Phrasebook.* 7th ed. Victoria, Australia: Lonely Planet Publications Pty Ltd, 2010.

Grun, Bernard. *The Timetables of History.* 4th ed. New York: Touchstone Press, 2005.

Gupta, Anil K. and Haiyan Wang. *Getting China and India Right: Strategies for Leveraging the World's Fastest-Growing Economies for Global Advantage.* San Francisco: Jossey-Bass, 2009.

Hall, Edward T. *The Dance of Life: The Other Dimension of Time.* New York: Anchor Books, 1984.

Hampden-Turner, Charles and Alfons Trompenaars. *The Seven Cultures of Capitalism: Value Systems for Creating Wealth in the United States, Japan, Germany, France, Britain, Sweden, and the Netherlands.* New York: Doubleday, 1993.

Hernandez, Ruben. *Presenting Across Cultures: How to Adapt Your Business and Sales Presentations in Key Markets around the World.* Tertium Business Books, 2013.

Hoare, James. *Culture Smart! Korea: The Essential Guide to Customs & Culture.* London: Kuperard Bravo Ltd., 2005.

Hodge, Sheida. *Global Smarts: The Art of Communicating and Deal Making Anywhere in the World.* New York: John Wiley & Sons, 2000.

Hofstede, Geert. *Culture's Consequences: Comparing Values, Behaviors, Institutions, and Organizations Across Nations.* 2nd ed. Thousand Oaks, CA: Sage Publications, 2001.

Hofstede, Geert, Gert Jan Hofstede, and Michael Minkov. *Cultures and Organizations: Software of the Mind-Intercultural Cooperation and Its Importance for Survival.* 3rd ed. New York: McGraw-Hill, 2010.

House, Robert J., Paul J. Hanges, Mansour Javidan, Peter W. Dorfman, and Vipin Gupta, ed. *Culture, Leadership, and Organizations: The GLOBE Study of 62 Societies.* Thousand Oaks, CA: Sage Publications, Inc., 2004.

House, Robert J., Peter W. Dorfman, Mansour Javidan, Paul J. Hanges, and Mary Sully de Luque, ed. *Strategic Leadership Across Cultures: GLOBE Study of CEO Leadership Behavior and Effectiveness in 24 Countries.* Thousand Oaks, CA: Sage Publications, Inc., 2013.

Inglehart, Ronald, Miguel Basáñez, Jaime Díez-Medrano, Loek Halman, and Ruud Luijkx. *Human Beliefs and Values: A Cross-Cultural Sourcebook Based on the 1999-2002 Values Surveys.* 2nd ed. Mexico: Fundacion BBVA, 2004.

Inglehart, Ronald, Miguel Basáñez, and Alejandro Moreno. *Human Values and Beliefs: A Cross-Cultural Sourcebook.* Ann Arbor, MI: University of Michigan Press, 1998.

Jablonski, Edwin F. and Barbara R. Wohlfahrt. *Authoritative Revelations on Tipping: Guidelines and Solutions.* Bloomington, IN: AuthorHouse, 2006.

Jadhav, Narendra. *Untouchables: My Family's Triumphant Journey Out of the Caste System in Modern India.* New York: Scribner, 2005.

Kim, Eun Young. *A Cross-Cultural Reference of Business Practices in a New Korea.* Westport, CT: Quorum Books, 1996.

Lefevre, Romana. *Rude Hand Gestures of the World.* San Francisco: Chronicle Books, 2011.

Leung, Kwok, Uichol Kim, Susumu Yamaguchi, and Yoshihisa Kashima. *Progress in Asian Social Psychology.* Vol. **1**. Singapore: John Wiley & Sons, 1997.

Lewis, Richard D. *When Cultures Collide: Leading Across Cultures* 3rd ed. Boston: Nicholas Brealey International, 2006.

Lewis, Richard D. *When Teams Collide: Managing the International Team Successfully.* Boston: Nicholas Brealey Publishing, 2012.

Luce, Edward. *In Spite of the Gods: The Strange Rise of Modern India.* New York: Doubleday, 2007.

Martin, Jeanette S. and Lillian H. Chaney. *Global Business Etiquette: A Guide to International Communication and Customs.* 2nd ed. Santa Barbara, CA: Praeger, 2012.

Martin, Jeanette S. and Lillian H. Chaney. *Passport to Success: The Essential Guide to Business Culture and Customs in America's Largest Trading Partners.* Westport, CT: Praeger, 2009.

Minkov, Michael. *Cross-Cultural Analysis: The Science and Art of Comparing the World's Modern Societies and Their Cultures.* Thousand Oaks, CA: SAGE Publications, 2013.

Molinsky, Andy. *Global Dexterity: How to Adapt Your Behavior across Cultures without Losing Yourself in the Process.* Boston: Harvard Business School Publishing, 2013.

Morrison, Terri, Wayne A. Conaway, and Joseph J. Douress. *Dun & Bradstreet's Guide to Doing Business Around the World.* New York: Prentice Hall, 1997.

Morrison, Terri and Wayne A. Conaway. *Kiss, Bow, or Shake Hands.* 2nd ed. Avon, MA: Adams Media, 2006.

Morrison, Terri and Wayne A. Conaway. *Kiss, Bow, or Shake Hands: Sales and Marketing—The Essential Cultural Guide from Presentations and Promotions to Communicating and Closing.* New York: McGraw-Hill, 2012.

Morrison, Terri and Wayne A. Conaway. *Passport to Global Business Etiquette.* New York: McGraw-Hill, 2010.

Nichols, Jonathan. *Myanmar for Foreign Dummies: The Businessman's 18 Point Guide to Myanmar.* Hong Kong: Asia Business Books, 2013.

Nisbett, Richard E. *The Geography of Thought: How Asians and Westerners Think Differently . . . and Why.* New York: The Free Press, 2003.

Nyi, U. *Practical Aspects of Buddhist Ideals.* Buckinghamshire, England: Author-House, 2010.

Plafker, Ted. *Doing Business in China: How to Profit in the World's Fastest Growing Market.* New York: Hachette Book Group, 2007.

Pollock, David C. and Ruth E. Van Reken. *Third Culture Kids: Growing Up Among Worlds.* Boston: Nicholas Brealey Publishing, 2009.

Pollock, Robert. *World Religions: Beliefs and Traditions from Around the Globe.* New York: Fall River Press, 2008.

Price, David Clive. *The Master Key to Asia: A 6-Step Guide to Unlocking New Markets.* David Clive Price Publisher, 2013.

Ricks, David A. *Blunders in International Business.* 4th ed. Malden, MA: Blackwell Publishing, 2006.

Rosen, Robert. *Global Literacies.* New York: Simon & Schuster, 2000.

Rugman, Alan M., ed. *The Oxford Handbook of International Business.* New York: Oxford University Press, 2009.

Sabath, Ann Marie. *International Business Etiquette: Asia & The Pacific Rim.* Lincoln, NE: ASJA Press, 2002.

Shaules, Joseph. *The Intercultural Mind: Connecting Culture, Cognition and Global Living.* Boston: Intercultural Press, 2015.

Shinomiya, Sue and Brian Szepkouski. *Business Passport to Japan.* Revised and updated edition. Berkeley, CA: Stone Bridge Press, 2008.

Silkenat, James R., Jeffrey M. Aresty, and Jacqueline Klosek, ed. *The ABA Guide to International Business Negotiations: A Comparison of Cross-Cultural Issues and Successful Approaches.* 3d ed. Chicago: ABA Publishing, 2009.

Steinberg, David I. *Burma/Myanmar: What Everyone Needs to Know.* New York: Oxford University Press, 2010.

Stewart-Allen, Allyson and Lanie Denslow. *Working with Americans: How to Build Profitable Business Relationships.* London: Pearson Education, 2002.

Tomalin, Barry, and Mike Nicks. *World Business Cultures: A Handbook.* 3rd ed. London: Thorogood Publishing, 2014.

Towson, Jeffrey and Jonathan Woetzel. *The One Hour China Book: Two Peking University Professors Explain All of China Business in Six Short Stories.* Cayman Islands: Towson Group LLC, 2013.

Trompenaars, Fons and Charles Hampden-Turner. *Riding the Waves of Culture: Understanding Diversity in Global Business.* 3rd ed. New York: McGraw-Hill, 2012.

Unkovic, Dennis. *Understanding Asia: Winning Strategies for Business Success.* Chicago: ABA Publishing, 2011.

Wee, Chow Hou, and Fred Combe. *Business Journey to the East: An East-West Perspective of Global-is-Asian.* Singapore: McGraw-Hill, 2008.

Yoshimura, Noboru and Philip Anderson. *Inside the Kaisha: Demystifying Japanese Business Behavior.* Boston: Harvard Business School Press, 1997.

Online Resources

U.S. Central Intelligence Agency (www.cia.gov): Government agency offering online library containing documents, periodicals, maps and reports on international affairs. Publications include:

The online directory of *Chiefs of State and Cabinet Members of Foreign Governments* (www.cia.gov/library/publications/world-leaders-1): Reference aid for information on foreign governments.

The World Factbook (www.cia.gov/library/publications/the-world-factbook): Database providing almanac-style information by country/world entity.

U.S. Department of the Treasury, International Resource Center (www.treasury .gov/resource-center/international): Provides resources with information on international economic affairs.

U.S. Department of State, Travel Resources (www.state.gov/travel): Provides information about passports and visas for U.S. citizens; travel warnings; information sheets; public announcements; foreign counselor offices in the United States; key U.S. officers at foreign office posts; and country background notes.

U.S. Department of State, U.S. Embassy (www.usembassy.gov): Your country's embassy is an important contact when traveling, especially in emergency situations. Embassies can also provide various services, including making appointments with local business and government officials. They may be able to advise you about local laws, trade regulations, customs, and to identify importers, buyers, and agents. In addition, they can provide data on the economy, political situations, technology, and the workforce.

U.S. Department of State, Country Commercial Guides (www.state.gov/e/eb /rls/rpts/ccg): Comprehensive annual reports on the commercial environments of foreign countries.

Transparency International (www.transparency.org): Nongovernmental organization that follows and reports corruption and bribery around the world. Research includes:

The *Corruption Perceptions Index* (www.transparency.org/research/cpi/overview): Annual report on perceived levels of public sector corruption in many world countries and territories.

U.S. Centers for Disease Control and Prevention, Traveler's Health (www.nc.cdc.gov/travel): Provides medical information, vaccination and other health requirements and resources vital for international travelers.

CultureGrams (www.culturegrams.com): Cultural reference products, including reports on the history and customs of more than 200 countries.

The World Clock—Time Zones (www.timeanddate.com/worldclock): Reference for information on time zones and current local time while traveling abroad or interacting with international colleagues.

The Akamai *State of the Internet Report* (www.akamai.com/stateoftheinternet): Quarterly report released by cloud services provider, Akamai Technologies Inc., providing global Internet statistics, such as connection speed and broadband adoption, at the country level.

British Broadcasting Corporation, BBC News (www.bbc.com/news): Online news coverage from the world's largest broadcast news organization. Provides country profiles with country-specific facts and information.

The World Bank, Country Profiles (www.worldbank.org/en/country): Profiles of world regions and countries providing the latest on economic news, programs, research and data.

World Bank Group, *Doing Business* project (www.doingbusiness.org): Provides comprehensive data on business regulation environments of world economies, including global, regional and subnational reports.

Encyclopedia Britannica Online (www.britannica.com): Encyclopedia Britannica online reference with articles, daily features and links to news reports.

United Nations Development Programme, Human Development Index (http://hdr.undp.org/en/content/human-development-index-hdi): Annual report measuring human development levels in many world countries and territories, based on life expectancy, education and income indices.

World Economic Forum, Global Gender Gap Index (www.weforum.org/issues/global-gender-gap): Annual report measuring gender equality in many world countries, based on economic, political, education- and health-based criteria.

McKinsey Global Institute (www.mckinsey.com/insights/mgi): Provides business and economics research on the global economy and in-depth reports on various countries and industries.

International Monetary Fund (www.imf.org/external/index.htm): Provides information, research and data on various economic and financial indicators.

Randstad Holding (www.randstad.com): Randstad Holding is a multinational human resource consulting firm.

Forbes, Lists (www.forbes.com/lists): Rankings of top companies, people, places and so on, including lists such as Global 2000 Leading Companies, Best Countries for Business, Asia's Fab 50 Companies, World's Most Powerful People, and Asia's Power Businesswomen.

The Hofstede Center (http://geert-hofstede.com): Provides insights into national and organizational culture from the research of Geert Hofstede and colleagues.

Japan External Trade Organization (www.jetro.go.jp): A Japanese government-related organization working to promote mutual trade and investment between Japan and the rest of the world. Useful resources on doing business in Japan are provided online.

Malaysian Investment Development Authority (www.mida.gov.my/home): The Malaysian government's principal agency for the promotion of the manufacturing and services sectors in Malaysia. Services include providing information on investment opportunities and facilitating project implementation.

Cultural Detective (www.culturaldetective.com): A system developed through collaboration among dozens of intercultural experts worldwide. The system enables individuals and organizations to gain cultural insight into an increasingly global and interconnected economy.

Contributors

Sharon and Liz would like to thank everyone who kindly agreed to be interviewed for this book. With every project there are those who contribute but wish to remain anonymous for cultural, safety or political reasons; we have respected such wishes. In addition to these anonymous individuals, we would like to thank the following people:

Arii Aoi: Tokyo, Japan.

Rowena Aquino: Associate vice president of operations, Eco-Merge Philippines, Inc.; environmental consultant, Philippines Department of Environment and Natural Resources, Department of Science and Technologies, and the Philippine Economic Zone Authority.

Colonel Hitendra Bahadur: Country head of human resources, administration, training, security, and government relations, Punj Lloyd Limited, Darussalam, Brunei.

Melanie Barnes: CEO, Texas Climate & Carbon Exchange, an emissions offsets mercantile established in 2011, Austin, Texas.

Mahesh Baxi: Founder and CEO, PurpleGear Software Pvt. Ltd.; author of *New Age Leadership: Practical Mantras on Leadership* (Jaico Publishing House).

Natalie Betts: Recycling economic development liaison, City of Austin; former global business recruitment and expansion coordinator, City of Austin Economic Development Department.

Marina Ong Bhargava: Executive director, Greater Austin Asian Chamber of Commerce, Austin, Texas.

Amanda Bohm: Former systems engineer, IBM, Los Angeles, California.

Dr. William I. Brustein: Vice provost of global strategies and international affairs and professor of sociology, political science, and history at Ohio State University, Columbus, Ohio.

Yu-Jin Chua: Principal, Panther Capital Asia, a private investment management firm specializing in project funding and asset management, Singapore.

Thomas Conry: International advisor in public affairs, communications and protocol; former director of U.S.-Japan relations, JETRO-Houston (Japan External Trade Organization).

Adriana Cruz: President, Greater San Marcos Partnership; former vice president of global corporate recruitment, Austin Chamber of Commerce; and director of marketing, Texas Governor Rick Perry's Economic Development & Tourism Office.

Rhea Dasgupta: Membership and operations manager, Asian Business Association of San Diego; former member services coordinator, Greater Austin Chamber of Commerce, Austin, Texas.

Arvind Datar: Senior advocate, Madras High Court; trustee of the Palkhivala Foundation, Chennai, India; director, Nani Palkhivala Arbitration Centre, Chennai, India; contributing author, *Courtroom Genius*.

Michael DeCaro: Managing director, Hiermeans, LLC; former chief audit executive and vice president of finance, Asia Pacific and Japan, for Dell, Inc.

Fermin Diez: Adjunct professor, Singapore Management University and Nanyang Technological University; and human resources executive, Singapore.

Robert Easson: Group CEO, Imagino Group Ltd., Myanmar.

Dr. Janet Ellzey: Vice provost, International Programs, and professor, Department of Mechanical Engineering, University of Texas at Austin.

Gary Farmer: President, Heritage Title Company of Austin, Inc., Austin, Texas.

William J. Flannery: President, the WJF Institute, Austin, Texas.

Errol Flynn: CEO of consultancy and advisory firm KPC & G International, Australia, and senior executive with Global Capital Markets (Lux), Europe/Asia.

Harvey Frye: Former vice chairman, Tokyo Electron America, Austin, Texas.

Dr. Tanvi Gautam: Founder and managing partner, Global People Tree, Singapore.

MaryAnn George: Human resources professional, Bangalore, India.

Gay Gillen: Owner, Gay Gillen Travel, Austin, Texas.

Rodney Gonzales: Deputy director, Economic Development Department, City of Austin, Austin, Texas.

Elizabeth Hay: Senior administrator, KPC & G International, Perth, Australia; administrative and senior level negotiator, Global Capital Markets.

Gabe Higham: Former hardware development manager, Dell, Inc., Taiwan.

Drew Hoeffner: Law student, American University and University of Texas at Austin.

Dr. Chi-Kao Hsu: CEO and chairman, SEFBO Pipeline Bridge, Inc.; EMR Construction, Inc.; Hsu Realty Company, Inc.; HKL Environmental Technology, Ltd. (Beijing); Jilin HG New Energy Development Company Ltd.

Sikh Shamsul Ibrahim: Director, Malaysian Investment Development Authority, Singapore; former director, Malaysian Investment Development Authority, Houston, Texas.

Yuan Jia: CEO, Internash Global Services, LLC, Austin, Texas.

Helen Jobes: Owner and principal of Gold Eagle Investments; investment sales broker in Central Texas, San Antonio, Houston, Dallas, and the Rio Grande Valley; named one of CREW Austin's Top 10 Women in Commercial Real Estate, and one of Austin's Top 25 Heavy Hitters by the *Austin Business Journal.*

Kevin Johns: Director, Economic Development Department, City of Austin, Austin, Texas.

Dr. Kelechi Kalu: Associate provost, Global Strategies and International Affairs; and professor, African American and African Studies, Ohio State University, Columbus, Ohio.

Looi Teck Kheong: Advocate and solicitor, Looi Teck Kheong (a law firm), Singapore.

Margie Kidd: Executive director, GlobalAustin (affiliated with the National Council of International Visitors); former director, University of Texas International Office.

Dr. Eun Young Kim: Founder, CEO International, Inc.; author of *Samsung 3.0* (2013) and *A Cross-Cultural Reference of Business Practices in a New Korea,* Austin, Texas.

Soraya Kim: Business development manager, Global Commercialization Group, IC^2, University of Texas at Austin.

Tatsuya Kitamura: Executive vice president and COO, Nikkei Business Publications America, Tokyo, Japan.

Aung Ko Ko: Human resources development manager, Premium Distribution, Myanmar.

Jordan Kostelac: Project manager, MovePlan Group, Hong Kong.

Eileen Kunkler: Assistant director, Center for Slavic and East European Studies, Ohio State University, Columbus, OH.

David Kuo: Director, Asian Operations, Adexa, Inc., Taipei City, Taiwan.

Naveen Lakkur: Co-founder and director, technology services firm, Compassites Software Solutions, Bangalore, India; author of *Inseparable Twins: Paired Principles to Inspire Young Minds* (Lone Trees Books).

Yeo Eng Lam: Managing director, Johnson Medical International Sdn. Bhd., Petaling Jaya, Selangor, Malaysia.

Young Lee: Financial manager, YERICO Manufacturing, Inc., Austin, Texas.

Dr. Steven Leslie: Special assistant to the president for medical education; former executive vice president and provost, Bauerle Centennial; professor, dean of the College of Pharmacy, and director of the Institute for Neuroscience, University of Texas at Austin, Austin, Texas.

Donna Lipman: "Life coach" and presentation-skills trainer; owner and cofounder, The Center for Seven Lights; instructor, Global Commercialization Group, IC² Institute, The University of Texas at Austin.

Adam Loewy: Attorney, Loewy Law Firm, Austin, Texas.

Katrina Lucero: Former Mandarin crypto-linguist, U.S. Consulate, Guangzhou, China.

Moe Lwin: Co-founder and senior consultant, Moe & Tun Associates; sales representative, Cooper Valves, Myanmar.

Marianne Martinez: Sister Cities International Program coordinator, City of Austin, Austin, Texas.

Chiara Mauri: Deputy Head of Mission, Embassy of Italy, Yangon, Myranmar.

Rajiv Mathew: Head of marketing, Compassites Software Solutions, Bangalore, India.

Madame Nie Meisheng: Chairwoman and former president, China Real Estate Chamber of Commerce; vice president of China Urban Water Association; and director, China Elite Real Estate Academy.

Jaime Melanson: Engineering manager for the Server Networking HW and Sustaining team, Dell, Inc., Austin, Texas.

John Melanson: Distinguished fellow, Cirrus Logic, Inc.; received Texas Inventor of the Year Award in 2007 from the State Bar of Texas, Austin, Texas.

Joy Miller: Marketing and outreach coordinator, City of Austin Small Business Development Program, Austin, Texas.

Ihn-Hong Min: CEO, YERICO Manufacturing, Inc., Austin, Texas.

Amir Mirabi: Director, Small Business and Exports, Office of the Governor, State of Texas; former manager, State of Texas Governor's Office International Business and Recruitment Division, Austin, Texas.

Joel Momberger: Former director, Korea Tech Innovation Program, The University of Texas at Austin.

Saiko Motonaga: Second general manager, Electronic Components and Materials Department, Electronic Materials Division, Hitachi High Technologies Corporation, Tokyo, Japan.

Lee Mozena: Owner and founder, Zena Consulting, a cross-cultural communication firm, Seattle, Washington.

Mark Murdock, J.D.: Consultant, Gerson-Lehrman Group, Austin, Texas.

Mary Scott Nabers: President and CEO, Strategic Partnerships, Inc.; co-founder, Gemini Global Group; statewide office holder, Texas; author of *Collaboration Nation*, Austin, Texas.

Jamie Nanquil: Creative director, Austin branch manager, and graphic artist, Social Media Delivered, a social media optimization firm based in Dallas, Texas, U.S. and Paris, France.

Nadirah Mohamed Nazri: Deputy director, Malaysian Investment Development Authority, Houston, Texas; former assistant director, Malaysian Investment Development Authority, Malaysia.

Jonathan Nichols: Entrepreneur and author of seven books, including *Puk Time Stories & Business Lessons on How to Make It Happen in Myanmar* and *My My Myanmar: Tales From the New Frontier of Capitalism*.

Yuki Ochiai: Vice consul, Consulate-General of Japan, Houston, Texas.

Carol Ong: Business owner and entrepreneur, Kuala Lumpur, Malaysia.

Dr. Amin Osman: Director, Taman Bijaya Pte. Ltd., Selangor Darul Ehsan, Malaysia.

Allison O'Sullivan: Director, Sourcing Travel, Events & Entertainment—Americas, UBS, Weehawken, New Jersey.

Miguel Ozaeta: Chairman, board of directors, All Medica Global Corporation, Manila, Philippines.

Mary Kay Park, PhD: Adjunct professor, Cook School of Intercultural Studies, Biola University, La Mirada, CA.

Deepali Patwadkar: Senior manager of quality assurance, SunGard, a software and technology services company, Pune, India.

Sarada Ramani: Founder, president, and CEO of Chennai-based Computers International; founding member and president, ITSME Association.

Ben Ramirez III: International economic development manager, City of Austin, Austin, Texas.

Dr. Charles A. Rarick: Professor of International Business, College of Business, Purdue University Calumet, Hammond, Indiana.

Hari Ratan: Director, LATERAL Management Services Ltd., an accounting services company based in Chennai, India.

Pam Reed: CXO, Texas Climate & Carbon Exchange; former Travis County commissioner; former commissioner, Texas Commission on Environmental Quality, Texas and Vermont.

Mike Rollins: President, Greater Austin Chamber of Commerce, Austin, Texas.

Nurul Shams Rusli: Director, Malaysian Investment Development Authority, Houston, Texas.

Akiko Sato: Event coordinator, Information and Cultural Affairs, Consulate-General of Japan, Houston, Texas.

Dominique Savariau: Senior consultant, Myanmar Carlton Consulting, Co., Ltd., Myanmar.

Reina Sawada: Manager, Showcase-tv, Inc., Tokyo, Japan.

Tsukasa Sawada: Officer of Ibaraki Longhorn Basketball; former Japanese Olympic Committee member, male enhancement coach, Tokyo, Japan.

Rajesh Setty: Co-founder and president of cloud-based platform, WittyParrot, Cupertino, California.

Dr. Joseph Shaules: Director, Japan Intercultural Institute (JII), Tokyo, Japan; author of *The Intercultural Mind: Connecting Culture, Cognition, and Global Living* (2015).

Sue Shinomiya: President, Business Passport; co-author of *Business Passport to Japan* (Stone Bridge Press, 2008), Portland, Oregon.

Dr. Patricia Sieber: Associate professor, Department of East Asian Languages and Literatures, The Ohio State University; former director, OSU East Asian Studies Center; and director, OSU Institute for Chinese Studies, Columbus, Ohio.

Dr. George Simons: World-wide consultant, creator and editor in chief of diversophy® intercultural training games, Nice, France.

Derrius Sims: CEO and founder, Tactus Imperius, a software consulting and independent game development company, Austin, Texas.

Allan Smith: Executive and senior foreign exchange trader, KPC & G International, Perth, Australia.

Phyllis Snodgrass: COO, Greater Austin Chamber of Commerce, Austin, Texas.

V. Srinivasan: Founder and director, SJS Enterprises, an automotive manufacturing corporation; former chairman, Indo American Chamber of Commerce, Karnataka Chapter, Bangalore, India (2012–2013).

Motokatsu Sunagawa: Chairman and CEO, Eco-Merge Philippines, Inc., Manila, Philippines, a renewable energy and green technology developer.

Jay Tang: General manager, Asia Pacific Region, Readen Holding Corp., Hong Kong.

Aung Thet: Lead analyst, Market Maker Realty & Investments, Austin, Texas.

Tony VanderHeyden: Business development director, Brewers Science, Tokyo, Japan.

AVIS Viswanathan: Founder and "chief dreamer" at A V Initiatives, a "workplace happiness consulting firm," in Chennai, India (www.avinitiatives .co.in); author of *Fall Like a Rose Petal* (Westland Books, 2014).

April Wareham: Cultural Consultant and Program Director, Great Wall China Adoption, Austin, Texas, USA.

Sharon Jackson Wendell, J.D.: Attorney, Vorys Legal Counsel, Houston, Texas.

Jerald Wrightsil: CEO, Eco Merge USA, a renewable energy and green technology developer, Austin, Texas.

Vivian Xiaowei Wu: Guide, China International Travel Service (CITS), Beijing, China.

Phoebe You: Director and chief representative, The Ohio State University China Gateway Ltd., Office of International Affairs, Shanghai, China.

Vicki Zhang: Guide, China International Travel Service (CITS), Beijing, China.

Index

359